The German Social Democrats in Opposition, 1949-1960

The German Social Democrats in Opposition, 1949-1960

The Case Against Rearmament

By Gordon D. Drummond

UNIVERSITY OF OKLAHOMA PRESS : NORMAN

Library of Congress Cataloging in Publication Data

Drummond, Gordon D. (Gordon Douglas), 1938-
  The German Social Democrats in opposition, 1949-1960.

  Bibliography: p. 351
  Includes index.
  1. Sozialdemokratische Partei Deutschlands—History. 2. Germany (West)—
Defenses—History. I. Title.
JN3971.A98S5824   324.243072   82-2731
                                             AACR2

Contents

Illustrations

Acknowledgments

Like every other author, I owe a great deal to a great many people. My first debt of gratitude is to Professor Gordon Craig, who suggested the topic and provided the inspiration for my research in modern German history. Once under way, I received encouragement and support from my colleagues in the Department of History at the University of Oklahoma. They read the many drafts of this manuscript and offered many suggestions, most of which I had the good sense to accept. I also would like to express my appreciation to three German friends— Georg, Maya, and Ulrich. Without their help my efforts to investigate the recent history of the German Social Democratic party would have achieved very little. Finally, there is a debt that every author must acknowledge and that is to those at home who patiently endure the absenteeism and the absentmindedness of one who is engrossed in writing. To those who know my wife, Janice, the extent of her contribution to the completion of this work is only too obvious.

GORDON D. DRUMMOND

Norman, Oklahoma

The German Social Democrats in Opposition, 1949-1960

Introduction

The German Social Democratic party (Sozialdemokratische Partei Deutschlands, SPD) is the oldest political party in Germany. Having been out of office most of its parliamentary life, it has been treated as Germany's opposition party par excellence. Only with the emergence of the governments of Willy Brandt and Helmut Schmidt did its image alter in any significant way.

Founded in the 1870s as a product of a merger between two struggling Socialist parties, the SPD with its Marxist ideology eventually attracted a loyal working-class following and grew to become the largest party in Parliament. Yet because of the state's authoritarian structure the SPD never had a chance to enter the government. Not until the collapse of the monarchy in November, 1918, did the SPD hold the reins of power. Even then it did not last long. After serving little more than a year in a coalition government, signing the Versailles Treaty and drafting the Weimar Constitution, the members of the SPD moved to the opposition benches, where they remained throughout most of the republic's short life. In May, 1933, the Nazis dissolved the party.

After the war the Social Democrats reemerged very quickly as an organized political group. They became the most active party in the Western zones and played a vital role in the founding of the West German Republic. The first general election, however, was a severe disappointment. They ran second to the Christlich-Demokratische Union-Christlich-Soziale Union (Christian Democratic Union Christian Social Union, CDU-CSU) and opted for opposition rather than attempt a compromise with the bourgeois parties. During the following decade the SPD deviated very little from its opposition course. The party members believed that the electorate would turn in despair from the coalition government organized by Konrad Adenauer, but in the 1953 and 1957 elections, although the Social Democrats gained votes on each occasion, the Christian Democrats gained even more. Gradually the hopes of the postwar period began to fade.

3

Since 1945 there had been forces at work in the SPD trying to promote party reform. Those forces had deep roots. They could be traced to revisionists like Eduard Bernstein in imperial Germany and to reformists of the parliamentary party in the Weimar period. In the Bonn Republic the reform movement grew in strength after the party's successive election defeats, but not until 1959 did the reformers triumph. At its Bad Godesberg conference the SPD threw the old Marxist baggage overboard, dropped its working-class image, and became a Volkspartei, a party for the entire nation. The following year the Social Democrats rallied behind a new leader, Willy Brandt, and prepared an election program that corresponded more closely to the domestic concerns and above all the security needs of the West German population. Although the immediate results were not spectacular, the party's electoral support grew steadily. Finally, in 1966, the Social Democrats entered a coalition government with the rival CDU-CSU. It was the first time in thirty-six years that they had been in office. Three years later, winning almost 43 percent of the vote, the SPD turned the tables on the Christian Democrats by forming a government with the tiny Freie Demokratische Partei (Free Democratic party, FDP). The 1969 election represented the greatest electoral triumph in the party's long history and opened a new era in the political life of the West German Republic.

Few political parties have received as much attention as has the SPD. It has been observed, researched, and analyzed throughout its long history. It has been used as a model for developing a theory of party organization, examined as a case study in the evolution of a Marxist party, and criticized or defended for the role that it has played in modern German history.[1] Still the literature continues to flow, and the party remains a subject of continued interest.

The purpose of this book is to investigate the reaction of the SPD to West German rearmament during the first eleven years of the Bonn Republic. Throughout this period the Social Democrats stood in opposition, first to rearmament as it was proposed by the Western powers in 1950 and then to rearmament as it was carried out by the West German government five years later. Although they quickly acknowledged the existence of a new German army, it was not until 1960 that they finally accepted West Germany's alliance with NATO. My main concern is to explain the role of the Social Democrats in the rearmament debate and to evaluate the impact of that debate on the evolution of the SPD from an Arbeiterspartei (workers' party) to a Volkspartei. In the process two related matters are examined: first, the problem of party leadership and party democracy, and, second, the role of the opposition party in a parliamentary regime.

The SPD is a mass political party. It has a large dues-paying membership, averaging over 680,000 members between 1946 and 1961, and a well-articulated party structure, with 22 regional divisions (Bezirke) and over 9,000 local organizations (Ortsvereine) in the Federal Republic. Leadership is in the hands of a party chairman, an executive board (Parteivorstand) and, beginning in 1958, a party presidium (Parteipräsidium) composed of the most influential board members. In addition there is a control commission (Kontrollkommission), which reviews the party's finances and serves as a grievance committee, and a party council (Parteiausschuss, renamed later the Parteirat), made up of regional party officials and state political leaders who help coordinate national and local affairs. The highest organ of the SPD is the party conference (Parteitag). Meeting once every two years, approximately 300 delegates from regional organizations convene for about a week to hear reports from the executive committees and the party's parliamentary delegation (Fraktion). Their most important task is to elect the party chairman and the executive board and to vote on resolutions relating to policy and organizational matters.

The SPD has always considered itself the very model of a democratically organized political party. Those who have studied the party, however, have not always shared this view. Beginning with Robert Michels, who investigated the Social Democrats of imperial Germany, political observers have commented on the oligarchical nature of the SPD.[2] Even today critics charge that the Social Democrats have done no better than their political opponents in meeting the recognized standards of intraparty democracy. They point out that in the SPD the flow of ideas and opinions is predominantly from top to bottom. As a consequence the average party member has very little influence on policy making. Party conferences, where discussion should prevail, have become little more than propaganda shows in which the delegates adopt resolutions drafted by the leaders. Even the election of party leaders has become less open because of the recruitment of candidates primarily from the upper echelons of the Bundestag Fraktion. It is this group that has come to dominate the party leadership and the policy-making process in the SPD. Critics charge that since the party has become a Volkspartei, the leaders have become more concerned with what the voters think than with what the members want. A study of the rearmament debate, however, shows that, whatever may have developed in the 1960s, during the previous decade the SPD leaders responded to pressure from the rank and file; in fact, they had to accept a number of compromise resolutions before formulating a new policy position

A question of considerable interest is the role of the SPD as an opposition party. In the late 1950s political scientists began referring to the "waning" of political opposition in Western parliamentary Regimes. Otto Kirchheimer pointed out that the British pattern of government-opposition relations, whereby the party out of power represents a clear alternative to the ruling party, had failed to take hold on the Continent. The trend was toward a convergence of policy positions leading ultimately to the creation of a cartel arrangement among the state-supporting parties that further reduced the area of political competition. In West Germany, Kirchheimer wrote in 1962 of a "vanishing opposition."[3] The argument is overstated and hard to sustain, as subsequent events in that country have shown, but it has influenced much of recent thinking about the behavior of the parliamentary opposition in West Germany.[4]

Much of the discussion about the changing role of opposition parties has been based on the so-called end-of-ideology debate. Political sociologists like Seymour Lipset have argued that with growing prosperity in the West a social system has emerged in which class conflict has been greatly reduced.[5] This has encouraged political parties, especially leftist parties, to broaden the base of their support by appealing across class lines, and in the process they have become more pragmatic and less ideological. This was certainly the case with the SPD, which abandoned its Marxist heritage in 1959 and adopted a new political style to be more competitive with the CDU. Nevertheless, the transformation of the SPD cannot be explained solely in terms of socioeconomic developments and the resulting deemphasis of ideology. As a discussion of the rearmament debate clearly reveals, it is necessary to take into account international events because they have played a greater role in West German politics than in any other West European country.

During the 1950s both the West German government and the SPD opposition acknowledged the primacy of foreign policy because both realized that a victory on that issue would determine the domestic structure of the new Germany. At first the contestants focused on how to regain freedom from foreign control and reestablish German sovereignty, but from the summer of 1950 on, the key issue was rearmament. Writing shortly before the second general election, Dolf Sternberger commented that no other political theme has "so unceasingly occupied the people, the parties, and the organs of government, so agitated and thoroughly shaken our entire political structure and so strained it to the limit of exhaustion and disintegration" as the struggle over rearmament.[6] Although the temperature of the debate cooled periodically in the following years, it shot up again in response to government initiatives in the military area.

Why was rearmament such a sensitive issue, and why did it remain so for an entire decade? First, a decision in favor of West German rearmament was by its very nature a decision against German reunification. Once the West Germans agreed to join the Western alliance, the Russians were certain to tighten their hold on East Germany and seal the division of the country. Second, rearmament meant that the young men of the nation would have to go back into uniform. After the losses and suffering of World War II, combined with a fear of militarism, most West Germans preferred not to think about creating another German army. In time the mood of the public changed as a majority, under the impact of events, came to accept both the division

6

of Germany and the necessity of a military contribution. But the major opposition party, the SPD, did not. The Social Democrats refused until 1960 to accept West Germany's military ties with the West, and during the fifties they kept the spotlight on the government's rearmament policy.

For the Social Democrats no other issue—not even the debate over the abandonment of its Marxist heritage—so agitated the party as Konrad Adenauer's decision to rearm West Germany. The explanation is not difficult to find. The Social Democrats opposed West German rearmament because it was Adenauer's policy. To them the chancellor was the spokesman of reactionary forces that, if restored to power, would destroy all hope of creating a new social and political order. They also opposed rearmament because it would block the restoration of German unity. During the 1950s the Social Democrats insisted that reunification was the primary task of German foreign policy, and they castigated Adenauer for "turning his back" on the eighteen million Germans imprisoned in the Soviet zone. Finally, there was the weight of party tradition. Throughout its long history the SPD never felt comfortable dealing with military questions and never established a relationship of mutual trust with the armed forces. It was a heritage that handicapped the party as much as, if not more than, its Marxist philosophy in competing with the CDU.

Until the Bonn era the Social Democrats never established a clear position on military affairs. They made positive declarations on national defense and even developed a conception of how a democratic army should be organized, but throughout the period from Bismarck to Hitler a negative attitude prevailed. Most Social Democrats wanted nothing to do with military matters. They held strong pacifist and antimilitarist views that the party leadership either shared or respected. As a result the SPD never came to grips with the military question.

The pacifist views did not stem from the party's Marxist heritage. On the contrary, Socialist thinkers concluded from their reading of Marx that war was the inevitable result of competition among the capitalist powers and the necessary catalyst of a proletarian revolution. Peace would be secured only when the capitalist system itself had been destroyed. The Social Democrats abandoned this strictly determinist view in the decade before World War I.[7] They did so in part because the Socialist movement in Germany had grown to such proportions that the SPD had more to lose than to gain from a European war, but even more because the majority of the party members believed in a reformist rather than a revolutionary path to socialism. In dealing with international affairs, they preferred to believe that peace—though not necessarily permanent peace—was possible before the advent of a Socialist world order. Furthermore, the Social Democrats had always been outspoken critics of power politics, and even in the Bismarck years they had condemned the chancellor's strategy of armed peace. At their Erfurt

party conference in 1890 they passed a resolution calling for the settlement of all international disputes by means of arbitration. This demand
was reaffirmed at subsequent party conferences and highlighted in the
massive peace campaign that the SPD unleashed in the immediate prewar years against imperialism and the arms race. The campaign came
to an abrupt halt in August, 1914.

The war greatly strengthened pacifist feelings within the party. In
its aftermath the SPD demanded that Germany not only renounce war
as a means of policy but forgo the game of power politics as well.
Hermann Mueller, a leading Social Democrat and foreign minister in
the second Weimar government, declared in 1919 that from then on "the
German sword will no longer count as an aid in the art of diplomacy."[8]
He urged the European powers to work for general disarmament, which
was the cardinal point of SPD foreign policy during the Weimar period.
In pursuit of this goal the Social Democrats supported the policy of
fulfillment, applauded Germany's entry into the League of Nations, and
praised both the Locarno and the Kellogg-Briand pacts. The extent to
which the 1928 peace pact corresponded to the pacifist mood of the
SPD was strikingly revealed the following year at the party's Magdeburg conference, at which a resolution was passed demanding that German youth be educated not in the lessons of war but in the spirit of
peace.[9]

The party's antimilitarist attitude was decisively influenced by the
political setting in which the SPD grew to maturity. Imperial Germany
was an authoritarian and militaristic state, created under Prussian guid-
ance. Even before unification the Social Democrats attacked Prussian
militarism and demanded the creation of a popular militia to replace
the standing army, which they labeled an instrument of "the monarchy
and class rule." In the Reichstag the Social Democrats expressed their
opposition to militarism by consistently voting against the military budget and by demanding that the appropriations be used to improve the
economic, social, and cultural well-being of the population. Defiantly
they vowed to contribute "not a penny, not a man" to protect the class
system of imperial Germany.[10]

The Social Democrats remained committed to the militia system
throughout the imperial period, praising it for a variety of reasons. It
was less dangerous, they argued, than a standing army because a militia
could be used only for defensive purposes; it was less expensive to
maintain, even with universal military training, because the citizen-
soldiers would be in uniform for only a short time each year, and it
was more effective as a fighting force because "the discipline of the
militia was the discipline of free men, not slaves." Actually the Social
Democrats showed little concern for the question of military efficiency
and viewed the militia primarily as a means of neutralizing the retali-
ative powers of a hostile regime. But the militia system became enshrined in party thinking as an article of faith which few bothered to
question.

After the war the Social Democrats had an unparalleled opportunity to reshape German military policy. They held the reins of power during the revolution but did nothing to lay the foundations of a new military system.[11] Part of the explanation is that the SPD leaders were preoccupied with restoring order in Germany, but, equally important, men like Friedrich Ebert and Philip Scheidemann exhibited no interest in military questions. They preferred to leave such matters to the constituent assembly, which they assumed would have a Socialist majority and would adopt the militia system. They assumed too much, however, because the Socialists failed not only to win a majority but also to persuade their coalition partners in the first Weimar government to support the creation of a militia. Furthermore, the workers shunned any form of military organization because of their experiences either at the front or at home under the military dictatorship of Erich Ludendorff and Paul von Hindenburg. The final blow for the Social Democrats came at Versailles, where the Allies decreed that Germany was to be limited to a 100,000-man professional army.

At that point the SPD was without a military policy, but not without a voice in military affairs. One of the party's parliamentary leaders, Gustav Noske, occupied the post of defense minister. Unfortunately, Noske lacked experience in the field and had to rely on the advice of the old officer corps. He also lacked support from his own party colleagues, who tended to view the officers as dangerous militarists and incorrigible reactionaries. They criticized Noske for being too closely associated with them, and when, to his chagrin, the army failed to defend the republic during the Kapp putsch, the party forced him to resign. Since no other Social Democrat was willing to take the post, the SPD gave up the chance to control the new army. As one writer noted, the Social Democrats were not forced out of the defense ministry: "They walked out."[12]

During the following years the SPD never overcame its mistrust of the army. In the press and in Parliament the Social Democrats remained the Reichswehr's severest critics, protesting against excessive military spending, condemning the political unreliability of the Reichswehr, and demanding a purge of the officer corps. At times they did offer constructive criticism and perceptive comments on conditions in the army, but since they were never again in a position to influence military policy, the only result of their efforts was to deepen the gulf between the army and the party. By 1933 the two stood further apart than ever before, separated by a deep, mutual antipathy.[13]

Despite their opposition to the military system in Weimar and imperial Germany, the Social Democrats never questioned the nation's right of self-defense. They always insisted that they would defend Germany because, as August Bebel said, "it is our country, because it is the land in which we live." Yet before 1914 they could not convince the imperial government that their patriotism was genuine. In 1907 when young Noske assured the Reichstag that in case of an attack on

Germany the Social Democrats would respond just as decisively "as the gentlemen sitting on the right of the chamber," the government remained unimpressed, and for obvious reasons. Within the SPD were many Social Democrats who objected to Noske's statement and in particular to the suggestion that they had anything in common with the Conservatives. In their minds there was a distinction between a defense of the fatherland and a war to preserve the state.[14] But when the conflict came in August, 1914, the party discovered that it was not possible to separate the German nation from the Junker-dominated German state. In a flood of patriotic sentiment nation and state suddenly became one. The Social Democrats voted unanimously for the war credits on August 4, and although a small group eventually broke away from the SPD to go into opposition, the majority held to the decision to support the war effort.[15]

After the war, the question of national defense hardly seemed relevant to the SPD. Peace was the issue of the day. Not until 1929, at the Magdeburg party conference, did the SPD reaffirm its support of a defensive war, and then it did so only indirectly. The resolution adopted by the conference stated that an army was necessary to defend German neutrality and "the political, economic, and social achievements of the working class [against the] power policy of the imperialist and fascist states."[16] For this purpose a reformed Reichswehr would be useful. The resolution also pointed out, however, that the establishment of a small, professional army would be a step toward general disarmament. From the course of the debate it was clear that the question of disarmament, not defense, was uppermost in the party's mind.

The lack of clarity in SPD's position on military questions was due in large part to conflicting opinions within the party. Before the war only a handful of Social Democrats—mainly revisionists and Reichstag deputies—saw the need for a military policy, and they were unable to convince their party colleagues. Most Social Democrats were content either to ignore military affairs or to repeat traditional pacifist antimilitarist slogans. The radicals were the major exception. They wanted an active policy but one of a different kind.[17] Karl Liebknecht, for example, declared that since militarism was "the strongest bulwark of capitalism" the SPD should unleash a massive antimilitarist campaign among German youth before they were drafted into the army. Without reliable troops, he said, the government would be unable to suppress a revolutionary proletariat. Rosa Luxemburg added that in case of a European war the Social Democrats should be concerned not with defending the Junker-capitalist state but with promoting revolution. By contrast, the party leaders were unprepared either to join the radicals in translating the party's Marxist rhetoric into revolutionary action or to support the moderates in working for a positive military program. Instead they attempted to reconcile the conflicting viewpoints at the biennial party conferences by drafting resolutions that everyone could accept. The tactic succeeded. Party unity was maintained, but in the process the SPD sacrificed clarity of purpose.

After the war the party was still deeply divided on the military question. Although the radicals had left the SPD for the new Communist party, there was a leftist element within the old party that opposed Socialist participation in a national-defense program, as well as Socialist cooperation with the Reichswehr because it was "an instrument of class rule." Rank-and-file Social Democrats were hostile toward the Reichswehr. They shared the antimilitarist views of the left and were even less willing than before to support an active military policy. Again only a few Social Democrats, mostly members of the parliamentary party, saw the need for positive measures. They urged their colleagues to establish better relations with the Reichswehr, to work for constructive military reforms, and to support national defense. Their argument was that, while under the empire the SPD could be an opposition party and nothing more, as a founding member of the Weimar Republic the SPD had a vital interest in its defense. Yet throughout the period the SPD leaders were very cautious not to press the members too hard. In 1929 they gained approval of a set of party guidelines on military affairs, but under pressure from the left they abandoned further discussion of the military question. The SPD leaders were concerned with maintaining party unity and increasingly, as the Communist challenge grew during the last years of the Weimar Republic, with appeasing the strong antimilitary sentiments of the German working class.[18] As a result, when the republic fell, the SPD still lacked a clear policy on military affairs.

CHAPTER 1

Kurt Schumacher and the SPD

With the collapse of the Third Reich, Germany as a political entity ceased to exist. There was no German state or central government, and with the sudden demise of the Nazi party national representation totally disappeared. The country was occupied by the victorious Allies and divided, on the basis of wartime agreements, into four zones of occupation. In Berlin the victors established a control council to co-ordinate Allied policies, but from the first days of the occupation they administered their zones separately and independently. As a result German political parties had to reorganize at the zonal rather than the national level. That is where the SPD began to rebuild. Although the Social Democrats were licensed first by the Russians, it was in the British zone, that the postwar party, under the forceful leadership of Kurt Schumacher, began to take shape.

Schumacher's Party

Schumacher played a vital role in the resurrection of the SPD. He united Social Democrats in the three Western zones, and, as party chairman from 1946 until his death in 1952, he provided the aggressive leadership and the will to power that the Social Democrats had so disastrously lacked during the Weimar period. It was Schumacher, more than any other Social Democrat, who set the course for the postwar SPD. Yet Schumacher was more than just a dynamic party leader. He was a powerful moral force in the democratic renewal of Germany and a courageous spokesman for the rights of his countrymen during the postwar years. Although unsuccessful in trying to convince the occupying powers of the virtues of social democracy and in competing with Konrad Adenauer for the right to govern the new West German state, he was nonetheless one of the most important men in Europe.

Schumacher was born in 1895 at Kulm, a small town in the former German province of West Prussia.[1] He served in World War I and lost an arm after being severely wounded in an early battle on the eastern front. Before the war ended, he began his college career and eventually received his doctorate in political science from the University of Münster. His political career began in 1918, when he joined the SPD. Although extremely combative and impatient, he had a moderate view of Marxism and sided with Ebert and Scheidemann against the radical left during the November Revolution.

In 1920 he went to southern Germany to serve as political editor of the party's newspaper in Stuttgart. He quickly established a reputation for himself as "a man with one arm and a dozen elbows."[2] Schumacher's aggressive political style was best reflected in his pointed editorial attacks on the antirepublican activities of the right. From the beginning Schumacher recognized the need to combat the Nazi movement. He led counterdemonstrations against the Nazis in the early twenties and even organized a paramilitary group of young Socialists to defend the Weimar regime against its enemies. At no time, however, did he ever contemplate an opening to the left in defense of the republic. To Schumacher the Communists were nothing more than "a red-laquered second edition of the Nazis." Not surprisingly, therefore, he very early became the most hated Social Democrat in Württemberg.[3]

In 1930, after serving six years in the state legislature, he won a seat in Parliament. His election to the Reichstag, however, coincided with the first spectacular triumph of the Nazi party, and the Brownshirts were there in force when the young deputy from Württemberg arrived in Berlin. It did not take Schumacher long to clash with the Nazis. He exchanged insults with them, even going so far as to label national socialism "an appeal to the inner swine in man."[4] When the Nazis came to power in 1933, they arrested Schumacher and held him in Dachau and other concentration camps for most of the next twelve years.

Schumacher survived the camps mainly because, as Lewis Edinger points out, he was not the sort of person "whose spirit could be broken even under the worst conditions."[5] Life in the Nazi camps did take its toll, however. At the end he "was a pitiful walking cadaver, with ulcers, yellowing stumps for teeth, flickering eyesight [and still carrying] in him seventeen pieces of shrapnel from World War I."[6] A developing thrombosis in his left leg made him lame; later the leg had to be amputated. Although pain was a constant companion for the rest of his life, Schumacher endured it because of his commitment to a cause. He believed in social democracy and identified himself fully with the struggle for its realization in Germany. There was no time for anything other than the political struggle. He was married to politics.[7] To his domestic opponents these qualities made him a fanatic—self-righteous, uncompromising, and intolerant—but to his friends and followers he was "the guardian of democracy" who gave "a life for Germany."[8]

After his release by the Nazis, Schumacher settled in Hannover to regain his strength and await the end of the war. It was there in April, 1945, during the last days of the Third Reich, that he made his return to politics. He immediately established a party office to make contact with the SPD organizations that were reappearing spontaneously across Germany, and in October he invited them to send delegates to a party conference at Wennigsen, near Hannover. This first postwar gathering of the SPD was a remarkable triumph for Schumacher. Local party leaders in the three Western zones and remnants of the party's Executive Committee in exile accepted his lead in reorganizing the SPD; however, the small delegation from the Soviet zone refused to concede the leadership to Schumacher. As early as June, 1945, a group of Social Democrats headed by Otto Grotewohl had established a central committee in Berlin. Claiming to be the legal heirs of the Weimar party, they had mobilized party functionaries in the east as Schumacher was doing in the west. Now at Wennigsen they offered themselves as the natural rallying point for a new Social Democratic party.[9]

Grotewohl had been encouraged by the Russians to reorganize the SPD and cooperate with other left-wing groups. He not only proved amenable to cooperation but even came out in favor of a merger with the Kommunistische Partei Deutschlands (Communist party, KPD). His proposal appealed strongly to those on the left who believed that a united working-class movement in Weimar could have prevented Hitler's rise to power. Schumacher, however, opposed any association with the Communists. He too remembered Weimar. He remembered that the Communists had tried to overthrow the republic and had made the Social Democrats, rather than the Nazis, their primary enemies. Now in 1945 he saw them as a fifth column of the Red Army. Their first allegiance was to Moscow, not to the German people, he warned, and they would attempt to make a unity party the instrument of Soviet policy in Germany. To the suggestion that Communists and Socialists were ideological brothers, he replied, "Yes, like Cain and Abel."[10]

Schumacher stumped the Western zones, proving himself a remarkable campaigner. As one reporter described him: "He would stand on a speaker's platform, pouring his whole life's energy into the dramatic, acid oratory which held huge crowds spellbound for two or three hours."[11] The effort worked. He gained the overwhelming support of party members in the West, though he was unable to influence events in the Eastern zone. Under strong Russian pressure and without consulting the party rank and file, Grotewohl joined with the Communists in April, 1946, to form the Sozialistische Einheitspartei Deutschlands (Socialist Unity Party, SED). Schumacher deplored the destruction of a free Social Democratic party in the Soviet zone and refused to recognize the new party as anything more than a continuation of the KPD. In his eyes it was still a quisling party.

The Social Democrats, now restricted to the three Western zones, saw themselves standing in the forefront of the struggle between the forces of totalitarianism and democracy. They tried to convince the Western powers that this was not simply a dispute between two political parties but a conflict which would directly affect the fate of European democracy.[12] When city elections were held in Berlin six months later, the SED received less than one-fifth of the vote, while the SPD, in the western sectors, won almost one-half. The party proudly announced the election results to be the first victory for freedom in the Cold War.

By his vigorous campaign against a merger with the KPD, Schumacher played a key role in frustrating Soviet efforts to establish a strong satellite party in the Western zones. The independence of the SPD was maintained, and a great tactical victory was won for the West, but it was a costly victory. Opposition to the merger meant that the party was cut off from traditional areas of Socialist strength in East Germany. Of course, once the Russians decided to create the SED, there was little that Schumacher could do except concentrate on rebuilding the SPD in the Western zones. Nonetheless, it was primarily as a result of his determined efforts that the Social Democratic party rapidly re-emerged as a strong, independent force in German politics.

In the turmoil of the postwar period Schumacher was a source of inspiration and strength for a party trying to drag itself from under the rubble of the Third Reich. He impressed party members with his political knowledge, his courage, and his passionate commitment to the creation of a social-democratic Germany. It seemed natural, therefore, that Schumacher should step into the vacuum left by the deceased or aged leaders of the Weimar period. At the first official party congress in May, 1946, Kurt Schumacher was elected chairman of the SPD.

The party organization which Schumacher took over in 1946 greatly resembled the one he had so roughly criticized in the Weimar period. The long blackout of the Nazi period had deprived the SPD of a trained corps of younger leaders; consequently, when the party began rebuilding after the war, mostly men and women in their fifties and sixties came to the first organizational meetings. In many instances, veteran party officials simply reassumed the positions they had occupied before 1933.[13]

Schumacher believed that a strong party was necessary to create a social-democratic Germany, but he knew that it was not enough simply to resurrect the old Weimar party. There had to be an infusion of new ideas and new blood into the organization. This Schumacher accomplished. He brought to the forefront new personalities, many of whom later came to play a vital role in the transformation of the SPD, and he attracted many new faces to the party.[14] In two years, largely because of his efforts, membership rose from about 600,000 to over 875,000. Young people in particular were drawn to the SPD by Schumacher's dynamic personality and his promise of a new Germany. They soon found the party atmosphere stifling, however. The old-timers were united by a strong ingroup feeling and generally treated the newcomers with suspicion. Disappointed at not being able to make their voices heard or to penetrate the power structure of local party organizations, many new members gradually drifted out of the party.[15]

At first glance it is somewhat surprising that Schumacher never attempted a thoroughgoing reform of the party organization, but he was primarily a public figure (Volkstribun) rather than a party politician. After some initial criticism of the bureaucrats, in which he told them to look forward, not backward, Schumacher turned his attention to national problems. In the heat of the battle against the Communists, the occupying powers, and the bourgeois parties, he had no time to deal with the party apparatus. He recruited a group of experts to deal with policy matters and a staff of organization men to run the SPD from party headquarters. Gradually he lost touch with the lower echelons of the organization, where old party officials had become firmly entrenched, but since they were loyal and provided him with a reliable instrument, he left the bureaucracy alone. As a result the SPD received a new head "but not a new body."[16]

Despite the differences between reformers and traditionalists, as well as between the leadership and the rank and file, there was considerable unity within the party. Pressure from outside brought the members closer together, and memories of the past helped them avoid the excessive factionalism of the Weimar period. Most important, however, was the unifying influence of the new party chairman. The SPD was Schumacher's party. There was no doubt, as one colleague said, that "he was the strongest power, that he had the greatest political brain, the most evident power of judgment."[17] His ideas, his spirit, and his leadership gave the old party a new look.

A Socialist Policy for Germany

The policy which Schumacher developed for the party stemmed from a close reading of the lessons of Weimar and a Marxian analysis of the German problem. However, he had an undogmatic view of Marxism. It was an analytical tool, he once said, not a catechism or an article of faith. Nonetheless, he relied on Marxian concepts, emphasizing the class basis of German politics and the importance of economic factors, and he allowed Marxism to shape his thinking much more than he was willing to admit.[18]

Speaking in Hamburg in 1946, Schumacher said that in the mature democracies it might be possible for democracy and capitalism to exist side by side but in Germany "democracy will be socialist or there will be none at all."[19] He explained that German capitalists would "always feel compelled to convert their money into political power and use it against democracy and peace." In the nineteenth century they had allied with Prussian militarists to defeat liberal democracy and to create an authoritarian regime with an expansionist foreign policy. The result was World War I. In the Weimar period these same antidemocratic forces had combined with a frightened middle class to resist the legitimate demands of the German proletariat, and together they had opened the door to Adolf Hitler and the Nazis. Now, after a second world war, Schumacher warned, peace and freedom would be secured only after the power of German capitalism had been destroyed once and for all.

His immediate impression of the postwar period was that Germany had entered a new phase in the historical class struggle. Because of the war's destructiveness and the occupying powers' shortsightedness, the division of society was deepening, and the gap between rich and poor was widening.[20] Under these conditions, Schumacher claimed, Germany was in a state of latent social revolution. Most Germans were anti-capitalist, which meant that socialism was "no longer the affair of the working class in the old sense of the word." It was "the program for blue-collar and white-collar workers, farmers, artisans, tradesmen, and the intellectual professions." The SPD, the party of the poor people, had become a home for those who opposed the exploitative capitalist class.[21]

Schumacher realized that members of the middle class, though impoverished, had not surrendered their traditional view of the SPD or their fear that socialism meant communism. His response was to urge the party to abandon traditional class slogans and to emphasize that democratic socialism meant freedom and individuality, not the slavery and uniformity of the "barracks socialism" of the Soviet Union. He asserted that businessmen who profited from their own labors had nothing to fear; in fact, they had everything to gain from an attack on the economic power of the old ruling elite. After all, it was the members of the middle class who had suffered most from the inflation of the early twenties, the depression of the thirties, and the catastrophic policies of the Nazis. He believed that if he could convince them that militarists and capitalists were responsible for Germany's destruction they would accept the socialist program of the SPD. Why they supported the party was unimportant. As Schumacher noted, it was not necessary to be a Marxist to believe in socialism. A person could become a Social Democrat through the "spirit of the Communist Manifesto or the Sermon on the Mount, as well as for philosophical or ethical reasons."[22] There was room in the party for everyone except unregenerate Nazis and capitalists.

Schumacher believed that there was a majority for socialism in Germany, but he never went so far as to predict its inevitable triumph. The party would have to go out to win the middle class. It could not wait passively for the forces of history, as the Social Democrats had done in 1918.[23] He warned that the capitalists would act promptly. They were already trying to exploit the miseries and anxieties of the middle class as a means of repeating the great swindle they had perpetrated in the early thirties; but whereas in the Weimar Republic they had tried to use nationalism and the Nazis to defend their interests, now they had a new cause, Christianity, and a new party, the CDU. Schumacher was also troubled by the support which the CDU and its Bavarian partner, the CSU, received from the Catholic church. In his eyes, party and church waged their campaign against social democracy in the name of a revived clerical fascism.[24]

Schumacher's distorted conception of the CDU stemmed from his critical view of the old Catholic Zentrumspartei (Center party) and his failure to understand the forces that made up the new party.[25] Unlike any previous German party, the CDU represented a political union of varied interest groups, including Protestants and Catholics, trade unionists and businessmen, Christian socialists and economic conservatives. It was his contention, however, that a party composed of such diverse elements could not survive for long. In time the Protestants and the progressives would break with the party's capitalist, conservative, and clericalist elements and seek a new political home. He assumed that they would turn to the SPD.[26]

Initially, therefore, Schumacher felt optimistic about the party's chances of playing a decisive role in shaping the nation's future. In the postwar period, however, the fate of Germany lay in the hands of the occupying powers. Schumacher had already seen the Russians intervene in favor of the KPD, and to his dismay he soon came to the conclusion that the Western powers preferred the party's domestic opponents as well. He complained that undue favoritism was shown the Christian Democrats in the assignment of local administrative positions and warned that, if the CDU succeeded in establishing a government, the opportunity to achieve a genuine democratic revolution would be missed. This time the blame would lie not with the German people, as it had after World War I, but with the occupying powers.

Schumacher never relinquished the conviction that only the Social Democrats had a legitimate right to govern postwar Germany, even after they lost the 1949 election. He based his demand for power not on the development of the dialectic according to Marx but on the moral superiority of the Social Democratic party. The SPD had always held firmly to the line of democracy and peace. "All the others needed the persuasive power of the war potential and superiority of Anglo-Saxon weapons to discover their love for democracy, [but] we would be democrats even if the English and the Americans were fascists."[27] Schumacher asserted further that only the SPD possessed a program which could meet the vital needs of the German people in the postwar period. The other parties offered nothing more than a restoration of the past and a round of "new crises, catastrophes, and wars." The existence and strength of the SPD, therefore, was not a partisan issue "but a vital necessity for the whole German nation and for Europe."[28]

A Patriotic Leader

Schumacher's view of postwar Germany was decisively influenced by his memories of the Weimar period. He not only feared a repetition of the mistakes of the past by victors and vanquished alike but also claimed to see some unpleasant similarities between past and present. The words "once again" were frequently on his lips. He pointed out, for example, that democracy in Germany was being imposed on an apathetic population by foreign powers, as had happened after World War I, and once again right-wing radicals financed by the big capitalists and national Bolsheviks sponsored by the Soviet Union were waging a two-front war on the SPD.[29]

Of greater concern to Schumacher was the attitude of the Allies toward Germany. As part of their security policy they had demilitarized the country, dismantled many factories directly and indirectly related to the arms industry, and severed slices of territory from the Reich. In the east the Russians had pushed Germany's frontier back to the Oder-Neisse Line, while in the west the French had sought to annex the Saar and control the Rhineland and the Ruhr. The Social Democrats said that, while they understood Europe's desire for security, it seemed to them that the victors were resorting to measures which had already proved to be an inappropriate basis for peace. According to Schumacher, Allied policy was based on an attempt "to overcome the mistakes of Versailles by repeating them in the most exaggerated fashion."[30]

At a party conference in 1946, Schumacher warned the occupying powers that they could not gain security by a policy of destruction. He agreed wholeheartedly with the Allied policy of dismantling factories involved in the arms industry but questioned whether it was also necessary to destroy industrial capacity used in the production of civilian goods.[31] A year later in San Francisco he told a labor convention that the dismantling process was having a disastrous psychological effect on German workers. Hungry, cold, and unemployed, they were becoming demoralized. Unless the situation improved, he feared that the masses could become prey to Communist propaganda.[32] Schumacher also warned that the seizure of German territory could lead to the revival of that aggressive German nationalism the Allies had fought a war to destroy. No German would accept the present boundary with Poland, he said, and certainly no Social Democrat would agree to any project which separated the Rhineland and the Ruhr area from the Reich. "We warn all victors, big and little, not to tear pieces off the body of the German people, leaving wounds which will fester for many years to come."[33]

Like many of his contemporaries, Schumacher felt that nationalism still had a strong emotional appeal in Germany, and he expected the political reactivation of the masses once the initial mood of apathy and demoralization had passed. When that happened, Schumacher wanted his party to be ready. He remembered that in Weimar the right-wing parties had been able to exploit the nation's resentment of the Versailles settlement and to accuse the SPD, which had signed the treaty, of weakening Germany for the benefit of foreign powers. The Social Democrats eventually had been isolated from the nation and crushed by the wave of violent nationalism which swept Germany in 1933. Schumacher vowed that nationalism would never again be used as a weapon against the SPD.[34]

There was general agreement among Social Democrats, especially those who had spent the Nazi years in exile, that the Weimar party had underestimated the importance of nationalism. Now in the first postwar days Schumacher did something about it. He cast himself in the role of a patriotic leader—a role which he played well because of his own strong national feelings—and he portrayed the SPD as the "political party of the German patriots." His strategy was to divert German nationalism into democratic channels and harness it "to social-democratic purposes." By denying the political right its traditional position, perhaps patriotism could become the common denominator to unite the discontented and the disillusioned behind the SPD.[35] His role as patriotic leader, however, was something more than a political tactic designed to mobilize popular support for the party. He believed that by guarding the legitimate rights of the nation the SPD might prevent the reemergence of a new mass radicalism on the right or the left. Schumacher, therefore, consciously presented himself to the German people as their champion, ready to defend the national interest against exploitation by foreign powers.

Under a different set of circumstances he might not have felt compelled to press his defense of German interests quite so aggressively. Seeing an occupied and divided Germany, however, in which the occupying powers were pursuing their own national interests, he believed that the Germans needed a spokesman more than ever. "It is of vital national importance," he told a Frankfurt audience, "for the German people to have a party that still has the courage to fight for the right to freedom and independence." The SPD would cooperate but would not subordinate itself to any of the great powers as the SED had done in the Eastern zone and the CDU in the West. "The SPD would be not a British, a French, a Russian, or an American party but a German party." Its policy would emanate from the German people and would not be a function of "a foreign will."[36]

Schumacher's declaration of independence was a courageous act, especially in the early years of the occupation, when the fate of Germany was still unknown, but it was bound to produce a number of serious encounters with the occupying powers. The Russians attacked him because of his opposition to the merger. To them he was "a loyal pupil of the fascist school" whose tactics included "materials from the arsenal of Josef Goebbels." The Western powers also disapproved of his policics and behavior. According to Willy Brandt, "for the Americans he was too socialistic, for the English he was too aggressive, and for the French too German. They all found that he was too independent."[37] Some in the West thought that he was playing a dangerous game by opposing Western policy on national grounds. While it was essential to keep German nationalism in a democratic channel, his strategy could backfire and "excite the very forces which destroyed his own body and made Germany a pariah among nations."[38] Schumacher disagreed. If there was a revival of right-wing radicalism in Germany, it was not because of his democratic defense of the rights of the German nation but because of the vindictive policy of the occupying powers.[39] Others criticized Schumacher for being too nationalistic. Adenauer compared him with Alfred Hugenberg, the leader of the German Nationalist party in the Weimar period, and according to one Frenchman, the only thing that kept Schumacher from becoming another Hitler "was his crippled left arm, which he could not raise above his shoulder."[40] The SPD leader responded in anger. He insisted that his party was merely defending the rights of the German nation, and he saw no reason why every German attempt at self-preservation should be viewed as a dangerous revival of nationalism.

Schumacher realized that he was often misunderstood, both at home and abroad, and he was sensitive to the charge that he had abandoned the party's traditional internationalism to pursue a selfish national policy. He claimed that the views he represented were patriotic, not nationalistic. To be patriotic was simply to love one's own country. A nationalistic view, on the other hand, was one which ignored the rights of other nations. If there was to be a new European order—stable and peaceful —the nations would have to be treated as equals. "Europe means equality," he said. Without equality there could be no self-respect. Without a minimum of self-respect democracy could not survive, and a nation could not live in peace with its neighbors. By defending the interests of the German nation, therefore, the SPD was guarding democracy and providing "the best proof of respect for the interests of other nations."[41]

According to Schumacher, internationalism was possible only in a world organized on a national basis. He considered this to be a realistic view because, as he told the Bundestag, "every country is above all concerned about its own position, and forward-looking men in all countries view freedom in the world in terms of their own needs."[42] For the Germans the most pressing need was to reunite Germany.

Schumacher's Reunification Policy

Schumacher realized that reunification could not be achieved by German efforts alone. There would have to be a four-power agreement because, in his own words, there was "no single German question which would not also be a European or international question."[43] Unfortunately the great powers were involved in a struggle and could not agree on how to handle the German problem. As early as the October, 1945, Wennigsen conference, he had pointed out that the world was being split into spheres of influence with the line of division running through the heart of Germany.[44] After the failure of the foreign ministers' conferences at Moscow and London in 1947, Schumacher had to admit that prospects for an agreement were very dim. He complained that the German question received little consideration because the great powers were concerned primarily with "power relations among themselves."[45] Although he remained suspicious of Western intentions, the SPD leader never doubted that the main obstacle to German reunification stood in the East.

Schumacher's attitude toward Russia had taken shape long before 1945. The people of the town in which he grew up, only twenty miles from the Russian border, and the members of the party he joined saw Russia as a threat to Western civilization. Throughout the Weimar period the Social Democrats were as suspicious of the Soviet Union as they had been of the czarist regime. Many Social Democrats, including Schumacher, firmly believed that the European Communist parties were agents of Soviet imperialism and that the Comintern was nothing more than a front for the continuation of Russia's traditional policy of expansion. When Schumacher returned to political life in April, 1945, and saw the position the Russians had won for themselves, there was little doubt in his mind about the nature and goals of Soviet foreign policy.

Schumacher believed that the Russians had designed two foreign-policy programs for the postwar period. Their minimum program was to gain security by creating a ring of satellite states in Eastern Europe and keeping Germany as weak as possible. However, if the circumstances were favorable, he assumed that the Russians would switch to their maximum program, which was to establish Soviet hegemony on the Continent. Before the end of the first year of occupation, Schumacher felt that the Kremlin had shifted the emphasis from security to expansion.

Writing in 1946, Schumacher warned that the Russians intended to keep "central and Western Europe in a state of constant unrest" to help the KPD find support among the demoralized masses. Schumacher believed that the Communists represented no serious threat by themselves, but he feared that the Western powers would unconsciously give aid to the Communist cause through a misguided security policy.[46] There was the danger that an impoverished middle class or, as Schumacher considered more likely, naïve German conservatives would be attracted by the idea of an alliance with the Russians as a means of restoring Germany's position in Europe. In the early postwar years some former generals and diplomats were already advocating an Eastern orientation.

To Schumacher an alliance between the far left and the right was a natural one because both the CDU and the KPD wanted to be "the two large millstones between which the SPD is crushed." If they succeeded, Schumacher predicted, the Communists would then turn on the German conservatives as the Nazis had done. With the victory of the KPD the Russians would be masters of Central Europe, and control of the entire continent would be within their grasp. Soviet policy was based on the thesis, advanced by Lenin, that "who has Germany, has Europe."[47]

The Soviet Union was not the only occupying power that concerned Schumacher. He believed that the British were not sensitive enough to German needs and that the Americans, though concerned, were too sure of the universal applicability of their own brand of democracy ever to understand the German situation. But among the Western powers the French troubled him the most. Even beyond the postwar period they treated the German problem as a security problem and viewed the Germans, rather than the Russians, as the greater threat to French security. Schumacher recognized the underlying cause of French fears but insisted that the price paid for giving satisfaction to France must not be the viability of the German nation. French policy was an attempt "to keep Germany down, to paralyze it, to make it impotent." It was a fateful continuation of the line established by Raymond Poincaré. As for the Franco-Soviet treaty negotiated by Charles de Gaulle in December, 1944, Schumacher pointed out that this was a return to the power politics and national rivalries of the prewar era.[48] Apparently the French had learned nothing.

After the war Schumacher's immediate concern was the danger of a European settlement at German expense. No doubt he was thinking of the Paris Peace Conference in 1919, but in his early statements he referred to the French experience after the Napoleonic Wars. At the Congress of Vienna, fearing that the victors would pursue a policy of revenge and deny France its rightful place in the world, Talleyrand had told the powers that "Europe is a system of states within which a certain balance must exist." Similarly, Schumacher warned the victors against atomizing the Reich, for a balanced European order could not function unless Germany as a whole was incorporated into the system of states. Security could not be gained by making Germany a glacis for the national defense of those powers who have hegemonial tendencies, he said, nor could the political testament of Richelieu or Peter the Great provide the basis for a lasting peace. What Europe needed was "a conception of collective thinking and a policy for creating general security."[49]

Schumacher, therefore, was not thinking of an isolated and nationalistic Germany. For him Germany was a part of Europe, and the European system was something more than a combination of powers existing in a state of equilibrium. He wrote in 1946 that Europe could survive only through the close cooperation of its member nations. A year later he told an American audience that economic integration was necessary to prevent the European countries from stumbling from one economic crisis to another, and he warned that these crises would occur regularly as long as international relations remained at the stage of nation-state competition. The only viable solution was the creation of a United States of Europe (Staatenbund) or, more specifically, a social-democratic federation of European states.[50]

Schumacher was rather vague about the structure and the membership of this new Europe. He did state explicitly, however, that the SPD could not be anti-Russian because "the exclusion of such a large country would make the creation of a lasting international community of peace impossible."[51] Schumacher realized, however, that there was no place in a Socialist Europe for Bolshevik Russia. Once the Cold War began, the dream of a free system of cooperating European states had to be abandoned, and the SPD leader had to focus his attention on the countries west of the iron curtain. For a time during 1947 and 1948 he still hoped that it might be possible to prevent the division of Europe into two power blocs by organizing Western and Central Europe, including Germany, as a third force between the Soviet Union and the United States. Indeed, the idea was popular among European Socialists. In a speech prepared for the third postwar party conference, Schumacher declared that Europe was a continent with its own character and that it had to find its own path of development.[52] By then, however, he could no longer deny that Europe was divided or ignore that the line of division ran not east of Germany but through the heart of the country.

As the Cold War intensified, Schumacher became more and more convinced that the worst problem facing Germans was "the victor problem," that is, how to convince the occupying powers that reunification was in the best interests of all concerned. Yet even that posed a dilemma for the SPD leader. Although Schumacher recognized the need for a four-power agreement, he could not suppress the fear that the powers might reach agreement at Germany's expense, and during the Berlin Blockade a vision of another Munich surrender appeared before his eyes.[53] He warned the party that the world was "quite capable of living without a united Germany" but added that if the Germans were denied national unity and exploited by foreign interests a series of problems would arise to poison the international atmosphere and keep Europe in a state of constant unrest. Without a united Germany there could be no peace in Europe.[54]

Schumacher suggested that if agreement could be reached on settling the German problem the powers should adopt a three-step approach to reunification. First, zonal boundaries would be abolished and the physical unity of the Reich reestablished according to the 1937 frontiers. Second, free elections would be held across the entire country on the basis of equal rights for all political parties. Third, the freely elected national assembly would draft a constitution and establish a government to negotiate a peace treaty with the victors. Schumacher vehemently opposed the idea that reunification could be achieved either by bringing together representatives of the individual German states (Länder) or of the various German political parties, as the Russians proposed in 1947. He objected to any system which gave parity to the SED and insisted that only free national elections could properly reflect the views of the nation. Once the vast body of Socialist support in the Soviet zone was reopened to the party, Schumacher assumed that the SPD would win the election and head the first postwar government.

The SPD leader never deviated from his demand for free elections. In fact, after the creation of the West German Republic, free elections remained an essential part of reunification policy for both the opposition and the government. Schumacher realized that the chances of receiving the Soviet Union's voluntary consent to this kind of reunification plan were small, but he believed that under pressure from the Western powers the Russians could be compelled to negotiate a settlement and surrender their hold on Germany.

After the failure of the Moscow conference in the spring of 1947, Schumacher conceded that the Russians had little immediate interest in reunifying Germany. He insisted, nonetheless, that the Western powers must not remain passive. At a party meeting that year Schumacher suggested that reunification could be achieved only by making conditions in the West so attractive that West Germany would act as a magnet on the people in the Soviet zone. This meant that Germans in the West would have to receive better treatment than that of their countrymen across the zonal border; thus the oppressed would see that real democracy did exist on German soil and that their homeland was "obviously treated with more respect [by the Western powers] than Moscow affords to any eastern country."[55] Furthermore, in contrast to the poverty and misery in the East, there would have to be economic prosperity and social justice in the West. Once these conditions were created, the disparity between the Eastern and Western zones would promote such discontent among the East German population that the Russians would find their position there untenable and would gladly come to the conference table to settle the German question. Schumacher remained optimistic. After all, the Soviets had reversed directions in the past—the Nazi-Soviet Pact was one very prominent example.[56] Before events could reach that stage, however, German relations with the West had to be placed on the proper footing. Schumacher assumed that he would be the man to handle such a task, but when the West German state was created in 1949, it was Adenauer, not Schumacher, who held power.

Schumacher and the West

Konrad Adenauer, leader of the CDU and first chancellor of the West German Republic, was an advocate of close cooperation with the West;

more than that, he was a firm believer in West European integration. He said on one occasion, "When you fall from the heights as we Germans have done, you realize that it is necessary to break with what has been." Germany could no longer play an independent role in Europe. For that matter, none of the European countries were in a position to defend themselves individually or to save Western civilization. The security of the West could be achieved "only if the West European nations form a political, economic, and cultural union and, above all, if they render any further warlike contests amongst themselves impossible."[57] Adenauer believed that a new Europe could be created only on the basis of a sincere reconciliation between France and Germany. As a result, he responded very enthusiastically in early 1950 to proposals made by the French foreign minister, Robert Schuman, for the integration of the coal and steel industries of Western Europe, and later he supported Premier René Pleven's plan for the creation of a European army.

On the basis of Schumacher's statements about the need for European unity, reason would dictate that the Social Democrats support the French proposals. On the contrary, the SPD "declared war" on them.[58] Schumacher charged that the Schuman Plan was the result of a pact between French and German capitalists which stemmed from nothing more than a desire to gain protection against social democracy. If established, the plan would create a "Europe Incorporated," dominated by the forces of "capitalism, clericalism, conservatism, and cartelism." An SPD spokesman warned that a Europe built on anything other than social-democratic principles was a Europe built on sand. Second, the party claimed that the proposals denied the Germans equality of status (Gleichberechtigung). They represented an attempt by the French in particular to maintain the victor-vanquished relationship by placing the human and material resources of the nation at the disposal of foreign powers. By demanding vital concessions from the Germans in return for a promise of equality in the future, Schumacher said, the Western powers were forcing the new West German state to repeat the fateful policy of fulfillment. The SPD leader believed that the pursuit of this policy by the Weimar regime had given rise to a sense of aggrieved nationalism in Germany. Its exploitation by the extremists had paved the way for the downfall of the republic. The party demanded, therefore, that the entry of the Federal Republic into any European organization had to be based on full equality from the start. Third, the SPD rejected the French proposals because they were based on a small Europe (Kleineuropa). Britain and the Scandinavian countries were not part of the original community, and without the support of their labor governments it would be impossible to create a Socialist Europe. Furthermore, the Pleven and Schuman plans not only excluded the northern countries, but also deepened the division of Europe. The iron curtain fell across Germany, and Social Democrats feared that these schemes for West European integration would raise the barriers to German re-unification even higher. According to Schumacher, reunification was "more pressing and more important" for the pacification and reconstruction of Europe than the integration of one part of Germany with other European countries.[59] Of course, Schumacher was not opposed to integration on the basis of Socialist principles. In fact, he believed that only a social-democratic Western Europe could exert the necessary magnetic force on the East European states to free them from Soviet domination. Adenauer's program could never unite Germany or liberate the countries behind the iron curtain.

Few doubted that the government viewed reunification as the most important goal of its foreign policy. The SPD questioned, however, whether the government saw reunification as "the most pressing demand" of the German nation.[60] Adenauer's response was that unity could be restored only in cooperation with the Western powers. The Federal Republic by itself lacked the strength to compel the Russians to release their hold on East Germany. To obtain Western support and to build a position of strength, West Germany would have to join the Western Alliance system. West European integration, therefore, became the first step on the road to reunification and, in Adenauer's view, the most immediate problem facing the government.

Schumacher criticized the chancellor for giving priority to his European program and accused him of treating the Federal Republic as a permanent fixture instead of a provisional arrangement (Provisorium)— a stopping place on the road to reunification. West European integration on the basis of the Schuman and Pleven plans would bind German hands for fifty years and block the path to reunification. Schumacher declared in January, 1952, that the SPD would fight against any agreement that did not "leave open, and even strengthen, the possibility of German unity." West Germany should keep to agreements of "a provisional nature."[61]

Despite these reservations, however, Schumacher sided wholeheartedly with the West. He warned the Germans that a choice between the East and the West was not open to them, nor was it possible to imitate the Weimar policy of playing one side against the other to promote German interests. In the Cold War there could be no political neutrality.[62] He knew that social democracy could be realized only in the West; thus, as long as the Soviet threat existed, Germany could find allies only among the Western powers. If Schumacher was "for" the West, however, he did not believe that it was necessary to be "with" the West under all circumstances.

Early in 1950 the Federal Republic was invited to join the Council of Europe at Strasbourg as an associate member. Adenauer readily accepted the invitation, but Schumacher demanded its rejection because of continued discrimination against the Germans. The SPD leader was offended by the subordinate status accorded the Germans and infuriated because an invitation had been sent simultaneously to the Saar, a German territory under French administration. If the French were asking the Germans to join them in the creation of a new Europe, why were they trying to separate the Saarlanders from their countrymen? Why were they pursuing a security policy against the Germans? On this basis any attempt to convince the German nation that Strasbourg represented the beginning of a new Europe would only give rise to a new mass nationalism. The lesson of Weimar was "the greater the illusion . . . the more destructive the reaction." Furthermore, if the French were permitted to retain control of the Saar, the political and moral position of the Germans in their struggle to win back the area east of the Oder-Neisse would be destroyed. An SPD spokesman advised, therefore, that it would be better to work outside the walls of Strasbourg for a real Council of Europe than to be inside bargaining for the revision of treaties as the Germans had done after World War I.[63]

Adenauer and Schumacher agreed on the need for solidarity with the West, but they differed on how it should be accomplished. While the chancellor felt that equality for the Germans would be the inevitable result of European integration, the leader of the opposition demanded that equality be the prerequisite for close cooperation with the Western powers. Adenauer believed that if Germany was to gain equality and full partnership in the free world it would be necessary first to win the confidence of the other nations. "We could neither demand nor expect full confidence at the outset," he wrote in his memoirs. "We had to be fully aware of the fact that confidence could only be regained slowly, step by step, and that we had to be careful to avoid everything that might awaken mistrust."[64]

Schumacher refused to accept the argument that the Germans could be granted equality only after they had proved themselves to be good democrats and peace-loving neighbors. Without equality, there would be no democracy and no peace, as the failure of the Weimar Republic clearly demonstrated. The chancellor emphasized the psychological aspect of his relations with the Western powers and thus the need to make concessions to create an atmosphere of trust. The leader of the opposition, on the other hand, expressed concern about the legal aspects of Allied-German relations. Fearing that conditions could be created which future German governments would be unable to revise—even for such a vital issue as reunification—he insisted that German foreign relations be placed on the proper footing right from the very beginning. He sharply criticized Adenauer's readiness to compromise, claiming that the chancellor had made concessions at the negotiating table without receiving anything in return and without pressing the Western powers to make reasonable counterproposals. The government, he said, should present a series of demands, not renounce vital interests to attain rights which already belonged to the German people. Schumacher remembered the success that he had had in winning concessions from the Western

powers during the debate on the West German constitution (Grundge-
setz, or Basic Law). In April, 1949, the Allies proposed that the powers
of the German states be increased, but Schumacher wanted a stronger
federal government, and he eventually won by refusing to compromise
with the military governors. As a result, when the subject of an international authority to control the Ruhr came up for negotiation, and
later, when the Schuman and Pleven plans were discussed, Schumacher
insisted that Adenauer give an uncompromising no to Western demands
until German conditions were met. He assumed that the Western powers
would be compelled to start negotiations on a new and more favorable
basis simply because the Cold War made it impossible for them to
ignore Germany's potential power. Although Adenauer warned against
a German policy which harped "on our indispensability," that was pre-
cisely what Schumacher expected the government to do. He admitted
that the Germans needed the economic assistance and military protection of the Western powers, but for the resistance of communism "they
need us to the same extent."[65] Thus the Germans would be throwing
away their trump card if they joined the Council of Europe or accepted
plans for European integration before their demands for equality had
been met.

A Munich newspaper commented that, although Schumacher's aggressive approach might force more concessions from the Allies than Adenauer's policy of conciliation, his political success would prove to be
a psychological failure. The policy Schumacher advocated would mean
an increase in suspicion and resistance to Germany which eventually
would have to be overcome if the new Europe was ever to become a
reality.[66] Schumacher realized that it would take time to establish a new
image for Germany after the Hitler era. He would not, however, buy
Europe's trust by sacrificing Germany's inalienable rights. If the Germans were still mistrusted by the outside world, it was not because
of the party's demand for equality but, in the words of his deputy,
because of the continued existence of the ideas of Hugenberg and Hitler
in the ranks of the bourgeois parties.[67] The fears and suspicions would
disappear only with the emergence of a social-democratic Germany.

Thus Schumacher guided the SPD through the ruins of the postwar
period and into the opening political battles of the Bonn Republic. He
played a decisive role in shaping party policy and in setting the SPD
on a course of intransigent opposition to the government and policies
of Konrad Adenauer. When he died in 1952, party leadership was transferred without hesitation to the men who had helped him run the SPD
from the first conference at Wennigsen. They proved to be "faithful
executors of the dead man's legacy."[68] Although there was some cooperation with the government on important pieces of domestic legislation, it was only after the party suffered jarring setbacks in the general
elections of 1953 and 1957 that the SPD began altering fundamental

aspects of Schumacher's opposition policy. A new program was adopted in 1959, and a new course was set the following year.

While Schumacher was chairman, his policy was supported enthusiastically by the Social Democrats. He symbolized their belief in the party's legitimate right to govern Germany, and he articulated clearly their recognition of the need for a more determined course of action than the SPD had pursued in the Weimar Republic. There were party members, of course, who disagreed with aspects of Schumacher's opposition policy and some who found his uncompromising attitude toward the bourgeois parties and the Western powers too hard to maintain. Wilhelm Hoegner of Bavaria, for example, saw the need for cooperation with other democratic parties, and Ernst Reuter, the mayor of Berlin, knew how vital it was not to alienate the Western powers as Schumacher appeared to be doing. The so-called Bürgermeister wing of the party—Max Brauer in Hamburg, Wilhelm Kaisen in Bremen, and Ernst Reuter in Berlin—supported the Schuman Plan and West German membership in the Council of Europe. They argued that Schumacher offered no constructive alternative to Adenauer's policy of cooperation with the West. As Brauer told the Hamburg party conference in 1950 during the Council of Europe debate, "If we ignore this opportunity, then we are pursuing a policy of self-isolation and passivity that will not move us a step forward. . . . Europe will not begin life as a perfect institution," but must be fought for day by day. The Bürgermeisters thought that Schumacher was too critical of Adenauer's step-by-step approach, and they regretted that the line had been drawn so sharply between the SPD and other parties. According to Kaisen, "We must pursue a policy that eases tensions rather than increasing them."[69] Greater cooperation among the parties was necessary to rebuild Germany. Despite these disagreements, however, no one was prepared to carry his differences with Schumacher to the point of upsetting the unity and the general consensus upon which the postwar party rested. There were varying degrees of enthusiasm about his policies, but no one questioned Schumacher's right to lead the SPD.[70]

Schumacher led the SPD into battle with a vigor and determination that was totally unknown to the Weimar party. It appeared, however, that he was obsessed with the mistakes the SPD had made in the past and that he was now trying to make the party play the role he thought it should have played in Weimar Germany. Fritz René Allemann, a Swiss journalist, wrote that Schumacher was the victim of "a false historical analogy,"[71] He made the SPD assume a position which was appropriate to the German mood in 1923, but not to the prevailing attitudes of 1949.

Soon after the party's defeat in the first general election, Schumacher held an executive meeting at Bad Dürkheim, where a sixteen-point program was adopted as a guideline for the party's opposition policy in the new Bundestag (Federal Assembly). It was clear even before the meeting, however, that there would be no grand coalition between the SPD and CDU. The growing animosity between the two party leaders made compromise difficult, but even more important were the political views of the two men. Adenauer preferred an alliance with the ideologically more compatible bourgeois parties to the arduous task of trying to reach an accommodation with the Socialists. Schumacher, for his part, believed that a coalition with the CDU could be justified only if the SPD could carry out its Socialist program. Anything less would give encouragement to the extremist parties and would mean a repetition of the mistakes made in Weimar. He felt that the Social Democrats had been too willing to enter coalition governments and accept responsibility for policies which they did not make. In the end it was the SPD that had to bear the blame for the economic and political instability of the Weimar regime. Therefore, when the American and British zones were merged in 1947, Schumacher refused to allow his party to participate in the five-man directorate of what was called Bizonia because the SPD was unable to secure the key offices of economics and finance. During the 1949 election campaign he said that the SPD would enter a coalition only if the party was so strong that it was indispensable for the formation of a national government and if the other parties fully accepted a concrete program presented to them by the SPD;[72] otherwise it would be better for the SPD to stand aside and let the bourgeois parties form a government. At least in this way there would be a clarification of the fronts between the government and the opposition, and the uncompromised position of the SPD would give the public a clear alternative to the bankrupt policies of the governing coalition. As a result, when the SPD failed to gain a majority or even sufficient political power to dictate its terms, the Executive Committee (Parteivorstand) withdrew to Bad Dürkheim to draft a "document for the opposition."[73]

Schumacher blamed the election results on the intervention of the Catholic clergy and the occupying powers, who he felt had deceived the masses, and on the unfair comparison of democratic socialism with bolshevism. He remained confident that his analysis of the German situation was correct. The CDU was a capitalist party (Unternehmerpartei) trying to defend an obsolete capitalism, and he expected that eventually the impoverished masses would see the 1949 election for what it was—a victory for heavy industry and the class society. The party's economic experts confidently predicted that Ludwig Erhard's free-market economy would create a series of problems which the capitalist system could not overcome. There was certain to be an intensification of the class struggle, and Schumacher warned that there would also be a nationalist reaction to the fulfillment policy of the Adenauer government. Although he was impressed with the similarities between the present situation and the Weimar period, the SPD leader remained confident that this time the Social Democrats could reach "the apolitical masses" before they fell prey to national bolshevism or a new right-wing radicalism.[74] The party was on the right track. It had only to remain true to its principles to receive the call from the people.

In the immediate postwar years there was considerable evidence to support his view of the German situation. Few German cities or towns had escaped the destructive effects of the war. Where once the nation had stood strong and united, now there were "only individuals who moved like shadows among the rubble, roaming the streets of the devastated and scorched country, cowering in cellars and bomb shelters."[75] Millions upon millions of desperate people were searching for food, shelter, and a way to make a living. Herbert Hoover, who made a survey of the country in early 1947, said that the standard of living in Germany was far worse than in any other part of Europe and that for many Germans living conditions were depressed far below anything in living memory.[76] Although conditions began to improve after the currency reform in 1948, the real upsurge did not come until more than four years later. In the meantime there remained a considerable disparity in living conditions between a wealthy few at the top and the impoverished masses below. Relatively little was done initially to deal with the plight of the largely dispossessed refugees or to aid those who had suffered heavy losses because of the war, the currency reform, and the sudden return to a free-market economy. The urban middle class suffered severely in trying to adjust to the new economic situation. Six months after the formation of the first West German government, the unemployment figure stood at two million, and as late as the summer of 1951 a joint American-German technical-assistance mission warned Adenauer that the gap between rich and poor in Germany was too wide. "No effort should be spared to relieve this condition, for it can become the cause of serious unrest in a democracy."[77]

It seems somewhat surprising, therefore, that Schumacher's call for rebuilding Germany on a new foundation did not receive wider acceptance among West Germans. The old social order had apparently collapsed, and millions had suffered great losses, both material and personal. Under the rubble which covered much of urban Germany, however, social attitudes remained intact. An American observer who visited Germany in 1946 was amazed at how middle-class people, "even without any material foundation, clung to their old class identification." All activities were oriented toward recovering as much as possible of the social status and prestige they had once enjoyed. Although the SPD won some support from the lower middle class, the majority tended to vote for the CDU in local elections. For most members of the middle class the CDU represented the maintenance or recovery of that "degree of social distinction which differentiates them economically from the lowest level of the social hierarchy."[78] They did not consider themselves proletarians, so they were relatively indifferent to Schumacher's warnings about a capitalist restoration. The great national issues which excited the SPD leader did not rouse their interest either, except temporarily when the question of rearmament was first introduced. The Germans were spiritually exhausted from the Nazi experience, and few expressed a desire to become involved in another crusade. Although they applauded Adenauer's European program, the general reaction to political matters was "a turning inward and a concentration on private affairs," such as a good job, a home, and a life which promised security and stability. The Germans wanted to put the hunger years of 1945 to 1948 behind them. Most were uninterested in politics and seemed content to leave political power in the hands of a responsible elite.[79] Adenauer drew the proper conclusions. He stepped forward with a policy that promised to satisfy the general desire for a return to normalcy, and he soon convinced the Germans that he was the only one who could guide them out of the chaos of the postwar years in a safe and orderly fashion. Even more important, he was on good terms with the Western powers. The Germans realized very early that cooperation with the West meant freedom, security, and prosperity.

Schumacher's failure to achieve the goals he pursued, above all the creation of a social-democratic Germany, was the result of many factors. The SPD leader was restricted in his political actions by the presence of the occupying powers and handicapped by his own inflexible personality,[80] but, more important, he misread the mood of the population. Because he viewed the postwar setting through a Marxist lens and based his judgments primarily on the party's Weimar experience, Schumacher saw a desire for radical change among the German people which really did not exist. Most Germans did not want a patriotic leader or a tribune, and national democratic socialism as espoused by Schumacher was unsuited to the demands of the majority and the realities of the German situation.

CHAPTER 2

The Opening of the Rearmament Debate

During the war the Allied Powers declared that they intended to demilitarize Germany so that country would "never again be able to disturb the peace of the world."[1] Soon after the war ended, however, the victors began to deal separately with the question of how to exploit German military potential. In 1945 the Russians established a Volkspolizei (zonal police force), and two years later they formed special militarized units. The decisive step toward the creation of regular armed forces in the Soviet zone came the following year, when former German army officers and reliable party members were employed to organize cadres for an East German army. The Russians justified remilitarization by charging that the Western powers, in violation of the agreements made at the Potsdam Conference had failed to demobilize all the Wehrmacht units in their zone. According to *Neues Deutschland,* the official newspaper of the SED, the Volkspolizei was necessary because of "the alarming preparations for a German civil war being made in West Germany."[2] The Western powers denied these charges. They admitted that demobilized soldiers had been organized into labor battalions (Dienstgruppen) to help clear war-torn areas but contended that these units possessed no military function. This was reaffirmed by the military governors in the British and American zones, who stated in late 1948 that the official Western position was to keep Germany disarmed.[3]

Although the Western powers publicly denied any interest in German rearmament, they discussed the matter privately. As early as the summer of 1947, American military leaders investigated the role Germany and Japan might play in the strategic balance between Russia and the United States, and the following year the National Security Council discussed the importance of a German military contribution to European defense. Even in Britain and France military men, such as Field Marshal Bernard Montgomery and General Pierre Billotte, advised their governments of the need for German military support.[4] Predictably, rumors of a West German rearmament continued to circulate.

The Initial German Reaction

In 1948 the West German press showed a very restrained interest in rearmament. Several commentators, writing under the impact of the Communist coup in Prague and the Soviet blockade of Berlin, pointed out that an effective defense of Western Europe was possible only with the addition of German troops, but they added that for political and psychological reasons no one dared to use them. The publisher of a pro-CDU newspaper, however, asked in November, 1948, whether the geographic position of the West German state then being organized would not justify granting it the right to form a defense force.[5] These discussions did not arouse much public interest until November 24, when Eugen Kogon, the editor of a Frankfurt journal, made some revealing statements about Western intentions.[6] He told a group of journalists that the Western powers were already creating a West German army without having first discussed the question with the Germans themselves. Apparently Kogon did not oppose West German rearmament but felt that if there was to be a new army the Germans had to control its development. There was, of course, no West German government at the time, only a parliamentary council meeting in Bonn to draft a constitution. Rearmament was not on the agenda.

At first the Social Democrats refused to discuss rearmament, but because of the seriousness of the international situation and the attention given to the rumors in late 1948, they felt it necessary to take a position on the issue. At an Executive Committee meeting in Bad Godesberg early in December, the SPD leaders passed a resolution on the military question.[7]

In drafting the resolution, the SPD leaders realized that the party expected them to oppose rearmament. Since the end of the war many party members had expressed strong pacifist sentiments, and now they demanded an end to all talk of a new German army. Carlo Schmid, a Tübingen professor who had joined the SPD after the war and become a leading parliamentary figure, told a local party rally in 1946 that, while other nations "may continue to rearm, never again do we want to send our sons into the barracks. If the madness of war should break out again somewhere, . . . then we would rather perish, knowing that it was not we who committed the crime."[8] The following year, at its national conference in Nuremberg, the party passed an antiwar resolution. As one delegate explained, it was time to banish war "from the minds and hearts of men" and win German youth for the "heroism of peace."[9]

A year earlier, at the Hannover party conference, the Social Democrats had declared that the Socialist program of the SPD offered the only real guarantee for maintaining peace and security in Europe.[10] By altering the economic structure of the country, socialism would destroy the political power of those who had led Germany into two world wars and would create an unalterable will for peace among the German people. With socialism triumphant over militarism and capitalism, the powers would no longer wish to pursue a policy of revenge against the Germans. They would not have to cripple German economic potential or detach vital pieces of territory from the Reich, and, instead of controlling the Ruhr for security purposes, they could socialize its industries as the first step toward the creation of a Socialist Europe. A Europe that was organized on the basis of a planned and integrated economy, with an international division of labor, would preclude the possibility of war.

By 1948 the dream of a harmonious Europe built on a Socialist foundation was fading fast. Europe was divided, and the rival powers were building military alliances to defend their spheres of influence. At their Bad Godesberg meeting the SPD leaders acknowledged the possibility that a new German army would have to be built, but they insisted on the fulfillment of certain conditions: first, that "representatives of the old militarism" would be excluded from discussions of the military question; second, that a new military system would be made dependent on the role Germany would play "in a future European community"; and third, that the entire discussion would be conducted in terms of "the absolute necessity" of creating a system of collective security. The vagueness of such statements led to confusion about the party's position.

On the subject of a new military system Carlo Schmid told the Parliamentary Council that the age of national armies had come to an end.[11] It was time to transfer Wehrhoheit (the right to raise and maintain an army) to an international body. He suggested that a system could be created in which security would no longer be "guaranteed exclusively by national military and industrial power potential" and the exercise of power, instead of being an act of national sovereignty, would become a matter of "collective self-defense by all those nations that are concerned with the maintenance of peace." As the executive instrument of this new community Schmid proposed the creation of an international army which would be something more than a "mosaic of national troop contingents" and to which the Germans could make a contribution.

Schmid was thinking of a global, or at least a European, security system, and he insisted that to be effective such a body had to include a reunited Germany. Erich Ollenhauer, the deputy party chairman, offered a different interpretation of the Bad Godesberg resolution. He implied that the Social Democrats had considered the possibility of German participation in a Western security system.[12] No doubt this matter had been discussed at the Bad Godesberg meeting, but Ollenhauer's comments hardly corresponded to the pacifist mood of the party or to the views of the party chairman.

Schumacher discussed remilitarization in an interview late in December with a reporter from the party newspaper, *Neuer Vorwärts*.[13] In contrast to Schmid's enthusiasm for international organizations, the SPD leader talked about the question of national sovereignty. He pointed out that in a democracy Wehrhaftigkeit (the courage and readiness to fight) could be only an expression of national sovereignty and international equality—and Germany possessed neither. Without them, however, the Germans would not be competent morally or legally to deal with rearmament or to join a collective-security system. Schumacher was also more skeptical than Schmid about the readiness of the powers to accept a collective-security system, especially at a time when the Russians were blockading Berlin. Even if they accepted such a system, the answer was not a German contribution to Western defense. "From the point of view of peace, national morale, and in the simplest terms, humanity," the idea of answering Russia's remilitarization of East Germany with the remilitarization of West Germany was unthinkable.

Schumacher could not overcome the suspicion that the Western powers wanted to take advantage of German military potential to secure their spheres of influence. He warned that they would treat a German army as nothing more than a foreign legion. It was not the Western powers, however, but the CDU that he blamed for the current discussion of rearmament. In exasperation he complained that "one cannot make it clear to German nationalists . . . that certain things are not for sale." He warned those Germans who still believed that something could be gained from a new war that any attempt to liberate the country by military means would lead to its destruction. At the very least rearmament would deepen the division of Germany. When NATO organized, therefore, Schumacher insisted on "the absolute necessity of military neutrality." He urged the West Germans, however, not to believe that they could remain politically neutral in the struggle against communism.[14] The task facing them was to create the political and social conditions needed to promote reunification. Working under the umbrella of security provided by the Western powers and the new Atlantic Alliance, West Germans could build a society that would act like a magnet, attracting people living in the Soviet zone.

Schumacher made no attempt to deal directly with military questions or develop a general security policy for the SPD; that could wait until Germany was reunified. In the meantime the occupying powers were responsible for a military defense of West Germany, and Schumacher was determined to keep the responsibility in their hands. The creation of a West German state did not shake his resolve to oppose West German rearmament.

The Plain Dealer

The formation of the first Bonn government in September, 1949, prompted renewed speculation about West German rearmament. Prominent military men on both sides of the Atlantic publicly expressed interest, and the press reported that NATO military planners were considering a German contribution to Western defense. When Secretary of State Dean

A meeting in the Bundestag office of Kurt Schumacher (lower left) with Carlo Schmid (center) and Konrad Adenauer, September 10, 1949. Such encounters were seldom so friendly. Courtesy German Press Agency.

Acheson visited West Germany in November, rumors circulated that plans were being laid for the creation of five West German divisions. Although the Allied high commissioners promptly denied that the subject of German rearmament had been discussed, the suspicion remained that it soon would be.[15]

Before the end of the year the rearmament debate received stimulus from an unexpected quarter. On December 3, Chancellor Adenauer granted an interview with an American newspaper, the *Cleveland Plain Dealer,* in which he expressed his opposition to the creation of a new German army and the recruitment of German mercenaries for a Western defense force. If the Allies demanded a German contribution, he said, "I would be prepared to consider the question of a German contingent in the framework of a European federation."[16] The chancellor's statement caused a sensation because it created the impression that the Western powers had discussed rearmament with him. Even more alarming, it conflicted with what Adenauer had said two weeks earlier. At the signing of the Petersberg Protocol, which revised the Occupation Statute to grant broader powers to the West Germans, the chancellor had pledged his government's "earnest determination to maintain the demilitarization of the federal territory and to endeavor by all means in its power to prevent the re-creation of armed forces of any kind."[17]

After reading the *Plain Dealer* interview, Erich Ollenhauer declared angrily that the SPD opposed not only rearmament but even a discussion of the subject.[18] He charged that Adenauer had created the impression that the Federal Republic was prepared to take military measures in its own defense. This was impossible because under the Occupation Statute the occupying powers were responsible for military matters and thus for the security of West Germany. Furthermore, the existence of the Volks-polizei, to which Adenauer alluded in the interview, did not justify a discussion of West German rearmament. These militarized police units in the Soviet zone, however, were a cause of great concern for the SPD. Schumacher pointed out that once the occupying powers withdrew, as the Russians had recently proposed, the only military forces left in the country would be the Volkspolizei.[19] "We do not want a civil war in which one side brandishes a pen and the other a rifle," or a situation in which the Communists could repeat the successful coup they had carried out in Prague. To establish a German balance of power, Schu-macher recommended "an equal degree of demilitarization and disarma-ment" in both zones, not the creation of a comparable West German military force. That would deepen the division of Germany. In the Bundestag, Ollenhauer explained that it was not a question of arming the West Germans or leaving them defenseless, since they had the pro-tection of the Western powers. The question was rather "what contri-bution can the Federal Republic make to a peaceful solution" of the German problem. Since its contribution could not be made in the mili-tary field, he urged the government to concentrate on building a social order in which freedom and justice prevailed.

In the months that followed, the Social Democrats took advantage of every opportunity to express their opposition to rearmament. Schu-macher told a press conference in January, 1950, that the SPD was against rearmament because it endangered peace and because the Ger-mans were not "morally, materially, or biologically" in a position to survive another war. Instead of talking about rearmament, he said, "It would be a good idea if all Germans kept their mouths shut."[20] When Winston Churchill suggested to the House of Commons in March, 1950, that the Germans could make a contribution to a European army, Carlo Schmid responded that "people should leave the Germans with the only victory they won in 1945—the victory over the army." Several weeks later he told a group of Social Democrats that remilitarization was a matter for the Germans to decide, and "we do not want any kind of remilitarization."[21] In May the Hamburg party conference passed a reso-lution empowering the SPD leaders to oppose by all means the rearma-ment of Germany.

The party's opposition to rearmament had clearly stiffened since the executive meeting at Bad Godesberg in December, 1948, but there seemed little reason for the Social Democrats to be so concerned. Adenauer had received no encouragement from the Western powers; in fact, in May, 1950, they had issued a declaration against German rearmament. Schumacher, however, suspected that they still wanted to raise a German army, and he was determined to bar that possibility or at least keep the decision on rearmament in German hands. He also expressed concern about the increased activity within nationalist and military circles following Adenauer's interview with the *Plain Dealer.* Their interest in a new German army would certainly cast doubts on the peaceful intentions of the government. Schumacher said that there were approximately 280 right-wing organizations in Germany and if they continued their "frightful nationalistic remarks" none of the great powers would support German unification.[22] Thus he recommended that the subject of rearmament be dropped.

The SPD discovered, however, that it could neither end the rearmament debate nor refrain from using military arguments to defend its position. At the end of March, 1950, the Executive Committee published a memorandum on the Ruhr and the security question in which the German policy of the Western powers came under heavy attack.[23] The Social Democrats supported all measures necessary to maintain German disarmament, such as the Military Security Board, but they objected to the continued employment of the Occupation Statute and the International Ruhr Authority as security instruments. In the words of Kurt Schumacher, the occupying powers should stop destroying men and machines and start relying on those who had a desire for peace and a belief in the future.[24] It was time, he said, to end "the hysterical misreading of the security problem." The West was threatened not by Germany but by 175 Russian divisions.

According to the memorandum, Russia's overwhelming superiority in conventional forces represented the basic problem facing Western military planners. If the Red Army attacked, the only strategy open to NATO was a retreat to the Atlantic to avoid a major battle until reinforcements could be landed on the Continent and American nuclear power brought to bear on the Soviet Union. Obviously such a strategy was politically unacceptable because Western Europe wanted to be defended, not liberated as it had been in World War II. The "radical remilitarization" of West Germany offered one alternative. With twenty or thirty motorized German divisions, supported by elite ground troops, the military balance would shift in favor of the West and ensure that the Russians would not overrun Western Europe. Such a radical solution to the security problem, however, would frighten Germany's neighbors and could force Russia to launch a preventive war. After all, a German army could also be used to spearhead an attack on the Soviet Union. If the Germans remained disarmed, however, and the West relied on a non-German army, there would be no reason for the Russians to feel threatened. "It is the idea of German rearmament alone which threatens peace" in Europe, Schumacher said.[25] Keeping the Germans disarmed, therefore, would be "the decisive contribution to the security of Germany and its western neighbors."

The Social Democrats offered political reasons for their opposition to rearmament, warning that even a partial rearming of the West Germans would increase international tension and, more important, deepen the division of Germany. They dismissed all military reasons advanced in support of rearmament as irrelevant because the Russians were "almost certain" to avoid an open attack on Western Europe within the next few years.[26] Fortunately for the party, most military observers in the West agreed with this assumption. With no immediate danger of Soviet aggression, the question of German rearmament could be treated as a matter for "speculation rather than active resolution" by Western leaders,[27] and the Social Democrats could focus their attention on other matters—the Schuman Plan, the Council of Europe, and the Saar. Priorities changed suddenly, however, with the outbreak of war in Korea on June 25, 1950.

An Offensive Concept for Western Defense

Many observers in the West feared that the North Korean invasion of South Korea signaled a change in Communist tactics from political to military means of expansion, and there was widespread public apprehension because of the similarities between the Korean and the German situations. Although most military observers minimized the threat of Soviet aggression in Europe, they realized nonetheless that NATO could not defend the Continent if the challenge came.

In the summer of 1950 there were only twelve undermanned and ill-equipped Allied divisions stationed in Western Europe, whereas there were approximately twenty-seven Soviet divisions in Germany alone and another seventy-five nearby. Western military leaders knew that if the Red Army marched it would take nothing more than a good pair of boots to reach the Atlantic. Until September, 1949, when the Russians exploded a nuclear device, the West had relied on the American monopoly of atomic weapons to deter Soviet aggression. Now it seemed only a matter of time until the Russians would achieve parity and with it the opportunity to use their vast superiority in conventional forces to overrun Western Europe without fear of nuclear retaliation by the Americans.

The Western alliance had the capability of strengthening its ground forces, but serious disagreement existed on how that might be accomplished. While the United States expected its allies to provide most of the manpower, the Europeans hesitated to shift funds from social and economic programs to the military budget because of the unfavorable reactions expected in their countries. The burden could be lightened by having the Germans share the defense load, but few in Western Europe were ready to trust them with another army so soon after the war. The French in particular, with memories of three German invasions in eighty years, had difficulty deciding which was the greater danger—German militarism or Soviet communism. Obviously any attempt to push West German rearmament in the face of these fears could destroy the alliance.

At a conference in London one month after the outbreak of war in Korea, Western officials agreed to strengthen the military posture of the alliance by raising NATO's standing force to thirty-six full divisions and to complete the building program within three, possibly even two, years.[28] The published report of the meeting, however, made no mention of a German military contribution. The European members of the alliance were apparently ready to accept a heavier defense burden, but they did so with strong reservations. Besides requesting considerable financial aid from the United States, the Continental countries demanded that the Americans and the British increase their troop strength in Europe during the military buildup to provide protection against the threat of Soviet intervention and to demonstrate their commitment to a strategy of defense rather than liberation. NATO planners had originally assumed that if they could mobilize enough divisions they would respond to a Soviet attack by retreating only to the Rhine, where they could regroup their forces for a massive counterattack. Even this strategy, however, had little appeal for the Dutch, the Danes, and, of course, the Germans, because they would have to suffer the horrors of a Russian occupation. They wanted a forward strategy, one that placed the line of defense somewhere beyond the Rhine.

Two days after conflict broke out in the Far East, Chancellor Adenauer asked the Western powers for a "binding security guarantee to cover the territory of the Federal Republic." He requested permission to establish a federal police force to counterbalance the Volkspolizei in the Soviet zone but failed to renew his previous offer of a German military contribution.[29] Several days later the SPD press service also pointed to the pressing security needs of the country and called for the stationing of more Allied troops in Germany. There was no mention, however, of rearmament or a federal police force.[30]

In late July, Schumacher finally commented publicly on the Korean conflict. Speaking with the full support of the Executive Committee, he stated that there was no real parallel between the situations in Germany and Korea and no good reason for creating paramilitary units to counter a threatened invasion by the Volkspolizei.[31] Korea was an unoccupied country, but if the East Germans marched on West Germany, it would mean an attack on the Western powers and the beginning of World War III. Moreover, Schumacher felt certain that the Russians preferred a war of nerves to a military encounter. What the West needed, therefore, was not the creation of German divisions but a strategy to counter a Soviet political offensive. The SPD leader spoke out sharply against those who thought of defense solely in terms of armaments and troop strength. What good were cannons and soldiers when behind them stood a million-man "army" of homeless refugees and unemployed workers? Schumacher pointed out that in Korea and China the Communists had enjoyed great success not because they had military superiority but because the poverty and misery created by a rapacious capitalism had "opened the gates to the invaders." The conclusions to be drawn from the conflict in the Far East were obvious: when living standards decrease, opportunities for Communist subversion increase. Therefore, "the only and the best contribution" that the Germans could make to safeguarding the peace was to concentrate on building a solidly democratic foundation for the Federal Republic.

Carlo Schmid used a similar argument in an address to the Council of Europe, which despite their initial opposition the Social Democrats had agreed to join. Speaking on August 10, Schmid warned that rearmament posed a serious threat to German democracy because the Bonn regime was not yet strong enough to control the military leaders of a new German army.[32] He also pointed out that German rearmament would provide the Russians with an excellent pretext for unleashing a preventive war. "We do not know what the intentions of the Kremlin might be. But . . . among all the causes of war, fear is one of the most potent." Schmid did not deny that a military threat existed; in fact, he told the council, it was the responsibility of every member state to make a reasonable and effective contribution to European defense. He warned, however, that care should be taken to "avoid exacting contributions which, instead of safeguarding peace and strengthening European unity, might be used to increase the chances of war and destroy the moral capital" that existed in Europe. By rearming the Germans, the Western powers would be making a grievous mistake. Germany's neighbors would find intolerable the creation of a new German army only five years after the war. Far from strengthening European defense, German rearmament "would prove to be a factor of disintegration and perhaps even of ruin." Therefore, he said, "Ask us for work, for manpower, industrial products, efforts in every field of economic and political activity, but do not ask us for German soldiers until an effective European supranational authority has been created."

The following day Winston Churchill introduced a resolution proposing the creation of a European army. It passed by a large majority. Although the Social Democrats agreed with the idea in principle, Schmid and the rest of the SPD delegation abstained. They felt that, until the other nations had overcome their fear of Germany and a European political authority had been created to control a European army, it would be better for the Germans to make a nonmilitary contribution to Western defense.[33]

One week later Chancellor Adenauer took advantage of the favorable response Churchill's proposal had received to comment on German rearmament. He knew that the NATO foreign ministers would discuss the subject at their September, 1950, meeting in New York and decided, therefore, to take the initiative. Adenauer asked, first, for the immediate strengthening of Allied forces stationed in West Germany to assure the Germans that their country would be defended and, second, for permission to create a defense force of about 150,000 reliable volunteers which, he said, could be organized by the spring of 1951.[34] The request was based on the chancellor's firm conviction that "Stalin was planning the same procedure for Western Germany as had been used in Korea." Adenauer admitted that Germany, unlike Korea, was still an occupied country, but he questioned whether the United States would respond by attacking the Soviet Union with atomic weapons if only the Volkspolizei marched. Fear of unleashing World War III could both paralyze and demoralize the Western powers in the face of such an attack. Although he requested a counterforce to the Volkspolizei, Adenauer denied that he wanted to create a German national army. If an international European army could be formed, the Germans were ready to make a contribution. A European army would strengthen the military position of the West, especially its conventional forces, and encourage the movement toward European unity. Uppermost in Adenauer's mind, however, was the belief that a military contribution to Western defense would have enormous political benefits for the Federal Republic; specifically, he expected the Occupation Statute to be replaced by a system of contractual agreements between the Federal Republic and the occupying powers as the basis for German sovereignty and equality within the Western community.[35]

On the morning of August 22, Adenauer presented his views on rearmament to the floor leaders of the three coalition parties. A CDU spokesman later announced that full agreement had been reached on the course to be followed by the government.[36] That afternoon the chancellor met with the leader of the opposition but failed to win his support for a bipartisan policy. The following day Schumacher held a press conference. It was there, and in speeches made during the following weeks, that the battle lines were drawn between the SPD and the government on the question of rearming the Germans.[37]

Before the Korean conflict Schumacher had expressed clear and unequivocal opposition to rearmament. Even in late July, one month after the war started, the SPD leader had refused to advocate rearmament for the Germans, and *Neuer Vorwärts* had continued to run headlines demanding "No German Remilitarization" and "Social Policy Instead of Rearmament." Now, at his August 23 press conference, Schumacher announced a startling change in the party's position. He did so, however, not in response to the military situation but to exploit the political implications of a military contribution to Western defense. He told reporters that under a certain set of conditions—which many journalists considered realistic—the SPD would support the creation of a new German army. The emphasis was on the conditions and on the party's differences with the government, but the SPD was apparently no longer categorically opposed to West German rearmament.

The initial point of difference between Adenauer and Schumacher concerned the question whether it was expedient for the Germans to offer a military contribution before the subject had been officially broached by the Western powers. Adenauer believed that the Americans were looking for some indication that the Germans were prepared to make a military contribution. He assumed that political concessions would follow automatically. Schumacher argued that by taking the initiative the chancellor was throwing away Germany's only trump card; once the Western powers had a German commitment, there would be no need for concessions. By waiting until the Western powers requested a military contribution, however, the Germans would be in a position to raise certain demands of their own about the Saar, the Ruhr Authority, and, above all, the Occupation Statute. Schumacher insisted that the Germans could not rearm until the occupation regime had been abolished. If the Germans made a commitment to Western defense before equality and sovereignty were restored, the Federal Republic would be nothing more than a satellite of the Western powers.

Schumacher also believed that Adenauer had erred in trying to promote rearmament on the basis of a comparison with events in the Far East. He argued, as he had a month before, that there was no real similarity between the two situations. "If the Volkspolizei marched, so would the Red Army," and that would mean World War III.[38] He saw no indication, however, that the Soviet Union planned to unleash a global conflict in the near future. At most the Russians had developed war plans "for a later date," but for the present peace would be maintained because "80 percent of the world's productive capacity lies in the West, and Stalin knows he will lose the last battle."[39]

Schumacher maintained that the West's military potential, while a powerful deterrent to Soviet aggression, could not provide absolute security for West Germany. After all, Stalin could be provoked by the attempt to rearm the Germans or tempted by the weakness of the Western defense position to seek a quick military decision in Central Europe. The Russians would then control all of Germany, and liberation by the Western armies would mean little more than the liberation of a corpse. No German could take comfort in knowing that the West would win the last battle. Schumacher demanded that the Western powers focus their attention on the first battle and defend their freedom in Germany by sharing the "same risks, sacrifices, and chances" as the Germans. There would be no war as long as the Russians knew that the Western powers were unwilling to surrender another inch of German territory, he said. "A guarantee against another Dunkirk is a guarantee for peace."[40] If the Germans rearmed before NATO had developed an acceptable strategy, they would simply be sacrificing themselves to safeguard the retreat of

45

their allies. Alone, the Germans could not stop the Red Army even if they carried out an "extraordinarily strong" rearmament program.[41] At best, commented Carlo Schmid, they could slow down the Russian drive so that "some people will have the opportunity to reach the Statue of Liberty."[42] What provoked Schmid's remark was the suggestion from Senator Robert Taft and former President Herbert Hoover that the United States concentrate on air and sea defense and leave to the Europeans the task of providing NATO's ground forces.

The French also criticized this point of view and insisted emphatically that the United States adopt a forward strategy, but Schumacher found little encouragement in the statement by French Defense Minister Jules Moch that for her defense France needed "an area of maneuver between the Rhine and the Elbe." West Germany could not be used as the outer perimeter of the Western defense system or a battlefield on which to destroy the invading armies from the east; it would have to be defended like the rest of Western Europe. Although NATO discussed the possibility of a defense at the Elbe, Schumacher found even that insufficient. He wanted protection for the people who lived in Berlin and the Soviet zone as well, and he argued that this could be achieved if the Western powers concentrated their forces in Germany so that they could respond to a Russian attack with such force that the decisive battle would be fought beyond the eastern borders of Germany. An offensive strategy that would seek a decision between the Vistula and the Niemen was "the most effective warning to the Kremlin" and the best means of preventing war.[43]

An offensive strategy was necessary, Schumacher added, not only to deter the Russians but also to persuade the Germans to participate in the Western defense system. If the Germans were to be called upon to defend their freedom and risk their existence as a nation, they would have to know that their fatherland, not simply the interests of other nations, was being defended. In Schumacher's words, "Those who believe that the Germans must pay for the sins of the Third Reich by sacrificing themselves for the Western powers are quite mistaken."[44] West Germany would make a military contribution when the Western powers had inextricably bound their own fate with that of the Germans. "It is up to them to create the facts so that we can say yes and amen."[45]

Finally, Schumacher insisted that the question of German participation in Western defense was "important only in terms of long-range planning."[46] It would take two to four years to prepare German troops for combat, whether or not a Soviet military threat was imminent. What was needed immediately, therefore, was an effective Western shield behind which the Germans could build a foundation for democracy so as to be able to make an effective military contribution to Western defense in the future.

In presenting his views to the public, Schumacher spoke with the assurance of one who could count on the full support of his party, and

Schumacher (left) discusses opposition to Adenauer's rearmament program with Pastor Martin Niemoeller, October, 1950. Courtesy German Press Agency.

indeed most observers interpreted his remarks as an authoritative statement of SPD policy. Yet Schumacher knew that he still had to convince the party that his offensive concept was the correct policy for the SPD. After all, the party had stated its unequivocal opposition to rearmament at the Hamburg party conference in May, 1950, and Schumacher had endorsed that view until his press conference in August. Therefore, on September 17 he met in Stuttgart with leading party officials from across the country to explain his new position.[47] He reaffirmed what he had said only four weeks before and urged his colleagues to take into account "the hard realities" of the situation. Pacifism, he said repeatedly, no longer represented a viable policy if the Social Democrats wanted to meet the full Soviet challenge. This did not mean, however, that the SPD's previous concern about the dangers of rearmament had become irrelevant. After calling for military measures, Schumacher added that rearmament could not replace a comprehensive program of social reform. Furthermore, after stressing the important role to be played by military specialists, he warned that civilians would have to remain vigilant to prevent the reemergence of a dominant military caste. What Schumacher demanded of his supporters, therefore, was recognition of the need for rearmament; what he offered them was the assurance that the SPD would accept rearmament only if its conditions were met. From

47

what followed the Stuttgart meeting it became clear that most Social Democrats had heard him say only why the SPD opposed rearmament under existing circumstances. They applauded his warning about the threat of militarism and his reference to the need for social reforms, but few heard him warn that a rejection of rearmament in principle and of the right of self-defense was an invitation to the Red Army to march across the Elbe. In the fall of 1950 most Social Democrats expected him to oppose rearmament and lead the battle against Adenauer's attempt to raise a new German army.[48]

The Pleven Plan

At the NATO Council meeting in New York in mid-September, 1950, Secretary of State Dean Acheson told the foreign ministers of the member nations that, in response to Europe's request for a firm American commitment to the defense of the Continent, the United States was prepared to continue providing financial aid for European rearmament, to reinforce American ground forces in Europe, to create a unified command structure for NATO, and to assign the role of NATO supreme commander to a ranking American officer.[49] This offer, however, was contingent on a more substantial contribution of ground forces by the other members of the alliance. Since the United States Joint Chiefs of Staff did not believe that the manpower needed for a forward strategy would be immediately forthcoming, they pressed for the creation of ten German divisions and soon convinced President Harry S. Truman of the need for an immediate start on German rearmament. It was up to Acheson, therefore, to convince the NATO foreign ministers. He assured them that the United States had no intention of permitting the Federal Republic to use a West German army as an instrument of national policy. The entire military force would be incorporated into NATO and controlled by the three occupying powers to ensure that it was used solely for a defense of the West.

Although the NATO members objected to the price demanded by the United States for its support of European defense, Acheson persuaded all but one of the foreign ministers to accept West German rearmament in principle. Robert Schuman of France argued that it was too early to raise such a delicate question and insisted that effective controls would have to be established before the Germans could rearm. Schuman admitted that the Soviet threat was pressing, but he feared that the American proposal could lead to the re-creation of a German national army and the eventual emergence of a powerful Germany pursuing its own foreign policy. Because of Schuman's opposition the official communiqué released on September 26 could only declare that Germany should be allowed to contribute to Western defense; it was left to the NATO defense committee to recommend the "methods by which Germany could most usefully make its contribution."

Realizing that German rearmament was imminent, the French government decided to produce a defense plan of its own. On October 24, Premier René Pleven proposed to the French National Assembly that the West European countries merge their military forces and create a defense community similar to the structure outlined in the Schuman Plan for the iron and steel industries. The Germans could make a contribution in the form of small combat teams—each about battalion strength—to the multinational divisions of a European army, but they would be denied a national army, a general staff, and a defense ministry. Although the Pleven Plan could be described as a distant cousin of the European army plans discussed earlier in the Council of Europe, the main reason for advancing the plan was to appease the Americans in a manner that would blunt the strong opposition in France to a German defense contribution. Pleven, therefore, linked German rearmament to the fulfillment of certain conditions: (1) the acceptance of the Schuman Plan, (2) the appointment of a European defense minister, and (3) the creation of a political assembly to watch over the minister's actions. In addition he requested that France be permitted to withhold from the European army divisions assigned to duties outside Europe and that military aid not be supplied to the Germans until the other national contingents had been equipped. The premier's proposal received only the reluctant approval of the National Assembly.[50]

Four months after the outbreak of the Korean War, therefore, NATO had two basic plans for rearming the Germans. The Americans proposed that a German army be incorporated into the Western alliance; the French, in an effort to deny the Germans direct membership in NATO, suggested the creation of a European defense community within the framework of the alliance. At the NATO Council meeting in Brussels in December, 1950, however, the Allies agreed to make the Pleven Plan, with minor modifications, the basis for West German rearmament.

In West Germany the initial reaction to the Pleven Plan was distinctly cool. A CDU deputy labeled it "an entirely unrealistic program for German participation in Western defense," and even the chancellor stated that it was filled with errors and absurdities. After conversations with the French, however, in which he was assured that there would be no discrimination against the Germans, Adenauer expressed his willingness to assist in developing the plan. He later told parliament that the Pleven Plan was a "worthwhile contribution" to one of the main objectives of German policy—European integration.[51]

The Pleven Plan had a different reception from the leader of the opposition, however. Schumacher described the French proposal as "thoroughly negative" and refused to accept it as a basis for discussion. Mistakes in the details of any plan could easily be corrected, but in this case the entire spirit of the French proposal was such that it had to be rejected. The SPD leader did not understand how the government could see in the Pleven Plan anything other than an expression of "the national egoism" of the French or in the whole conduct of the Allied discussion of German rearmament anything more than "the spirit of un-conditional surrender."[52]

Adenauer ignored Schumacher's caustic comments, but even he felt uneasy about the way the subject of West German rearmament had been treated. He noted that the Western powers had failed to ask whether the Germans wanted to make a defense contribution; they had then compounded the insult by concentrating solely on military matters without considering the changes that had to be made in the political sphere. Speaking to the press on November 24, Adenauer suggested that the Occupation Statute be replaced with a treaty so that relations between West Germany and the Western powers could be based on mutual agreement. A month later Adenauer received the answer he wanted. The NATO Council authorized the Allied high commissioners to discuss rearmament with the chancellor, "as well as any changes in the present occupation arrangements which might logically attend a German defense contribution."[53] In March, 1951, as a promise of things to come, the occupying powers agreed to a small revision of the Occupation Statute.

While these negotiations were in progress, the Western powers invited the Germans to attend parallel conferences in Bonn and Paris dealing with the question of rearmament and Western defense. Adenauer viewed this as a positive development, but Schumacher saw no real change in the Western attitude toward Germany. He accused the Americans of sacrificing German rights to appease the French and of adopting a defense plan which would "leave to the Europeans, and primarily the Germans, the role of ground troops while they mobilize all their strength for the air force and navy."[54] At a press conference in January, 1951, Schumacher emphasized that Western Europe could be defended only with the full cooperation of the United States. Neither a German army nor an all-European army, as proposed by the French, could stop the Russians. Furthermore, if the Germans rearmed on the basis of the Pleven Plan, they would be inadequately equipped, placed under foreign command, and used as cannon fodder to cover the retreat of others. "The acceptance of this plan would be the greatest sin that one could commit against the German nation."[55]

In early February the SPD leader attempted to convince the chancellor that the Germans had a strong bargaining position and did not have to rearm under present conditions.[56] Adenauer, however, doubted that the Western powers would grant any substantial concessions without first receiving from the Germans a commitment to Western defense. In response Schumacher referred to a recent statement by General Dwight D. Eisenhower, supreme commander of NATO, in which he told Congress that political equality should precede discussions about the inclusion of German units in a Western defense force. "Certainly," Eisenhower argued, "I want no unwilling contingents, no soldiers serving in the pattern of the Hessians in our Revolutionary War, in any army of my command."[57] The Social Democrats interpreted Eisenhower's statement as confirmation of their policy, and also as proof that they recognized more clearly than did the government the possibilities open to the Federal Republic in negotiations with the Western powers. Schumacher proudly stated that the firm attitude of the SPD had once again saved the nation from taking a catastrophic step.[58]

Eisenhower's statement was important to the SPD for yet another reason. In October, 1950, the Soviet-bloc countries met in Prague to discuss the German problem, specifically, the threat of a rearmed Germany. They passed a resolution recommending the maintenance of German demilitarization as outlined in the Potsdam Agreement, the establishment of a constituent assembly with an equal number of members from both East and West Germany authorized to draft a German constitution, the conclusion of a peace treaty with a united Germany, and the withdrawal of all occupation forces within a year. Immediately after the Prague Conference Soviet Foreign Minister Vyacheslav Molotov proposed that the four powers meet to discuss the Prague recommendations. Several weeks later East German Premier Otto Grotewohl sent a series of letters to Bonn urging support for the establishment of a German constituent assembly. Although Grotewohl was rebuffed by the West Germans, Molotov succeeded in persuading the Western powers to reopen four-power negotiations. A preliminary conference convened in January, 1951, to prepare the way for a formal meeting later in the year.[59] The Social Democrats welcomed the prospect of a new four-power conference, especially after Eisenhower's remarks. They assumed that pressure on the Germans to rearm would be relaxed and that the Western powers could go to a four-power conference without fear of the Soviet Union coming as the plaintiff. *Neuer Vorwärts* stated that by not pressing ahead with German rearmament the Western powers had made it possible to discover more clearly what Soviet intentions really were. They could now bring forward the demand for free elections in Germany, and the Russians would have to show their hand.[60]

Schumacher had no illusions about Soviet intentions and did not believe that, at present, the Russians were prepared to accept free elections. Their goal was to make Germany "a Russian province with German inhabitants. If the circumstances necessary for the achievement of this aim do not, or do not yet, exist, then Russian policy is and remains to hinder German unity."[61] Schumacher warned the party that the Soviets would probably enter four-power talks with the purpose of dragging them out to delay Western defense preparations and promote neutralist sentiment by exploiting the unpopularity of rearmament in West Germany. Although the neutralists in Germany had only a small following, there was considerable sympathy within the country for a neutral position between the two competing power blocs. Even the SPD had its neutralist spokesmen.

Fritz Baade, a prominent Kiel Social Democrat, told a university audience in February, 1951, that there were only two real possibilities for a defense of Europe.[62] West Germany could rearm and join a Western defense system, but that could provoke the Russians and would certainly end all chances for reunification. Or West Germany could forgo the chance to build an army in order to pursue reunification. Baade believed that the Russians might agree to free elections in Germany, even though it would mean certain defeat for the Communists, if the Germans agreed to remain unarmed and nonaligned. By observing military neutrality, he added, the Germans would not be left unprotected. German security would be based on the superior air power of the United States; the sobriety of Stalin, who "realizes that he will lose the last battle and suffer the destruction of the Soviet system"; and the mutual fear of a third world war now that both sides possessed atomic weapons. Baade concluded that if the two countries signed an honest agreement, based on respect for their own interests, "the security and integrity of such a free and unarmed Germany could be guaranteed for a long time."

Although Schumacher had also spoken in favor of military neutrality when the subject of rearmament first arose, he now rejected the idea because it no longer seemed a realistic alternative for West Germany. As for a reunified Germany, he warned, neutrality was an exceedingly dangerous course, because the English would withdraw across the Channel and the Americans across the Atlantic, while the Russians would retreat no farther than Poland. From there they could easily march back into Germany. Schumacher viewed the whole discussion of neutrality as a Soviet attempt to weaken the democratic forces in West Germany, but he added that the Western powers were helping the Russians by refusing to treat the Germans as equal members of the democratic community. "The way to take this propaganda weapon out of Communist hands is to give the Germans equality."[63] He suggested that the Western powers could begin with the defense question.

Schumacher was a very critical observer of the rearmament talks being conducted in Bonn and Paris. Throughout the period of negotiation, which lasted from January to July, he insisted that there was nothing to discuss because the Western powers had brought forward no reasonable proposals.[64] The French had their Pleven Plan, but that offered the Germans neither equality nor security; on the other hand, the British and the Americans "still had not presented a clear military and political conception" of Germany's role in the Western alliance. Thus there was no indication that the Western powers were ready to share the same "chances, risks, and rights" with the Germans. During these months Schumacher presented the same arguments that he had used in August, 1950, when he first announced his conditional acceptance of West German rearmament; in fact, his position had not changed except that it had hardened. He was more insistent on the need for granting the Germans full political and military equality and more intransigent in holding to the view that the Western powers had to create the conditions under which the Germans could rearm. There could be no compromise. He had stated his terms; now it was up to the Western powers.

The Western powers concluded their discussions of West German rearmament at a September meeting in Washington, D.C. They agreed that German rearmament would be carried out within the framework of a European army, as the Pleven Plan had originally proposed, and that German participation in Western defense would entail "the establishment of a new relationship with the Western powers and the abrogation of the Occupation Statute." Adenauer was, of course, exceedingly pleased with the results of the Washington conference. By accepting the Germans as partners in Western defense and by granting them sovereignty and equality, he said, the Western powers had "drawn a line through the past."[65]

Naturally the leader of the opposition did not share the chancellor's optimistic view of Allied-German relations. Schumacher described the Washington resolution as a blatant attempt to perpetuate the protectorate-like status of the Federal Republic and to deny the Germans sovereignty and equality. He pointed out that the political changes promised by the Allies were tied to German acceptance of the Schuman and Pleven plans, both of which were designed to exploit the economic strength and human potential of the Germans. Furthermore, there could be no talk of military equality because, except for one minor concession permitting the Germans to raise units of twelve thousand instead of five thousand men, the Western powers maintained the discriminatory policy of the Pleven Plan. For example, only the Germans were compelled to place all their forces "at the disposal of Mr. Pleven"; the other nations could maintain armies. Only the Germans were denied access to the decision-making body of the alliance; the other nations sat on the NATO Council. Schumacher concluded that the Western powers had adopted "a pro-French line" and had given their support to a foreign policy which ever since 1945 "has been haunted by the ghost of Richelieu."[66] Speaking at a political rally in the Rhineland, Schumacher said that it was time to ask the French whom they feared. If it was the Russians, then a Western defense system had to guarantee the security and respect the rights of all its members. "We are just as valuable and worth defending as France and Britain." If it was the Germans, then "people should stop discussing a German military contribution."[67]

Schumacher's criticism of the French, though severe enough, was mild in comparison to his treatment of Chancellor Adenauer. The SPD leader charged that Adenauer had always shown a willingness to accept whatever the Western powers offered him. From the Petersberg Agreement in November, 1949, through the negotiations on the Saar, the Schuman Plan, and now the Pleven Plan, the chancellor had failed to defend the rights of the German nation. This time the Germans had to stand firm. On the question of rearmament it was a matter not of moving forward step by step through a series of small successes but rather of making a decision that would be difficult to alter once "the train of German policy was set on this track." Schumacher was confident, however, that even if Adenauer accepted the Washington resolutions the decision would not be final until the German people expressed their opinion. Because of the widespread opposition to rearmament in West Germany he assumed that the public would reject the chancellor's policy.

The Demand for New Elections

On November 8, 1950, Chancellor Adenauer told the Bundestag that the Germans could not expect others to "assume the sacrifices that arise from the creation of a defense front while Germany makes no contribution at all. I believe that it is an imperative duty for every German to defend his home and freedom."[68] The West Germans, however, failed to respond with any enthusiasm. According to a poll taken by a Frankfurt newspaper in December, almost 70 percent were opposed to remilitarization, and no more than 17 percent were in favor of contributing German units to a European army.[69] Surveys made over the next two years recorded similar results. The unwillingness of the Germans to rearm seems somewhat surprising, because they were deeply shocked by the Korean War, and many feared that war would soon follow in Europe. The reasons for their opposition to rearmament are clear, however. In 1950 the destruction caused by the last war was still visible in the rows of bombed-out buildings in scores of gutted towns and was even more poignantly represented by the millions of disabled veterans and fatherless families. Furthermore, many questioned whether the Western powers could, or even would, defend Germany against an attack by the Red Army. There was considerable support for the belief that, if the Germans rearmed, the Western powers would treat them as expendable mercenaries and use Germany as the battleground. Perhaps, as some suggested, the Germans' only hope for survival was to duck their heads and let the storm pass over. Carlo Schmid captured the mood when he told a Munich audience in October, 1950, that if the Western powers could offer nothing more than a strategy of retreat to the channel then "it would be better to be bolshevized as a healthy man living in a house that still stood than to sit as a cripple in the cellar of a bombed-out building."[70]

Opposition to rearmament was strongest among young people, especially those in the age-group between eighteen and thirty. This generation had been mobilized by the Nazis and trained to believe in the cause of a greater Germany. Now, however, with the Third Reich condemned and Germany in ruins, these young Germans refused to make a commitment. Most of them were part of the so-called *ohne mich,* or "count-me-out," movement. They recognized the existence of a military threat and the need for the social and political reconstruction of Germany, but they preferred to leave the responsibility to someone else. A former general commented, with some sympathy, that men of military age "are interested only in providing for themselves and their families. They have no ideal for which to fight."[71]

Most of the large organizations—the Protestant churches, the trade unions, the refugees' and veterans' groups—were opposed to rearmament or at least to giving it priority.[72] Among the former soldiers were some who wanted to go back into uniform and some who joined with angry refugees in talking of a revanchist policy; most veterans and refugees, however, shared the general revulsion toward war. Furthermore, they disliked the idea of transferring funds from resettlement and pension programs to a defense budget. The trade unions, which were no longer directly affiliated with the SPD, also believed in the priority of social policy over military affairs. According to a statement issued in November, 1950, by the executive committee of the Federation of German Trade Unions, "The decisive means for guaranteeing lasting peace and security is the establishment of conditions which are socially just and economically sound so that it will be worthwhile for all elements of society to defend this country." The trade-union leaders, therefore, did not exclude the possibility of or even the need for a military contribution, but to rank-and-file unionists rearmament was a deadly threat to German democracy and the chances for German reunification. Opposition became so vehement that union leaders decided to adopt a neutral position by declaring, in July, 1951, that rearmament was a question for Parliament, not the unions, to decide. The leadership councils of the Protestant churches also tried to avoid taking a stand. In contrast to the Catholic church and Catholic lay organizations, who spoke of the need for a military defense against communism, the Protestants claimed that rearmament was not a religious question but a political matter which each person would have to decide for himself. There were exceptions, of course. Some Protestant leaders publicly supported rearmament by emphasizing the nation's right of self-defense; others, like Pastor Martin Niemoeller, called on their fellow churchmen to oppose Adenauer's military policy.

Niemoeller, a maverick within the German Confessional church, entered the political arena in search of allies and soon established contact with the Social Democrats. At Darmstadt in late October, 1950, he met with Schumacher and other SPD leaders. The two sides differed considerably in their point of view—Niemoeller, for example, advocated a policy of neutrality for Germany—but according to the communiqué issued at the end of the meeting, agreement was reached on a number of important matters and "was unanimous on one point, namely, that only a newly elected Bundestag can speak for the nation in this question of rearmament."[73] Although the alliance with Niemoeller faded quickly, the SPD viewed his call for new elections as a great tactical gain.

The Social Democrats first mentioned the need for new elections in September, 1950, and they pressed their demand with increasing vigor during the following year. They argued that because rearmament had not been an issue in the first general election the people had a right to express their opinion on a matter of great national importance. In a democracy, Schumacher told the Bundestag, Parliament should have the courage to go to the voters and let them determine the fate of the nation. To the objection that general elections would set a precedent for the dissolution of Parliament every time a difficult problem arose Schumacher responded that rearmament was a step which once taken "could scarcely be corrected." A German defense contribution would alter "the political psychology of the nation and the whole economic and social structure of the country."[74] He rejected a plebiscite because there was no provision for it in the constitution and because it had been misused by extremist parties in the Weimar period. Further, there were the problems of separating Socialist opposition to the government's policy from Communist agitation and of preventing such a complex issue as rearmament from being reduced to a simple yes or no. More important, Schumacher preferred a new election because that was his only path to high political office, and he strove for power with every "nerve and fiber" in his crippled body.[75]

In response to the SPD's demand for new elections, the chancellor pointed out that Parliament had the right and duty to deal with those issues that arose during its period of existence, "whether or not they were foreseen at the time of the election."[76] For whatever reason, however, Adenauer had no intention of facing the public in the fall of 1950. He realized that if new elections were held the SPD would easily upset the government's narrow majority and become the strongest single party in the Bundestag. In the three state elections held in November, the Social Democrats based their campaign mainly on the rearmament issue and made significant gains at the expense of the CDU. On the average their total vote rose by 8 percent, while that of the Christian Democrats fell by 6 percent. In the spring of 1951, although its state election gains were less impressive, the SPD continued to improve its political position relative to the CDU. *Neuer Vorwärts* wrote of the "Götterdämmerung" of the CDU, and Schumacher predicted that the Social Democrats would have about fifty more seats than the Christian Democrats after new federal elections.[77]

The Social Democrats pressed the demand for new elections with greater urgency during these months, arguing that it was essential to force a change in government before negotiations had progressed too far on the Pleven Plan. As Schumacher told the press in May, new elections had become an absolute necessity to take the pen from the hand of a man who signed every piece of paper the Allies placed before him.[78] After their impressive showing in the state contests the Social Democrats felt confident of doing so.

Adenauer did face a serious situation. Besides losing popular support, he appeared to be in trouble with members of the coalition over a number of issues, including rearmament. Interior Minister Gustav Heinemann, a member of the Protestant wing of the CDU, resigned in October, 1950, because he feared that rearmament would severely diminish the chances for reunification. His resignation, coming at a time when Niemoeller was actively campaigning against rearmament, suggested the possibility of a Catholic-Protestant split within the CDU. Adenauer's troubles also extended to the trade-union section of the party, where there was increasing criticism of his domestic policies. Among the coalition parties the Free Democrats were the most dissatisfied with the chancellor. They criticized his style of leadership and openly opposed both the Pleven and Schuman plans. It was possible for Schumacher to assume, therefore, that under pressure the coalition would crumble and pave the way for a new government through new elections. Whether Adenauer could have been overthrown is difficult to say, because Schumacher never used the opportunities that were available. He was absolutely convinced of the correctness of his own views and would not compromise with disgruntled members of the coalition, insisting that any new government would have to adopt the SPD program.[79] Since that was even less acceptable to the coalition parties than the chancellor's policies, they preferred to take their chances with Adenauer rather than risk an alliance with Schumacher.

Regardless of his relations with the other political parties, Schumacher felt confident that Adenauer could be stopped. He knew that the chancellor's military advisers were concerned about the unpopularity of rearmament and that they had advised the chancellor to seek the support of the SPD for a bipartisan policy.[80] Furthermore, Adenauer had publicly admitted that the final decision on rearmament would have to be made by Parliament.[81] He realized, as Schumacher did, that, because the constitution made no reference to military matters, an amendment would have to be passed before the government could begin its rearmament program. Since a constitutional amendment required a two-thirds majority, which the government parties could not muster, the SPD could block Adenauer's rearmament policy. Schumacher's decisive weapon, however, remained outside Parliament. He established contact with the veterans, the refugees, and the trade unions, and initially there appeared to be room for considerable agreement on both rearmament and socioeconomic issues. More important were the state elections, which he viewed primarily as a "lever" to shake the people's confidence in the reliability of the Adenauer government.[82] The SPD leader hoped that in time public dissatisfaction would become so great that the coalition would feel compelled to seek a dissolution of Parliament. In new general elections the tide of popular opposition would be strong enough to sweep Adenauer out of office and bring the SPD to power.

When rearmament became a prominent issue in the fall of 1950, a German newspaperman commented that "Schumacher thinks his turn has come."[83] The press generally agreed that on this question he was more in step with public opinion than Adenauer but there was growing concern about the course pursued by the SPD. Critics charged that SPD opposition was negative, irresponsible, and opportunistic.[84] One writer pointed out that Schumacher's electoral strategy could produce a loss of public confidence both in the government and in the whole parliamentary system. Instead of political tension, what the country needed was domestic peace. The success of the neo-Nazi Sozialistische Reichspartei (Socialist Reich party) in the May, 1951, Lower Saxon state elections pointed to the dangers that still faced the young republic. There were limits, however, to Schumacher's opposition policy. Although he exploited the antirearmament mood of the population, he nonetheless warned that the *ohne mich* movement was "foolish and ill-considered"; and although he allied with "antirearmers" like Niemoeller, he did avoid the Communists. With them there could be no alliance.[85] Still, according to his critics the problem was not the extent of his opposition; of greater concern was the lack of a clear and realistic alternative to the government's policy.

Schumacher was very sensitive to such criticism, but on close examination there was less clarity in the party's position than he was willing to admit. From the beginning he had emphasized that it was not a question of remilitarization or pacifism. The rearmament debate was between those who would press their demands regardless of the rights and needs of the German nation and those who would demand the fulfillment of certain conditions before giving their consent to the creation of a new German army. After the state elections in November, 1950, Schumacher said that the voters had approved the party's "temporary no" on rearmament until "all necessary prerequisites" had been met.[86] Although that was Schumacher's position, it is questionable whether the electorate, or even the party, interpreted the SPD's position in this manner. In state elections the party conducted its campaign on a platform of unqualified opposition to rearmament. Election posters read: "Barracks or Hospitals! CDU or SPD!" A piece of literature handed out by the party at election time contained the slogan "Vote against remilitarization! Vote for peace, social justice, and freedom. Vote Social Democrat!" To any candid observer it appeared that the party was fundamentally opposed to a defense program, but that was not the case—at least not according to Schumacher. Yet one could legitimately ask whether Schumacher could have carried out his own rearmament program if the SPD had won a general election. Could he have convinced his own party to accept the need for a new German army? There is room for doubt.

In the fall of 1950, Schumacher warned his colleagues that pacifism could not be the basis of SPD policy, and he admonished them not to think that "social formulas alone" could stop the Red Army. There is little evidence, however, that the party was listening, because early in 1951 he still faced demands for a declaration of total opposition to West German rearmament. Those demands he rejected, but thereafter he rarely confronted the party about facing its responsibilities in the military area. No doubt he was sensitive to the party's mood and, like SPD leaders before him, responsive to pressure from below,[87] but there were other reasons for his failure to challenge the party. Increasingly, because of his ill-health and his involvement in the struggle against Adenauer and the Allies, he found less and less time for party matters. Those like Erich Ollenhauer who managed the party for him shared to a great extent the antimilitary sentiments of the rank and file, and thus they were content to focus attention on Schumacher's policy of intransigent opposition. At the end of the first year of the rearmament debate, therefore, the Social Democrats still had not come to grips with the military question. They had simply taken up where they had left off in the Weimar period.

Schumacher's ideas on the military question were bold and imaginative. From all that he said on the subject, however, it is not clear what kind of army he would have supported. He treated the military question as primarily a political problem and approached the task of creating a new army in terms of the party's continuing struggle to prevent a restoration of antidemocratic forces in Germany. Rearmament, he told the Bundestag, was not simply a technical problem which could be handed over to those with skills and experience in the military area—that is, the old officer corps. The Weimar Republic had organized a highly efficient military force but then allowed the Reichswehr to become a state within the state—an end in itself. A new German army would have to be motivated by the notion of service to the people and dedication to a great idea: "The ethos of an army in modern mass society is the feeling of political and national freedom and the will to serve a great international idea, a great human idea. Military organizations without ethical bonds are a source of danger for domestic and foreign affairs and for those outside and inside Germany who would press for their formation."[88]

Schumacher's concern about a new German army stemmed in part from his Weimar experiences but to a greater extent from the demands being raised by former army officers, some with neo-Nazi connections, and from the manner in which rearmament was being treated by Adenauer and the Allies. He was appalled by the readiness of the Americans to enlist the support of anybody who proclaimed himself an anti-Communist, as though all that concerned them was the creation of an army as rapidly as possible. Schumacher doubted that Adenauer, with his lack of experience in military matters, possessed the determination to resist the assaults of the old officer corps and to democratize the army. Thus with the threat of a revived militarism and the lack of a realistic defense plan for Germany, Schumacher was not surprised that so many Germans opposed rearmament. When a reporter asked him to comment on the report that a million young men would try to avoid military service, he replied that if the SPD was responsible for creating a new military organization there would be no conscientious objectors.[89] Unfortunately Schumacher avoided a public discussion about the kind of army that was best for West Germany. Privately, however, he spoke in favor of a democratic people's army (Volksarmee) and against both a volunteer army and a militia system; the latter did not meet "the needs of the German situation" while the former, "without roots in the nation," was a threat to democracy.[90] In March, 1951, an SPD newsletter acknowledged the party's preference for a Volksarmee and stated that, "if all other premises are fulfilled, the citizen must recognize an obvious duty in the defense of the state."[91] That was Schumacher's view, but he told the press in Bremen, "Before we can talk about military service [Wehrpflicht] we must decide first of all whether there is going to be a German defense contribution."[92]

Schumacher realized, of course, that at some time in the future the Germans would rearm and that it would be necessary to use former officers of the Nazi Wehrmacht to help create the new army. Although he attacked the officer corps for its cooperation with the Nazis, he judged the officers on an individual basis and was prepared to make contact with those military leaders who had not been irretrievably compromised by their behavior toward Hitler. In the fall of 1950, Schumacher held a series of meetings with prominent military men, among them General Hans Speidel and Adolf Heusinger, who advised the chancellor. There was much to be gained from these meetings. Since the generals shared many of his arguments against existing plans for German rearmament, the SPD leader hoped to win their support against the government. Their opinions would carry a good deal of weight with veterans' organizations and would be listened to by politicians faced with making a decision on rearmament. In addition the generals could provide valuable ammunition for the party to use in the rearmament debate. Simply by demonstrating the feasibility of Schumacher's forward strategy, they could prove the correctness of his opposition course. Since the SPD leader was not opposed to rearmament in principle, however, there must have been another reason for the meetings. Perhaps he was thinking of the day when he would become chancellor, and negotiations with the Western powers would be carried through to a successful conclusion. At that time the experience and technical skills of reliable officers would be needed to create an army for the republic. These contacts could also help prevent a recurrence of the Weimar situation, in which the working class and the officer corps had displayed a deep mutual antipathy. Whatever the value of these meetings, however, Schumacher found it very difficult to justify them to the pacifists in the party and to reconcile them with the vigorous campaign the SPD was waging against rearmament. The meetings continued until the summer of 1951, when they were terminated except for several later conversations with Heusinger.[93]

The generals were impressed by Schumacher's knowledge of and interest in military affairs. Correspondents who followed his political career also commented on his firm grasp of power politics. Schumacher, however, was afraid that the German public would get the wrong impression about his views. There was a good deal of confusion, for example, about the meaning of "offensive strategy." Some believed that Schumacher wanted to wage a war of liberation to reconquer the lost territories in the east, but that was definitely not the case. He told the Bundestag in November, 1950, that no German could think of military power in terms of preparing for another war.[94] Military strength could have its justification only in the preservation of peace, and that idea would have to be inculcated in the mind of the nation. Turning to the parties sitting on the right, he questioned whether they clearly understood the dangers involved in power politics. Schumacher realized, of course, that his own party tended to make the opposite mistake of underestimating the role of power in international affairs. To the SPD and the nation, therefore, he offered his forward strategy as an alternative to the policies proposed by those who would rearm under any circumstances and those who sought peace at any price.

Schumacher's insistence on a forward strategy was not an unreasonable demand. Hans Speier describes his concept of defense as one of the few genuine military alternatives to the strategy of nuclear retaliation advanced during the early years of the rearmament debate.[95] Certainly there were excellent political and military reasons for insisting that the Western nations meet the Soviet challenge as far east as possible. First, the development of an atomic bomb by the Soviet Union had forced military men to reconsider the possibilities of another Normandy-style landing on the Continent; second, the Western strategy of retreat in response to a Russian attack had little appeal for those Europeans who would be abandoned to the Red Army. With the heightened international tension following the outbreak of war in Korea, the need for a forward strategy became even more pressing.

Schumacher realized that the Germans were greatly concerned about the strength and proximity of the Red Army, and he feared that they would be tempted to remain neutral unless the Western powers adopted his forward strategy. If they did, he confidently predicted, not only would neutralist sentiment be destroyed but also those who were trying to exploit those sentiments would be dealt a severe blow. He proudly stated that the Communists had properly understood the meaning of his concept when they said that his goal was "to relieve the people from the pressure of fear."[96]

By demanding a strategy which would carry the main battle beyond the borders of Germany, Schumacher also had an opportunity to make political profit by showing the Germans that he knew how to defend the national interest better than Adenauer did. His forward strategy, however, was more than a tactical gesture. He believed that the Western powers were pursuing a selfish policy in defense of their own interests without regard for Germany, and he saw in their actions a consistent effort to exploit the Germans. In response he demanded that the Western powers share the same risks and sacrifices as those the Germans had to make, that they commit themselves to the defense rather than the liberation of Europe.

Schumacher's demand for an offensive strategy has been described by some as purely demagogical and by others as nothing more than a red herring.[97] Schumacher himself conceded that war was not imminent, yet he insisted that the Western powers, mainly the Americans, mass their forces on the Elbe. But was it realistic to raise such a demand, especially when American troops were on the road south from Seoul to Pusan, and the American government was desperately trying to obtain greater military support from its NATO partners? In any event, Carlo Schmid had already told the Council of Europe that the Allies were incapable of helping the Germans rearm because "they are so short of modern arms that they have the greatest difficulty in equipping their own troops."[98] One could assume, therefore, that because of its predicament the West would be willing to grant the Germans sovereignty and equality in return for a defense contribution.

The bargaining style was typical of Schumacher. From the founding of the Federal Republic he had insisted that Adenauer use the trump cards in his hand to win concessions; now he demanded that the chancellor be as defiant and steadfast as the Social Democrats had been in April, 1949, when they had forced the occupying powers to accept their views on the constitution. In a letter to the SPD leader Adenauer warned that undue resistance from the Germans could antagonize the Americans to the point that they would not only abandon the cause of German reunification but eventually withdraw into isolation, leaving the Continent under Soviet influence. Schumacher replied that there was no need to rush into negotiations because the Americans could not afford to lose their position on the Continent. Firmness and unanimity by the Germans in maintaining the conditions laid down by the SPD would produce the desired results.[99]

Some observers have suggested that in his attempt to bargain with the Western powers, Schumacher did not appreciate the unrealistic nature of his demand. The SPD leader, however, claimed that he was under no illusions. As he told the Bundestag, if his demand was utopian, then the whole idea of a defense of Europe had "a utopian character."[100] Although Schumacher never stated in public how many divisions his forward strategy would require, Carlo Schmid said later that it would take about fifty British and American divisions to make German rearmament worthwhile. He claimed that similar figures had been used by Generals Heusinger and Speidel to justify a defense contribution.[101] In 1951, however, the United States indicated that it would send no more than six divisions to Europe. The Social Democrats immediately interpreted this as an attempt to burden the Germans with the defense load and to avoid the risks and sacrifices that would be required for a real defense of Europe. It can be argued that if the Western powers carried out the military buildup demanded by Schumacher the Russians would have responded with a military buildup of their own in East Germany, thereby destroying whatever chances still existed for German reunification. The evidence suggests, however, that Schumacher viewed Western rearmament not as a barrier but as a means of opening the path to reunification.[102]

In the November, 1950, foreign-policy debate, Chancellor Adenauer stated that negotiations with the Soviet Union would stand a chance of success only when the Western powers had built a defense front strong enough to deter Soviet aggression.[103] Although Schumacher sharply criticized the chancellor's handling of the rearmament question, in that debate he did not question Adenauer's idea of building a position of strength in order to negotiate with the Russians. The SPD leader merely pointed out that with the Pleven Plan the Germans would never attain equality, and the West would not create the strength needed to meet the Communist challenge. During the following year, as Adenauer developed his policy of strength, Schumacher continued to attack its components but not its basic premise. The necessary components, of course, could be produced only in cooperation with the West, and for that reason Schumacher attacked the Western powers for their attempt to use small means in dealing with the great questions of the day. According to Klaus-Peter Schulz, an SPD member from Berlin, Schumacher wanted the whole border area from Lübeck to Passau converted into a huge international garrison. The SPD leader himself demanded a concentration of military forces on German soil that would make the power and resolution of the Western democracies "strikingly visible."[104]

Although he was aware of other trouble spots around the globe, the SPD leader insisted that Western power—above all, American power—had to be concentrated at the decisive point, which was Germany. "We must convince the Americans that . . . the loss of Germany would mean the loss of the whole European continent." If that happened, the United States would find itself involved in a war of continents against three-quarters of humanity. Schumacher added that in facing the Communist challenge the Western powers had to do more than defend their sphere of influence in Germany, thus accepting the final division of the country. "The price for such a policy [would be] paid [not] by Germany alone but by the cause of freedom throughout the whole world." It was essential, therefore, that the Western powers convert what was basically a defensive posture into an offensive position if they were to win the Cold War.[105]

The focal point of the offensive which Schumacher had in mind was the demand for free elections in Germany. He wanted to make this demand "a formula of the European and world democracies" for countering Soviet propaganda.[106] Of course, the Russians were certain to reject free elections because acceptance would mean the loss of Soviet influence in Germany. By forcing them "to respond to a realistic offer," however, the Western powers could reveal Communist agitation in favor of German unity for what it was—a fraud. Schumacher insisted that if the Western powers agreed to his demands for equality they could then go to a four-power conference and demonstrate to the enslaved peoples of Eastern Europe that in comparison to life under Soviet rule freedom and justice reigned in the West. They could also show that it was the Russians who had refused to support disarmament measures and had depressed living standards by their pursuit of the arms race. It would not be hard to demonstrate which side possessed a desire for peace. With this kind of political offensive, based on a new set of power relations in Central Europe, Schumacher assumed that in time the Russians would come to the conference table prepared to negotiate their withdrawal from Germany—perhaps even from Eastern Europe—as part of a general redivision of spheres of influence in the world.[107]

One can only speculate about the possible results of Schumacher's offensive concept, because it was never tried. Whether it could have been brought to fruition, however, is doubtful. In 1950 the Western powers were not ready to accept the Germans as full partners. The Americans, who were the most likely of the three powers to support this kind of policy, were not prepared to make the extensive commitments that Schumacher demanded. There were influential figures like John Foster Dulles who indulged in the rhetoric of rolling back Communism, and even Acheson spoke of the need to build situations of strength—which sounded deceptively similar to Schumacher's demand for a concentration of Western power—but the government did not believe that vital American interests were to be served by taking the offensive. It was committed to a policy of containment. Thus, whereas Schumacher wanted to win the Cold War, American foreign policymakers were determined not to lose it. It was this acceptance of the status quo that the SPD leader wanted to alter. Even if he could have won the support of the Americans, as well as the British and French, however, reunification could have been achieved only if the Russians had been compelled to relinquish their hold on Germany. Later, when the Western powers did attempt to negotiate from strength, the Russians responded with an increased determination to compete with the West. The result was a stalemate and a deepening of the division of Europe.

One may also question the manner in which Schumacher approached the task of trying to win support for his offensive strategy. He did not seem to appreciate the limitations placed on German leaders by Western attitudes toward Germany, and his defiant national stance, although founded on a democratic base, alienated many potential allies. Adenauer, on the other hand, was more sensitive to Western opinion. He believed that Schumacher's demand for a massive power concentration on German soil as a prerequisite to German rearmament was totally unrealistic.

Although the chancellor requested Allied protection, he was willing to rearm and to accept guarantees from the Western powers to show his faith in their good intentions. Schumacher wanted facts, not promises. He insisted that "our contribution could only be the second step after the others have taken the first to guarantee our security."[108] He informed the chancellor that an essential difference of opinion also existed over whether equality should come "at the beginning or at the end of the road to rearmament."[109] Whereas Adenauer would rearm in order to obtain equality, Schumacher would rearm only after the Germans had become equal partners in the Western community.

By the end of the first year of the rearmament debate Schumacher realized that the Western powers would not meet his conditions, and from the Washington conference of September, 1951, he knew also that they would not wage a political offensive for German unity. At this point, therefore, the SPD leader introduced an argument that had not been heard since before the Korean War. He warned that rearmament would threaten the chances for reunification. The danger was obvious from the very beginning, but now, because his attempt to persuade the Western powers to adopt an offensive strategy had failed, he stiffened his opposition to rearmament and assailed Adenauer for accepting Western integration before German unity.[110] Yet had the Western powers agreed to his demands—that they bind their fate with that of the Germans—the result would have been the same. Schumacher resolved the contradiction by insisting that integration on the basis of his offensive strategy would open the path to reunification whereas the integration schemes accepted by Adenauer would rob the Federal Republic of its "attractive power" in the East. The SPD, therefore, refused to compromise or even to consider negotiations on rearmament until its conditions were met. Since, however, Adenauer was prepared to accept the Washington resolutions and to ignore the Social Democrats if necessary, the distance between the government and the opposition grew wider and wider. By the end of 1951 the SPD found itself immobilized in a policy of intransigent opposition.

CHAPTER 3

The European Defense Community

Following the Washington, D.C., foreign ministers' conference in September, 1951, the Western powers and the six member nations of the proposed European Defense Community (EDC)—France, Italy, West Germany, and the Benelux countries—convened to draft a pair of treaties, one to replace the Occupation Statute, the other to establish the new defense system. By January, 1952, agreement had been reached on the military aspects of the treaties, but progress on political matters proved to be more difficult.[1] While Adenauer insisted that the occupation regime be scrapped and replaced by a totally new arrangement based on the idea of partnership, the occupying powers wanted to maintain as much influence as possible on the conduct of German affairs. Eventually the British and the Americans reduced their demands to gain German acceptance of the treaties, but the French hesitated to grant further concessions. They feared that the Germans, freed from the occupation regime, would soon withdraw from EDC and "go their nationalist way—armed and intransigent." As a result the French demanded a series of security measures: the exclusion of West Germany from NATO, the separation of the Saar from Germany, and the assurance of Anglo-American support against German secession from EDC.[2] The problem facing the negotiators, therefore, was to reconcile the conflicting interests of the Americans, who wanted German troops for Western defense; the French, who wanted security against a rearmed Germany; and the Germans, who wanted sovereignty and equality in return for a military contribution to Western defense.

During these difficult negotiations with the Western powers Konrad Adenauer felt heavy pressure from both the government parties and the opposition. The Free Democrats were especially critical of his handling of foreign policy. Although they accepted the Schuman Plan, which Parliament ratified in January, 1952, they subsequently joined with the opposition to force a full parliamentary debate on rearmament.

The General Treaty and the EDC Treaty

On February 7, Chancellor Adenauer opened a hectic two-day debate with an appeal to Parliament and to a large radio audience at home for support of the government's foreign policy.[3] Adenauer promised that with the signing of the treaties the Federal Republic would receive virtual sovereignty. There was, he said, another reason for continuing the present course: "The point of departure for our considerations, and the cause of all that has happened in recent years, is the policy of expansion and aggression pursued by the Soviet Union." To meet the Soviet challenge, Adenauer proposed a policy of integration with the West. He offered the European Coal and Steel Community and the proposed defense community as complementary aspects of an effort to create a united Europe and a secure Western world.

Speaking for the ailing Kurt Schumacher, who had suffered a paralytic stroke in December, Deputy Chairman Erich Ollenhauer blasted the chancellor for conducting a policy of fear. Turning to the government bench where Adenauer was sitting, he said, "You and I know, Herr Bundeskanzler, that the present situation gives no cause for filling the people with such alarm."[4] Ollenhauer pointed out that the chancellor was using the same arguments in favor of rearmament that he had employed in November, 1950. At that time Adenauer had warned of the Soviet menace and the danger of American withdrawal into isolation unless Europe united and the Germans rearmed. Since then nothing had happened. The West had grown stronger, not weaker, and the threat of Soviet aggression had, if anything, diminished. Certainly the French saw no need to press ahead with EDC; in fact, said Ollenhauer, no one in the West saw cause for panic—except the chancellor.

Although he acknowledged the existence of a Soviet threat, Ollenhauer argued that the extent to which the Russians were actually planning to wage war remained "in the realm of speculation." The reality of the existing situation was the Cold War. In the Kremlin, he said, policymakers thought in terms of political infiltration, not military confrontation. As a result the Western powers could no longer pursue the arms race at the expense of living standards, and in West Germany social security would have to take precedence over a military contribution to Western defense. Under present conditions "a hundred new homes are more important for the defense of German democracy than a hundred soldiers."[5]

The SPD came under sharp attack from the government parties for giving priority to the social question. With 180 Soviet divisions facing the West, the military threat was obviously real, and if the Germans were unwilling to make a defense contribution now, the burden would have to be shouldered by the other Western nations. The Christian Democrats insisted that West Germany had a moral obligation to share the burden.[6] The Social Democrats responded defensively that by emphasizing the social question they were not suggesting that the Germans stand aside with their hands in their pockets while other nations defended German democracy. At present, however, rearmament had to be seen as a political matter, as a question of whether the policy pursued by the government could lead to meaningful cooperation in a European defense system. The Social Democrats denied that it could, and they demanded that the government negotiate a new set of treaties based on the idea of "equal risks and equal chances for all."[7]

At the end of the debate the Social Democrats voted against a resolution in support of the government's foreign policy because none of the conditions they had laid down for a German defense contribution had been met. The coalition parties, however, gave Adenauer a vote of confidence—though they provided a list of conditions to be met by the Western powers. Armed with this commission, Adenauer returned to the conference table. Several months later he signed the treaties.

The General Treaty, which established a new basis for Allied-German relations, represented a major step toward sovereignty for West Germany. Except for certain rights retained by the Western powers in relation to the city of Berlin, the question of reunification, the signing of a peace treaty, and the right to declare a state of emergency in case of external attack or internal subversion, the Federal Republic had full control of its own affairs. The EDC Treaty represented the key to the entire arrangement because only after its ratification would West Germany gain the political freedom provided for in the General Treaty. For the French, however, neither the direct connection between the two treaties nor the restrictions placed on German rearmament by the EDC Treaty were sufficient to remove all their fears. At the last moment Britain and the United States had to guarantee "the unity and integrity of EDC" which meant preventing the Germans from withdrawing, in order to gain French acceptance of the treaties. The General Treaty was signed in Bonn on May 26, and the EDC Treaty in Paris the following day.[8]

Before the negotiations ended, the Allies had to remove some reservations on the German side. In Bonn the coalition parties expressed concern about certain aspects of the treaties. Adenauer had failed to keep them informed about the details of the negotiations, and although not all members of the coalition agreed with the chairman of the Deutsche Partei (German Party) that the General Treaty was a "second Versailles," they were dissatisfied enough to inform the chancellor that the draft agreements were unacceptable.[9] The coalition parties objected in particular to the emergency clause of the General Treaty, which permitted the Allies to resume full political control if the stability of the democratic order in West Germany was threatened, and to the revision clause, which would transfer to the government of a united Germany the obligations undertaken by the Federal Republic. They had assumed that all traces of the occupation regime would be completely removed.

Furthermore, they had expected the Western powers to deal promptly with such questions as the release of war criminals, the return of the Saar, and the admission of West Germany to NATO. The chancellor, however, proved adept at calming his coalition partners. Although he was unable to gain satisfaction on all of the troublesome issues, in the last stage of the negotiations he won important concessions from the Western powers, for example, redrafting of the two disputed clauses, which was sufficient to satisfy his supporters, or at least to answer their objections for the moment.

The Social Democrats, however, refused to remain silent. They labeled May 26, the day Adenauer signed the General Treaty, "a black day for Germany." A party spokesman warned that the Germans could expect not freedom but a petrification of the occupation regime; not equality but continued discrimination; and, above all, not unity but a deepening of the division of Germany.[10] Schumacher wasted no words: "Whoever signs the General Treaty ceases to be a German."[11] There were attempts later to deny that he made the statement, but when pressed by the government parties, the Social Democrats refused to disclaim it. During the EDC debates in December, 1952, Adenauer quoted from an interview that Schumacher had given earlier in the year, in which the SPD leader had said: "I will fight the signing of the EDC Treaty. If it is signed, I will campaign against it while the soldiers are being mobilized. If I were elected chancellor, I would repudiate the treaty as soon as possible." The Social Democrats responded with loud applause, and an SPD deputy called out, "It could not have been said any better."[12] This was three months after Schumacher's death.

No one could give more forceful expression to the party's rejection of the treaties than Kurt Schumacher. Even he, however, realized that his words were often too strong and sometimes alienated possible supporters. They created the mistaken impression that the SPD was an extremist party. The Social Democrats had no intention of repudiating international treaties or going beyond the bounds of legality in their dispute with Adenauer, but they were determined to stop him from rearming West Germany. The question was how.

The SPD Goes to Court

Once it became clear that Adenauer would sign the General Treaty and rearm West Germany on the basis of the EDC agreement, the Social Democrats had to formulate an opposition strategy. Several possibilities existed. They could resort to extraparliamentary action—rallies, marches, and demonstrations—to mobilize public opinion against the government, they could press their demand for new elections, or they could take their case to the Federal Constitutional Court (Bundesverfassungsgericht, BVG) to set up legal roadblocks to the chancellor's rearmament policy. The SPD leaders investigated all three courses of action.

In December, 1951, Gustav Heinemann wrote to Schumacher asking his support in a nationwide campaign to gather signatures for a petition against rearmament. Ollenhauer, who was substituting for the ailing party leader, responded four weeks later that Adenauer could be defeated only at the polls, that petitions or plebiscites were worthless. He warned Heinemann that such a campaign would attract the Communists and give the government a chance to accuse its opponents of pursuing a pro-Soviet line.[13] On February 5, two days before the Bundestag's foreign-policy debate, an SPD deputy also urged that the party go directly to the people. Again Ollenhauer opposed the idea. Not until after the debate, in which Adenauer secured a vote of confidence from the majority parties, did the SPD Executive Committee examine the possibilities of waging an extraparliamentary campaign.[14] The time seemed opportune. During the following months refugee groups demonstrated in Bonn to express their dissatisfaction with the government's relief program; the trade unions demanded action against the government's handling of the factory council bill; some unions even spoke of a political strike. On the military question local union officials pressed the national leaders to support a radical antirearmament campaign, and local SPD groups pledged their support for a more active opposition policy, including "the development of a broad national movement (Volksbewegung)" against rearmament.[15] In May, when Schumacher vowed to continue the fight against the treaties, it seemed that the SPD would embark on a radical course of action. Even within the Bundestag delegation sentiment in favor of extraparliamentary action was building. The SPD leader, however, had no intention of taking to the streets against the government; other options were open to the party.[16] Either the Bundestag or the Bundesrat, or if necessary the courts, could be used to block Adenauer's rearmament program, thereby forcing new elections.

One of the most consistent themes in the SPD's opposition campaign was the demand for new elections. In the February, 1952, debate, for example, Ollenhauer called for a dissolution of Parliament on the grounds that the Bundestag elected in 1949 no longer represented the "will of the nation" and therefore lacked the moral authority to carry out rearmament.[17] Although Adenauer still refused to pay any attention to SPD demands, the Social Democrats had an opportunity the following month to take their case to the people in the Baden-Württemberg state election. The election offered an important test for both the government and the opposition. A victory for the CDU could be interpreted as confirmation of Adenauer's foreign policy; on the other hand, an SPD victory would provide a degree of legitimacy to its demand for new elections as well as provide the party with enough votes in the Bundesrat to block ratification of the treaties. With this in mind Schumacher told a radio audience that if the electors "are at their posts the worst can still be avoided."[18]

In the Baden-Württemberg election the Social Democrats continued to improve their position against the CDU. The Christian Democrats, however, won the most votes in this election and, together with the Free Democrats, their allies in the Bonn coalition, held a majority of the Landtag seats. To everyone's astonishment the state leader of the FDP, Reinhold Maier, formed a coalition government with the SPD and the Bund der Heimatslosen und Entrechteten (Refugee party, BHE).[19] This was an important tactical victory for the Social Democrats. They had strengthened their position in the Bundesrat and became more confident of their ability to stop Adenauer. Their trump card, however, was the Federal Constitutional Court (BVG), which they assumed would deliver the coup de grace to the chancellor's policy.

As early as October, 1950, Schumacher had warned that the government could not carry out its rearmament policy on the basis of the majority vote in Parliament. A constitutional amendment would have to be passed, with the required two-thirds majority, because the constitution made no reference to an army or the right to raise an army (Wehrhoheit).[20] The Social Democrats, however, waited until January, 1952, before taking action. In an attempt to block the chancellor, who was arguing that a simple majority would suffice for ratification of the treaties, they filed a petition with the BVG in Karlsruhe, requesting the high court to declare that Parliament would have to amend the constitution before West Germany could rearm.

Adenauer had no intention of letting the Social Democrats forestall his foreign policy by an appeal to the constitution, and he casually dismissed their appeal to the BVG as "superfluous and hopeless."[21] According to the chancellor, the Parliamentary Council of 1948-49 not only had discussed the military question and the possibility of war but also had envisaged the creation of German armed forces. After all, those who drafted the constitution would not have declared in article 26 against preparations for an offensive war unless they believed in the possibility of a defensive war. The Social Democrats responded that this article represented nothing more than an unequivocal declaration of the nation's will for peace at a time when memories of the war were still fresh.[22] Why then, asked Adenauer, did the constitution makers state in article 4 that protection would be given to conscientious objectors, unless they were thinking of conscription? What the Parliamentary Council had in mind, claimed the Social Democrats, was to protect young Germans, like those in the labor battalions, from being forced by the Western powers to bear arms against the Germans in the Soviet zone. The Parliamentary Council had been drafting a constitution for a state without the right to build an army of its own. Finally Adenauer referred to article 24, which permitted the Federal Republic to transfer its sovereign rights to an international organization and join a collective-security system to preserve peace. Since EDC served this purpose, the treaties could be ratified by a simple majority. Not so, said the Social Democrats. The Federal Republic could transfer sovereign rights to an international organization only if it became a member of that organization. Since NATO was the decision-making body of the alliance and since the Germans had been excluded from NATO membership, conceding West Germany's rights to EDC made no sense. Furthermore, EDC hardly corresponded to what the Parliamentary Council had in mind when it drafted article 24. EDC and NATO were systems of collective self-defense organized by the Western nations against the threat of Soviet aggression. A system of collective security would include all members of the world community and would designate the aggressor only after the act of aggression had been committed. Logically, if this distinction was maintained, Germany could not make a military contribution to Western defense, but the Social Democrats refused to go that far. They were content to prove that Adenauer had no legal basis for rearmament.

The coalition parties conceded that the constitution contained no explicit authorization for rearmament. Since the right of self-defense was one of the implied powers of government, however, they argued that the Federal Republic did possess Wehrhoheit and the coalition could proceed with the creation of a new military force without amending the constitution. The Social Democrats were not so politically naïve as to deny West Germany's right of self-defense. They concentrated instead on the gaps in the constitution.[23] For example, it said nothing about the powers of the Federal government in military matters or about the organizational structure of the armed forces (Wehrverfassung), that is, what kind of army the country would have—conscript or volunteer; who would be the commander in chief—the president or the chancellor; and who would decide when the armed forces could be used—the parliament or the commander in chief. Finally, every individual who entered military service had to surrender certain basic rights, but the constitution made no provision for a change in the legal status of German citizens. Therefore, an amendment would have to be passed before there could be a German army or German contingents in a European army.

The Social Democrats, along with the deputies of the Föderalistische Union (Federalist Union), filed their petition with the BVG on January 31, 1952. Nothing happened for several months. The high-court justices tried to avoid making a decision, viewing the entire affair as a political rather than a legal matter. Finally in late July they rejected the SPD's petition on the grounds that judicial review could be exercised only on legislation which had been formally enacted by Parliament. Court action at this time would be interpreted as interference in the legislative process and would violate the constitutional principle of the separation of powers. The SPD, therefore, would have to resubmit its petition after the treaties had been ratified.[24]

The verdict shocked the Social Democrats. They insisted that unless the BVG acted before ratification West Germany could face international obligations which were contrary to the law of the land. Besides, it would hardly be possible "to unarm divisions after they had been formed or to take German units out of a European army once it had been organized."[25] According to Fritz Heine, the SPD press secretary, the nation faced a state crisis because of the court's failure to act.[26]

The situation was not as desperate as the Social Democrats claimed. Even after ratification it would take at least two years to raise a German army, and that was sufficient time for the BVG to act on a petition from the SPD. Furthermore, there was little chance for ratification that summer. Although Adenauer wanted Parliament to ratify the treaties before the summer recess, the coalition parties refused to be rushed. They wanted time for a more thorough examination of the treaties, and the most they would agree to was a first reading in July, with the second and third readings to follow sometime after Parliament reconvened in September.

In addition to the trouble brewing in the Bundestag, Adenauer faced a difficult situation in the Bundesrat. The chancellor had originally hoped to bypass the upper house, except for minor aspects of the treaty system, but the state governments insisted on their right to participate in the ratification process. On June 20 the Bundesrat went one step further and announced that it would deal with the treaties only when their constitutionality had been established by the BVG. Furthermore, President Theodor Heuss had already asked the high court for an advisory opinion. The president asserted that he wanted to be able to act, one way or the other, once the treaties were presented to him for signature. Indirectly, therefore, the Social Democrats would get an answer from the BVG.

Despite the storm warning Adenauer remained confident that the treaties would have a safe passage through Parliament. The first reading was held in July, and although the treaties remained in committee longer than expected, they finally passed their second reading on December 4. Ordinarily the Bundestag would have completed its work the following day, but Adenauer suddenly postponed the third reading and directed the coalition parties to submit a petition to the BVG. The chancellor, hearing rumors that the court's advice to the president would be unfavorable, embarked on a complicated legal maneuver designed to preclude a decision on the president's request for an advisory opinion. When the court refused to cooperate, Adenauer urged Heuss to withdraw his request, which he did on December 10.[27]

The Social Democrats immediately accused the chancellor of provoking a constitutional crisis. They charged that to avert certain political defeat Adenauer had exerted "massive pressure" on the president and had attempted to manipulate the Federal Constitutional Court for partisan political purposes.[28] At a press conference on December 12, Ollenhauer declared that the only solution was for the government to join the Bundestag and the Bundesrat in submitting a joint request to the BVG for an opinion on the constitutionality of the entire treaty system. He urged Adenauer to delay further the final reading of the treaties because Parliament would end its four-year term in a few months. Besides, the "approval of the treaties by a slight majority, a majority which in this question certainly does not express the will of a majority of the nation, provides no basis for the execution of laws of such wide range." Holding new elections before a third reading was the most sensible course of action.[29] Adenauer, however, had no intention of conceding to the SPD. He wanted the treaties ratified before a general election, and he would avoid Karlsruhe as long as chances for a favorable verdict seemed unlikely. Since the Social Democrats could neither force new elections nor appeal to the BVG until after the treaties had been ratified, they had no choice except to wait for Adenauer to make the next move.

Although Adenauer's actions sparked the political controversy in December, 1952, the Social Democrats bore the brunt of the blame because they were the ones who initiated the legal battle. The party's critics accused them of using the courts to "continue politics by other means"[30] and of waging a "war of nerves" to force new elections. It can be argued, however, that, since the constitutionality of rearmament was in question, the SPD did have a right to its day in court. According to the Social Democrats, their appeal to the BVG stemmed from a genuine concern for the preservation of constitutional legality because of what had happened in Weimar Germany. They also realized, of course, that if the court decided in favor of a constitutional amendment the government would suffer a devastating defeat. It was in this sense an astute political move. The Social Democrats, however, were motivated not only by political competition with Adenauer but also by their concern about the impact of rearmament on the chances for reunification. They treated reunification as the most urgent task facing the nation, and in time they made opposition to Adenauer's rearmament policy for the sake of German unity a party principle.

Rejection of the Policy of Strength

After signing the General Treaty on May 26, 1952, Adenauer proudly declared that the Germans had now taken the "first step toward reunification." Through integration with the West they were building a platform from which to launch a policy leading ultimately to the restoration of German unity.[31] The Social Democrats disagreed with the government's list of priorities. They argued that the nation should work first to reunify the country and then to promote European integration. Without reunification, said Carlo Schmid, other national goals would remain incomplete, and "this tiny Little Europe [Kleineuropa] would become nothing more than a possible bridgehead for the Americans."[32]

This line of argument, not a new one, emerged gradually after the Washington conference of September, 1951. It was a response to the party's belief in the primacy of reunification and an expression of its attempt to maintain a consistent policy of opposition to the chancellor. At first the Social Democrats indicated that they were opposed only to current plans for Western integration. As Schumacher told a radio audience in October, 1951, German unity and Western integration did not have to be mutually exclusive. Two months later he still felt that integration could strengthen the chances for reunification if it was carried out on the basis of social-democratic principles. But in January, 1952, when Parliament accepted the European Coal and Steel Community and Adenauer brought negotiations on EDC closer to completion, the Social Democrats declared that integration could only mean a "capitalist, clerical, and conservative" Europe. Schumacher took the predictable step of declaring that the SPD would "fight against attempts to integrate any part of Germany with other nations in advance of German reunification."[33]

By giving absolute priority to the question of unity, the Social Democrats had to oppose any action which could transform the provisional West German state into a permanent structure. That included not only commitments which would bind West Germany to Western Europe but also, if the argument was carried to its logical conclusion, the acquisition of sovereignty by the Federal Republic. Sovereignty would give legal recognition to the division of Germany and free the Western powers of their responsibility for reunifying the country. By implication it would also give the East German regime the right to claim sovereign status. These developments alarmed the SPD. Gerhart Luetkens, the party's foreign-policy expert, told the Bundestag in October, 1951, that sovereignty was neither politically possible nor desirable before reunion with the Soviet zone.[34]

However logical Luetkens's declaration may have been, the Social Democrats found it a difficult position to defend, and Ollenhauer quickly took the podium to explain that the SPD deputy was expressing a personal opinion.[35] As a West German political party the Social Democrats had to demand an end to the occupation regime and a restoration of German sovereignty. They emphasized, however, that West Germany's sovereign status could be only a temporary condition, lasting until Germany was reunited. They also demanded that in dealing with the West the government "keep to agreements of a provisional nature."[36] In this way the Germans could hold open the path to reunification and maintain a free hand in dealing with the occupying powers.

While the Social Democrats assumed that the Western powers would accept such an arrangement, Chancellor Adenauer saw more realistically that the Germans could not expect to play an independent role. The Western powers were still suspicious of their former enemy and apprehensive about the reemergence of a powerful Germany. Obviously they would support reunification only if they were sure the Germans would remain loyal allies. It was up to the Germans, therefore, to win their confidence and thus gain a voice in the councils of the Western Alliance, which Adenauer said could best be done by accepting EDC and the General Treaty. The chancellor denied, however, that his policy represented a conscious choice between unity and integration, as the Social Democrats charged. To achieve reunification, he said, the West would have to be united and strong. The Russians "were not going to give us reunification in freedom as a present," he told the Bundestag. They had to be confronted with the overwhelming strength—in particular, the military strength—of a united Western front. Only then would there be a "genuine point of departure for peace negotiations to free not only the Soviet zone but all of enslaved Europe east of the iron curtain." There was no other possibility.[37]

The Social Democrats did not share the chancellor's faith in a policy of strength. They accused him of playing at power politics and indulging in the kind of "illusionary thinking which certainly does not lie in the German interest."[38] Of course, in condemning Adenauer's approach, the party took leave of Schumacher's forward strategy. By May, 1952, however, the SPD leader himself had joined the chorus, pointing out that "German unity was not a matter of power politics."[39] This was a surprising statement from a man whom journalists only two years earlier had called a Realpolitiker. Yet his attack on the chancellor's policy was not based on a conversion to the antimilitary attitude of the party rank and file because he still understood the importance of the power factor in international affairs. It is possible that after the severe stroke he suffered in December, 1951, Schumacher no longer possessed the strength to maintain his forward strategy against those who took over the reins of the party.[40] Although Ollenhauer and the men at party headquarters insisted in January, 1952, that "what Schumacher said fourteen months ago is still valid," they were now warning "German democrats to beware of arguments from the world of power politics."[41]

Schumacher was certainly under pressure from party colleagues to abandon a policy of strength, but more compelling reasons accounted for his decision. To begin with, the SPD leader realized that the Western powers would not meet his conditions for a German military contribution or his demands for an offensive strategy. At first glance this seemed an unduly pessimistic view because NATO, at its meeting in Lisbon in February, 1952, had agreed to provide about fifty divisions "in appropriate conditions of combat readiness" before the end of the year and a total of ninety-six divisions, including twelve from West Germany, by 1954.[42] The Lisbon goals were too ambitious, however, and the universal public response was one of skepticism. A writer for the *Times* (London) pointed out on February 26, that the proposed figures would not impress the Russians, "who know the true state of affairs." In the following months the NATO allies demonstrated that they had no intention of meeting their commitments. Fear of Soviet aggression was beginning to diminish in Europe, and although the arguments in favor of greater conventional strength appeared sound, the Europeans remained unconvinced. They continued to view NATO's ground forces, whatever their number, as a trip wire to trigger an American nuclear attack. As a result, in December, 1952, the NATO Council decided to reduce substantially the Lisbon goals and to concentrate on improving the quality of existing military units.

The Social Democrats promptly pointed out the lack of good faith shown by the Western powers in demanding something from West Germany that they themselves refused to deliver.[43] The Social Democrats, however, expressed little concern over NATO's failure to achieve the Lisbon goals. First, they were opposed to a defense plan based on EDC, and, second, they believed that NATO had misread the nature of the Soviet challenge. *Neuer Vorwarts* commented in an editorial that it was foolish to allocate more funds to the defense budget when communism was already thriving on the lack of social-reform programs in countries like France and Italy. Unfortunately, the paper said, Adenauer still failed to see the mistake of relying on military means alone to provide security. Furthermore, his rearmament program threatened to paralyze "the most effective defense contribution of the Federal Republic in the Cold War, namely, the consolidation of democratic powers of resistance by policies of social justice."[44]

Besides criticizing Adenauer for giving primary emphasis to military matters, the Social Democrats questioned the chancellor's claim that by rearming the Germans the West could build a position of strength for negotiations with the Russians. In an interview in late May, Schumacher pointed out that twelve German divisions would not tip the balance in favor of the West.[45] If the Federal Republic joined the Western Alliance, he said, the Russians would respond by incorporating East Germany into the Soviet bloc and raising an equal number of East German divisions. Nothing would be achieved except that the level of arguments would be driven higher. The Germans, therefore, should put aside arguments about a threatened use of force and help promote East-West negotiations as soon as possible. "We stand at the crossroads," SPD deputy Fritz Erler told the Bundestag. "One road leads to an attempt at the peaceful reunification of Germany and the reduction of international tension; the other leads to the heightening of existing tensions and the transformation of the two zones into fortresses of the two power blocs."[46]

The Soviet note of March, 1952, provided one final reason for abandoning the policy of strength. Since the Western powers refused to adopt his offensive strategy, and for the present the Russians could not be frightened into surrendering their hold on East Germany, the SPD leader felt that it was necessary to examine closely any Soviet proposal on the German question.

The Soviet Note of March, 1952

From the opening of the rearmament debate Soviet interest in German reunification varied in direct relationship to the West's determination to rearm the West Germans. After the NATO meeting in New York in September, 1950, the Russians invited the Western powers to discuss the German question at a four-power conference. They also directed the East Germans to begin conversations with the Bonn government. These efforts to initiate either four-power or all-German talks continued through the early months of the following year but were relaxed once it became apparent that the NATO allies disagreed on how to rearm the Germans. When the Western powers finally decided to proceed with EDC, the Russians and the East Germans reopened their political offensive. The day after the Washington conference East German Premier Otto Grotewohl warned that the remilitarization of the Federal Republic would threaten chances for peace and reunification. He suggested that an all-German conference be convened because agreement among the Germans was the basic condition for restoring German unity. In the following months the East German regime made similar appeals, all seconded by the Soviet occupation authorities, but Adenauer and the Allies refused to accept the Communist slogan "Germans at One Table."[47] When NATO called for an accelerated armament program at its Lisbon meeting in February, 1952, the Russians returned to the idea of a four-power conference.

In a series of notes delivered between March and September, the Russians urged the Western powers to join them in an attempt to settle the German question.[48] They offered a detailed draft of a peace treaty and suggested, as the first step toward reunification, the formation of an all-German government composed of representatives from Bonn and East Berlin and the signing of the treaty, followed by free elections and the withdrawal of all foreign troops from German soil. The frontiers of this reunited Germany would be those established by the Potsdam Conference; specifically, the Russians wanted German recognition of the Oder-Neisse Line. Reversing their earlier demand for German demilitarization, the Russians agreed to the creation of a limited military force on the condition that a reunited Germany would not "take part in any coalition or military alliance directed against any power" that had fought against Nazi Germany. That meant a neutral Germany.

In reply the Western powers demanded a different procedure in settling the German question. They wanted to begin with free elections, followed by the formation of a new German government and the negotiation of a peace treaty with the occupying powers. The Western powers characterized the creation of a German national army as "a step backward," insisting that a reunited Germany should be free "to enter into any associations compatible with the principles and purposes of the United Nations," by which they meant EDC or NATO. This last proposal was totally unacceptable to the Russians. They had not initiated the campaign against West German rearmament in order to deliver all of Germany to the Western Alliance. On the other hand, the Western powers could not be expected to help create a situation which would open up Central Europe to Soviet domination. Many Europeans feared that the treaty proposed by the Russians would lead to the withdrawal of American troops from the Continent and invite Soviet forces stationed across the Oder-Neisse Line to intervene in German affairs. The Western powers, therefore, "had to weigh the uncertain and risky prospect of a neutralized Germany against the certainty of a Western increment of power at a crucial stage in the Cold War."[49] Without hesitation they decided to continue strengthening their position in Europe by completing the treaty system being negotiated with the Federal Republic.

Adenauer voiced complete agreement with the decision to delay negotiations with the Soviet Union. He viewed the entire Soviet offensive as little more than a blatant attempt to disrupt Western defense efforts, and he urged that the treaties with the West be completed as quickly as possible. The treaties constituted the basis of Adenauer's foreign policy. He wanted to forge the closest possible ties between Germany and the West because, he said, "our future lies in this partnership alone."[50] For the moment only the Federal Republic could be integrated with the West, but he assumed that the Soviet Union would eventually agree to the reunification of Germany and its inclusion in the Western community. Although the Russians showed no sign of weakening, Adenauer declared nonetheless that his policy of strength was beginning to show results. Six days after the first Soviet note was delivered to the Western powers, he told a CDU audience at Siegen, "If we continue to help make the West strong, the point will soon be reached when the Russians are ready to negotiate sensibly."[51]

The government parties shared Adenauer's suspicions of Soviet intentions and accepted his argument in favor of close cooperation with the West. Yet the deputies and the public at large felt uneasy about choosing Western integration before German reunification. Some feared that this could be the last chance for discussing the German problem with the Russians. The Free Democrats, along with several prominent members of the chancellor's own party, urged that the March note be closely examined at a four-power conference before ratification of the EDC and General treaties,[52] but Adenauer persuaded the coalition to accept his strategy that negotiations should follow rather than precede ratification.

The Social Democrats were most insistent that the government delay

Schumacher (right) with West Berlin Mayor Ernst Reuter, 1952. Courtesy German Information Center.

ratification until after the four powers had met to discuss the Soviet proposals. As a matter of fact, when the Eastern offensive began in September, 1951, the Social Democrats urged the Western powers to make the Russians "lay their cards on the table."[53] Schumacher told a radio audience immediately after Bonn received Grotewohl's letter that, although the Kremlin's goal was still the creation of a Soviet Germany, this "most recent variation in Soviet strategy" was worth investigating. He pointed out that in discussing reunification Grotewohl had mentioned free elections but had omitted the demand for equal representation of the Bonn and Pankow regimes in an all-German conference. This was new and could not simply be ignored by the West; otherwise, it would appear that only East Germany wanted reunification. The Russians, he said, would like nothing better than to be able to show the East Germans that the Federal Republic had subordinated reunification to Western integration. It was up to the Western powers, therefore, to clarify the situation by discovering through four-power negotiations what "stands behind the gestures of the Pankow marionettes."[54]

As the Eastern offensive gained momentum, the Social Democrats began speculating about the possibility of a change in Soviet policy toward Germany. Just before Christmas, Schumacher insisted that the

United Nations' investigation into the question of all-German elections had placed great moral pressure on the Soviet Union which the men in the Kremlin could not escape.[55] Of greater consequence was the political situation in East Germany, where, according to the Social Democrats, the SED held a very precarious position. *Neuer Vorwärts* reported in a banner headline on March 7 that there existed a "crisis of the Soviet-zone regime" because of rising popular opposition to the Communists. Thus three days later, when in a diplomatic note Joseph Stalin offered to discuss the German question, the SPD eagerly pressed the Western powers to accept the Soviet invitation.

The Social Democrats quickly became disillusioned with the Stalin note because it proposed a dictated peace settlement rather than negotiations between a freely elected German government and the four occupying powers. Moreover, it made no mention of the free elections that the Social Democrats treated as the essential first step toward reunification; the Russians insisted instead on direct talks between Bonn and Pankow. With some regret Ollenhauer admitted that the note could be only a tactical maneuver designed to prevent the incorporation of West Germany into the Western Alliance, either by exploiting French opposition to EDC or by offering German nationalists an army and German neutralists a chance to withdraw from the East-West conflict. Yet he insisted that the Soviet note had its positive side because it offered a proposal for immediate talks and a chance to see what the Russians really wanted.[56]

As the exchange of notes dragged on through the summer of 1952, the Social Democrats became more and more concerned about the failure of the Western powers to bring the Russians to the conference table. It appeared to them that the West was blocking negotiations by its insistence on certain preconditions and priorities. Ironically, the Social Democrats agreed with the Western procedure for reunification, but they insisted that the purpose of a four-power meeting at this stage was to investigate "the possibilities" for holding serious conversations on the German question. It was a matter of finding out whether the Russians had made a rigid offer or merely raised certain demands for bargaining purposes.[57]

The Social Democrats had grave doubts about whether Adenauer and the Allies really wanted to see Germany reunified. They noticed a considerable gap between the declarations made in favor of German unity and the actual energy expended by the Western powers in trying to achieve it, and they asked why Adenauer showed less zeal in pursuing reunification than in promoting rearmament. Their answer was simple. Fearing that reunification would open the large reservoir of Socialist support in the Eastern zone and bring the SPD to power, the chancellor was using the division of Germany to protect the reactionary forces in Bonn and to bind the Federal Republic to a clericalist and capitalist Kleineuropa.[58] As for the Western powers, they too were committed to a defense of the status quo, either by a deal with the Russians or by a permanent freeze in the Cold War.

Throughout the EDC debate the Social Democrats made good use of the West's ambiguous attitude toward the question of German reunification to challenge the chancellor's assertion that the treaties bound the Western powers to an active reunification policy. If anyone was bound, they said, it was the Germans. SPD spokesmen pointed out that the treaties would remain in effect for fifty years and that, although the General Treaty had a revision clause, changes could be made only with the consent of all the signatories. The Social Democrats assumed that the French would veto any step toward German reunification.[59] Furthermore, since the Western powers wanted to extend the treaty system to cover all of Germany, and had so informed the Soviet Union, ratification of the treaties would be interpreted by the Russians as a negative reply to their offer of a four-power conference. "If it had been planned intentionally to prevent the Russians from agreeing to free elections," said Carlo Schmid, "no better way could have been chosen."[60]

In mid-July, Fritz Erler wrote a letter to the *Deutsche Zeitung* in which he tried to answer the question how the Russians could be persuaded to accept free elections.[61] He dismissed an appeal to moral arguments because they "suffice as little as armaments." What counted was the price the Western powers would be willing to pay to compensate the Russians for the loss of an important piece of territory. Since free elections would mean the end of Communist rule in East Germany, the only acceptable price for the Russians would be "the renunciation of German participation in the Western alliance system." For that matter, any attempt to draw Germany into either of the competing power blocs would destroy chances for reunification.

The policy of nonalignment proposed by Erler can be interpreted as a logical outgrowth of the SPD's insistence on the primacy of reunification, but it contradicted arguments used by the party in recent months. For example, in January, Ollenhauer had reiterated Schumacher's earlier warning that neutrality was either "a fantasy or a conscious attempt to support Communist expansion." Three months later Carlo Schmid referred to armed neutrality as an "absurd idea" even though it was the basis of the Stalin note on reunifying Germany.[62] Erler, who had recently been elected to the executive committee of the parliamentary party (Fraktion), took the position nonetheless that military nonalignment was both necessary and safe.

Speaking to the students at Bonn University, Erler suggested that Germany could follow the example of Austria in identifying politically with the West without becoming a military ally of the Western powers. Austria was able to hold free elections, establish a single government, maintain close economic ties with the West, and avoid Communist interference in its affairs. Although Erler did not state publicly how the problem of German security could be treated, he did offer a plan to the party leadership. He proposed that the Germans build a small army for domestic purposes—in case of an attempted putsch from the left or the right—and obtain a security guarantee from the great powers against the threat of external aggression.[63]

The SPD leaders turned down Erler's proposal. While they agreed with him that Russia would never permit Germany's inclusion in the Western alliance, they insisted nonetheless that the status of a reunited Germany would have to be the subject of negotiations between a freely elected German government and the occupying powers.[64] Furthermore, Erler's proposal amounted to the neutralization of Germany and the denial of equal rights to its people, which was one of the party's major criticisms of EDC. During the first reading of the treaties an SPD deputy had suggested that a reunited Germany could join a world-security organization like the United Nations as an equal member and thus avoid the perils of neutrality. The SPD leaders, however, made no effort to develop this idea during the summer months.[65] Their main concern was to get the powers to the conference table without complicating matters by raising another issue. Presumably once the Russians agreed to free elections as the first step to the creation of an all-German government, then all other problems would find an easy solution.

The Soviet note of March, 1952, thus helped strengthen the SPD's opposition policy, but without clarifying it. The Social Democrats demanded that integration be delayed until the Russians had been sounded out. After all, said Ollenhauer, the West Germans could not bind their hands for fifty years in an alliance with the West unless they were 100 percent certain that the Russians were unalterably opposed to free elections.[66] The party's concern was understandable, but the urgency with which the Social Democrats pressed their demand for a four-power conference hardly corresponded to their estimation of Soviet intentions. At an Executive Committee meeting in January, Ollenhauer said that the Russians wanted to open negotiations and keep them going—but without coming to a conclusion. Although he later suggested that a timetable be established to prevent the Russians from filibustering, others in the party pointed out that, since the Americans had negotiated for a year and a half over the release of several thousand prisoners of war in Korea, they could certainly devote as much time to the liberation of eighteen million Germans.[67] To the question how long negotiations would last, Schmid answered that, once the Russians had made it absolutely clear that they wanted Germany as "a Russian province" a new situation would be created. Then "one must consider what has to be done next."[68] In the summer of 1952 the Social Democrats knew only that, whatever it was, it could not be EDC.

Rejection of EDC

According to the treaty, the European Defense Community would have an integrated military force of forty-three divisions, twelve of which would be German.[69] Integration would be carried out at the division level—a vast improvement over the original Pleven Plan—but the national divisions would not have their own support units, and no two divisions of the same nationality could be combined in the same army corps. Further integration would be carried out through the standardization of equipment and the use of common uniforms and officer training schools. This six-nation force would then be placed within the command structure and strategic planning of NATO.

To administer EDC, the treaties called for the creation of a council of ministers, a parliamentary assembly, and a board of commissioners. The board was to be the executive arm of the community and would consist of nine members appointed for six years. It would act as a kind of defense department, handling all aspects of the organization, training, and supervision of the European army, as well as preparing the budget and the armament program in consultation with the various national ministries. The parliamentary assembly was to be composed of deputies elected by the member nations' parliaments. Although it would have no legislative responsibilities, the assembly would review the work of the executive and could overthrow the board of commissioners by passing a vote of no confidence. It was the council of ministers, however, which was to exercise direct control over the board by virtue of its right to give unanimous approval to the most important policy matters. The six members of the council would act as "protectors of the sovereign rights" of their respective states, but they were expected to harmonize the policies of their governments with the activities of EDC.

The Social Democrats expressed great dissatisfaction with the organizational structure of EDC. They charged that it provided neither the proper safeguards for the separate interests of the member states nor the necessary means for the democratic control of an international army. Above all they criticized the exclusion of the national parliaments from the construction and operation of the defense community. The council of ministers failed to provide an effective instrument of control. For example, the German delegate represented the government rather than the Bundestag, and his vote "behind closed doors" could plunge Germany into another war.[70] Even less satisfactory was the parliamentary assembly, which Erler called a "caricature of a parliament." He pointed out that the commissioners could act without consulting the assembly while the deputies could dismiss the board only by a two-thirds majority. The EDC Treaty, therefore, was nothing more than an "Enabling Act for the technocrats, in this case, the military."[71] When the deputies from the six member parliaments assembled later to discuss the treaty, Erler expressed dismay at the lack of concern shown about the undemocratic aspects of EDC. It appeared to him that the Germans were the "most concerned democrats"—thanks to their own "painful experiences."[72]

The Social Democrats also criticized the economic aspects of EDC.

In particular they pointed to the control powers granted to the board of commissioners over the production of armaments and munitions. They feared that the board would discriminate grossly against German industry and force the Germans to purchase most of their military supplies abroad. Furthermore, since the Americans were not going to equip twelve German divisions and the other EDC nations could hardly be expected to help with German defense costs when they balked at paying their own, the Germans would have to finance rearmament themselves. The Social Democrats considered this impossible. In no other West European country, said Ollenhauer, were the extremes of ostentatious luxury and wretched poverty more strikingly visible. To pay for rearmament the government would have to raise taxes, further lowering living standards, and divert funds from such vital areas as aid to Berlin and to the millions of refugees and war victims living in West Germany.[73] Although the Bundestag passed a resolution in February, 1952, asking the Western powers to take these matters into consideration when assessing West Germany's defense contribution, the Social Democrats doubted that the government parties were fully cognizant of the dangers involved.

The purely military aspects of EDC were treated at some length by Fritz Erler in a pamphlet entitled *Should Germany Arm?* Erler became involved with the military question in August, 1950, when Schumacher asked him to "get interested" in military matters.[74] Why the SPD leader selected Erler remains unclear; the young deputy, whose training was in public administration, had little military experience. In fact, he had been in the army only a few months in 1938 when he was arrested by the Nazis. He spent the next six years in prison. On the other hand, Erler possessed a clear, well-disciplined mind and a sober understanding of the importance of the military question. In the fall of 1950 he made contact with former army officers and later brought them together with prominent Social Democrats, including Carlo Schmid and Herbert Wehner. Erler organized these meetings to prevent a repetition of the Weimar situation, in which the army sided with the right-wing parties against the Socialists and the republic. It was also an opportunity for Erler to become acquainted with the thinking of German military men and to formulate ideas of his own. When the Bundestag formed a committee in July, 1952, to study the military aspects of the EDC Treaty, Erler quickly established a reputation as an expert in the field. His pamphlet, which the party published two months later, summarized his views on EDC.[75]

Erler offered some severe criticism of EDC. He pointed out that the Western powers planned to build an international army without regard for national differences or preferences and that, since the defense community would determine the internal structure of the army, there was no opportunity to create a new military system based on "modern German ideas." Erler was referring to the work of certain military reformers in the Blank Office (Dienststelle Blank), an embryonic defense ministry attached to the chancellor's office and headed by a former trade-union official, Theodor Blank. He applauded their reform plans, especially their attempt to replace the militarism of the past with the concept of the citizen in uniform. Because of the SPD's growing concern about how Adenauer would use the Blank Office, however, Erler demanded both a parliamentary committee to control its activities and a guarantee from the government that Parliament would be included in all decisions on rearmament.[76] It was essential, he said, that everything be done to prevent a revival of the reactionary caste spirit of the old army. Unfortunately, the EDC Treaty "offers very little security against it."

Continuing his critique of EDC, Erler complained bitterly of the second-class status assigned to the Germans within the defense community. He pointed out that they were the only ones who had to assign all their forces to the European army. The other member states could maintain a national army to defend their interests outside Europe. What would happen, Erler asked, if an EDC member became overcommitted abroad, as the French could in Indochina? Obviously EDC would be weakened by the heavy drain on French military resources, but the losses could not be made up by raising more German troops because, according to the treaty, France always had to have a larger contingent in EDC than West Germany. Simply by keeping the French involved elsewhere, the Russians could weaken the entire West European defense system.

To Erler the exclusion of the Germans from NATO constituted blatant discrimination. Echoing Schumacher, he charged that without access to the NATO Council the Germans would be nothing more than a "foreign legion" at the disposal of the Western Alliance. Germany would supply the troops, while "the others decide what they will do, where they will be used, and what territory they will defend."

The Social Democrats hammered away at the lack of equality in EDC and the continued discrimination by the Western powers against the Germans. They pointed to Adenauer's failure to establish a basis for mutual trust upon which a genuine defense effort could be built. As it stood, said Ollenhauer, the proposed defense community was a dangerous experiment that would fail in "the hour of danger."[77] Since the Germans stood at the front, they were certain to suffer most in the event of a Soviet attack.

Trying to sell the treaties to the German people, Chancellor Adenauer claimed that by joining EDC the Germans would become part of the most comprehensive defense system in the world. As a member of the Western alliance system they would gain the greatest imaginable security. The chancellor warned, however, that any delay in ratifying the treaties would leave Germany unprotected against the threat of Soviet aggression.[78] To the Social Democrats this was a gross distortion of the facts. Adenauer possessed no inside information on Western defense plans. For that matter, the Western powers had delayed a decision on a defense strategy for Western Europe until after the presidential elections in the United States. Furthermore, even if the Federal Republic ratified the treaties, EDC would be no closer to realization because, as Ollenhauer pointed out in November, 1952, the French would deal with the treaties sometime the following spring and the Italians in the summer. After the six member nations had ratified the treaties, it would still take the Germans another two years to become combat-ready—1955 at the earliest.[79] What protection was there for the Federal Republic in the meantime? According to the Social Democrats, none at all. There was no guarantee of automatic military assistance in the event of an attack from the east. At best the French would use the area between the Elbe and the Rhine as a battleground for the defense of France. As for the Americans, Erler told the Bundestag in December, 1952, that they still planned to use the Germans as partisans and to blow up the Rhine bridges while they withdrew their own troops toward the Atlantic and Channel ports. Schumacher commented caustically that in a European army "orders to attack will be given in German, but orders to retreat in another language." By joining EDC, therefore, the Germans would gain only the "illusion of security" while sacrificing their land and their blood in the defense of foreign interests.[80]

To the Social Democrats, EDC and the General Treaty demonstrated the bankruptcy of Adenauer's foreign policy. The Social Democrats pointed out that the alleged benefits of the General Treaty would be granted to the Germans only on the condition that they provided soldiers for the Western Alliance. This meant that the Germans were being denied the free decision that was part of any genuine partnership, while being forced to join a defense system that provided neither equality nor security. As for sovereignty and freedom, the treaties changed nothing in West Germany because the occupying powers remained the ultimate source of authority. According to Schmid, the Western powers "wanted to abolish the Occupation Statute but not the regime."[81]

One of the primary objectives of Adenauer's foreign policy was to create a new set of relations between Germany and the West, based on a sincere reconciliation between the Germans and the French. By 1952 he had made progress toward a formal agreement on West European integration, but, as the Social Democrats pointed out, France's traditional fears of a strong Germany remained. The French still viewed German rearmament as a threat to their security rather than a contribution to Western defense, and they made their acceptance of EDC contingent on the fulfillment of certain demands, including the exclusion of the Germans from NATO and the separation of the Saar from Germany. The SPD considered these conditions totally unacceptable. One Social Democrat asked how the French would feel if the Germans made the return of Alsace and Lorraine a prerequisite for their acceptance of the treaties.[82] French demands for the Saar greatly embarrassed Adenauer, but he pressed ahead with the treaties, believing that in time this matter, as well as the question of German membership in NATO, would resolve itself.[83]

The Social Democrats warned the chancellor against accepting an unfavorable settlement with the hope that in time it could be modified; that would compel the Germans to pursue a revisionist foreign policy as they had in the Weimar period. The consequences of such a policy, said Schmid, "are well known."[84] While admitting that the resentment which many Europeans felt toward the Germans would take time to overcome, the Social Democrats argued that it would be a mistake to bring West Germany into a partnership with the free world in stages, by gradually dismantling the occupation regime. If a basis of confidence and mutual understanding could not be established at once, "then so-called European projects had better wait." Any other procedure would risk compromising the idea of a unified Europe for generations.

Adenauer responded that if the Bundestag rejected the EDC and General treaties it would force the Western powers to seek an alternate course of action. They had several options: they could maintain the occupation regime and deny freedom to the Germans; if they lost confidence in the Germans, they could seek a compromise with the Russians; failing that, the Americans and the British could withdraw into isolation and abandon Germany to the Russians. Thus, in voting on the treaties, the deputies were dealing with a question that involved the destiny of Germany. "We have the choice of slavery or freedom. We choose freedom."[85]

Adenauer's remarks provoked an angry response from the Social Democrats. They objected to the implication that those millions of Germans who opposed the treaties wanted slavery instead of freedom. With this kind of thinking, said Ollenhauer, the chancellor "surpasses even the arrogance and ignorance of Kaiser Wilhelm II, who once characterized the Social Democrats as *vaterlandslose Gesellen* (men without a country)."[86] As for the need to ratify the treaties immediately, Ollenhauer argued that the Germans had no reason to rush into an agreement with the West because "nothing has been decided yet." The international situation was in a state of flux, which meant that a four-power conference on Germany was still possible, and within the Western Alliance there was no fixed agreement on the treaties. The French felt uneasy about EDC, the British refused to join it, and the Americans viewed it simply as a means of raising German troops.[87] As for the threat of an American withdrawal from Europe if the Germans rejected the treaties, SPD Deputy Adolf Arndt commented that to maintain its world position the United States had to prevent the Russians from seizing the rest of Germany. After all, "It is not our beautiful eyes that keep Americans in Europe but our industrial potential."[88] They would have to reopen negotiations with the Germans on a new basis once the present treaty system had been rejected.

Throughout 1952 the party's critics freely admitted that the SPD frequently brought forward important objections to the treaties but could offer no clear alternative. In the Bundestag, for example, SPD speakers were unable to silence coalition deputies who heckled them with calls of "Well, what would you do?" Their replies were unclear, often unrealistic; in fact, because of the "aura of indefinition" which surrounded their position, it was difficult to determine exactly where the SPD stood on West German rearmament.[89] According to Herbert Wehner, a former Communist who joined the SPD after the war and became a member of Schumacher's inner circle, there were three prerequisites for a German defense contribution: real security, genuine equality, and an open road to reunification.[90] From the party's arguments, however, it was hard to explain how all three could be met simultaneously.

The Social Democrats declared that the immediate goal of any German policy had to be the reunification of Germany. It was primarily for this reason that they opposed the General Treaty and EDC. As the debate progressed, however, they began arguing as though rearmament, rather than a specific set of treaties, was endangering the chances of reunifying Germany. They warned that rearmament would lead to an arms race and a sharp rise in international tension, whereas to achieve reunification the Western powers would have to pursue a policy of detente. "We need a policy which does not pour oil on the fire," said Erler.[91] But how was this to be reconciled with the party's demand for security? Writing in June, 1952, Schumacher demanded that Germany be defended "the same as any other country," and in the following months his colleagues continued to criticize the Western powers for their failure to develop a strategic concept which would guarantee the security of Germany.[92] The Social Democrats also demanded complete political and military equality for the Germans. In EDC the Germans were denied the rights of other member nations; in particular, they did not have a voice in the decision-making process of the Western Alliance. Genuine equality could be achieved only if the Germans had a seat in the NATO Council. But the Social Democrats, although they constantly made reference to the Federal Republic's exclusion from NATO, did not want to join the alliance—at least not yet.[93] The first step had to be a four-power conference on the German question to determine whether or not the Russians would agree to free elections.

At best, the party's position on rearmament was "not yet." SPD leaders stated that they approved rearmament in principle, and before the first reading of the treaties Ollenhauer reminded the party of its obligation to contribute to the defense of the German democracy.[94] After he listed the conditions for a defense contribution, however, the SPD's yes in principle became a clear no in practice, which was what the rank and file wanted. One could argue, therefore, that the Social Democrats were without a defense policy for West Germany in 1952. Throughout the year they moved further and further away from the military basis of Schumacher's offensive strategy, and, beyond the demand for a policy of social security first, they had nothing tangible to offer the West Germans. Rearmament would have to wait until the four powers had dealt with the question of German reunification.

In contrast to the SPD's uncertain attitude about rearmament, Adenauer urged the West Germans to rearm in cooperation with the West. With his policy of strength he promised concrete gains for the West Germans, in particular, immediate progress toward West European unity and, most important, security for the Federal Republic. Although Adenauer exhibited a certain amount of self-deception in asserting that this policy would also lead to a unified Germany, it was a deception that most West Germans seemed ready to share.[95]

The Social Democrats warned that Adenauer's policy of strength, with its reliance on military means alone, constituted a dangerous course for the Germans. A show of Western military might would fail to impress the Russians, and a war of liberation would lead to total destruction. The only alternative was four-power negotiations. At the conference table the United States and the Soviet Union could settle their differences and agree on spheres of influence.[96] But why would the Russians surrender their hold on East Germany? Erler, who was the only Social Democrat to pursue the question at length, suggested that they might be interested in a German settlement because of the political situation in the Soviet zone or because of the pending alliance between "German military potential and American industrial strength." Schumacher had already warned that if the West went ahead with EDC the Russians would respond with the rearming of East Germany. It was essential, therefore, to negotiate. In the meantime, Erler said, "the narrow path of German foreign policy lay somewhere between an unconditional no to any military contribution, which would make us a satellite of Soviet policy, and an unconditional yes to the treaties, which would make us a satellite of American policy."[97]

Such a prescription for West German foreign policy was thoroughly unrealistic. The Western powers were not going to grant West Germany the freedom of action the Social Democrats wanted, and an SPD-led government holding to an inflexible bargaining position would only create a state of open tension in Allied-German relations which the Social Democrats, like the Christian Democrats, wanted to avoid. Ultimately, an SPD chancellor would be compelled to do what Adenauer had done. As for the SPD's reunification policy, the Social Democrats had nothing to offer except a call for negotiations with the Russians. They rejected Adenauer's policy of strength, but in its place they offered nothing more than "a naïve internationalism" which downplayed, if it did not ignore, the role of power in foreign affairs.[98] Unfortunately for the Social Democrats, their departure from Schumacher's earlier position came at a time when most West Germans were coming to accept the validity of Adenauer's foreign-policy views. The Social Democrats, however, refused to concede anything to the chancellor. They became more deeply entrenched in their opposition course and in the process allowed tactical arguments to harden into party principles.

Soon after the treaties were signed, Schumacher stated that the SPD based its opposition policy on the interests and vital needs of the German people. Since reunification was the most urgent task facing the nation, SPD opposition to the treaties was not an act of obstruction but an example of a German party "doing its duty." Furthermore, an active opposition was a necessary counterforce to the government and an essential part of any well-functioning parliamentary system.[99] The Social Democrats readily admitted that the Bundestag had played a less effective role than parliaments elsewhere, but the fault, they said, lay with the government. Ever since the founding of the Federal Republic, the Social Democrats had complained of Adenauer's failure to consult or inform the opposition leader about foreign affairs. Indeed, the chancellor did go his own way, formulating policy without regard for Parliament or for the views of the SPD. Although he made several appeals for cooperation between the government and the opposition on vital foreign-policy issues, the Social Democrats charged that he never considered taking them into his confidence and that he "steadfastly refused" to provide them with information on the state of negotiations with the Western powers. As a result the gap widened until, as the SPD press service wrote in June, 1952, "there no longer existed any common ground between the government and the opposition on foreign-policy matters."[100]

Others commented at the time on how deep the differences were, but there was no unbridgeable chasm separating the government parties and the SPD. The Social Democrats cooperated in passing most of the government's domestic legislation and found room for accommodation on certain foreign policy matters as well.[101] For example, although they voted against German membership in the Council of Europe and the European Coal and Steel Community (ECSC), the party sent deputies to Strasbourg and later to the parliamentary assembly of the ECSC. Similarly, the Social Democrats did not boycott the Bundestag's EDC committee, despite a pledge to reject any military proposal made by the government "irrespective of its actual content."[102] Led by Fritz Erler, a small group became deeply involved in the committee's work. They discussed with coalition deputies the problem of creating a democratic army that would be subject to parliamentary control and civilian influences; however, because of their own party's opposition to any detailed discussion of rearmament—the issue for most Social Democrats was not how but whether the Germans should rearm—these SPD deputies found it expedient not to publicize their activities. They stressed the reasons for their opposition to Adenauer's rearmament program with the result that outside the committee room the SPD's image as the uncooperative and uncompromising opposition party remained intact.

More than anyone else Kurt Schumacher was responsible for the party's intransigent opposition in the rearmament debate. He set the course in August, 1950, and the party followed. Even when he was too ill to direct party affairs, the men around him reiterated his original conditions for a West German defense contribution. In 1952, when the unity question became the focal point of SPD opposition, it was Schumacher who provided the battle cry, insisting that the Social Democrats would fight the government's policy of rearmament before re-unification. That, however, was only part of his legacy to the SPD. By refusing to leave military affairs to the government, as the Weimar party had done, he assured that the SPD would play a part in West German rearmament. Unfortunately, as the Social Democrats geared for war against the treaties, the positive aspects of Schumacher's opposition campaign fell more and more into the background until it became questionable in the public's mind whether the SPD could handle defense matters. Since a sound security policy was absolutely essential for success in West German politics, the SPD needed to alter its image and resolve the contradictions in the Schumacher legacy before the 1953 general election.

CHAPTER 4

In Search of a Security Policy

On August 20, 1952, Kurt Schumacher died. His death was a severe loss to the party, but the course had been set, and his followers acted promptly to maintain it. Only one month later, at its biennial party conference, the SPD adopted a program inspired by Schumacher and elected his deputy, Erich Ollenhauer, chairman.

The new party chairman came from a working-class background in the city of Magdeburg, now in East Germany. He entered the party by way of its youth movement, devoted his time to Socialist activities, and eventually became chairman of the German branch of the Socialist Youth International. Soon after Hitler came to power, the SPD leaders brought Ollenhauer into the Executive Committee and then sent him abroad as part of a leadership corps in exile. He returned to Germany in 1946, settling in Hannover, where he helped Kurt Schumacher combat the proposed merger with the Communists. Ollenhauer never doubted who should lead the SPD. At the first party conference held in the Western zone, he gladly accepted the post of deputy chairman and served as a perfect second to the fiery Schumacher. Calm, mild-mannered, and accommodating, he worked best behind the scenes, rather than out front as Schumacher had done. Ollenhauer was always more an administrator than a politician, and he became indispensable to Schumacher because of his ability to manage the party and smooth out differences between SPD headquarters and the local organizations. After Schumacher's death the many contacts Ollenhauer had established in the party, most dating back to the Weimar period, helped make him the leading candidate for the party's highest office.[1]

Some observers expected the party to select one of the SPD Bürgermeisters—Brauer, Kaisen, or Reuter—if only because of Ollenhauer's colorless political personality. *Der Spiegel* noted that his career as a politician appeared "deadly boring even to his comrades," so it could hardly be expected that the German public would find him any more

Kurt Schumacher shortly before his death in August, 1952. Courtesy German Information Center.

attractive.[2] Schumacher, however, had preferred Ollenhauer as his successor,[3] and the party met his wishes.

The Dortmund Party Conference

Most people assumed that the change from Schumacher to Ollenhauer would have a moderating influence on the party's position, changing the tone, if not the substance, of SPD opposition. The new party chairman, however, immediately crushed any suggestion that the SPD would do things differently. He told the press that the policy of Kurt Schumacher was the policy of the SPD, "yesterday, today, and tomorrow."[4] Yet something was different. Ollenhauer was anything but militant; even when he used the same words Schumacher had used, they did not have the same effect. Furthermore, the men who surrounded Ollenhauer were incapable of maintaining Schumacher's aggressive political style. Wilhelm Mellies, the new deputy chairman, was "a puritanical functionary" a strict sort of Calvinist, Schumacher had called him—who also served as secretary of the parliamentary party. Mellies had mastered the techniques of doing business in the Bundestag, but he was not an inspirational leader, and he shunned the political spotlight.[5] As for the rest of the leaders, the new Executive Committee was composed mainly of good party men and loyal Social Democrats. The only prominent political personalities on the twenty-five-member board, Carlo Schmid and Ernst Reuter, had little influence at party headquarters.

The party conference at Dortmund revealed how little the party had actually changed since 1945. Despite the bold promise of a new beginning, most Social Democrats had retained a deep attachment to traditional Socialist goals and sentiments. They had willingly followed Schumacher, but they had placed his powerful arguments within the framework of their own conventional thinking and made little effort to broaden the political base of the party. As a result the SPD remained predominantly a workers' party.

If the old party had survived, however, it had experienced new impulses and heard new ideas. Under Schumacher's protection a small group of reformers had come to the fore, especially in the parliamentary party. They had a more flexible approach to doctrinal matters than older party members had and a greater desire for political power. At Dortmund they urged the adoption of a program that would make the SPD more attractive to young voters and the middle class. Although the delegates at the party conference conceded that something had to be done to improve the SPD's chances in the 1953 general election, they were reluctant to alter the party's working-class image or accept any dilution of its Socialist principles. It was left to Ollenhauer and the leadership to mediate a compromise, which they did without much difficulty.

The program accepted at Dortmund was called an Aktionsprogramm,

Erich Ollenhauer shortly after he succeeded Schumacher as party leader, 1952. Courtesy German Information Center.

which listed the specific demands of the SPD, rather than a Grundsatz-programm, which would have provided the theoretical basis for these demands. Although the old-line Socialist majority would have preferred an orthodox Marxian analysis of current conditions, the Executive Committee pushed for a set of practical rather than theoretical guidelines for the 1953 campaign and had little trouble gaining adoption of the program at the conference. Significantly, the Dortmund program served as the first concrete step in an evolutionary process that led the SPD to a new political and ideological position.[6]

Whatever it augured for the future, the Dortmund program showed no deviation from the Schumacher course. In speech after speech the delegates expressed strong opposition to the policies of the government, especially its foreign policy, and demanded that reunification be treated as an immediate rather than a distant goal. Echoing their sentiments, Ollenhauer declared that the SPD's main task was "the establishment of a united, free, democratic and socially progressive Germany in a Europe based upon freedom and equality."[7] He added that a Social Democratic government would pursue a different foreign policy from that of the Adenauer regime and, in the words of the Dortmund program, "strive for a radical revision of the treaties . . . by means of new negotiations on a new basis." Yet from the original draft of the program prepared by the Executive Committee,[8] it was difficult to discern what the Social Democrats would offer in place of the existing treaty system or how they would guarantee the security of the German people.

In preparing for the Dortmund conference, local party organizations gave little attention to the problem of devising an alternative to the government's security policy. If they discussed it at all, they generally expressed alarm over the dangers of rearmament. The Frankfurt party, for example, warned that a new German army would constitute a threat to peace and democracy. The Social Democrats in Essen declared categorically that reunification must precede rearmament.[9] A group from Berlin, however, which included Willy Brandt, urged the conference to state clearly under what conditions the SPD would support a defense contribution. Conceding that West Germany had to do more than rearm, Brandt warned the delegates that the security problem also had a military side that they were ignoring. He reminded the delegates that "we live in a world that would be much worse than it is today if only Moscow had divisions."[10]

Earlier in the summer Ollenhauer had stated that he could not imagine a situation in which the SPD would take "a purely negative attitude" on the question of a German defense contribution,[11] but now, at Dortmund, he hesitated to ask the party for a positive statement. Ollenhauer had his hand on the pulse of the party, and he knew that most Social Democrats vehemently opposed the rearmament of West Germany. The Executive Committee decided that it was safer, therefore, to offer a declaration stating the SPD's readiness to stand with the West in a defense of freedom against Soviet totalitarianism without making reference to a military contribution. As the conference progressed, however, the leaders came under pressure from a group of party politicians who wanted a policy statement that would show the electorate that the SPD had a defense plan to replace the treaty system negotiated by Adenauer. Finally, on the last day of the conference, the editorial committee, under the chairmanship of Willi Eichler, drafted a statement declaring that the SPD would work for "an effective system of collective security in which Germany would participate as an equal without endangering her reunification." Eichler presented it to the conference, without comment, as a "certain addition" to the foreign-policy section of the program.[12]

At Dortmund the Social Democrats made no attempt to clarify their position on rearmament. What they accomplished, and what concerned them most, was a reaffirmation of their commitment to the primacy of reunification and a demonstration of their total opposition to the treaties. They adopted the idea of a collective security system almost as an afterthought and without giving it concrete shape; in fact, they avoided a discussion of the proposed security system. Ollenhauer feared that if he opened the subject to debate it would disrupt the sense of unity which pervaded the conference. Thus the most elementary questions remained unanswered, including the obvious one: whether the system was designed for the Federal Republic or a reunited Germany. The statement in the Dortmund program was open to either interpretation, though it seemed to imply that the Germans could join a collective security system before reunification—at least that was the opinion of the party's press service one day after the conference adjourned. The press service confused the issue, however, by suggesting that a contribution to the security system could be economic as well as military.[13] As a result, no one knew where the Social Democrats stood on rearmament or what they meant by an effective system of collective security. They still had to provide Parliament and the public with a clear explanation.

A Concrete Proposal

In the period immediately following the Dortmund party conference, the Social Democrats made no serious effort to develop their idea of a collective security system. They seemed reluctant to discuss it while a chance remained of promoting reunification. Speaking to the press in Berlin on October 27, Ollenhauer remarked in passing that "no suitable basis [exists] at present for West Germany's joining a collective security system." First on the agenda was the further examination of the prospects for a four-power conference. When asked whether the SPD would review its position if the Soviet Union continued to oppose the creation of a united and free Germany, the SPD leader refused to speculate in anticipation of a Russian *njet*.[14] During the second reading of the treaties the Social Democrats referred more frequently to a collective-security system but did so without clarifying their position. Brandt spoke favorably about NATO, noting that the Atlantic Alliance, with its loosely organized military structure, was vastly superior to either a national army or a highly integrated international force like EDC. Arndt, however, speaking soon after Brandt, pointed out that NATO was a system for collective defense rather than collective security. Ollenhauer added that the SPD had not "expressly" asked for NATO membership. In his address to the Bundestag the SPD leader referred to a possible West German role in a collective security system, if all efforts to promote reunification failed. In conclusion he spoke of a global security system, which obviously applied to a reunited Germany. Following the debate the SPD leader stated that the Social Democrats were prepared to join with other free nations in the defense of the free world and to do their part within the framework of a collective security system. When pressed by reporters to explain what the SPD meant by a collective security system, Ollenhauer confessed that he had nothing more to say because "we ourselves have not yet made up our minds about the details in any concrete way."[15] This was a shocking admission. Three months after the Dortmund party conference the Social Democrats were still without a security policy.

In early January, 1953, the party leaders finally organized a committee to study the question of German participation in a collective security system. The committee faced a difficult task because of the wide diversity of views within the party on foreign-policy matters. A German news-paper commented on the "discordant sounds produced by the SPD foreign-policy orchestra," especially on the theme of rearmament.[16]

Willi Eichler, a prominent party official and a member of the Execu-tive Committee, expressed the feelings of those Social Democrats who, though they accepted rearmament in principle, were advocates of what amounted to a pacifist policy. Eichler believed that there had to be a better way of achieving security than through an arms buildup. Writing in the Socialist journal *Geist und Tat,* which he edited, Eichler warned repeatedly that a policy of strength would only deepen the division of Germany, accelerate the arms race, and increase the danger of war. The only answer was reasonable discussion among the powers on the great issues of the day, because when cannons face cannons, "reason is forced to remain silent."[17]

Fritz Baade, who had spoken earlier in favor of German neutrality, argued that rearmament should follow, not precede, reunification. In a journal article published in September, 1952, Baade stated that West Germany would not gain real security by joining the Western Alliance because "a defense of Europe was no longer possible." Security could be achieved only by preventing another war, and that could best be done by reunifying Germany. Once reunified, he said, Germany would avoid the competing power blocs and become a contributing member of a worldwide security organization—the United Nations. At the Dortmund party conference Baade had offered this scheme to the delegates as the only possible solution to the problem of world peace.[18]

Fritz Erler, who advocated a policy of nonalignment for a reunited Germany, disagreed with Baade. He argued that rearmament could come before reunification and warned against accepting West German neutrality as the price for negotiations on the German question. If the Russians tried to maintain control of East Germany, he said in March, 1953, then they could not expect to keep West Germany out of a West-ern security system as well. Willy Brandt, who shared Erler's views on rearmament and reunification, told a Berlin party audience in May that the SPD should make it clear to the Kremlin that "a Socialist-led govern-ment will not pursue a powerless policy but a policy of cooperation with the Western world."[19]

Very few in the party saw the need for such a positive statement, but the Bürgermeisters were among those demanding greater realism in foreign policy. They believed that the Germans should make a mili-tary contribution to Western defense; in fact, Brauer thought that they were morally obliged to do so. As he told a Hamburg audience, one could not expect American and English youths to stand guard so that citizens of the Federal Republic could sleep calmly. From Berlin, where the Soviet threat was more visible, Reuter advised the party against a pacifist or *ohne mich* attitude. He believed that the West had to be strong militarily to bargain with the Russians, but at the same time he warned against making rearmament an end in itself. The goal was German reunification. In his eyes the Western powers concentrated too much on "cannons, divisions, and bombs" and too little on negotiations with the Soviet Union. He insisted, nonetheless, that the Germans had to play their part in strengthening the Western defense system, preferably as members of NATO, and he urged the party to decide quickly on a security policy.[20]

The special committee which had been organized to deal with security policy needed little encouragement to begin its investigations. The members included Ollenhauer, Mellies, Schmid, Wehner, Arndt, and Luetkens —all prominent Bundestag deputies and conscious, therefore, of how difficult it was to operate against the government without a practical alternative to EDC. In a memorandum to the committee Herbert Wehner suggested to his colleagues, first, that they base their deliberations on the current situation in international affairs, which centered on the rivalry between the United States and the Soviet Union, and, second, that they decide what to do if, in spite of SPD opposition, EDC and the General Treaty came into effect. Since nothing could be gained by a policy of pure negation, Wehner suggested that the Social Democrats prepare a list of concrete demands for the step-by-step revision of the treaties negotiated by Adenauer. He warned, however, that the Western powers would insist on their "basic conception of the treaties," and the SPD would have to develop a security policy which kept West Germany within the framework of the Western Alliance.[21]

Although the committee never published its findings, some committee members discussed their ideas publicly. They all agreed that EDC was unacceptable and that the re-creation of an independent German army was neither desirable nor feasible. According to Mellies, defense would have to be a cooperative effort because no West European country could guarantee its own security. He suggested the creation of a European defense system in which the member states would raise their own troops but coordinate defense measures through "reasonable treaties." Speaking in Kiel, the deputy chairman emphasized that coordination could not mean integration; otherwise countries such as Britain, Denmark, and Norway would refuse to join the defense system. If the nations worked for a coalition arrangement, however, negotiations on a new set of treaties could be completed within six months.

Mellies's proposal was mistakenly labeled "the defense plan of the SPD."[22] The committee had not developed anything that precise; further, the Social Democrats still viewed West German defense as a secondary consideration—the primary task remained the restoration of German unity. Mellies himself had warned that, "before the conclusion of any new treaties, all possibilities for convening a four-power conference on the German question must be exhausted." The Germans would have to know that the Russians alone were to blame for the continued division of Germany. Even then West Germany could join only a defense system that left open the path to reunification.

Gerhart Luetkens suggested that West German forces could join a West European coalition army modeled on the Brussels Pact of 1947. The pact contained none of EDC's integrative schemes to combine military units from the member nations; rather, it offered the possibility of military and political cooperation at the command level. In this way West Germany could make a contribution to Western defense, receive the assurance of military assistance in the event of an attack from the east, and still retain the freedom of action necessary to promote reunification.[23] Neither Luetkens nor his colleagues, however, saw any need to hurry with the task of West German rearmament. Certainly there was no reason to ratify the treaties now, as the chancellor contended. The French had become more disenchanted with EDC, and the Americans, according to Ollenhauer, would accept new negotiations because they had never viewed EDC as the "only solution" to the problem of European defense.[24]

On February 5 the American Secretary of State, John Foster Dulles, arrived in Bonn for a one-day visit. He spent most of his time with Chancellor Adenauer, meeting for only forty-five minutes with Ollenhauer, Schmid, and Wehner. The encounter proved to be a disaster for the Social Democrats. They had hoped to convince Dulles of the need for a four-power conference and, if the powers disagreed, for a coalition of national armed forces to replace EDC. Before Ollenhauer could finish presenting the SPD case, however, Dulles interrupted him to point out that holding a four-power conference made little sense unless there was a chance of success, and Soviet policy to date had given little evidence of that. Dulles went on to say that the situation would change only when the West had built a strong defense front. He emphasized, however, that a German national army represented neither a military nor a political alternative to the plans for creating a European army. At that point the conversation ended.[25]

In spite of the setback the Social Democrats conceded nothing. Ollenhauer told the press that the SPD's proposals would eventually become of decisive importance because further conflicts over the treaties were inevitable. In the long run he was correct—the integrated army of EDC was replaced by a close-knit coalition of national armies—but for the moment the Social Democrats had to contend with Adenauer's determination to have Parliament ratify the treaties as soon as possible.

On March 19 the Bundestag held its third and final reading of the treaties. Adenauer went ahead with the debate in spite of a plea from the SPD to delay ratification until the Federal Constitutional Court had ruled on the constitutionality of the treaties or at least until the EDC signatories had dealt with a recent French request for greater control over French forces assigned to the defense community. According to the Social Democrats, there was an even more important reason for delay. Joseph Stalin had died on March 5, 1953. Since no one knew what effect his death would have on the course of Soviet foreign policy, Ollenhauer urged the Bundestag to wait until the situation had been clarified. There was time to pause, he said, and thus an opportunity to investigate the possibilities of a four-power meeting. The chancellor, on the other hand, felt that the West European countries should act immediately to strengthen their defenses through EDC because Stalin's death had "increased the instability of the world situation and the danger in which we live." As for the German question, Adenauer still insisted that reunification would be achieved only on the basis of a policy of strength, which EDC would help establish.[26]

In response Ollenhauer methodically restated the reasons for his party's opposition to EDC and a policy of strength. The SPD leader said nothing new until the conclusion of his address, when he attempted to offer an alternative to the chancellor's security policy. Basing his proposal on recommendations made by the special committee on security matters, he told the Bundestag that West German participation in a European security system, whose relationship to NATO was "still to be determined," would be possible under the following conditions: the Germans would be free to pursue reunification; the Federal Republic would be treated as an equal partner and sovereign member of the security system; a strategy would be devised to give West Germany, including Berlin, the same measure of security as other member states; the security system would be established on the broadest possible basis so that Britain, Norway, and Denmark could join; finally, in recognition of the Federal Republic's special position, social security would be viewed as equally important as the military side of defense. And that, said Ollenhauer, "is a concrete proposal."[27] The government parties remained unimpressed, however, and the treaties passed their third reading by a vote of 224 to 166.

Ollenhauer's Bundestag speech received a mixed response from the press. Some observers thought that it was the clearest statement to date from the SPD, lifting the fog which had covered its foreign-policy program for so long. Others felt that Ollenhauer had offered nothing more than "a series of related principles and demands" which in no way constituted "an alternative to a concrete policy." Even if the Social Democrats had offered something in place of EDC, they had failed to explain how a new security system could be realized under existing political conditions.[28] How, for example, could French and American opposition to a German national army be overcome? And what would be the relationship of this European security system to NATO? In the debate Ollenhauer consciously avoided the latter question, and four weeks later he had to admit that the SPD was still not in a position to give a final answer.[29] Actually the Social Democrats preferred to ignore the matter because, while they knew that a European security system could be effective only with NATO backing, they also feared that NATO membership for West Germany would destroy what chances remained for promoting reunification. They called on the Western powers, therefore, to exhaust every possibility for serious conversations with the Russians before engaging in further discussions of a West German defense contribution.

Before the Decision

After the Bundestag had ratified the treaties, Adenauer sent them on to the Bundesrat for approval. He could not expect an easy passage for the treaties because the balance of power in the upper house rested with Reinhold Maier, the FDP minister-president of Baden-Württemberg, who headed a state coalition of the Refugee party (BHE) and the SPD. Although Maier came under strong pressure from the national committee of the Free Democratic Party to vote with the government, he refused to jeopardize his own position for the sake of a treaty system he found hard to accept. As a result, on April 24 he supported a proposal that the Bundesrat withhold its vote until the Federal Constitutional Court had given an opinion on the treaties. This was exactly what the SPD leaders in Bonn wanted, for they felt certain that the court would render a favorable verdict. To their dismay, however, several weeks later Maier reversed his position and agreed to immediate ratification.[30] On May 15, the Bundesrat ratified the treaties by a vote of 23 to 15.

One day later Ollenhauer told the press that the Social Democrats would withdraw from the Maier government in protest over the Bundesrat vote. Only one Social Democrat resigned, however. The other SPD ministers, with the support of the state party organization, argued that resignation would be a futile gesture. Since the treaties had already been ratified, nothing would happen except that the state government would be handed over to the CDU. Ollenhauer and Mellies went to Stuttgart to convince the party in Baden-Württemberg that national issues had to take precedence over local matters, but they made no impression. Theo Pirker, a former party member, commented bitterly that the local organization considered a state coalition more important than the "credibility" of the party's campaign against the treaties.[31]

The leader of the state party was Erwin Schoettle, who had spent the war years in London with Ollenhauer and later worked with Schumacher in rebuilding the SPD. In the February, 1952, debate it had been Schoettle who had presented a resolution to the Bundestag declaring the SPD's uncompromising opposition to Adenauer's Western policy. Now, although he continued to oppose the treaties, Schoettle could no longer accept the implications of the party's uncompromising stand. His differences with the party leaders in May, 1953, dramatically revealed the dilemma the SPD faced. The party wanted to maintain Schumacher's opposition course and at the same time share in the work of building a new German society. While Schoettle and the Social Democrats in Baden-Württemberg could resolve the dilemma by separating state and federal matters, the national party felt compelled to continue the war against the chancellor's policy.

In May, 1953, after President Heuss signed the treaties, the SPD went back to Karlsruhe and asked the Federal Constitutional Court for an opinion on their constitutionality now that they had been formally ratified. The court, however, had no intention of reopening the case at that moment. With federal elections only four months away the justices would have been catapulted back into the center of the political arena. They decided instead to await the people's verdict. The Social Democrats, therefore, turned their attention to the upcoming election.

They viewed the September general election with considerable optimism. According to Deputy Chairman Mellies, the SPD looked forward to a decisive victory and the formation of "a pure Social Democratic government."[32] Even when it became clear, however, that no single party could win an absolute majority, the Social Democrats remained confident. They assumed that popular dissatisfaction with the Adenauer regime was so great that the SPD, as the only real alternative to the CDU, would become the largest parliamentary party and organize a new coalition government. Their election strategy, therefore, was to give the voters a clear choice by placing the SPD in direct opposition to the Adenauer regime.

At an election rally in Frankfurt on May 10, Ollenhauer drew the battle lines along which the party would wage its campaign. Although he said nothing new, most observers were surprised by the sharpness of his language.[33] He attacked the government for pursuing a reactionary, class-oriented policy at home and a policy of subservience to the Western powers abroad. The year 1953 was a year of decision for the Germans, he said. The people of the Federal Republic would have to decide whether they wanted to continue to be governed by the forces of conservatism and clericalism or preferred to rebuild Germany on a new basis under SPD leadership.

The main issue of the election campaign was foreign policy. The CDU and its coalition partners argued that through the chancellor's policy of West European integration a position of strength was being established which would guarantee German security and offer the only realistic starting point for negotiations with the Soviet Union. The Social Democrats countered, as they had throughout the debate on the treaties, that Adenauer's policy would provide neither security nor equality for the Germans. Above all, West European integration would deepen the division of Germany.

The Social Democrats tried to discredit Adenauer's policy as a whole by offering the people a choice between Western integration and German reunification. They made no major effort to exploit antimilitary sentiment as they had in the 1950 and 1951 state elections, in part because they viewed such action as irresponsible but also because they found it less profitable. On the basis of public-opinion surveys, the SPD leaders came to the conclusion that reunification was the main concern of most West Germans and therefore a more promising platform from which to wage an election campaign.[34] Of course, the party still needed a clear statement on national defense, but unfortunately party speakers said very little during the campaign about how the SPD would deal with security matters.

Early in the year the party published the *Handbook of Social Democratic Policy*. In the entry on collective security the handbook recommended that a reunited Germany make its contribution to the maintenance of world peace by becoming a member of the United Nations. The discussion of West German security, however, consisted largely of what Ollenhauer had said recently in the Bundestag, and the party made no further effort to clarify its position. At election rallies Ollenhauer simply assured the large audiences gathered to hear him that his party would discuss West German participation in Western defense "if a four-power conference failed to produce positive results." He saw no pressing need to deal with West German security. Speaking to the party's parliamentary delegation in early August, Ollenhauer stated that the Soviet Union was incapable at present of conducting "an aggressive, war-menacing policy."[35] The Social Democrats could feel safe in treating defense as a secondary consideration while devoting their attention to the question of unity. Reunification was the party's goal and its policy.

From March to September, 1953, the Social Democrats stressed the need for four-power negotiations. They insisted that the unsettled nature of Soviet policy in the months immediately following Stalin's death offered the West a chance to press for a settlement of the German question. After the East German uprising on June 17, the Social Democrats became even more convinced that the time for serious negotiations had arrived. Reuter declared that the Soviet position had been "suddenly and dramatically weakened," and he urged the Western powers to take advantage of this "historic opportunity" to reunite Germany. The chance, he said, might never recur.[36]

During the following months the four powers exchanged notes but did not go to the conference table as the SPD had hoped. Differences between East and West remained as they were in 1952, particularly over the question of free elections. For the Social Democrats this was the crucial issue, and they could only express disappointment when the Russians refused to accept free elections as the first step toward German reunification. They nonetheless insisted, as they had the year before, that a four-power conference was necessary in order to make certain that every effort had been made to secure Russian consent to reunification in freedom.

The Social Democrats maintained that they had no illusions about Soviet intentions, but they tended to blame the West for the failure to organize a four-power conference. Ollenhauer complained that the Western powers remained passive when opportunities arose to drive the Russians onto the defensive, almost as though they were waiting for the Bolshevik colossus to collapse by itself.[37] When the United States finally proposed a four-power conference, the Social Democrats deplored the decision to wait until fall before meeting the Russians. They charged that the decision "was based not on the factual necessities of the present situation but on the importance of the forthcoming West German elections." The Americans seemed more concerned with reelecting Adenauer than with reunifying Germany.[38]

As the campaign progressed, the SPD complained more and more about American intervention in favor of the chancellor, and in fact Washington indicated that it preferred a continuation of the Adenauer regime to an SPD government. The Social Democrats responded by charging that Adenauer was conducting a policy "considerably more American than German," and they warned that, given the crusading zeal of the American secretary of state, this would reduce the chances for a peaceful settlement of the German question and increase the danger of war. The Social Democrats insisted, however, that, far from being anti-American, they simply opposed "dictation from abroad" in matters of foreign policy.[39]

The Social Democrats directed their sharpest criticism at Chancellor Adenauer. They claimed that as a Rhinelander he had no real attachment to the territory beyond the Elbe and felt more at home in Paris than in Berlin. He also feared reunification, they suggested, because he knew that in free elections the SPD would win an absolute majority of the votes in East Germany. According to the Social Democrats, therefore, the chancellor tried to prevent the convening of a four-power conference, under the pretext that there was something wrong with the Russian proposals. Adenauer was an expert, wrote Eichler, at finding "the famous hair in the soup."[40]

As for Adenauer's policy of strength, throughout the election campaign the Social Democrats warned that the Russians would not surrender East Germany under threat of force; if anything, the chancellor's policy would lead to war. Only a few days before the election Ollenhauer conceded that, while no one would suggest that Adenauer desired war, nonetheless "war has often resulted from the policy of men who in no way wanted it."[41] He advocated the exercise of the greatest caution in dealing with the question of German rearmament. To rearm in the face of aggression was necessary; however, any exaggeration of that principle, especially when coupled with political demands, represented an incalculable risk for the German people. As for the course the Federal Republic should follow, Ollenhauer pointed out that "the weaponless rebellion" of the German working class in the Soviet zone had done more to strengthen the political position of the West than twelve West German divisions in EDC could ever have done. He added that the recent elections in Italy had demonstrated clearly that military divisions alone were an insufficient basis for building a democratic state. The radical right and left in that country had made electoral gains because of the government's failures and omissions in the area of social policy. Thus, instead of concentrating on rearmament, Chancellor Adenauer should be concerned with social questions and especially with four-power negotiations, which represented the only path to a peaceful settlement of the German question.

The charges the Social Democrats leveled at the government did not go unchallenged, for, just as the SPD attempted to portray Adenauer's foreign policy as dangerous and mistaken, the government parties described the Social Democrats as naïve and weak in the face of the Soviet threat and, ultimately, as advocates of a pro-Soviet line. In early August the Christian Democrats unleashed a major attack in the form of four questions to the SPD on reunification. The questions, which were cleverly constructed and patently designed to embarass the SPD, served as the main theme of the CDU's campaign on the foreign-policy question in the last weeks before the election.

The Christian Democrats asked if the SPD believed that reunification in freedom could be achieved without working in cooperation with the democratic forces of the free world. The Social Democrats answered no but added that the question was "how, not whether" the Germans should cooperate with the Western powers.[42] Then the CDU asked whether the SPD saw possibilities for cooperation with the West other than those already established by the government. The SPD said yes. The alternative to Adenauer's policy of Western integration was a system of cooperation based on genuine equality, real security, and continued promotion of the chances for German reunification. The Christian Democrats asked whether the SPD believed that the Russians could be persuaded to accept reunification without strengthening the international position of the Federal Republic, as the government had done. In their reply the Social Democrats denied first that Adenauer had improved the German position and second that a policy of strength would lead to reunification. Finally, the CDU asked whether the SPD thought that Germany should cooperate with neither the Soviet Union nor the Western powers. The Social Democrats responded that they were opposed to neutrality but insisted that Germany's relations with the great powers would have to be given special consideration. It was this last point that provoked the sharpest clash between the government and the opposition.

On August 28, nine days before the election, Fritz Erler and Willi Eichler met the press to advertise a new party pamphlet entitled *The European Policy of the SPD*. The pamphlet itself contained nothing new, but Erler's comments at the press conference provoked such a stir that the party was hard-pressed to defend itself.[43] Erler stated that, because neither side would let the other incorporate Germany into a hostile military bloc, reunification was possible only if the four powers could agree on the future military status of a united Germany. As a basis for agreement, Erler suggested that the powers make Germany a member of the United Nation's worldwide security system.

The government immediately pounced on Erler's statement, charging that the SPD now advocated a settlement dictated by the great powers. Trying to save the situation, Ollenhauer responded that the SPD still insisted on the right of a freely elected German government to determine the future status of the country through open negotiations, but even he believed that this amounted to a mere formality.[44] For over a year the Social Democrats had been warning that the Russians would not agree to free elections if the West attempted to draw a united Germany into EDC or NATO. Ollenhauer did not deny this assertion; he underlined it.

In the press conference Erler had also mentioned that representatives from East and West Germany could get together to discuss the technical details of an all-German election once the four powers had agreed on a settlement. He added that the question of Germany's eastern frontier could be left to a future peace conference, which a freely elected German government would attend, instead of letting this "thorny problem" delay a four-power agreement on free elections. Several days later Adenauer charged that the SPD had deserted its previous position on negotiations with the East German regime and in so doing had betrayed the German people. As for the question of the Oder-Neisse Line, he said, the SPD had no policy at all. Ollenhauer angrily rejected the chancellor's accusations. The SPD, he declared, had been the first party to oppose recognition of the Oder-Neisse Line as Germany's eastern frontier. The Social Democrats, furthermore, had no intention of sitting down with the "Pankow persecutors" to negotiate Germany's future, but there would have to be technical arrangements on election procedures. The chancellor's charges, Ollenhauer said, were "the crowning piece in his campaign of vilification" against the SPD.[45]

The main thrust of the government's criticism centered on the charge that the SPD had proposed the neutralization of Germany. Speaking to the Foreign Press Association in Bonn, Adenauer described Germany as the principal obstacle for the Russians in their attempts to gain control of Western Europe. If the West accepted the SPD proposal, Germany would "be on her way to the gallows," and the rest of Europe would soon fall under Soviet domination.[46] In response the Social Democrats stated again that Germany would not be neutral, because of its strong political, economic, and cultural ties with the Western world. Who could question that "we belong to the West," asked Ernst Reuter, "especially the East Germans after their experiences with the Russians?" They had demonstrated their readiness to fight for freedom. Germany, he assured a Berlin audience on August 30, would not become "an easy prey for the Soviets."[47] Unimpressed, Adenauer closed his election campaign by warning that an SPD victory would be a Russian victory.[48]

On September 6 the West Germans went to the polls. The results disappointed the SPD greatly. Although the party gained a million more votes and 20 more seats than they had won in 1949, its percentage of the popular vote fell slightly, and its role as the opposition was reaffirmed. In the Bundestag the balance of power shifted abruptly in favor of the government parties. The CDU-CSU alone won 243 of the 487 seats, and, with the aid of the smaller parties, a two-thirds majority was within its grasp. Adenauer had achieved an impressive victory.

After the Decision

There were several reasons why Adenauer won again in 1953. The chancellor benefited from the tremendous economic recovery that West Germany had undergone since 1948. People could remember very well the devastation, the hunger, and the misery of the first postwar years, and they now shared the government's pride in having achieved what seemed like the beginning of an economic miracle. The government could also point to a successful foreign policy. Instead of being treated as a pariah, West Germany had won the respect of the Reich's former enemies in the West and gained security against the threat of aggression from the East. The key factor, however, was the chancellor's public image. He symbolized the nation's accomplishments since the war, and, as a strict but kindly father figure, "Der Alte" (the old one) created a feeling of confidence among West Germans that progress with stability would continue. In many ways the electoral victory represented a personal triumph for Konrad Adenauer.

No one could question the electoral strategy of the Christian Democrats. They campaigned on the government's record, stressing the leadership qualities of Chancellor Adenauer, and they won. The Social Democrats, on the other hand, focused on the alleged failures and mistakes of the government. They assumed that the West Germans wanted a change. Where the SPD read discontent, however, there was a growing satisfaction with conditions in the Federal Republic and with the policies pursued by the government, especially in the area of foreign policy.[49]

At the opening of the campaign the SPD had proclaimed that the decision on election day would be a decision for or against German unity. Most voters, however, never considered reunification a crucial issue. At election rallies the candidates always raised the issue, and audiences dutifully applauded, but most West Germans "considered their own personal well-being much more important than the loss of East Germany."[50] Besides, Soviet behavior gave them little cause for optimism about the chances of achieving reunification in freedom—if anything, the brutal suppression of the East German revolt revived their fears of Soviet intentions.

At an election rally in mid-August, Ollenhauer declared that the threat of Soviet aggression could "be eliminated peacefully only if one takes into account as a political reality the security requirements of the Soviet Union." Most West Germans, however, viewed Russia as a power bent on world conquest and thus without legitimate security interests,[51] a view which was forcefully reconfirmed by the sight of Soviet tanks in the streets of East Berlin during the June 17 uprising. It made no sense, furthermore, to criticize the Western powers as the Social Democrats did throughout the campaign. The exchange of notes in the summer of 1953 demonstrated that the West was willing to negotiate on the basis of free elections; the Russians, on the other hand, raised demands unacceptable to even the Social Democrats. Yet despite the evidence, the Social Democrats continued to call for a four-power conference. Fritz Erler revealed how badly they misread the public mood when, late in August, he told the press that Germany should be given an alliance-free status within the framework of an international security system. In self-defense Erler wrote later that he had said nothing new. He had simply wanted to give "the clearest possible formulation" of the party's foreign policy position,[52] but his efforts hardly improved the party's chances at the polls. To many voters it appeared that those same Social Democrats who in the past had criticized Adenauer for giving away so much to the Western powers were now proposing a settlement which would leave a defenseless Germany at the mercy of the Soviet Union. Given the prevailing climate of opinion in West Germany, this was an unpardonable sin—even for such a staunchly anti-Communist party as the SPD.

Some observers have suggested that the party lacked more than anything else an attractive candidate for chancellor. Whereas Winston Churchill could describe Adenauer as "the wisest German statesman since Bismarck," no one could see Ollenhauer as anything other than a colorless party bureaucrat and loyal Social Democrat.[53] The SPD also suffered from its inability to overcome a negative image. For most West Germans it was easier to say what the SPD opposed than what it favored, and even when the Social Democrats developed an alternative to the government's policy, it raised more questions than it answered. The SPD's foreign policy, in particular, took too long to explain and relied on too much speculation about Soviet intentions. Adenauer's policy, on the other hand, was easy to grasp.[54] "With Adenauer and the West," read a CDU election poster, "For Peace and Security." It was a policy for West Germany, one that dealt with the problems of today, not the promises of tomorrow.

Although distressed by the election results, the Social Democrats had a simple explanation for failing to achieve their political goal. They charged that the anti-Socialist forces had run a smear campaign against the SPD, exploiting the Cold War and appealing to the most primitive fears of the West German population. The CDU, for example, had an election poster which tried to associate democratic socialism with Soviet communism by warning: "All Paths of Marxism Lead to Moscow." The Christian Democrats also benefited from massive American assistance, including Dulles's statement only three days before the election that Adenauer's defeat would be disastrous for Germany.[55] On September 11, in *Neuer Vorwärts,* editor Gerhard Gleissberg warned all those people, especially foreigners, who viewed the election as a triumph for democracy to look again. True the neo-Nazi parties had suffered a crushing defeat, but Fascist elements in West Germany had found a refuge within the ranks of the coalition parties. Willi Eichler added that whereas it took the antidemocratic and anti-Socialist forces of the Weimar Republic ten years to unite, in the Bonn Republic the process was virtually complete in three.[56]

Several days later Chairman Erich Ollenhauer told a group of party officials gathered in Bonn not to be discouraged about the SPD's performance in the election.[57] He reminded them that in the 1907 election the SPD had suffered a similar disappointment but five years later had achieved an electoral triumph that no Social Democrat would ever have dreamed possible at the time. Now, as then, he said, the Social Democrats would have to learn from their mistakes in order to be better prepared for the next campaign. In the name of the Executive Committee Ollenhauer introduced ten reform measures dealing mainly with organizational matters, but he saw nothing fundamentally wrong with the party's position on domestic and foreign-policy questions. Throughout his address the chairman repeatedly emphasized to the party functionaries that the SPD had won eight million votes and now, conscious of its responsibilities toward those who had voted for the party, the SPD would remain loyal to the principles it had enunciated during the campaign.

Although most party members shared the chairman's view of the situation, not all did so. In the weeks following the election, while the party prepared for the opening of the new parliamentary session, there was some grumbling in the ranks about the election results and some quiet talk about the need for major alterations.[58] Some concerned Social Democrats called on the leadership to reduce the influence wielded by party bureaucrats and to abandon outworn slogans and practices in order to broaden its popular appeal. Above all, they warned that unless the party achieved greater clarity in presenting its views to the public the SPD would be condemned to play eternally the role of an opposition party.

The most outspoken critic was Ernst Reuter. At the party meeting in Bonn on September 17 he attacked the feeling of self-satisfaction that pervaded the speeches of many officials as they pointed to the million new votes won in 1953, and he severely criticized the attempt to explain away Adenauer's landslide victory as the result of certain "technical faults" in the party's propaganda and organization.[59] According to Reuter, the main problem lay in the basically negative accent of SPD policy; the solution was to tell people what the party favored rather than what it opposed. The party wanted reunification to be the primary goal of West German foreign policy, but it also supported national defense. Although Ollenhauer had frequently mentioned that the SPD would defend Germany, Reuter noted that it was always made as an aside and treated as a respected principle rather than a practical policy measure. It was time for the party to make a positive declaration.

In a rare moment of postelection candor, the party's press service stated that the SPD "had not fully appreciated the elementary nature of the preconceptions and concerns which dominated the electorate." Even Ollenhauer admitted that the SPD had underestimated the anxiety many West Germans felt about their "individual and national existence."[60] He doubted, however, that the situation could be improved by a declaration in favor of West German rearmament because real security for the Germans was to be found only in reunification. This was what the party had maintained throughout the election campaign. Now, as the Social Democrats prepared for the upcoming legislative session, they saw no need to change course; rather, they held the firm conviction that the main points of their election program remained "unalterably true and correct."[61]

To the Berlin Four-Power Conference

On October 28 the Bundestag held its first regular meeting of the new session. Considering how sharply Christian Democrats and Social Democrats had opposed each other during the election, the debate was a surprisingly mild affair, with both sides showing considerable restraint. Ollenhauer expressed the hope that it might be possible to normalize relations between government and opposition, perhaps even to cooperate on important foreign-policy questions. To remove the existing differences, however, he said that it would be necessary for the government "to keep the opposition informed, currently and comprehensively, of international developments and of its own plans and activities." Such an arrangement "would merely correspond to the practices observed as a matter of course in the democratic nations of Europe . . . and in the United States."[62]

The following day several newspaper commented on the SPD leader's moderation, noting in particular that "the biting sarcasm and the titanic all-or-nothing attitude of Kurt Schumacher" had been replaced by a readiness to compromise. It appeared that the SPD, chastened by an unsuccessful election campaign, was now moving cautiously toward a new policy.[63] On the contrary, the Social Democrats distrusted Adenauer too much ever to believe that he would listen to "appeals and arguments" from the opposition party. In spite of its "strikingly quiet tones,"

Ollenhauer's speech offered nothing new, lacking even the trace of a constructive foreign-policy proposal. Other than supporting the chancellor's insistence on sovereignty for the Federal Republic, Ollenhauer riveted his attention on reunification.

A week earlier Adenauer had declared that the inclusion of a reunited Germany in EDC would mean security for all—for the Germans because they would be assured of military assistance and for their neighbors because German rearmament would be controlled. Ollenhauer quickly pointed out that the Russians would never accept such a plan because of its Western orientation. "We must find a path," he said, "that the Germans, in common with the Western powers, can accept, in order to maintain Germany's position as part of the West, and at the same time satisfy the security needs of the Soviet Union." The answer was German membership in the United Nations. In this world organization a free and united Germany would have "the same possibilities for security" as other member states, and they in turn would receive assurances against any possible threat of German aggression.[64]

The Social Democrats had advanced this idea before. In 1952, Erler and several other SPD deputies had made similar proposals—even the party handbook included a reference to UN membership—but only after the election did the Social Democrats treat unity and security as complementary aspects of their reunification policy. They now insisted that free elections, together with an agreement on the future military status of a reunited Germany, were the prerequisites for the restoration of German unity.

When Ollenhauer presented his proposal to the Bundestag, the coalition parties immediately expressed their disapproval. Eugen Gerstenmaier of the CDU called it "dangerous and unrealistic." After all, the threat of aggression would remain undiminished even if the Germans joined the United Nations. Gerstenmaier referred specifically to the threat of Soviet aggression and warned against risking Germany's national existence in a security system built on nothing more than "wishful thinking."[65]

Following the debate, Fritz Erler attempted in a series of speeches and articles to defend the position advocated by Ollenhauer.[66] He pointed out that in 1952 the Soviet Union had wanted Germany to join the United Nations, and he argued that because of their interest in a relaxation of international tension the Russians would now be willing to discuss the German question. Erler also pointed out that the Russians, remembering World War II, wanted to prevent the creation of an alliance that would place American military equipment in the hands of German soldiers. To eliminate this possibility, they would have to pay "a suitable price," which according to Erler could be extracted by skillful diplomacy. The price he had in mind was free all-German elections and German membership in the United Nations. On this basis would Germany be secure? Erler replied affirmatively. He pointed to Korea, where, with UN assistance, the aggressor had been repulsed and an armistice negotiated. This, however, was a poor example. From the very beginning of the rearmament debate the Social Democrats had argued against a war of retreat and counterattack, such as the UN forces had fought in Korea, because it would mean the destruction of Germany. The key to German security, therefore, had to lie elsewhere. Erler's answer was that real security "lay in the knowledge that an attack on Germany would unleash a third world war." The threat of American intervention would deter Soviet aggression. Even this trump card, however, which Erler had drawn from Schumacher's deck, could not be played with absolute certainty. In a mid-November editorial Gerhard Gleissberg expressed concern about the growing danger of an American withdrawal from central Europe in favor of a peripheral strategy based on the concentration of American air and sea forces on the rim of the Continent. A severe critic of Western policy, Gleissberg added that the French were weakening the defense front by sending military units stationed in the Federal Republic to Indochina.[67] Thus at a time when Erler assumed that a Western deterrent was already operational, Gleissberg was raising serious doubts about the effectiveness of a Western security guarantee.

On the question of security for West Germany the Social Democrats were equally vague and contradictory. According to Luetkens, the SPD would support a military contribution to Western defense "under the condition that it would neither block the reunification of our country nor sharpen the tension between East and West." Erler noted that Prime Minister Winston Churchill had suggested in early October that if EDC should fail Germany could become an associate member of NATO. In this way, Erler said, West Germany would be part of a security system, with equal rights and duties, and at the same time possess the freedom of action to respond to situations which could lead to the restoration of German unity. Luetkens, however, commented several days later that the Russians viewed NATO as an offensive alliance directed against the Soviet Union. Faced with West German divisions linked to NATO, he said, Moscow would "consolidate its position" in Eastern Europe.[68] The Social Democrats, therefore, had not settled on a West German security policy. For the moment, the conflicting views of Erler and Luetkens, or of Erler and Gleissberg, seemed unimportant. The Social Democrats were hoping for a four-power conference. Until it convened, everything else would have to wait.

The Social Democrats closely followed the exchange of notes which began in the summer of 1953 between the Western powers and the Soviet Union. Initially little progress was made toward convening a four-power conference, and as late as November the Social Democrats had to admit that the Soviet attitude was "not encouraging." They insisted nonetheless that it was necessary to "seek clarification in direct negotiations of whether and on what basis an understanding about the German problem can be attained among the four powers."[69] When the powers finally agreed to meet in Berlin in January, 1954, the Social Democrats tried to take a realistic view of the situation. Ollenhauer spoke only of a chance to investigate the possibilities of reunification, and he counseled the party to observe a "cautious optimism."[70] As the conference date approached, however, neither he nor his colleagues could resist the temptation to portray the Berlin meeting as "a rare chance" for reunifying Germany. Gleissberg went so far as to declare that the upcoming conference would mean either an end to the Cold War or the prelude to a world catastrophe. It would be a test, therefore, not only of the peaceful intentions of the Soviet Union but also of "the political foresight and diplomatic skill" of the Western powers. He advised them to abandon their attempt to bind the Germans to EDC and adopt the SPD plan of incorporating a reunited Germany in a world security system.[71]

Appeals from the SPD had little effect on the Western powers. Although some Western officials wanted to test the new Kremlin rulers to see whether an agreement was possible, most doubted that progress could be made at Berlin. They were skeptical of Soviet intentions and declared very early that NATO and EDC remained the foundation of their common policy.

When the conference convened on January 25, the Russians proposed that representatives of the Bonn and Pankow regimes form a provisional all-German government to help the occupying powers prepare a peace treaty for Germany.[72] Several days later Foreign Minister Molotov submitted a draft treaty almost identical to the one presented by Stalin in March, 1952. The Russian draft called for a united but neutral Germany. Free elections would be held to create an all-German parliament, which would then ratify the treaty negotiated by the occupying powers and the provisional government. On February 10, Molotov introduced a second proposal, by which the four powers would agree to withdraw their forces from Germany within six months, except for "limited contingents" needed to perform certain control functions; of course, in the event of "a threat to security in either part of Germany" the occupying powers would have the right to return to their respective zones. For the normal tasks of "internal order and frontier defense" the two German states would have police units whose strength and armaments would be determined by the four powers. Thus Germany would remain divided but neutralized while the negotiations continued. Finally, Molotov proposed the signing of a collective security treaty by all the European countries, including the two Germanys, until a "democratic" Germany could take its place in the security system. The member states were to renounce the use of force, offer mutual assistance in case of aggression, and refrain from joining alliances or undertaking obligations "which are contrary to the purposes of the treaty." The United States was invited to participate as an observer in this European security system.

The Western powers rejected the Molotov plan. Speaking for the West, Anthony Eden of Great Britain insisted on the absolute priority of free all-German elections. There could be no dealings with any provisional government, only negotiations with a freely elected all-German government. Furthermore, the Western powers argued that the new German government should be granted complete freedom of choice in foreign-policy matters—as long as that choice, said Secretary of State Dulles, was "compatible with the security of the rest of us. Since, in fact, Germany wishes to associate herself with the western countries of Europe, it is essential to peace that she be allowed to do so." The Germans, therefore, should have the right to reunification and security on a basis not of neutrality but of alliance with the West.

After the conference adjourned on February 18, *Punch* carried a cartoon showing four phonographs on a large circular table, all blaring away at each other. This was the Berlin Conference. Neither side listened to the other; in fact, the dialogue between East and West on the German question had become "increasingly doctrinaire and unrealistic."[73] The Russians wanted to manipulate German domestic affairs through treaty arrangements, as well as to oust the Americans from Europe, while the West expected the Russians to surrender East Germany and accept a Western promise that EDC would guarantee the Soviet Union against the threat of aggression. At Berlin the powers made no serious attempt to see whether a viable alternative could be found. A two-Germanys solution was clearly emerging.

Immediately after the conference the Western powers issued a statement in which they blamed the lack of progress toward a solution of the German question on the unwillingness of the Soviet Union to permit free elections.[74] The Western powers declared that they would continue to work for the reunification of Germany. As long as the military power of the Soviet bloc remained intact, however, the three powers would refuse "to be deflected from their efforts to develop the system of defense on which their survival depends."

Konrad Adenauer firmly supported the Western position. On February 25 he told the Bundestag that the Berlin conference had revealed how determined the Soviet Union was to dominate Europe.[75] The free world now had the task of making it absolutely clear to the Russians that they would never succeed. The sooner that was done, the sooner the Russians would be ready for serious negotiations. His statement that all Germans owed a debt of gratitude to the three Western foreign ministers for "the excellent way in which they represented the cause of German reunification" drew loud and sustained applause from the coalition deputies.

The Social Democrats were considerably less pleased with the performance of the Western powers at Berlin. They agreed that Molotov had made some unacceptable proposals—on the procedure for reunification and on the nature of a European security system—yet so had the Western powers. Both sides, said Wehner, had raised demands, made charges, and introduced plans, but they had "not yet negotiated." The Western foreign ministers had not really tested Molotov's willingness to make concessions. They had made no attempt to see whether he would consent to free elections in return for a Western guarantee that Germany would not be incorporated into EDC. Since the Russians knew that free elections would mean the end of the Pankow regime and of Soviet influence in Germany, they wanted to be sure that the Germans did not join a hostile coalition. That was the key issue. The question of German reunification, said Ollenhauer, "cannot be separated from European security and the status of a reunited Germany in an international security system."[76] At Berlin the Western powers had refused to recognize this fact.

To the Social Democrats, therefore, the Berlin conference was a disappointment rather than a failure. At Berlin the four powers had established certain points of contact. They had recognized the need for further talks on disarmament and the control of atomic energy, and they had agreed on a conference in April to discuss Asian problems. The very fact that the powers had begun talking, said Ollenhauer, "was of fundamental and far-reaching significance" because it offered a chance for a relaxation of tension between East and West. In the words of the SPD leader, the Berlin conference represented "the beginning and not the end of international negotiations."[77]

After the Berlin conference the Social Democrats received strong criticism in the press and in Parliament for their failure to face the facts. *Die Zeit* accused Ollenhauer of lacking the political courage to admit that he had been wrong about the prospects for reunification. The government parties called him naïve. They charged that, although Ollenhauer had rejected Molotov's security plan he had offered in its place a security system that would lead directly to the situation he supposedly wanted to avoid—the Sovietization of Germany. According to Thomas Dehler of the FDP, the Social Democrats assumed the existence of an "almost idyllic world in which the states are as meek as lambs." It was time, therefore, for them to wake up to the realities of the international situation and get behind the government's foreign policy.[78]

The Social Democrats refused to be pressed into altering their list of priorities. They argued that it would be wrong to forsake an active reunification policy for membership in the Western Alliance system, and in a letter to Adenauer, Ollenhauer called on the chancellor to avoid any action that could prevent further negotiations among the four powers.[79] The SPD clung to its insistence on the primary importance of reunification for a number of reasons, not the least of which was the party's belief that reunification was the surest means of overcoming the handicaps of the existing political situation. Now, as in Weimar Germany, the Social Democrats saw themselves waging a two-front war against implacable foes—the Communists in the East and the bourgeois parties in the West—and they believed that free elections would open the way to a Socialist victory. The Social Democrats were motivated by more than self-interest, however. They believed that someone had to take up

117

the cause of German unity. If the SPD adopted the government's Western policy, said Herbert Wehner, "where would the stimulus for reunification come from?"[80] This was a legitimate concern, but to make it effective the Social Democrats had to develop a realistic reunification policy. They had to do more than point out the errors of Adenauer's policy of strength or suggest, as Ollenhauer did, that the alternative to negotiations was a hot war.[81] Even he did not believe that the Cold War was about to heat up. As for negotiations, whatever could be said about the inflexibility of the Western powers, the Russians showed no willingness whatsoever to concede free elections on terms acceptable to the West. Thus the SPD was left with little more than hope, and that, noted the *Manchester Guardian* on March 4, was "a currency which recent Soviet actions have debased."

Within the SPD a few outspoken members argued that it was time for the party to reassess its foreign-policy position. One of the first to speak out was Wilhelm Kaisen, the mayor of Bremen, who declared at the close of the conference that the Russians obviously did not want to see Germany reunified through free elections. He recommended that in view of the Soviet Union's "negative attitude" West Germany should work for European integration, including the creation of EDC. Several days later Kaisen received support from Karl Schiller, one of the party's economic experts, who argued that the SPD demand for four-power negotiations before integration had been met and the Russians had responded negatively to the test. A continuation of the party's policy of negation, he said, would not bring Germany closer to reunification; it would only lead to "the endless road of Moscow delays." The Berlin conference had demonstrated that the Social Democrats needed to turn their attention positively to the question of European integration.[82]

The party leadership responded quickly and critically to these suggestions. At a meeting in Bonn the SPD leaders refused to consider EDC as an acceptable alternative or to treat reunification as anything less than an immediate goal of German policy.[83] Yet even though they clung to the old slogans, they also took steps to deal more effectively with certain accomplished facts, specifically, the institutional connection between West Germany and the other West European states. They agreed, for example, to the formation of a committee to coordinate the activities of those SPD politicians involved in European organizations, such as the Coal and Steel Community and the Council of Europe.[84] As for rearmament, they realized that recent events compelled the SPD to take a more positive approach. The Berlin conference had demonstrated the four powers' unwillingness to change their current policy, which in the West meant the integration of German troops into the Western defense system; moreover, right after the conference the chancellor had secured passage of a constitutional amendment designed to remove all doubts about the legality of rearmament. Under the circumstances the Social Democrats could not afford to stand aside.

In the parliamentary debate of February 25, Ollenhauer told the Bundestag that his party's rejection of EDC did not mean "the rejection of a policy of military security for our people." He indicated that the SPD would support West Germany's entry into a security system before the restoration of German unity, on the basis of complete equality and real security, which he said meant "commitments linking the defensive power of the United States and Great Britain with that of the Federal Republic," as well as full support for German efforts to promote reunification. He hoped that this statement would finally silence the "nonsensical chatter" about the SPD's alleged *ohne mich* attitude or neutrality policy. The following day Carlo Schmid again carefully explained to the Bundestag the SPD's readiness to support rearmament before reunification.[85] Schmid found it difficult to contain his impatience with those coalition deputies who claimed not to understand the SPD position, but neither he nor Ollenhauer seemed to realize how tentative their commitment to West German rearmament appeared to be.

Actually the Social Democrats had made very little progress in dealing with the rearmament question during the year and a half since the Dortmund party conference. At best they had advanced from a position of "not yet," to one of "yes, but." Before the Berlin foreign ministers' meeting they had insisted that rearmament be delayed until the four powers had an opportunity to discuss fully the German question. After the meeting they still called for negotiations but conceded that rearmament was possible under certain conditions. The SPD leaders, however, failed to explain how these conditions could be met; they never even described what they considered to be a proper alternative to Adenauer's policy of integration with the West through EDC. As a result the party's position on West German rearmament remained unclear and unconvincing. But within the SPD there were several prominent Social Democrats who recognized the need for clarity. They now challenged the party to alter its opposition course and take a more positive view of rearmament.

CHAPTER 5

From EDC To NATO

During the winter of 1953-54, the Social Democrats concentrated on more than the Berlin conference. Even as the foreign ministers convened, they continued to discuss the party's performance in the September election and debate the question what could be done to improve its political chances. Although most Social Democrats saw nothing fundamentally wrong with the party—its structure, its policies, or its ideology—there emerged within the SPD a growing number of reformers who wanted to modernize the old party to make it more competitive.

As a group the reformers cannot be identified with any particular geographic region or age-group, though an impressive number of younger members were involved. They included many political figures—Bundestag deputies Carlo Schmid and Fritz Erler, along with Länder leaders Georg August Zinn and Wilhelm Kaisen. These politicians were genuinely shocked at the results of the election and recommended that the party change its political style by selecting as leaders men who could speak to the public as well as to the party. In the words of the party organization in Hamm, "It was time to give up the idea that modestly talented men, with good character and a sufficient period of membership in the party, can replace men with above-average abilities." It was also time to abandon outmoded symbols such as the red flag, the Socialist songs, and the term "comrade." By their behavior, Erler said, the Social Democrats gave the impression that they wanted to "be by themselves."[1]

The reformers also believed that the party would have to relinquish the view of the SPD as a proletarian party fighting for workers' rights in a hostile environment. German society had changed, and so had the attitude of the German worker. To keep in step the SPD would have to modernize, that is, break out of "the nineteenth century ideological eggshell" in which it had been born, drop the Marxian concepts of class consciousness and class struggle, and become a people's party, appealing to all classes with a broad program of social reform.[2]

When the intraparty discussion began in the months immediately following the election, Chairman Ollenhauer encouraged a frank reappraisal of the party's performance. Before long, however, he became concerned about the thrust of the discussion and spoke out in favor of the old party. At a meeting in Elberfeld he told local party officials that "the SPD without the symbol of the red flag would be a party without a heart, . . . and a party without the fighting songs, one which does not address its members as comrade, would be a party without blood."[3] Since these sentiments were shared by most Social Democrats, Ollenhauer felt safe in resisting demands for radical change. Yet in spite of his attachment to party tradition, he realized that on some issues the reformers offered sound recommendations. On the issue of rearmament he accepted some of their advice, or at least as much as he thought the party would tolerate.

The Sicherheitsausschuss beim Parteivorstand

Late in 1953 the Adenauer government drafted a constitutional amendment to remove the last internal barrier to rearmament. Since the coalition had the necessary two-thirds majority, the amendment would pass, and the Social Democrats would soon face legislative proposals from the government on the creation of a new German army. Unfortunately, the party had no military policy. Only a handful of SPD deputies had dealt with the military question. They had worked on the Bundestag's EDC committee since its founding in July, 1952, and they now urged the leadership to take positive steps to prepare the party for what lay ahead.

In December, Friedrich Beermann wrote a letter to Ollenhauer expressing concern about the political dangers facing the party because of its continued opposition to West German rearmament.[4] Beermann, a former army officer who had joined the SPD after the war, warned that unless the SPD supported West Germany's right to raise military forces, the officer corps would be alienated from the party before the first troops even assembled. Beermann advised against treating "the professional officer as an a priori opponent," as the Weimar party had, and urged the SPD instead to make every effort to win his support. He called for a clear policy statement on military affairs, which, of course, could be achieved only if the leaders gave up the attempt to satisfy everyone in the party—supporters and opponents of rearmament alike.

One month later the government introduced its constitutional amendment, and the pressure on Ollenhauer for a decision increased. Helmut Schmidt, one of the party's young military specialists, told him after the first reading that because of the disposition of forces in the Bundestag it was no longer a matter of whether the Germans would rearm but rather of how they would rearm. Schmidt warned Ollenhauer that under the circumstances the SPD had to deal "very quickly and very concretely" with the military question.[5]

In spite of the urgency of the situation, Ollenhauer took no immediate action. He continued to temporize and to advise enthusiasts like Schmidt that for the moment it would be sufficient to restate the SPD's support of rearmament in principle. He preferred to allow the party conference, scheduled for Berlin in July, to decide "whether and in what form" the general statement in the Dortmund program should be expanded.[6] This would mean avoiding a decision, as Erler pointed out, because the rank and file saw nothing in the Dortmund program that committed the SPD to support a military contribution; in fact, the average party member still used pacifist arguments to combat the government's rearmament program. Only a few members of the Executive Committee—Arndt, Schmid, and Wehner—shared the concern of the military experts; most preferred to avoid a confrontation with the rank and file.[7] As a result, when the Bundestag held its final readings of the government's bill in late February, the parliamentary party (Fraktion) had nothing concrete to offer.

Of the Social Democrats who participated in the debate, only Fritz Erler addressed the question how the Germans should rearm.[8] He began by warning that an army could not be built one piece at a time or left to Parliament to add or change a piece at will, as the government's bill would allow. The basic structure of the armed forces would have to be written into the constitution. Furthermore, measures to establish civilian control of the military would have to be secured on a constitutional basis as well. These would include a parliamentary committee to watch over the military, a personnel committee to select officers of democratic persuasion, and a parliamentary commissioner to protect the soldiers' basic rights.

In concluding, Erler indicated that although the Social Democrats would vote against the bill they would support the formation of a democratic military system. This was a bold statement by Erler because he, more than anyone, knew how the party felt about rearmament. As he told the Fraktion at a meeting on March 4, the party had not yet recognized the importance of developing its own military program. He warned his colleagues that unless they acted promptly the government would create an army according to its own wishes and without the SPD.[9]

Two days later Helmut Schmidt wrote to Ollenhauer suggesting that the party leaders create a standing committee on security policy. The committee could draft a comprehensive policy proposal for the upcoming party conference and, more immediately, prepare the SPD for the legislative work on rearmament. Urged on by Erler and Wehner, Ollenhauer finally consented. On April 1 the Executive Committee agreed to the formation of a subcommittee, the Sicherheitsausschuss beim Partei-vorstand, to advise the SPD leaders on security questions.[10] It is sig-nificant that the initiative for creating such a committee came from concerned members of the Fraktion rather than from the party leader-ship.

Initially the SPD leaders made little use of the security committee. They prepared a security-policy recommendation for the Berlin party conference without consulting the committee, and they drafted the rec-ommendation—which did not go much beyond Ollenhauer's "concrete proposal" of March, 1953—before the committee even held its first meeting.[11] Once the committee met, it concluded very quickly that the party needed a more explicit statement. In Schmidt's words people still wanted to know whether the SPD was for national defense—"yes or no?"[12]

At a meeting on June 19 the security committee discussed the ques-tion how to handle military policy at Berlin.[13] Erler suggested that Ollen-hauer, in his opening address, could present a more precise formula-tion of the party's position than that contained in the security-policy recommendation. Once the conference had accepted the recommenda-tion, however, Erler saw no need to involve the delegates in a dis-cussion of military policy. He feared that in an open debate the party's deep-rooted antipathy toward military matters would come to the sur-face and paralyze all attempts at constructive action in Parliament. Ulrich Lohmar, president of the German Socialist Students' Union (SDS), disagreed with Erler. He thought the party should be kept informed so that there would not be a revolt of disgruntled party members once the Fraktion became engaged in military legislation. Ollenhauer's posi-tion was closer to that expressed by Erler. He also wanted to avoid a major debate on the military question, but for a different reason. His concern was party unity. While he conceded that the SPD needed a more concrete statement on rearmament, he insisted that it be accept-able to the overwhelming majority of the party.

In the weeks leading up to the Berlin party conference, Ollenhauer sought to enlighten the party about the need for an SPD military policy, but encountering a generally negative attitude toward SPD involvement in the actual rearmament process, he tended to avoid a frank discussion of the subject. The man who made the most determined effort to con-vince the party was Fritz Erler. He spoke at local party conferences and wrote numerous articles for the party's newspaper chain, trying in a measured and tactful way to inform party members of the need for a more realistic approach to the military question.[14] He told them that in a divided Germany it would be a mistake to make West German se-curity dependent on the decisions and benevolence of the Western powers. The Federal Republic would have to contribute to its own de-fense and, as an equal partner, to the common defense of the West. The Germans should, however, refuse full membership in NATO because that would upset the Western Alliance system in case of reunification, and "We should not offer the Soviets so much." Erler recommended a special agreement between West Germany and NATO, one that contained a revision clause releasing West Germany from its obligations should a chance for reunification arise. Finally, Erler urged his fellow Social Democrats to recognize the need for SPD participation in the military legislation which Adenauer would soon bring before parliament. As a responsible political party the SPD had to participate, to see that "the dangers for democracy were eliminated and the rights of the individual citizen were protected."

Erler received public support from other party reformers. Willy Brandt, now the SPD's floor leader in the Berlin municipal assembly, spoke favorably of a possible West German connection with the Western Alliance, and several members of the Fraktion, including Carlo Schmid and Helmut Schmidt, called on the party to play an active role in building a new German army.[15] As the conference approached, however, there was little indication that these last-minute appeals were having any noticeable effect on the antimilitary attitude of most Social Democrats.

The Berlin Party Conference

The party's sixth postwar conference opened in Berlin on July 20. Naturally, the subject of party reform stood high on the list of priorities, but what captured the attention of the delegates was the military question. Local party groups submitted twenty-nine proposals on rearmament, ranging all the way from the demand of the Berlin SPD for party action in favor of a democratic military organization to the Marburg Social Democrats' insistence on the rejection of West German rearmament in any form.[16]

The conference promised to be a severe test of Ollenhauer's leadership abilities. Two years before, at Dortmund, the delegates had avoided controversy to maintain the strong sense of party unity which existed following the death of Kurt Schumacher. Now he would have to deal with an issue guaranteed to provoke a bitter dispute within the party.

In his keynote address on opening day, Ollenhauer declared that the restoration of German unity in freedom and by peaceful means remained the primary task of the SPD. He told the delegates that the Berlin foreign ministers' conference, despite its negative outcome, had not sealed the division of Germany. The German question was still "an open question," and the SPD should strive to keep it high on the agenda of international politics. By maintaining the primacy of reunification over a policy of Western integration, Ollenhauer said, the SPD had the support of "a considerably greater part of the German people than the election figures of September, 1953, would lead one to believe." The party was justified, therefore, in continuing its opposition to Adenauer's foreign policy and to EDC in particular. Yet the rejection of EDC did not mean the rejection "of a military contribution to the defense of the free world in all circumstances," he said. The party had to face the possibility that all efforts to negotiate a settlement of the German question could fail. "If that happened, we would not be able to avoid cooperating in a defense of the free part of Germany. Any other decision would be an unrealistic one." Ollenhauer added that the Social Democrats would have to work with the government parties, if only to assure the "democratic development and democratic control" of the armed forces.[17]

In the ensuing debate, Ollenhauer's call for a constructive approach to the military question received strong support from prominent SPD politicians. They argued that the SPD would abdicate its role as a responsible political party if it abstained from the military debate. After all, said Herbert Wehner, the Social Democrats would have to deal with defense policy if they were in office. Being in opposition was no different. Helmut Schmidt reminded the conference that in Weimar the SPD had let itself become alienated from the Reichswehr, with disastrous results for the party and for German democracy. Others argued that, in view of the Soviet military threat, the Germans had an obligation to contribute to the defense of freedom. As for the effect of rearmament on reunification, Erler commented that nothing would be gained by keeping the Federal Republic disarmed. If anything, a defenseless West Germany would keep the Russians in East Germany. Rather than disarmament, he said, the Social Democrats now faced the prospect of Adenauer's rearming West Germany in spite of SPD opposition and Russia's refusing to permit free elections. To continue to say no to West German rearmament under those conditions would mean capitulation—possibly to the Russians, certainly to Adenauer and the militarists.[18]

The military question occupied the attention of the delegates throughout most of the second and third days of the conference. In all, thirty-four different speakers participated in the debate, twenty-one of them expressing opposition to rearmament. Significantly, those opposing rearmament received the loudest applause. Some appealed to the party's deep-rooted antimilitary and pacifist sentiments, though only a few speakers, such as Fritz Wenzel, advocated a pacifist policy for philosophical reasons. Others argued that, while the SPD was not a pacifist party, in the age of the hydrogen bomb it was "realistic, not utopian, to be a pacifist."[19] Some saw rearmament as a threat to peace. Willi Birkelbach of Frankfurt warned that, if West Germany agreed to rearm now, the twelve German divisions which the Americans were demanding would become twenty, thirty, or forty divisions, and war would be more likely.[20] Many, like Heinz Kühn, who opposed rearmament did so because they believed that it was impossible to build a democratic army in Germany. The officers for the new army would have to be drawn from the leadership corps of the Nazi Wehrmacht, and, given the political situation, it would be impossible for the SPD to prevent the resurrection of the old military spirit. Furthermore, as one delegate warned, "It will infect even the Social Democrats who join the army."[21] Most of those who spoke against West German rearmament expressed concern about its impact on the chances for reunification. They warned that rearmament, by increasing international tension, would prevent a four-power agreement on the German question. A vote against rearmament, therefore, was a vote for peace and reunification. Before the debate on the military question ended, the antirearmers introduced motion 113, rejecting West German rearmament in any form.[22] Surprised by this outburst of opposition, Ollenhauer went to the podium at the conclusion of the debate to assure the delegates that the party's policy remained the same.[23] The SPD, he said, still opposed EDC and would continue to work for peace. Its chief goal was, as before, the restoration of German unity. Ollenhauer added that the chances for four-power talks had improved and should be promoted but emphasized that "the demand for negotiations cannot by itself be the party's political program, at least not if we want to remain a political factor in the coming debates and discussions on domestic and foreign affairs." The SPD had to be prepared to make a defense commitment in case efforts to promote reunification should fail. The Executive Committee, however, was not recommending that West Germany should rearm today, he said, but rather at some point in the future and only after the party's conditions had been met. Ollenhauer's remarks had the desired effect; less than a third of the delegates voted for the motion introduced by the antirearmers. The Executive Committee's recommendations on foreign policy and security were then passed on to an editorial board for revision before being submitted to the conference in the form of a resolution.[24]

In its final form the resolution called for "energetic efforts by the Western powers" to promote negotiations with the Soviet Union to reunite Germany and establish a collective security system in which a reunited Germany could contribute to the maintenance of peace. Should these efforts fail, however, then the SPD would support a West German defense contribution under the following conditions: (1) attempts to restore German unity would be continued; (2) efforts to create a European security system within the framework of the United Nations would be maintained; (3) treaties signed by the Federal Republic would be terminated if they should become impediments to reunification; (4) equality of rights would be granted to all members of the security system, as well as equal chances for security; (5) democratic and parliamentary control of the armed forces would be secured. After noting that EDC failed to meet these conditions, the resolution stated that in any event the SPD would demand a democratic military organization should West Germany rearm.

In spite of the opposition voiced during the debate, the resolution received the approval of an overwhelming majority of the delegates, including over half of those who had voted for motion 113.[25] The readiness of the delegates to support the policy position advocated by the Executive Committee can be explained in part by the strong sense of solidarity which pervades SPD conferences but also in this case by the leadership's willingness to accept a clause in the resolution stating that a special conference would decide whether the conditions had been met. Originally the SPD leaders had assumed that the decision would be theirs, but the conference refused to give them a blank check. In the words of one delegate, "Party policy is decided by the cooperation of all members, and the party conference is the place where the decisions are made."[26] Without question, rank and file members were aroused. They applauded loudly for those delegates who asserted the rights of party members, and the leaders felt compelled to listen. As one reporter noted, this party conference was "the hour of the little man from the local district."[27]

Before the conference ended, the delegates had one more opportunity to express their views. They had the task of electing the men who would lead the SPD during the next two years. As expected, Ollenhauer gained reelection as party chairman, and Mellies returned as deputy chairman, but both men received fewer votes than they had at the Dortmund party conference.[28] The real surprise came in the balloting for the twenty-three-member Executive Committee. Willy Brandt and Fritz Erler were obvious candidates, considering their growing political reputations, but they were identified with the reform movement and in particular with the demand for an active military policy. As a result, neither won election; instead, the delegates chose three antirearmers, Kühn, Birkelbach, and Wenzel.

What most impressed observers in Berlin were the restrictions placed on the leadership. According to the *Times* (London), "the SPD leaders are left with their hands tied; before they can support any German military contribution to Western defense they are bound to face, and convince, a full party conference."[29] Ollenhauer confirmed this view when he assured the delegates, as the conference ended, that the party would be asked to decide if the conditions had been met. On the day after the conference, however, Fritz Erler told a radio audience that the Berlin party conference "explicitly demanded" that even if its conditions were not fulfilled the SPD had the obligation to fight for democratic and parliamentary control of the armed forces.[30] If the government went ahead with rearmament, then "in the interests of the German nation and of democracy" the SPD would have to participate in the military legislation. This the resolution "clearly stated."

Erler's interpretation of the Berlin resolution was understandable. As the party's military expert, he wanted the SPD to be ready when Adenauer began to rearm West Germany. If the Fraktion had to appeal to a special conference before the deputies got involved in the military legislation, there would be further compromises with the antirearmers and many delays before the party reached agreement; on the other hand, the conference could declare that the party's conditions had not been met and thus force the SPD to remain on the sidelines while Adenauer built a new German army.

Ollenhauer understood Erler's position, and, although he was willing to listen to the reformers, he refused to push the party too hard. He knew that the delegates at Berlin would oppose an open declaration in favor of West German rearmament, and thus for the sake of party unity he asked only that they state the conditions under which the SPD would support a defense contribution. This tactic satisfied the overwhelming majority of the delegates.

Karl Schiller, who pleaded for a clear policy statement, described the party's approach to the military question as a conflict between "reason and emotion."[31] Most Social Democrats wanted to avoid "the ticklish and difficult question of security," but Ollenhauer, much as he shared their feelings, realized that the SPD had to become involved. To satisfy the reformers, he sponsored a resolution that gave the Fraktion a chance to participate in the military legislation; to appease the antirearmers, he maintained the party's opposition course. As the product of an intraparty compromise, therefore, the Berlin resolution reproduced the half-yes, half-no answer which had characterized the SPD's attitude toward the military question since the rearmament debate began.

Nonetheless, the Berlin party conference made progress in several areas. The conference amended the Dortmund program in a liberal direction and so continued the gradual process of modifying the party's ideological position. On the military question the conference went one step beyond what had been said at Dortmund, setting out the conditions for SPD support of a defense contribution. The Social Democrats, however, never said what they would offer in place of EDC, or when they would consider their conditions fulfilled—especially those conditions relating to reunification. Ollenhauer admitted frankly that it would "always remain a difficult question to decide when the time for rearmament [had] come." Because of its commitment to reunification, the party could only accept West German entry into the Western Alliance with "a heavy heart."[32] It is difficult to see, therefore, how the Social Democrats could have made a decision in favor of rearmament without a push from Adenauer and the French.

The London Agreements

At a press conference in Bonn on August 24, soon after the Western nations rejected another French demand for treaty revision, Ollenhauer announced the impending death of EDC.[33] He called for a new Western policy and for a more determined effort from the Western powers to promote German reunification. According to him, the Soviets had expressed renewed interest in the German question. Thus a chance existed for holding four-power talks. He also indicated, however, that if negotiations failed the SPD would be ready on the basis of recommendations made at the Berlin party conference to join the Western defense system. When asked by a reporter whether the SPD would respond positively to a proposal that West Germany join NATO as an equal partner, Ollenhauer replied that with the international situation in a state of flux it would be unwise to give a simple yes or no. The party would wait.

Six days later the long, futile struggle to create a European army finally ended when the National Assembly voted against French participation in EDC. Upon hearing the news, Ollenhauer issued a statement urging the Western powers to open negotiations with the Russians on the related questions of European security and German reunification. He conceded that at the same time the Federal Republic could undertake negotiations with the Western nations to discuss political and military relations.[34] Two weeks later the Executive Committee confirmed that the SPD approved of parallel sets of negotiations but added that obviously a four-power meeting would determine the importance of any Western meeting[35] and thus the Western powers should avoid any hasty decisions. More specifically, the committee warned them against inviting West Germany to join NATO, because, as Ollenhauer later told the press, West German entry into the Atlantic Alliance "would, more clearly and unequivocally even than participation in EDC, bar any chance for the restoration of German unity." The SPD leader pleaded for a four-power conference as the only sensible step after the failure of EDC.[36]

The Western powers had ideas of their own. At a nine-power conference, held in London from September 23 to October 3, they proposed inviting the Federal Republic to join NATO. Three weeks later in Paris the West Germans and the NATO powers signed the necessary agreements, which the member parliaments ratified during the following months. The so-called Paris Accords went into effect on May 5, 1955.

The French gave their consent to the new arrangement, including the creation of a German national army, on the condition that the other Western powers limit German rearmament, support a Saar settlement, and locate troops on the Continent for fifty years. To meet French demands, British Foreign Secretary Anthony Eden proposed that the Brussels Treaty among Britain, France, and the Benelux countries, signed in 1948, be expanded to include West Germany and Italy. It could then be reconstituted as the West European Union and used as the arms-control agency of the alliance. As for the Saar, Konrad Adenauer and French Premier Pierre Mendes-France agreed that the territory could be placed under a European statute and kept in close association with both France and West Germany. Finally, to satisfy the French, Britain and the United States made a firm commitment to remain in Europe, even though it represented a radical change in British foreign policy and, for the United States, another link in the "entangling alliance" with Europe.[37]

Immediately after the London conference, Chancellor Adenauer delivered a report to the Bundestag on the nine-power agreement.[38] He claimed that on the basis of this agreement West Germany would become an equal partner in the Atlantic Alliance and gain complete control over its domestic and foreign affairs, except for certain rights reserved to the three Western powers. Furthermore, he said, the agreement would maintain the unity of the free world, which was suddenly threatened by the French vote against EDC and by the possibility of American withdrawal from Europe. "Believe me, the danger was very great and very serious." Adenauer reminded the deputies that without unity in the West there could be no freedom, no security, and no chance of reunifying Germany.

Two days later, on October 7, the Bundestag held a major foreign-policy debate. The coalition parties pointed out that the agreements satisfied many of the objections which the SPD had to EDC and that further opposition to West German rearmament was unnecessary. In his response Ollenhauer agreed that the London Agreements represented a certain improvement over EDC, especially in securing British participation and "complete renunciation of the supranational integrative principle," but he deplored the continued emphasis on military factors as the basis of Western unity. He called for cooperation on a broader basis—economic, political, cultural—and added that a comprehensive policy of social security still had more meaning for strengthening the free world than German rearmament. Besides, a military contribution "no longer [had] the urgency which it may possibly have had in the past." There were signs of detente and of a growing Soviet willingness to discuss the German question, as demonstrated only the day before in East Berlin, where Foreign Minister Molotov had talked again of four-power negotiations. If this was the case, then West Germany should not surrender "an opportunity to negotiate reunification in favor of a speedy rearmament." The Social Democrats, he said, "are of the opinion that the Federal Republic should not assume new obligations in connection with the Western defense system . . . before a new and serious attempt has been made by way of negotiations with the Soviet Union to clarify whether it is possible to solve the problem of German reunification on the basis of free elections and the incorporation of a reunited Germany in a collective security system."[39]

The debate, which lasted eleven hours, was conducted routinely until the closing moments, when the deputies were suddenly aroused by an angry exchange between government and opposition speakers. The clash arose over a question directed at Ollenhauer by CDU Deputy Eugen

Gerstenmaier. Ollenhauer had said in his concluding remarks that the Russians would agree to German reunification only on the condition that Germany remain free of any military alliance. Gerstenmaier wanted to know whether freedom from alliances (Bündnisfreiheit), a term SPD Deputy Adolf Arndt had used earlier in the debate, meant the neutralization of Germany.[40] The question irritated Ollenhauer. Thinking that the Christian Democrats were trying to label him a neutralist, he snapped back angrily that the Social Democrats were "not secret agents of the Soviet Union." When pressed by Gerstenmaier for an answer, the SPD leader replied that to him neutralization meant the exclusion of Germany from political, economic, and military affairs and the creation of a vacuum in Central Europe. "Such a conception is absolutely unreal and conforms in no way to the views of the SPD." The Social Democrats proposed the creation of a European security system which would be acceptable to the four occupying powers and to a freely elected, all-German government.

Adenauer intervened to ask whether Russia would be a member of this European security system, pointing out that, if the United States belonged as well, it would not be a European system, and that if it included only Russia, then Europe would be at the mercy of the Red Army. The chancellor quoted a warning by Herbert Wehner in November, 1953, that the Kremlin's goal was "to isolate us." If so, asked Adenauer, what security was there for Germany in the security system proposed by the SPD?

This time Ollenhauer made no effort to respond, and for a moment there was an embarrassing silence on the SPD side of the house. Finally Schmid and Erler came to his rescue. They explained that the SPD wanted German participation in a European security system within the framework of the United Nations. In this way an American connection with Europe would be maintained, the details of which could be worked out in later negotiations. The coalition parties found this explanation unacceptable because, in the words of an FDP deputy, the SPD had based its security system on an illusion—the United Nations had already collapsed in the face of Soviet aggression. For Fritz Erler that was the last straw. He turned to the coalition deputies, declaring that if they wanted reunification then they would have to give up the idea "that a reunited Germany must be a military camp for American troops." The Russians would agree to German reunification only with the assurance that a reunited Germany would not join a hostile military coalition. For that reason Germany would have to renounce its right to join one of the competing military blocs and accept a status of Bündnisfreiheit, which, unlike neutrality, would allow Germany to become a member of a collective security system. Unconvinced, Adenauer commented that to him it still sounded like the neutralization of Germany.

The debate was a tremendous disappointment to the Social Democrats. If they succeeded in clarifying their position somewhat, they failed to make it more acceptable to the other parties or to the West German public. Certainly they failed to slow down the chancellor's rearmament program. Several weeks later in Paris, Adenauer signed the new treaties with the NATO powers, and in mid-December he presented them to Parliament for ratification. For the Social Democrats the struggle had begun all over again.

In the two months between the foreign-policy debate on the London Agreements and the Bundestag's first reading of the Paris Accords, the Social Democrats unleashed a major attack on the chancellor's policy. Their strategy, as explained by Ollenhauer to the Fraktion, was not to focus on the various aspects of the treaties but rather to highlight the impact of the treaties as a whole on the chances for reunification.[41] Of course, the party would protest against the so-called emergency clause, which meant in practice that the Western powers would grant the Federal Republic "only as much sovereignty and freedom as was needed to effectively accomplish its military contribution to NATO, but nothing more." The SPD could also point out that Adenauer signed the Saar Agreement simply "to obtain French assent to the establishment of West German divisions." Furthermore, the SPD could legitimately ask what security the Germans would receive when NATO still viewed the Federal Republic as a "lost territory" which in case of war would be surrendered and possibly retaken within five years. Yet much more was at stake, Ollenhauer said, than the question whether it was meaningful or reasonable in terms of West German security to raise half a million troops and incorporate them into the Western Alliance—even if, admittedly, there were certain advantages to NATO membership over EDC. What really counted was that "the implementation of the Paris Accords would mean the inevitable abandonment of an active reunification policy and probably the destruction of all chances for reunifying Germany in the foreseeable future as well."

Working under the impact of the Paris Accords, the Social Democrats pressed more urgently than ever for four-power talks. They recognized the West's determination to devise a system this time that would bind West Germany to NATO—a determination reflected in the sudden negotiation of the London Agreements and in the empty declarations issued by Western leaders about the need for German reunification. The Social Democrats also feared that the Russians were becoming less interested in reunifying Germany. Ollenhauer noted with deep concern that Soviet leaders had declared frankly that if the Paris Accords came into effect West Germany would no longer be considered a peace-loving state, and further East-West negotiations on a relaxation of international tension would be in terms of the status quo, that is, on the basis of a divided Germany. The German question, Ollenhauer said, "would thereby be pushed back to third or fourth place on the agenda of international politics."[42]

The Social Democrats came under heavy attack for their opposition stance. They were accused of following a pro-Soviet line in their advocacy of Bündnisfreiheit and criticized for adhering to a negative and unrealistic position, especially now that Adenauer was about to begin rearmament. High Allied officials appealed to the Social Democrats, warning that their cooperation was essential to prevent the reappearance of a "reactionary Wehrmacht." Even other European Socialists intervened to point out that West German rearmament was a necessary evil which had to be faced.[43] The Social Democrats, however, remained adamant; if anything, their position had hardened. Now instead of parallel sets of negotiations they insisted that first there would have to be four-power talks. Only after it had been proved conclusively that Russia opposed reunification would they consent to join the deliberations on rearmament. Negotiations would have to come first.[44] When Adenauer continued to ignore their demands and proceeded with the ratification of the Paris Accords, Ollenhauer warned him in a private conversation that the SPD would "use every means at its disposal" to prevent the precipitate incorporation of the Federal Republic in the Atlantic Alliance.[45] The party soon revealed what those means would be.

The Paulskirche Movement

The Bundestag began its first reading of the Paris Accords on December 15, in what amounted to a continuation of the October foreign-policy debate. This time, however, the tone was considerably sharper. There were frequent interruptions by angry deputies, who heckled and harassed opposing speakers and few indications that either side would be willing to compromise. The outcome of the debate, of course, never stood in doubt. After two days of heated discussion the coalition parties voted to send the accords to committee in preparation for the final readings.

The Social Democrats now faced the task of trying to decide on a course of action. They insisted on negotiations before ratification, but since the coalition had a two-thirds majority in the Bundestag, they had to find another way to stop Adenauer. The Social Democrats discarded the idea of appealing to the Federal Constitutional Court as they had done in the campaign against EDC because on the basis of its earlier ruling the court would act only after the accords had been ratified. They decided, therefore, to take their case directly to the people, in hopes that a ground swell of public opposition would compel coalition deputies to delay the ratification process.

The Social Democrats felt certain that a growing number of people outside the party supported their position in the debate. As evidence they pointed to recent state elections in Schleswig-Holstein, Hesse, and Bavaria, where the SPD had recouped the losses they had suffered during the 1953 general election. Since foreign-policy questions played a major role in the elections, the SPD interpreted the results as confirmation of their opposition course.[46] Furthermore, in a public-opinion poll conducted in January, 1955, respondents had been asked what they considered the most urgent task facing the Bonn government. Almost half replied "The reunification of Germany."[47]

The Social Democrats also noted the continued and widespread opposition to West German rearmament, especially among young people. Most German youths adopted a frankly *ohne mich* attitude, but late in 1954 the fear that Adenauer would finally succeed in rearming West Germany provoked some to take political action. Those who most vehemently opposed rearmament held demonstrations and marches, and on several occasions they broke up political rallies and public meetings conducted by government officials. During the Bavarian state elections, Defense Minister Theodor Blank was shouted down in Augsburg by a crowd of angry youths and had to be escorted from the meeting hall by the police. According to the press, trade-union and Socialist youth groups played a prominent role in these antirearmament demonstrations.[48]

Between September and November, 1954, the youth organizations sponsored by the Trade Union Federation (DGB) and the Social Democratic Party passed resolutions expressing their opposition to rearmament before reunification.[49] More than young workers and Socialists took a strong stand, however. In early October, at its national conference in Frankfurt, the DGB spoke against a West German defense contribution until all possibilities for negotiating a settlement of the German question had been exhausted, and during the following months some local unions called for radical action, including a general strike, to prevent rearmament. In January the executive committee of the DGB issued an appeal for the formation of a popular movement (Volksbewegung) against the Paris Accords.[50]

SPD leaders also found themselves under pressure from their followers to take the offensive against the government's attempt to ratify the accords. In late 1954, *Neuer Vorwärts* published many articles by party members who feared the consequences of rearmament. They warned that it would mean the end of democracy, the sharpening of international tension, and the danger of a German civil war—if not a world war. Most expressed alarm about the threat that rearmament posed for reunification.

In contrast to the rank and file, the SPD leaders never equated the struggle for German reunification with a total rejection of West German rearmament. They indicated that the SPD would stand by the military resolution passed by the Berlin party conference, which stated that the Social Democrats would support a West German defense contribution after a sincere effort had been made to reach agreement with the Russians on German reunification. The party paid little attention to the resolution, however, and for that the SPD leaders had no one to

Die Nächsten bitte . . .

"Next please . . . ." Cartoon, *Vorwärts,* November 19, 1954.

blame but themselves. Ever since the collapse of EDC, Ollenhauer in particular had behaved as though he believed that this was the last chance for reunification. It was now or never. As a result opposition to the Paris Accords became a crusade for many party members, and they expected Ollenhauer to lead them into battle against the Adenauer regime. In early October, during the Bundestag debate on the London Agreements, the press had expressed concern about the strong anti-military sentiments in the SPD Fraktion and about Ollenhauer's ability to keep the party on a responsible line.[51] During the first reading of the Paris Accords, even Ollenhauer could no longer ignore the antag-onistic mood of the party. He responded, however, by calling for action rather than restraint.

On January 7 the party's press secretary, Fritz Heine, announced that the SPD would initiate a public campaign against the Paris Ac-cords.[52] Just one week later, in Mainz and Worms, SPD deputies from the Bundestag and the Rhineland-Pfalz Landtag went into the streets to distribute leaflets, while party volunteers began posting antirearma-ment placards on billboards and kiosks. During the following weeks local party organizations took similar action in other towns and cities across West Germany, and speakers from party headquarters went on the road to explain what the SPD hoped to achieve by going directly to the people. At a rally in Hesse, Mellies stated that if opposition to the "fateful policies" of the chancellor were made more visible and if among the population "a storm should unfold, then the plans of the government would be made impossible." The fate of Germany, he said, depended on the ratification or rejection of the Paris Accords.[53]

At the very moment the Social Democrats unleashed their campaign against the Paris Accords, the Soviets again proposed a four-power conference to discuss the German question. Adenauer saw no reason to give serious consideration to the Soviet offer, but Ollenhauer insisted that the Western powers must respond. The SPD leader told a radio audience that the Soviets were deadly serious when they warned that ratification of the Paris Accords would preclude further negotiations on reunification.[54] The problem, however, was to convince Adenauer of the danger. Since personal contact with the chancellor had produced no results, Ollenhauer resorted to political pressure. In mid-January he joined the trade-union and church officials who also opposed the Paris Accords in laying plans for a mass rally at Paulskirche (Saint Paul's Church) in Frankfurt, where in 1848 a German parliament had met in an attempt to bring freedom and unity to a divided Germany.

On January 29 more than six hundred prominent figures from various walks of life gathered at Paulskirche to issue an appeal for German reunification. Although Ollenhauer was the only Social Democrat on the rostrum, there could be no doubt that the SPD was the driving force behind the Paulskirche meeting. The Social Democrats consciously tried to remain in the background to make it look like a national rather than a party affair. The speakers included a DGB executive committee member, a Catholic theologian, a Protestant minister, a professor of sociology, and the leader of the neutralist Gesamtdeutsche Volkspartei (All-German People's Party), Gustav Heinemann. The speeches were restrained, and the meeting, which lasted only an hour and a half, was conducted in a dignified and solemn manner. At the conclusion Ollenhauer read the "German Manifesto," a declaration calling for negotiations before ratification, which everyone present was asked to sign.

The Social Democrats viewed the Paulskirche meeting as a great success. They had gained considerable publicity for their campaign and, according to Ollenhauer, demonstrated to the government that "opposition to rearmament went far beyond the ranks of the SPD." To prove it, they decided to ask the people to sign the manifesto, in hopes that if they obtained enough signatures the coalition deputies would feel compelled to delay the government's ratification schedule.[55] As early as February 11, the SPD daily newspaper, now called *Vorwärts*, reported that SPD volunteers had found "a strong echo" across the country, with people of all classes and professions signing the manifesto.

The coalition parties criticized the SPD severely for its opposition campaign, charging that it amounted to an attack on the constitutional order. According to Adenauer, the campaign represented an attempt to transfer decision-making powers from the Bundestag to the streets, and he alluded to a similarity in tactics employed by the Social Democrats and the Communists. The Social Democrats responded angrily that they had nothing to do with the Communists and in fact had pointedly rejected overtures from the SED.[56] Ollenhauer added that the

Meeting in Paulskirche (Saint Paul's Church), Frankfurt, January, 1955, to protest the Paris Accords. The delegates are voting for the "German Manifesto." Courtesy German Press Agency.

Paulskirche movement represented no threat to Parliament's authority. In a democracy every citizen has a legitimate right to express an opinion on a vital national issue and, in the words of Max Brauer, it would contradict the spirit of parliamentary democracy to ask the voter to cast his ballot at election time and then remain silent for the next four years.[57] In these crucial times, not calm but "alarm was the citizen's first duty."[58]

In the period immediately following the Paulskirche meeting, the SPD accelerated its extraparliamentary activities. Ollenhauer spoke to large rallies in various sections of the country, while Social Democrats combined with trade unionists in cities like Frankfurt and Munich to organize marches and demonstrations. Regardless of what the SPD said or did, however, Adenauer held to his schedule for ratifying the accords. The final readings began on February 24.

The parties said nothing new. In the words of one German reporter, the arguments from both sides could be reduced to the simple formula: "I am of the opinion, as I was before, that your opinion is wrong."[59] The SPD began by introducing two motions: one to delay ratification until after a four-power conference, the other to negotiate a new Saar agreement. The coalition parties rejected both motions. Standing by the government, they voted for the accords, which were ratified on February 27 and sent to the Bundesrat for approval.

One week later the leadership committees of the SPD met at party headquarters in Bonn. They agreed that in spite of Adenauer's triumph in Parliament the SPD would continue the opposition course it had been following since the failure of EDC. In his address to the party leaders Ollenhauer spoke optimistically about the party's political chances, insisting that its position was "extraordinarily good." He declared proudly that the impact of the Bundestag debate on the West German public went far beyond all expectations. The people had followed the proceedings on radio and television with great interest, which clearly revealed their concern for the question of reunification, and they now identified the SPD as the party of German unity. The SPD leader claimed that this stemmed from the party's role in the Paulskirche movement. The movement itself he labeled an "undisputed success." The percentage of those signing the manifesto in the various polling areas far exceeded the vote received by the SPD there in the 1953 general election. Ollenhauer believed that the party had also gained strength in Parliament because of growing criticism of the chancellor's policy among coalition deputies, the Free Democrats in particular. For the first time in the life of this Bundestag, Ollenhauer said, the political forces had begun to shift, and "who knows what new combinations might possibly be produced." The SPD leader admitted that Adenauer still held a strong position, but problems lay ahead for the chancellor. The Bundesrat could prove uncooperative, especially on the Saar question, and it was by no means certain that the French would ratify the accords. It was still "a completely open question if and when the accords would come into force." The SPD, therefore, should continue its efforts to demonstrate public concern for reunification. The people had not given up hope, Ollenhauer said, and neither should the SPD.[60]

Ollenhauer remained optimistic during the next two months; in fact, by late April he still saw no reason to revise the foreign-policy theses of the SPD. Abroad, the possibilities for convening a four-power conference seemed brighter than ever; at home, the SPD had strengthened its position, as evidenced by the results of the state election in Lower Saxony.[61] But in spite of supposedly favorable conditions, Ollenhauer made no attempt to maintain the momentum of the Paulskirche movement. To begin with, the SPD found it difficult to sustain public interest or to organize an unending round of rallies and demonstrations. Second, although some local party organizations showed continued enthusiasm for extraparliamentary action, prominent SPD politicians warned Ollenhauer of the political dangers of going too far with the Paulskirche movement. The SPD leader responded by assuring them at a Fraktion meeting that the SPD had no intention of violating the principles of parliamentary democracy.[62] He had no answer, however, for those who expressed concern about the campaign degenerating into a general attack on rearmament and thus creating the impression that the SPD favored an *ohne mich* policy.[63] Finally, whatever popular success Ollenhauer might claim for the Paulskirche movement, it was having absolutely no effect on the government's determination to ratify the Paris Accords. Adenauer secured the assent of the Bundesrat and the signature of the president without much difficulty, and on May 5, following ratification by the NATO states, the accords came into effect.

It seems surprising that the SPD leaders failed to recognize beforehand both the dangers of extraparliamentary action and the unlikelihood of delaying ratification. Some leftist critics have suggested that the party leadership viewed the Paulskirche movement as nothing more than an escape valve to release the pressure building up within the party.[64] No doubt the leaders considered this aspect, but they also wanted to find a legitimate means of preventing Adenauer from ratifying the accords because of their impact on the chances for reunification, as Russian warnings made clear. Furthermore, if the West Germans shared the SPD's concern for reunification, which Ollenhauer believed they did, then an appeal to the public seemed opportune as well as necessary. In going to the people, however, the Social Democrats hardly enhanced their reputation. It made them appear misguided, even irresponsible, especially since most West Germans doubted that reunification—though a matter of concern—could be achieved any time soon. The party's image suffered further damage from its treatment of a new element in the rearmament debate—atomic weapons.

Carte Blanche

In June, 1955, West Germany experienced its first atomic alarm. It was triggered by a NATO exercise, code name Carte Blanche, in which tactical air units simulated a nuclear exchange between invading Soviet forces and the Western allies. Although NATO observers considered the exercise a great success, it failed to reassure the Germans about their security. According to newspaper accounts, the mock battle involved the dropping of 335 bombs in the crowded area between Hamburg and Munich, with civilian casualties numbering over five million, excluding those affected by radiation. The exercise shocked the West Germans severely. They had thought very little about the possibility of a nuclear war and then, mainly in terms of an American attack on targets in the Soviet Union. Now, however, they knew that nuclear weapons could be used in Germany to stop a Red Army attack.[65]

Carte Blanche stemmed from the NATO Council's decision in December, 1954, to adopt a defense strategy based on the immediate use of tactical nuclear weapons against an attack from the east. The decision itself came in response to technological developments and to the unwillingness of the NATO powers to meet the goals agreed upon at the Lisbon conference in 1952. Because of overstrained budgets and diminished fears of Soviet aggression, European governments balked at spending more money on defense. Even in the United States the Eisenhower administration announced its intention of bringing economic and military necessities "into some kind of realistic focus," or, as the press stated, of getting "more bang for the buck." That could be achieved by reducing the number of active American divisions and by employing nuclear weapons against attacks by conventional forces. Secretary of State Dulles formally announced the so-called "new look" in American defense policy in January, 1954, when he threatened massive nuclear retaliation against Communist aggression. Throughout the following months NATO military planners discussed the idea of a tactical nuclear response to conventional attacks in Europe. They came to the conclusion that, "because of the limitations on men and conventional weapons dictated by economic and political considerations," the only way of counterbalancing Soviet numerical superiority would be the use of unconventional weapons.[66] In December the NATO Council adopted a nuclear strategy.

NATO leaders agreed, however, that even with nuclear weapons the alliance would still need large conventional forces to maintain both a balanced defense and a credible deterrent. These forces-in-being would have to be strong enough to discourage local attacks by Soviet or satellite units and, in the event of a major attack, to prevent a quick breakthrough. NATO military planners believed that the decisive phase of a future war would be fought at the beginning. What counted, therefore, was the mobility and firepower of active units rather than the supporting strength of reserve forces as contemplated in the Lisbon plan. The NATO Council, however, failed to specify the number of divisions that would be needed to make its nuclear strategy effective, but the military men viewed the existing force level—about fifteen divisions in Central Europe—as insufficient. The key was the expected German contribution of twelve battle-ready divisions.

Konrad Adenauer accepted the new NATO strategy with ease. In February, 1955, he assured Parliament that West Germany would enjoy absolute security once it became a member of the Atlantic Alliance, adding, "If we are in NATO, then Germany will no longer be the battlefield."[67] Since NATO intended to use tactical nuclear weapons in the event of a Soviet invasion of West Germany, the chancellor either failed to understand the new defense concept or, as was more likely, refused to concern himself with military strategy and technology. He concentrated on the political aspects of German entry into NATO, accepting the West's assurance that NATO membership meant security.[68] The coalition parties also avoided a discussion of strategic issues and joined the chancellor in giving attention to political rather than military matters. Unfortunately for the government, the Blank Office, which served as a shadow defense ministry, was unable to provide the necessary corrective to the chancellor's ready optimism. The military men who worked in the office held views curiously out of step with the thinking of NATO's military planners, and, although recognizing the destructive power of nuclear weapons, they insisted nonetheless that the decisive battles would be fought by ground troops as in the last war.[69]

When Carte Blanche exploded on the scene, the Social Democrats were no better prepared than the government for a frank and intelligent discussion of NATO's new strategy. Until 1954 they had given little attention to nuclear weapons except to express horror at those "weapons of mass destruction" and on occasion to show concern about the impact of a nuclear-arms race on the chances for German reunification—especially after the Russians exploded a thermonuclear device. Following Dulles's statement on massive retaliation, however, the Social Democrats began to talk more and more forcefully about the need for a strategy of peace. They warned that in the atomic age, because no one could win the next war, the great task facing the West was to prevent a nuclear holocaust. The first step was to open negotiations with the Russians on disarmament and detente.[70] In his 1954 May Day message to the party Ollenhauer wrote that because of the threatened extermination of the human race in a nuclear war "the old Socialist demand for the prevention of war [has] taken on a new and deeper meaning." Maintaining peace had become a simple command of reason and general disarmament a pressing necessity. These sentiments were shared by rank-and-file party members, who loudly applauded Ollenhauer at the Berlin party conference when he declared that war, even without atomic weapons, was abominable and horrible.[71]

The only Social Democrat who offered a different evaluation of the impact of nuclear weapons on the defense question was Fritz Erler. He expressed concern about the American "new look," but unlike his party comrades he rejected the idea that nuclear weapons made war inconceivable or conventional forces unnecessary. Who knows, he said, whether the new weapons would be used? "And who wants to take on the responsibility of having one's own nation wiped out by so-called classical weapons" because no defense was prepared against a nonnuclear attack?[72] Whatever the logic of Erler's argument, most party members ignored it because they had found in nuclear weapons a powerful argument against rearmament. Following the NATO Council decision in December, 1954, even Erler found it necessary to modify his views.

In the period between the NATO Council meeting and the Carte Blanche exercise, the Social Democrats continued to register warnings about the perilous danger of atomic weapons. Their warnings became so severe that it seemed questionable whether SPD leaders could still justify the conditional acceptance of rearmament made by the party at Berlin in July, 1954. An article in *Vorwärts,* for example, described modern weapons as a means of self-destruction rather than self-defense and claimed that even the word "soldier" was an outdated concept because the citizen called to arms could no longer protect the civilian population. The party's press service concluded, that, after Carte Blanche, no one could possibly justify the raising of German troops for Western defense.[73]

Immediately after the public reports on the NATO exercise, the Social Democrats questioned the government in the Bundestag about what the Western powers had learned from Carte Blanche and from a similar exercise carried out in the United States, Operation Alert. Responding for the government, Defense Minister Blank said that he saw no evidence that conventional forces had been made superfluous by the development of nuclear weapons or even by NATO's nuclear strategy; on the contrary, the alliance needed them for mopping-up operations and for occupying enemy territory after a nuclear strike. Furthermore, exercises held in the Nevada desert by the American army had demonstrated that ground forces could survive a nuclear attack and that armored units could quickly reenter the target area. Obviously unimpressed, Herbert Wehner called out: "Where are *we* going to find a desert?"[74]

The coalition sent some of its best speakers to the podium during the debate, but the results were unimpressive. Cabinet member Franz Josef Strauss suggested that with more conventional forces the West would no longer be compelled to respond to a Soviet attack, at whatever level, with nuclear weapons. Erler responded that nuclear weapons formed the basis of American strategic planning and that the United States planned to reduce its ground forces in proportion to its reliance on these weapons and to the number of troops provided by the Federal Republic. The twelve German divisions, therefore, were designed to replace, not supplement, American forces in Europe. Strauss also offered the argument that the more awesome nuclear weapons became the less likelihood there was that they would be used. The resulting nuclear stalemate would increase the danger of local conflicts and with it the need for conventional forces. Although Erler had earlier spoken in similar terms, he now quoted Basil Liddell-Hart to prove that a clash between the great powers would escalate into total war. Keeping to the party line, Erler argued that since NATO had gone nuclear the twelve German divisions lacked any great importance, and he advised the government to pay greater attention to the civil-defense needs of West Germany.[75] Ollenhauer went one step further by adopting the view of Adalbert Weinstein, military writer for the *Frankfurter Allgemeine Zeitung,* who recommended that the whole defense budget be used for civil-defense purposes now that Germany faced the prospect of becoming an atomic battleground.[76] The SPD leader reminded Adenauer of his statement earlier in the year that, if the Federal Republic joined NATO, Germany would never be a theater of war. It seemed to the

Social Democrats that Carte Blanche had proved the very opposite to be true.

In presenting their case against the government's military policy, the Social Democrats used a number of witnesses, quoting active military men like Alfred Gruenther and Bernard Montgomery, who affirmed that nuclear weapons would be used in Germany, and scientists like Albert Einstein and Otto Hahn, who warned that a nuclear war would mean the end of civilization. Most of the witnesses were reliable, but the SPD made some questionable choices—in particular, a Colonel Bogislaw von Bonin.[77]

A former officer of the German General Staff, Bonin has been described by some as an ardent supporter of Adolf Hitler and by others as a military specialist of the old school for whom technical matters were always more important than politics. Whatever his record, he joined the Blank Office in June, 1952, and remained an active military planner until his dismissal three years later. From the beginning Bonin clashed with other members of the staff. He opposed the work of the military reformers, questioned the military worth of EDC, and criticized NATO's strategy for European defense because, he said, it would lead to the devastation of Germany. In July, 1954, he drafted a memorandum on German defense policy in which he proposed the creation of a defensive perimeter thirty miles wide along the zonal border. The area would be patrolled by a West German force of about 150,000 volunteers organized in armored divisions and highly mobile antitank units operating independently of NATO. While the NATO units formerly deployed in Germany would be withdrawn across the Rhine, Bonin assumed that in case of a Soviet attack they would come to the assistance of the West German army, at a position farther east than originally planned.[78]

Although Bonin received a favorable response from some officers, the government's military advisers rejected the plan on the grounds that it offered too little protection for West Germany. The government considered the Bonin Plan politically dangerous because it placed West Germany outside the framework of the Western defense system; Adenauer opposed any scheme which would separate the Federal Republic from the Western powers. When Bonin persisted with his plan, especially after the NATO Council decision of December, 1954, Blank asked for his resignation.

When the Bonin Plan first came across Ollenhauer's desk, he rejected it.[79] The Social Democrats had always been highly suspicious of Bonin, viewing him as one of the militarists in the Blank Office. Soon after the plan was made public, the party's press service stated that Bonin's militaristic supporters had tried to sell the plan to the SPD by pointing to its compatibility with an active policy of reunification, but the party would not be fooled.[80] Yet some members of the SPD leadership favored cooperation with Bonin. They received permission to establish contact with the colonel, and by summer the Social Democrats were using his ideas in their campaign against the government.[81]

On July 1, *Vorwärts* gave full-page coverage to a speech Colonel von Bonin had made before an SPD meeting in Munich. The paper noted with great satisfaction that in his opening remarks the colonel had declared that although he was not a member of the SPD he viewed the party's foreign policy as the correct one for Germany. According to Bonin, NATO offered no security because in the event of a Soviet attack the Allies, with their nuclear strategy, would destroy rather than defend Germany. For the Federal Republic, a policy of detente represented the most sensible course. The first step would be to remove all nuclear weapons and foreign troops from German soil, while permitting the two German states to maintain small defense forces. The second step would be reunification and an alliance-free status for Germany, which Bonin described as the best means of reducing international tension and thus eliminating the threat of war. *Vorwärts* presented the colonel's statements under the headline: "There Is No Security in NATO."

The party had nothing to gain by associating with Bonin. After all, he and the SPD stood at opposite ends of the political spectrum, and besides, the colonel advocated a policy which would have led to the neutralization of Germany. Yet the Social Democrats ignored all this in order to gather support against the government's defense policy. Unfortunately, they offered nothing in its place; if anything, they argued against the possibility of a successful defense strategy.

In the period from January, 1954, to June, 1955, the Social Democrats continued to oppose Adenauer's rearmament program and to insist, as they had previously, that there was no immediate need to rearm. If at times they showed a greater willingness than ever before to accept the possibility of rearmament, as for example at the Berlin party conference, they soon returned to the course of intransigent opposition in the Paulskirche campaign and during the atomic alarm set off by Carte Blanche. This persistently negative attitude stemmed directly from the party's fear of a revival of German militarism and its growing awareness of the threat of nuclear war, but above all from its deep concern for the question of German reunification.

For the sake of reunification the Social Democrats adopted a policy which could be described as an appeal for "one more conference." They declared that their consent to West German rearmament could be given only after it had been proven conclusively that the Russians refused to allow free elections in Germany. By no means a new demand, it had been raised by Kurt Schumacher and pressed with growing urgency by the SPD after the note from Stalin of March, 1952. Even after the unsuccessful Berlin foreign ministers' conference of January, 1954, the Social Democrats insisted that the question of Soviet consent to free elections remained open. In the following months they warned the government against relying on EDC to open the path to reunification because the Russians would not be intimidated by a policy of strength. When EDC finally died in August, 1954, the Social Democrats immediately assumed that one of the greatest obstacles to four-power agreement had been removed, and their hopes for a conference rose markedly—thus their dismay when Adenauer and the Allies decided to fit West Germany into NATO before opening negotiations with the Russians.

The Social Democrats clung tenaciously to their demand for negotiations in the face of Western resistance and, more remarkably, in spite of their own deeply held suspicions of Soviet intentions. Early in 1955, after the Russians had offered to discuss the German question again at a four-power conference, Ollenhauer told the Bundestag that "I do not know if this proposal [has been] raised as a means to prevent ratification. No one surpasses us in mistrust of the Communists, but in such a vital national question, it is necessary that we investigate every chance that seems to exist and not merely push it aside."[82] In calling for negotiations, the Social Democrats did not suggest that the Soviet Union was more willing to accept a settlement than before; rather, they emphasized that the Russians might be less willing to negotiate later.

Naturally the Social Democrats wanted the Western powers to act quickly. They also expected the German government to do whatever was necessary to promote four-power talks. As Ollenhauer explained, "We cannot expect the governments of other lands to do more for reunification than we ourselves are ready to do." Adenauer had done nothing to convince the Western powers of the need for an active German policy and, according to the Social Democrats, would do nothing because he accepted the existing situation. For Germany to be reunified, therefore, "Adenauer had to go."[83]

In April, 1955, when Austrian Chancellor Julius Raab successfully negotiated a treaty with the Soviet Union leading to the restoration of Austrian independence and the evacuation of foreign troops from Austrian soil, the Social Democrats immediately pointed to Raab's diplomacy as an example of what could be done for Germany. The key to the agreement, said Erler, was Raab's readiness to declare that Austria would neither join a military alliance nor allow its territory to be used by foreign powers for military purposes. The Soviets demanded this, and the Germans would have to accept as much if they wanted reunification.[84]

The coalition parties failed to see how Germany could learn from the Austrian example. To begin with, Austria and Germany differed completely in size, geographic location, and potential power and in the way they had been divided and occupied. More important, Austria had been neutralized. Ollenhauer responded that the SPD was not trying to make a direct comparison between Germany, a nation of seventy million, and Austria, with its seven million inhabitants; nor was the SPD of the opinion that the Austrian solution could be applied to Germany. Nevertheless, he said, Raab had demonstrated that "where there's a will there's a way."[85]

In spite of Ollenhauer's denials, the idea of neutralizing Germany to achieve reunification interested the Social Democrats. During the second reading of the Paris Accords, for example, Erler suggested that world peace would be more secure if the heavily armed military blocs were separated by a belt of states circling the globe from Scandinavia through Germany, Austria, the Near East, India, Burma, and Japan. Certainly there would be less chance of a conflict if Russian and American soldiers no longer stood face to face across the iron curtain.[86] Belgian Foreign Minister Paul van Zeeland made a similar suggestion, but he talked of a divided Germany and of allowing the two German states to maintain limited forces of their own after the occupying powers had withdrawn. The party rejected the plan,[87] and Ollenhauer opposed the idea of a neutral belt of states in Europe because Germany—even if reunified—would be isolated between the competing military blocs without any guarantee of its security. Furthermore, Ollenhauer warned that a reunited Germany, denied equal status with its neighbors, would undergo severe nationalist pressures and eventually become an explosive element in international affairs.[88]

In early May, 1955, after the Western powers had agreed to a summer meeting with the Russians at Geneva, the SPD Executive Committee published a statement on German reunification and four-power negotiations in an attempt to clarify the party's position.[89] Most of what the Social Democrats said had been heard before. They emphasized, as they had before the Berlin conference, that German reunification and European security had to be treated together. Before there could be free elections, the Russians would have to agree on the international status of a reunited Germany. Obviously, they would not accept German membership in NATO any more than the West would agree to the inclusion of Germany in the Soviet bloc. Bündnisfreiheit, therefore, was the prerequisite for German reunification, and the incorporation of Germany into a UN-supported regional security system was the best means of meeting the security needs of the four powers and the Germans.

In their comments on the projected four-power meeting the Social Democrats warned against any attempt to base an agreement on the status quo. International tension would be heightened rather than reduced. Furthermore, if West Germany entered NATO, then East Germany would be drawn into the Soviet bloc, and the division of Germany would be deepened. To reduce international tension and promote the reunification of Germany, the Social Democrats proposed that the Paris Accords be implemented only after the powers had conducted thorough negotiations.

146

The SPD policy statement came under heavy attack from coalition deputies. They charged that on the basis of the security measures proposed by the SPD the American presence in Central Europe would be replaced by a mere promise of support, and instead of a united Western front the Germans would have to rely on Soviet goodwill. The government parties reminded the Social Democrats that they themselves had pointed out the expansionist aims of Soviet foreign policy.[90] In response the SPD conceded that a Soviet threat existed, though considerably reduced, and asserted confidently that Germany would receive full protection from the Americans. As proof Adolf Arndt quoted Dulles as having said that the United States could not be defended without Europe. As Richard Jaeger (CSU) pointed out, however, what counted for the Germans was where the Americans would defend Europe—at the Rhine or from air bases in Spain or Great Britain.[91] According to the government, German security could be assured only on the basis of the closest possible ties with the West, that is, through membership in NATO. "Had we listened to the SPD and rejected the Paris Accords," said Adenauer, "there would have been no Western solidarity, no Geneva summit conference, and . . . we would have been led like lambs to the Soviet slaughterhouse."[92]

Although pressed onto the defensive, the Social Democrats refused to abandon their reunification policy. They believed that their position remained valid, and they insisted that the government alter its inflexible line of "rearmament first" in order to see what chances existed for promoting reunification.[93] As for the security question, the Social Democrats rejected the charge that by giving priority to reunification they were ignoring the security needs of West Germany. After all, they had stated over and over again that, once it had been demonstrated conclusively that the Russians would not accept German reunification in freedom, the SPD would support a West German defense contribution. The Social Democrats insisted that this had been recorded at the Berlin party conference in July, 1954, along with the party's specific conditions for supporting rearmament. Months later, while addressing the Bundestag, Herbert Wehner assumed that everyone knew the SPD stood "ready to defend our land and nation."[94] Throughout this period, however, the Social Democrats hardly dealt with the question of West German rearmament. They spoke at length about the role a reunited Germany could play in a European security system, while coalition deputies addressed themselves to the Soviet threat and the defense of West Germany. It appeared that they were participating in two different debates. Furthermore, the SPD's promise to deal with West German rearmament once the Russians had been tested rang hollow because the Social Democrats could never say when the results of a four-power conference would be recognized as final. On the few occasions that the SPD discussed West German defense, they insisted that NATO could provide no security, yet they offered no alternative except four-power negotiations.

When Carte Blanche focused public attention on nuclear weapons, the Social Democrats emphasized the need for civil defense rather than an active military defense, and throughout this entire period they reiterated the theme that social rearmament was more important than military rearmament.

During the ratification debates the Social Democrats expressed grave concern about the impact of rearmament on "the resistive strength of German democracy" to the Cold War tactics of the Kremlin. They warned that Adenauer's attempt to raise an army of half a million men in only three years would result in a serious economic and financial crisis.[95] Although the government dismissed such predictions as grossly exaggerated, independent observers—including economists and businessmen—pointed to the danger of inflation and the threatening shortage of manpower if the army called up significant numbers of men from the existing labor force.[96] The Social Democrats paid considerable attention to the costs of rearmament, and they deplored publicly the government's readiness to accept heavy defense spending at a time when its allocation of funds for social legislation was grossly inadequate. One Socialist writer warned that the burden placed on the German workers, because of higher taxes and fewer consumer goods, would drive the workers into radical action. "The result, given the mentality of the German propertied classes, inevitably means . . . more trumps for Moscow. And how will it be when the generals are once again in command?" he asked.[97] In the light of these dangers, Ollenhauer concluded, "a comprehensive policy of social security [had] more meaning for strengthening the free world than raising new divisions."[98]

The Social Democrats insisted that, given the existing state of international relations, their list of priorities was perfectly justified. As proof they advanced the argument that the conflict between East and West was basically a power struggle between the two superpowers. In such a contest a German military contribution would have no affect on the balance of forces because the United States and the Soviet Union already possessed the means to destroy each other.[99] They were, in the words of President Eisenhower, like two scorpions in a bottle—if they fought, they would kill each other. Thus, Erler said, it was no longer a question of making defense preparations in case of war, but one of removing the very possibility of an armed conflict.[100] Furthermore, because NATO was a military alliance, created "in the spirit of power politics" and designed primarily to serve American interests, it could not provide the basis for a lasting peace. Rather than enter the Atlantic Alliance, therefore, the Social Democrats proposed that the Federal Republic work for a settlement of the German question which if successful would represent "the greatest single contribution to the reduction of international tension."[101]

In the early summer of 1955 the Social Democrats were no more ready to deal with the creation of a West German army than they had

FROM EDC TO NATO

been five years before when the rearmament debate began. Although some party members—notably Erler and Helmut Schmidt—understood the technical aspects of rearmament, most Social Democrats knew little and cared less about military matters. They still stood under the shadow of the Paulskirche movement, viewing the fight against rearmament as a crusade for reunification, democracy, and peace. The SPD leaders had contributed to this misconception. True, they had resisted the most radical implications of the movement, but they gave the impression— as one coalition deputy put it—that if the nation followed the Social Democrats "it would not be necessary to wear a steel helmet; instead everyone would be able to stroll along the Rhine in his Socialist straw hat."[102] Now, however, the issue could no longer be avoided, for Adenauer was about to introduce the government's military legislation. What would the Social Democrats do? Would they fold their arms and watch while the coalition parties built a new German army, or would they roll up their sleeves and take a hand in the legislative work?

CHAPTER 6

The New German Army

On April 1, 1955, former editor Friedrich Stampfer published an article in *Vorwärts* on Otto Gessler, who had succeeded Gustav Noske as defense minister in 1920. Stampfer noted that Gessler had remained in office for eight years and during that time the army had become "an alien body within the republic." The tragedy of the Gessler episode was that the Social Democrats had abandoned the defense post willingly in 1920, without attempting to find a successor to Noske within their own ranks. Even worse, they had allowed an understandable dislike for the rigors of army life to be transformed into a rejection in principle of all things military. According to Stampfer, the failure even to try to build a loyal army was the great omission of the SPD in Weimar. "Let us hope that we have learned from the mistakes of the past."

In the following weeks *Vorwärts* received a flood of letters in response to Stampfer's article. Some agreed with him, but most thought that any attempt by democratic forces to control the new army would be completely futile. Since Adenauer and his reactionary friends held the reins of power, they would occupy the key positions in the army. Moreover, the military in Germany had a logic of its own. "What chance has the SPD to exert its influence?" asked a party member from Göttingen.[1]

Coming on the heels of the SPD's abortive Paulskirche campaign, the Stampfer letters added to the growing doubt in West Germany about the party's readiness to cooperate in the military legislation. Rumors were already circulating about a boycott of Parliament or even more radical action by the SPD. Ollenhauer denied that the SPD would resort to illegal means, but he never clarified the party's position.[2] Some observers speculated that the chairman had come under strong pressure from opponents of rearmament and, to maintain party unity, had to avoid any declaration on the military question. In the view of one reporter Ollenhauer was paying the price for getting involved in the Paulskirche movement.[3] Of course, he also had to listen to those who warned him about the dangers of a policy of abstinence. Led by Fritz Erler, they campaigned vigorously for SPD involvement in the upcoming legislative work.

By this time Erler had gained recognition as more than just a military expert. He was an established parliamentarian, respected by coalition deputies for his intelligence and objectivity and by his own colleagues, who, impressed with the compelling logic and clarity of his arguments, had elected him to the executive committee of the Fraktion. Above all, Erler was realistic about the party's chances, and now, after the ratification of the Paris Accords, he argued that the party had to face the facts of the situation. Adenauer intended to carry out his plans for West German rearmament, and he had the parliamentary strength to do so. When asked by a reporter what the SPD would do if Adenauer introduced military legislation, Erler said that the SPD would vote against it, but added that "of course, we will try to influence the contents of every law which the Bundestag passes; in fact, we will fight for every centimeter of civilian supervision, parliamentary control, democratic reliability, and human dignity in these military laws."[4] Although Erler recognized the need for such action, as did many leading SPD deputies,[5] he still had to convince the party. Unfortunately, Adenauer gave him little time. The chancellor announced in early May, 1955, that he expected to have the first piece of military legislation through the Bundestag before it adjourned in midsummer.

The Volunteers Bill

It had been Adenauer's original intention to introduce a comprehensive Soldiers Law defining the rights of soldiers and the position of the armed forces in the state. The basic outline of the law had been worked out by Theodor Blank's office, in consultation with the Bundestag Committee for European Security Questions (the Security Committee). Soon after the Paris Accords came into effect, however, the chancellor decided to begin the legislative program not with a draft of the Soldiers Law but with a bill that would give the government authority to enlist immediately a number of volunteers for the new army. Adenauer altered his tactics in response to pressing diplomatic considerations. The Geneva Conference was only two months away, and Adenauer wanted an army, however small, as a bargaining tool. He knew that the Soldiers Law, with its more than fifty paragraphs, would never get through Parliament before the summer recess, so he devised the so-called Volunteers Bill, which would be rushed through as quickly as possible. As justification for the government's haste, Adenauer claimed that the implementation of the Paris Accords was an essential step in building Western unity and strength, prerequisites for successful four-power negotiations. His immediate concern, however, was to gain a voice in the decision-making

council of the Western Alliance by the prompt delivery of German soldiers. Along with many other Germans, he feared that if the great powers
reached agreement at Geneva, it would be at Germany's expense. The
Volunteers Bill represented the chancellor's insurance policy against an
unfavorable settlement.[6]

Presented to the Bundestag on June 27, the Volunteers Bill consisted
of three short and deliberately vague paragraphs empowering the government to enlist six thousand volunteers. According to Defense Minister
Theodor Blank, military personnel were needed immediately to staff
the new Defense Ministry, attend NATO conferences, take charge of
military supplies being shipped from the United States, and open the
military installations which would be occupied by the new German
forces. Adenauer gave his assurance that the Volunteers Bill, a provisional measure, would be replaced shortly by more comprehensive legislation.[7]

The Social Democrats protested immediately. A spokesman for the
SPD charged Adenauer with "deplorable recklessness" in taking a step
which would "diminish the chances for reunification" at the upcoming
four-power conference in Geneva.[8] In the Bundestag on May 27, the
Social Democrats tried to block the chancellor's path by introducing a
motion calling for the postponement of all measures involved in the
implementation of the Paris Accords until after negotiations with the
Russians had been completed. The coalition parties disposed of the
challenge by defeating the motion.[9]

In the following weeks the Social Democrats protested both the timing
and the content of Adenauer's Volunteers Bill. It was another "Enabling
Act", they argued, giving the government complete freedom of action
without any real parliamentary control. In effect, the Volunteers Bill
and the cadres the government planned to form would determine "the
future shape of the armed forces which later legislation could not affect."
The Social Democrats pointed out that the dangers of a cadre army,
free from parliamentary control, had already been demonstrated in the
Weimar period by the antirepublican activities of the Reichswehr.[10] If
the government was now allowed to go ahead with rearmament on the
basis of the Volunteers Bill, asked *Vorwärts,* "could we rely on Adenauer
to handle the Prussian officer corps?"[11] The party stated frankly that it
had no confidence in the chancellor's ability to defend the democratic
order against the militarists.

The party's military experts placed great emphasis on the initial legislative step in the rearmament program. If that was wrong, the whole
course of West German military policy would be set on a false track.
As Erler told the Bundestag, if it failed to establish the place of the
armed forces in the state, then the military men would do it "according
to the needs of the armed forces and not those of parliamentary democracy." Erler recommended that, to secure parliamentary control and
civilian supremacy, the Bundestag create a Defense Committee to re-

view the officer candidates for the new army. He warned against leaving the selection process to the Defense Ministry because the new military leaders had to be judged on more than their professional competence. The new army needed republicans as well as technicians.[12] Before the Volunteers Bill could even be considered, furthermore, a whole range of questions must be dealt with; for example, who would be the commander-in-chief of the armed forces? What powers of control over the military would be granted to the Bundestag Defense Committee? How would the Defense Ministry be organized, and how would it be controlled? Adenauer's bill dealt with none of these questions. Unless the Bundestag asserted itself now, Erler said, it would "cease to be a Parliament." When asked by coalition deputies whether the SPD would help prepare the necessary legislation, Erler hinted at the possibility but emphasized that his party would under no circumstances vote for the Volunteers Bill.

On June 28, when the Bundestag opened debate on the Volunteers Bill, the Social Democrats wasted no time registering their opposition to the government's rearmament policy. Speaking for the SPD, Ollenhauer asked how the government could introduce military legislation at a time when the great powers were preparing to deal with the problem of German reunification, and after Carte Blanche had demonstrated that "neither these six thousand volunteers nor the twelve divisions foreseen by the Paris Accords will or can contribute anything worth mentioning to the security of West Germany?" As for the Volunteers Bill itself, the SPD leader called it "a monstrosity," an attack on Parliament by the combined front of military and bureaucratic forces, which should be withdrawn. He demanded that the government present Parliament "all the main legislative proposals for serious and thorough examination" before the first German was put into uniform. If Adenauer went ahead with the bill and created an army without the support of the SPD—a party "which represents the core of the industrial working class and embraces a substantial part of the younger generation"—he would deepen the divisions within the nation and eventually bring about the collapse of German democracy.[13]

The coalition parties interpreted Ollenhauer's dire warnings as nothing more than an attempt to delay West German rearmament. They intended to give Adenauer the troops he needed to get rearmament started and to pass an appropriate military bill before the summer recess. They voted to send the Volunteers Bill on to the relevant Bundestag committees. Many coalition deputies, however, had doubts about the merits of the bill; they expressed particular concern about the lack of parliamentary control. In the Bundestag the Free Democrats had applauded Erler's call to action, and Richard Jaeger, a member of the CSU and chairman of the Bundestag Security Committee, stated bluntly that in its present form the bill would "not receive the approval of my political friends." The Volunteers Bill would have to be revised so that the rights of

Parliament would be preserved and civilian control of the armed forces assured.[14]

Since that was what the Social Democrats wanted as well, it seemed logical to assume that they would cooperate with the coalition parties now that the bill had reached the committee stage; yet it was by no means certain. The influential *Süddeutsche Zeitung* reported that the Social Democrats were still considering a boycott of committee meetings,[15] and in fact there was considerable difference of opinion within the SPD over what course the party should follow. Erler and the members of the party's security committee advocated a policy of active cooperation, but many SPD deputies doubted that the coalition parties were actually working for civilian control of the new army. It was not until a week after the Bundestag debate, when Adenauer finally agreed to a substantial revision of the original bill, that Erler found the evidence he needed to convince his colleagues.[16]

At a caucus of the SPD Fraktion on July 7, Erler argued successfully against a policy of abstention which the antirearmers defended with great fervor. The deputies decided instead to cooperate with the coalition parties.[17] Many remained skeptical, however, about the chances of effectively influencing the government's legislation; others feared that by agreeing to cooperate with the coalition parties the SPD would appear to have given up its opposition to rearmament. After the caucus a party spokesman informed the press that the decision to cooperate in no way meant that the SPD had capitulated to the government. He added that SPD cooperation would be dependent on the readiness of the coalition parties to accept a real discussion of the issues and to deal with a number of specific conditions laid down by the SPD. The party wanted a Personnel Review Board established, and such matters as the position of commander-in-chief settled, before the Volunteers Bill was passed.

In committee the SPD and the coalition parties quickly reached agreement. Seeking to ensure democratic controls and assert the rights of Parliament, they agreed first to create the Personnel Review Board, which would screen officer candidates for the new armed forces. The Social Democrats wanted all officers screened but accepted a compromise—the board would review applications for the rank of colonel and above—because the coalition parties had agreed to establish the board by federal law rather than allow the government to organize a federal agency for the purpose as Adenauer had proposed. The Bundestag Security Committee then completely redrafted the Volunteers Bill. Reporting to Parliament, the committee stated that it felt obliged "not only to change the bill in form, and substantially to expand its scope, but also to amend its substance in such a way that it now presents a practical legal basis for preparing the establishment of the armed forces."[18] The new bill recorded the number of volunteers that could be enlisted, restricted the duties they could perform as well as the length of time they could be employed, and declared Parliament's right to determine the organization of the Defense Ministry and the armed forces in later legislation. These measures, revising the Volunteers Bill and creating the Personnel Review Board (Personalgutachterausschuss), represented an impressive demonstration of parliamentary solidarity and proved the correctness of the SPD's policy of cooperation.

When the bills reached the floor of the Bundestag on July 15, the question was not whether but how they would pass; the result never stood in doubt. The coalition parties voted unanimously for the Volunteers Bill and, except for the German Party, which opposed the wide powers granted the Personnel Review Board, they supported the second bill as well. The Social Democrats, however, faced a dilemma. They could not vote for the Volunteers Bill because it would be interpreted as a vote for rearmament; on the other hand, they could not vote against the bill creating the Personnel Review Board because it was designed, in Mellies's words, to protect the armed forces from those people who had learned nothing from the past.[19] The SPD therefore decided to support that bill and to oppose the Volunteers Bill. In the latter case, it made no difference. The chancellor got his military bill through Parliament, though in a significantly altered form. It passed the Bundesrat with ease and received the president's signature before the end of the month.

The debate on the Volunteers Bill has been celebrated as a triumph for the Bundestag because it was the first time that the parliamentary parties—the coalition and the opposition—combined to impose their will on the Adenauer regime.[20] What facilitated the victory was the working agreement established by the parties, in the Bundestag committees especially by Richard Jaeger and Fritz Erler. These two men had participated in the Security Committee's earlier deliberations on EDC, and now, during the discussions of the Volunteers Bill, they conferred informally about the need for more comprehensive legislation. When the bill reached the committee stage, Jaeger and Erler worked behind the scenes to improve it and to draft the controversial bill on the Personnel Review Board.[21] Ultimately SPD participation in the committee work paid great dividends. Besides influencing the final shape of the two bills, the Social Democrats helped create a greater sense of unity among committee members and thus assured themselves a voice in future military legislation.

Despite the obvious advantages of a policy of cooperation, however, many Social Democrats still questioned the need to become involved in the military legislation. After all, they had been told that a German army was militarily senseless. It would cost money, "mountains of money, and give the Germans neither sovereignty, nor freedom, nor security,"[22] yet now SPD deputies were cooperating with members of the coalition to create a committee to select military personnel for a new army. The SPD, it seemed, was helping Adenauer build his army. The party leaders disagreed. They argued that the Volunteers Bill, not the bill on the

Personnel Review Board had created a German army, and the SPD, had voted against it. Even members of the Fraktion, however, found it difficult to maintain a distinction between legislation creating the new armed forces and that guaranteeing civilian control. In the Bundestag balloting ten SPD deputies abstained rather than vote for the Personnel Review Board.[23]

In defending the policy of cooperation, Erler pointed out that the Fraktion had kept well within the bounds of the military resolution laid down at the Berlin conference. The deputies were responding to the threatening situation created by Adenauer's introduction of an enabling act for military affairs. Erler reminded the party that Adenauer could have built an army on the basis of the February, 1954, constitutional amendment, without any reference to parliamentary control whatsoever. Under such conditions, asked *Vorwärts,* what else could the party do except join with the coalition parties in defense of the right of parliament? The newspaper called on party organizations around the country to support this "historic decision of the Fraktion," a decision which had produced "a considerable success for the SPD."[24] Although the deputies received support from some local organizations,[25] most party members remained unconvinced and thoroughly disillusioned with the party's course of action.

The Geneva Conferences

The Social Democrats expressed relief when the debate on the Volunteers Bill finally ended. Now the government could put aside military matters and focus its attention on the German question, which moved to the center of the international stage. On July 18 the leaders of the four great powers met in Geneva for a summit conference. In terms of practical results the conference accomplished very little. There was a brief moment of detente—the so-called spirit of Geneva—and, more concretely, an agreement that the foreign ministers would reconvene in October. There was, however, a deadlock, on the German question. Both sides indicated that they could live with the status quo. The Russians even hinted at a two-Germanys solution. After the conference Soviet leaders Nikita Khrushchev and Nikolai Bulganin stated that reunification could be achieved only through a rapprochement between the two German states and only if a reunited Germany became "democratic and peace-loving."[26]

Although they recognized the change in the Soviet position, the Social Democrats refused to accept it. They remained adamantly opposed to direct negotiations with East Berlin, insisting that reunification was a four-power responsibility, and they clung to the hope that the Russians would discuss the German question if the Western powers would relinquish the notion of trying to incorporate a reunited Germany into

NATO.[27] More immediately, they tried to persuade Adenauer to abandon his rearmament policy, though without success.

On October 12 the government presented Parliament with another military bill, the proposed Soldiers Law, which would establish the legal status of the soldier and provide directives on such matters as enlistment, promotion, the oath and solemn pledge, political activities and voting rights, discharge, and retirement benefits. After a brief debate the government's bill passed the first reading. The coalition parties voted for it, though with the intention of taking a closer look at it when the bill reached the committee stage. The Social Democrats, of course, voted against it. Hans Merten of the SPD told Defense Minister Blank that his party found the bill completely inadequate in dealing with a number of basic questions, and he urged the government to prepare a proper constitutional basis for the soldier and the armed forces. Although Merten implied that the SPD would do its share of committee work, he deplored the government's decision to present Parliament with a military bill only two weeks before the Geneva Foreign Ministers' Conference.[28]

After the first reading of the Soldiers Law, the Social Democrats turned their attention to the upcoming four-power negotiations. They drafted an elaborate set of proposals, which they hoped the government would adopt as official German policy, and sent observers to Geneva when the conference opened.[29]

The Geneva Foreign Ministers' Conference proved an even greater disappointment for the SPD than the Berlin meeting of January, 1954. The powers made no progress toward a settlement of the German question, and there seemed little likelihood that they would do so any time soon. At first the SPD blamed the Western powers, claiming that they had failed once again to test the Soviet Union. Later Ollenhauer conceded that the Soviet government "did not consider the solution of the German question to be urgent," but he insisted nonetheless that there was much to be gained by "clarifying the situation" through negotiations, that is, by compelling the Russians to give an unambiguous answer to the essential question of what constituted for them an acceptable military status for a reunited Germany.[30] Party spokesmen warned repeatedly about the danger of resignation in the West because of the difficulties of negotiating with the Russians, and they demanded that the Germans strive to "place the question of German reunification on the international agenda again and again."[31]

The Social Democrats came under heavy criticism for their assessment of the Geneva conferences and for their "deplorable lack of any sense of reality." According to a government spokesman, the Russians were unwilling to surrender the East German regime through free elections and would consent to reunification only if it led to a bolshevized Germany. Molotov made that perfectly clear at Geneva. Speaking with what a government spokesman called "brutal candor," he said that in the Soviet view neither the Paris Accords nor the military status of a reunited Germany represented a serious obstacle to German reunification. The real obstacle, commented the CDU press service, was the Soviet attempt to force the Germans to accept a regime "which from the bottom of their hearts they abhor." For this reason the West German government would continue its policy of "close and trusting cooperation" with its Western allies, a policy constituting the only path to reunification in freedom and security.[32]

Soon after the Geneva Foreign Ministers' Conference, Adenauer urged the coalition parties to complete the final readings of the Soldiers Law by mid-December. The chancellor needed the Soldiers Law to replace the Volunteers Bill, which was only a temporary measure, expiring on March 31, 1956. Furthermore, the Volunteers Bill permitted the government to raise only a few thousand troops. Adenauer now wanted to build a cadre for the new army by enlisting 150,000 professional soldiers as soon as possible.

The Social Democrats tried to dissuade Adenauer from proceeding so rapidly with rearmament. They argued that his policy of strength had already proved itself a tragic failure by "hardening the Soviet attitude toward reunification." As for German security, the Social Democrats claimed that no immediate threat of war existed and that even if the Red Army stood ready to attack, the Germans could do nothing; in fact, as a result of modern weapons technology, the military worth of German rearmament had become "more questionable . . . than ever before." Ollenhauer added that, given the state of international affairs, it would make more sense to work for general disarmament than for twelve German divisions. He saw no political or military reason why Adenauer would "answer Geneva with an accelerated rearmament program."[33]

Fortunately for the SPD, the government's attempt to ram the military legislation through parliament before Christmas ran into a brick wall. The Bundesrat refused to deal with the Soldiers Law while the rights of the states in military matters remained unclear. In the Bundestag the Security Committee protested against the unnecessary haste with which the government approached the task of building a new army. Jaeger, chairman of the committee, insisted that before the Soldiers Law could be passed the government would have to introduce a constitutional amendment as well as solve a number of technical problems relating to the organization, command, and control of the armed forces.[34]

Once again, therefore, the SPD had an opportunity to exploit the differences between the government and the coalition deputies in the Security Committee. There could be little doubt about the course the party would follow. By participating in the committee work, the Social Democrats could slow down Adenauer's rearmament program and, as was the case with the Volunteers Bill, assure the preparation and passage of the best military legislation possible. Thus while publicly the party deplored the government's actions, behind the scenes SPD members of the Bundestag Security Committee began laying the foundation for another compromise with the coalition parties.

The Soldiers Law

In September, 1955, the SPD Fraktion organized a working group (Arbeitskreis) to deal with security questions. The Fraktion already had working groups for other policy areas to prepare the deputies for committee sessions, and Erler persuaded the leadership to do the same for rearmament now that Adenauer was about to introduce his major pieces of military legislation. Along with Erler as chairman, the committee enlisted several members of the Parteivorstand's advisory committee on security questions—including Executive Committee members Schmid and Wehner. This meant that the party's military experts had a direct line of communication with the leadership, as well as a means of coordinating policy planning and application through the partly interlocking membership of the two bodies.[35] Most of the members, furthermore, had served on the Bundestag Committee for European Security Questions and developed certain ideas about German military policy.[36] As a result, when the Soldiers Law passed its first reading in October, 1955, the Social Democrats entered the parliamentary committees armed with proposals of their own.

According to Erler, who wrote a great deal on the subject, the SPD wanted to find a place for the new armed forces within the framework of the democratic state which would assure that they served, rather than dominated, the nation.[37] This could be done by establishing four basic principles: civilian direction of the armed forces, parliamentary control of military affairs, legal protection of the soldier's basic rights, and rigorous screening of officer candidates. The Social Democrats wanted to see these principles legislated into action and anchored in the constitution before the Soldiers Law was passed.

The Social Democrats demanded, first, that, instead of a general curtailment of the soldier's civil rights, as was the case in the Weimar period, the constitution should state specifically what rights had been restricted so that "the soldiers knew where they stood." Second, they wanted the annual review of the budget to go beyond a mere accounting of how the money was to be spent; it should include a precise statement of the numerical strength and organizational structure of the armed forces. These questions, said Erler, had to be discussed publicly by the Bundestag, not arranged secretly "in the darkroom" of the Defense Ministry. The selection of officers had already been settled by the creation of the Personnel Review Board in July, 1955. Five months later the board received warm praise from the Social Democrats when it rejected the applications of four colonels who had worked in the Blank Office.[38] Third, the Social Democrats wanted to prevent the misuse of the armed forces for domestic political purposes by specifying in the constitution the conditions necessary for declaring a state of emergency (Notstand). Fourth, the Social Democrats proposed that the defense minister be made responsible to Parliament. Fifth, they urged the creation of a Bundestag Defense Committee with the powers of a permanent board of investigation. Finally, they called for the appointment of a defense commissioner (Wehrbeauftragter) who would survey conditions in the armed forces as the "eyes and ears of Parliament." In presenting their ideas to Parliament, the Social Democrats found broad agreement on the need for "democratic controls" but considerable disagreement among the parties on the specific role to be played by the Defense Committee, the defense commissioner, and the defense minister.

The interest shown by the Social Democrats in a strong Defense Committee stemmed from their desire to strengthen parliamentary government in a country where the civilian authorities had too often been dominated by the military. They had first proposed granting extensive powers of control to a Bundestag Defense Committee during the February, 1954, military debate, but to no avail. In June, 1955, when the government introduced the Volunteers Bill, the Social Democrats raised the matter with greater urgency because of Adenauer's "preference for secrecy and aversion to public criticism." Erler claimed that, to ensure parliamentary control of the military, the Defense Committee should have the authority to meet, even between sessions, and to investigate matters on its own without waiting for a request from the Bundestag.[39] Within the existing Committee for European Security Questions many coalition deputies shared Erler's interest in converting it into "a kind of parliamentary watchdog" for surveillance of the Defense Ministry.[40] It remained unclear, however, whether the coalition parties would agree to such a powerful committee or to the SPD's request for a constitutional amendment to secure the committee's powers.

The idea of creating a defense commissioner originated with SPD Deputy Ernst Paul, who proposed during the EDC debate that the Security Committee investigate the role of the plenipotentiary for military affairs in the Swedish army. Although the committee undertook an investigation, nothing further developed.[41] The Social Democrats returned to the idea in the military debates of 1954-55, when Erler explained in great detail what the SPD wanted. The defense commissioner would be the agent of Parliament rather than of the government. He would be given access to all military documents, installations, and personnel, while servicemen could send petitions and complaints to his office without interference by their superiors. With these powers, which would also be anchored in the constitution, the defense commissioner could guard the basic rights of the citizen-soldier and help Parliament control the armed forces.[42] Although Erler received a favorable hearing in the Security Committee, coalition deputies showed greater interest in extending the committee's powers than in creating the post of defense commissioner.[43]

Of the demands raised by the SPD, those relating to the defense minister proved to be the most controversial. The Social Democrats insisted that the Bonn constitution be amended to allow the Bundestag to pass a vote of no confidence against individual cabinet members as well as the chancellor. Since the defense minister held a key position, controlling the armed forces and spending about one-third of the budget, Parliament had to be able to replace a man who had lost its confidence without provoking the fall of the whole cabinet. The SPD asked for a provision that dismissal follow as a result of a simple majority rather than the two-thirds vote needed to remove the chancellor. Erler reminded the coalition parties that during Weimar the defense minister had allowed the Reichswehr to develop into a state within the state. That could now be prevented if Parliament could remove anyone who failed to maintain civilian control of the armed forces.[44] Erler added that it was also necessary to ensure that the Defense Ministry would be run by civilians rather than military officers operating from separate departments or from "a new OKW" (Hitler's high command) outside the ministry. To prevent this, Helmut Schmidt prepared a very elaborate organizational scheme for the Defense Ministry which he urged the coalition parties to adopt.[45] The coalition parties, however, neither shared the SPD's fears nor agreed with the argument that without a defense minister responsible to Parliament the whole effort at parliamentary control of the armed forces would be endangered. They warned that the SPD plan would destroy the existing political system, based on the constructive no-confidence motion, and plunge Germany into another period of governmental instability.[46]

Despite their differences, plenty of room for agreement still existed between the SPD and the coalition parties. If the Social Democrats wanted a voice in shaping the military legislation, however, they would have to remain flexible, because some influential members of the coalition considered cooperation with the SPD unnecessary. They argued that the simultaneous passage of the Soldiers Law and the constitutional amendments for securing parliamentary control of the armed forces was desirable, but hardly essential, as the SPD claimed. Under the constitutional amendment of February, 1954, the government could pass the Soldiers Law by a simple majority.[47] Fortunately for the Social Democrats, some members of the CDU-CSU believed that the Soldiers Law should be accompanied by a series of constitutional amendments and wanted to gain broad popular backing for a new German army by winning the support of the SPD. Their readiness to compromise was limited, however. They believed that the Soldiers Law must be passed before March 31, when the Volunteers Bill expired; otherwise, the government would be unable to recruit more soldiers.[48] Thus if the Social Democrats refused to compromise, the Soldiers Law would be passed, and the various elements of parliamentary control would be secured only in modified form and as a federal law rather than a constitutional amendment.

Through January and February, 1956, the Social Democrats negotiated with the coalition parties about how the military legislation should be drafted. While Erler and Jaeger continued their discussions in the Security Committee, now officially the Defense Committee, Ollenhauer held conversations with the chairman of the CDU Fraktion, Heinrich Krone.[49] Their initial meetings were inconclusive, but in mid-February *Vorwärts* hinted at the possibility of a compromise settlement.[50] The breakthrough came in North Rhine-Westphalia, where, on February 20, the Free Democrats withdrew from the CDU-led state coalition and joined the SPD in forming a new government. Several days later in Bonn most of the FDP deputies went into opposition, depriving Adenauer of his two-thirds majority. This meant that the Social Democrats could combine with the Free Democrats in the Bundestag and the Bundesrat to block passage of any constitutional amendments. Since Adenauer could still pass the Soldiers Law with a simple majority, alliance with the FDP offered them few advantages. The Social Democrats stood to gain, however, from the impact of events in Düsseldorf and Bonn on those Christian Democrats who now more than ever wanted SPD support in asserting the rights of Parliament against the government. With both sides ready to compromise, therefore, Ollenhauer and Krone reached an agreement on February 24. As part of the bargain the SPD gave up its demand for the parliamentary responsibility of the defense minister, while the CDU-CSU agreed to help establish the position of the defense commissioner and the powers of the Defense Committee as the SPD requested.[51]

On March 6, 1956, the Bundestag held the final readings of the Soldiers Law and of the fourteen constitutional amendments which accompanied it. The SPD voted for the amendments, Mellies said, because they dealt "with freedom, democracy, and human rights" and against the Soldiers Law because it was another "link in the chain of laws" emanating from the Paris Accords.[52] Many members of the SPD Fraktion found it difficult to make such a distinction, and they expressed their doubts to the leadership. Just before the debate the deputies caucused in "an almost bitter atmosphere." Although the Fraktion leaders—specifically Ollenhauer, Wehner, and Erler—succeeded in persuading the majority to compromise with the CDU-CSU, twenty deputies maintained that a vote for the amendments constituted a vote for rearmament.[53] They registered the only negative votes against the amendments in the Bundestag. Observers noted that this was the first major piece of legislation to produce a split in SPD ranks during the second parliamentary period, and some claimed that the party now faced the growing threat of internal division.[54]

Outside the Fraktion most Social Democrats questioned why the SPD had struck a bargain with the Christian Democrats. It seemed to them that the party had given up the struggle against rearmament to play godfather at the birth of a new German army. Gerhard Gleissberg, a former editor of *Neuer Vorwärts* who had left the paper and the party over rearmament, charged that the Social Democrats had now become "fellow travelers" of the Bonn regime.[55]

The SPD leaders denied that they had made the party an accomplice to Adenauer's rearmament policy. No agreement existed between the CDU-CSU and the SPD on military affairs; on the contrary, "the laws to create an army were forced on the SPD by Adenauer; [those] to secure freedom were carried through by the SPD against the will of Adenauer."[56] Walter Menzel, parliamentary whip of the SPD Fraktion, reminded his fellow Social Democrats that the Berlin resolution directed the party to work for a democratic military organization if the government continued with its rearmament plans. Since Adenauer had the constitutional power to rearm, he had only to prepare the appropriate legislation to call up the first soldier. That he tried to do with the military bills of June and October, 1955, both of which the SPD opposed. The constitutional amendments of March, 1956, represented nothing more than an attempt to secure democratic controls of the new armed forces. By voting for the amendments, Menzel said, the SPD Fraktion was faithfully fulfilling the mandate it was given in Berlin.[57]

Although such an interpretation of the Berlin resolution could be defended, the resolution had also referred to a special conference at which the party could decide what had to be done. The SPD leaders, however, had no intention of calling the party together because they feared that the rank and file would either paralyze the Fraktion at a time when decisive action was needed or produce such tension that a split would become inevitable. The next biennial conference was scheduled to meet in July, and the leadership preferred to wait until then to confront the party on the military question. In the meantime the SPD leaders braced themselves for the equally unpleasant task of dealing with the next piece of legislation in Adenauer's rearmament program.

Conscription

In early February, Adenauer won cabinet approval for the draft of a new conscription law. The chancellor wanted to maintain the momentum of his rearmament program, and once the first reading of the Soldiers Law had been completed, he sent the conscription bill to the Bundesrat as the first step in the legislative process. The upper house sent the bill back to the government on March 23 with its consent but with the recommendation that the period of military service be reduced from the proposed eighteen months to only twelve months. For Adenauer the reaction of the state governments was a warning of things to come.

In the following weeks, Defense Minister Blank tried to explain the government's position to the coalition parties, who were uneasy about the bill, and to the general public, which strongly opposed the reintroduction of a universal military obligation.[58] Blank argued that to meet its treaty commitments West Germany had to raise an army of 500,000 men. Since less than half that number could be secured by voluntary enlistments, conscription became essential. Blank insisted that West Germany needed half a million men in uniform because even with the development of nuclear weapons there had been no appreciable reduction of ground forces by either side. In view of the Soviet threat, therefore, the West needed large forces-in-being. As for the eighteen-month service period, Blank pointed out that with the more sophisticated weapons and equipment used by military forces, the modern soldier needed a longer training period. Finally, Blank adduced political reasons for conscription. He warned that a professional army, lacking the constant influx of new recruits, stood in danger of becoming a state within a state. Besides, defense in a democracy was the task of the whole nation.

The Social Democrats made their objections known very soon. Early in March, at a meeting in Bergneustadt, the party leaders passed a resolution condemning the government's bill and warning that conscription would greatly aggravate the situation in Germany. They then commissioned the security committee of the Parteivorstand to "examine carefully how far the government's ideas on conscription correspond generally to the current state of political and technical development."[59]

The security committee made its recommendations to the party leaders on April 11.[60] No one expected the committee to recommend acceptance of the government's bill; on the other hand, it could hardly be expected to discard the party's long-standing commitment to a people's army (Volksarmee). But that is exactly what it did. The committee proposed that as long as Germany was partitioned the SPD should "oppose the formation of a standing army of 500,000 men by conscription in favor of a small volunteer force." The latter was preferable because conscription would deepen the division of Germany. Moreover, it would offer no greater guarantee of German security because in the event of a major European conflict Germany would be the battlefield regardless of the size of a West German army. The only suitable task for the West Germans was to counterbalance any military force organized in the Soviet zone, and that could be done without a large standing army. Besides, West Germany's treaty commitments said nothing about raising a half-million-man army or introducing conscription. The committee also expressed concern about the impact of conscription on the current disarmament talks. The powers were apparently discussing the subject in earnest, and it would be advisable for the Germans to avoid rearming "beyond the scale likely to be allocated to Germany." Furthermore, because of recent technological developments, it would be senseless to plan for a conscript army. Modern armies needed a high percentage of long-term professionals. Finally, the committee insisted that a volunteer army was no longer a threat to German democracy. Because of the constitutional amendments fought for and carried through by the SPD, the Germans could "subordinate any kind of army to political direction by the government and to direct control by Parliament." The security committee stated in conclusion that these recommendations could also

Adenauer signals his interest in disarmament, but at the same time signals that he will go ahead with conscription. Cartoon by Leger, *Vorwärts,* April 6, 1956.

apply to a reunified Germany operating within the framework of a collective security system.

In a commentary the security committee investigated the effectiveness of a small German professional army in several defense situations.[61] These included (1) a strategic attack by Soviet-bloc forces stationed in East Germany and Czechoslovakia with the specific goal of destroying NATO forces east of the Rhine; (2) an attack from the east, following a massive concentration of forces, with the objective of sweeping all the way to the English Channel and the Atlantic coast; and (3) a clash with East German forces during the process of reunification in which the great powers stood aside. The committee considered a small professional army suitable for the first situation. It could contribute to a Western deterrent that would make a lightning attack by Soviet forces "improbable." The second constituted the worst possible situation. Against a mass attack by Soviet-bloc forces the approximately twenty NATO divisions in Western Europe, strengthened by the proposed twelve German divisions, would be unable to hold the line. Even with atomic weapons the West would need more ground troops, and the Germans would have to make a contribution of significantly more soldiers than could be raised on a volunteer basis. On strictly military considerations, therefore, the second situation would require a military system based on conscription. Because of "higher political reasons," however, the committee members rejected this solution and proposed instead a professional army of about 200,000 to 250,000 men. They described it as "especially suitable" for the third possible situation, in the event of an attempted Communist putsch, for example, such as had happened in Czechoslovakia. In conclusion the committee pointed out that as a security policy its recommendation of a professional army raised by volunteer enlistments was "an expedient" dictated by political considerations.

When the Parteivorstand held its monthly meeting, the SPD leaders decided to shelve the security committee's recommendations for the moment. In doing so, they seemed less concerned about abandoning the concept of a people's army than about adopting the extraordinary idea, for Socialists, of a professional army. A German newspaper reported that Ollenhauer was having difficulty trying to reconcile himself to the new military policy suggested by the party's military experts, and indeed he was,[62] but he also knew that the local party organizations had little sympathy with the idea of creating another Reichswehr. It seemed expedient and proper, therefore, to leave the final decision to the highest authority in the SPD, the party conference, which was scheduled to meet in July. This meant, however, that the SPD would have to face the first reading of the conscription bill in May without an alternative to the government's military policy.

In an address followed closely by the entire house, Fritz Erler explained to the Bundestag on May 4 why the SPD opposed conscription.[63] He began by denying that West Germany had an obligation under the Paris Accords to raise an army of 500,000 or to introduce conscription. The government was "merely using these alleged obligations to avoid an embarrassing debate on the appropriateness and necessity of introducing conscription." With reference to conditions in East Germany, Erler warned that if conscription was introduced in the West the Communist regime would draft tens of thousands of young Germans who until now had avoided being drawn into the Volkspolizei. The end result of the government's bill, therefore, would be the creation of two large German armies, the deepening of the division of Germany, and the growing threat of a civil war. To avoid the tragic conflict of conscience which the younger generation would have to face, Erler urged the government to consider the possibility of creating a volunteer army. He called it "a reasonable alternative" to conscription. Before concluding, Erler dismissed as a misreading of the facts Blank's warning that a professional army could more easily become isolated from the rest of society and thus develop into a state within a state. The spirit of an army, Erler said, depended on the attitude of the officers, who would be the same in a volunteer or a conscript army, rather than the disposition of the men in the ranks. "If responsible men firmly control personnel policy, it must be possible under any form of military organization to train the kind of officer who will remain loyal to the democratic constitution." If the civilian leaders surrender their powers of control to the military, then a few thousand conscripts handed over to the army for training could not save the situation. For the Social Democrats, however, the

Fritz Erler speaking during the May, 1956, military-policy debate. Adenauer and Gerhard Schroeder are conversing on the government bench. Courtesy German Press Agency.

decision for or against conscription ultimately rested on the more general question of the effect rearmament would have on the chances for reunification.

The Social Democrats complained again and again that the Adenauer regime had done absolutely nothing to promote the cause of German unity. Passivity on the German question, Wehner said, had been raised to the level of a political principle. Now the Germans had to take the initiative.[64] The Social Democrats had been watching events in the Soviet Union, in particular the Twentieth Party Congress, and they had come to the conclusion that Russian interest in peaceful coexistence—disarmament and detente—presented new possibilities for solving the German question. With discussions on disarmament under way, the Social Democrats predicted that an arms agreement would improve the chances for a solution simply by reducing international tension and by giving the powers an opportunity to discuss the military status of a reunited Germany. Speaking earlier in Strasbourg, Erler had referred to "the inseparable connection between disarmament, European security, and German reunification." Progress in one area would automatically lead to advances in other areas; therefore, the Bonn government should avoid any action that would make an arms agreement more difficult. For example, the powers were discussing the possibility of setting a limit of 200,000 men for the armed forces of states the size of West Germany. If this could be agreed upon, then it made no sense for the government to insist, "like Shylock demanding his pound of flesh," that the Federal Republic's right to raise 500,000 men be carried out "to the last grenadier."[65]

The coalition parties disagreed with the Social Democrats in their estimation of the international situation and even more in their treatment of conscription. Coalition deputies defended the government's policy by referring to the Weimar period, when the Reichswehr had become closed to "the free democratic spirit and the fresh air of civic responsibility." Taking the offensive, Hasso von Manteuffel quoted August Bebel and Gustav Noske to show that the Social Democrats had always emphasized the citizen's responsibility to bear arms in defense of his country, but Helmut Schmidt responded that these statements had been made at a time when Germany was united. Richard Jaeger countered by noting that, after 1949, Kurt Schumacher had warned against the dangers of re-creating a professional army and that even Erler, as late as November, 1955, had spoken of the political advantages of having an army which was drawn from all sections of society.[66]

In spite of their differences over the conscription bill, the Social Democrats and the Christian Democrats still had much in common. The SPD's military experts planned to work with their CDU counterparts if nothing could be done to prevent passage of the unwanted bill. On the other side, the Christian Democrats in the various Bundestag committees intended to cooperate with the opposition party, and once

Erler (right) confers with Richard Jaeger (CSU) during the May, 1956, military debate. Courtesy German Press Agency.

again they disagreed with the government over aspects of the legislation. A major problem arose over the period of military service. The government asked for eighteen months, Christian Democrats like Richard Jaeger preferred twelve months, and the Social Democrats wanted to keep it as short as possible. In June the two major parties reached a compromise.[67] They agreed that the final readings of the conscription bill would be held early the following month but the bill would only

169

establish the principle of a universal military obligation without mentioning the service period. Thus the government would have a conscription law without the authority to call up a single conscript.

Even after its agreement with the CDU, the SPD continued to protest that the government had no legitimate reason for requesting passage of the bill before the summer recess. There were plenty of volunteers to fill the ranks; in fact, the Defense Ministry was still processing applications for the 150,000-man allotment permitted by the legislation of March, 1956. More important, Defense Minister Blank still lacked sufficient barracks, uniforms, and equipment for the new German army. Erler added that because of government pressure the Personnel Review Board had so many officer candidates to screen that only a perfunctory investigation of their qualifications was possible. This benefited neither the candidates nor the people, "whose trust we must win for the new army." Besides, there was no need for haste. "The Soviets are not knocking at the door."[68] The Social Democrats realized, of course, that Adenauer had accelerated the rearmament program for political rather than military reasons; that is, the chancellor wanted to complete the major pieces of military legislation before the 1957 election. The Social Democrats wanted to slow him down.

The Bundestag held its second reading of the conscription bill on July 4 in an atmosphere of crisis. Even before the debate began, the CDU and the SPD plunged into an angry verbal duel over the agenda. The clash arose over a request from the Social Democrats that the second reading be postponed so that Parliament could study the thirty amendments the SPD now submitted to the government's bill. When the Christian Democrats refused to delay the proceedings, insisting that the bill should be passed before the summer recess as Adenauer had requested, Ollenhauer asked for a short recess so that the SPD could discuss the situation.

Excitement ran high in the caucus room of the SPD Fraktion.[69] The handful of resolute opponents of rearmament argued vehemently that the SPD had to stop compromising with the government and assert its opposition to conscription in dramatic fashion by refusing to participate in the debate. Others saw no need for the SPD to return to the Bundestag because the coalition parties obviously had no intention of discussing the issues. Wehner, however, countered that such a drastic step would be meaningless unless the SPD went into the streets and mobilized the people against the government, a course of action which he opposed. Ollenhauer also spoke for moderation. While conceding that the government's bill would pass with or without the Social Democrats, he insisted that they should be in their places because, as a responsible political party, the SPD had to do everything possible to protect the young men who would be drafted into the armed forces. The deputies debated the issue for ninety minutes, finally agreeing to participate in the Bundestag session by a vote of 84 to 58.

When the SPD returned to the chamber, Ollenhauer went to the podium to tell the house that the Social Democrats would fight the bill "point by point." They contested each line of every paragraph, and after eight hours of debate only a fourth of the bill had been completed. Their filibustering tactics failed to work, however, because the Christian Democrats refused to compromise. In disgust the Social Democrats marched out of the Bundestag, and the coalition parties completed the second reading without interruption. Two days later, with Social Democrats back in their places, the conscription bill passed its final reading after another bitter debate.

Along with the conscription law the government had introduced regulations dealing with the rights of conscientious objectors. The subject greatly interested the Social Democrats, but they objected to the conditions laid down by the government for determining who would be exempted from military service. The Social Democrats maintained that every individual had the right to refuse military service for reasons of conscience, even those who suffered a conflict of conscience because of the circumstances. In a divided Germany that included those who objected to fighting against fellow Germans, those who had relatives still living in the Soviet zone, those who had recently returned from Russian prisoner-of-war camps, and those who had lost their families because of the war or Nazi persecution. Walter Menzel suggested that the right to declare oneself a conscientious objector should also be extended to cover certain wartime situations, for example, to those who opposed the use of nuclear weapons. Menzel pointed out that the American airmen who had bombed Hiroshima and Nagasaki had suffered "the agony of a tortured conscience long after the event."[70]

To this broad interpretation of the exemption rule coalition deputies responded that the SPD was trying to open the door to all kinds of evasions. Jaeger stated that in addition to rights the citizen had duties, in this case to defend his country, and in passing legislation that Parliament had to be concerned not only with the conscience of the citizen but also with the survival of the state. A state which would open the right to refuse military service to everyone would be committing suicide.[71] The Social Democrats deplored the coalition's appeal to reason of state (Staatsräson). They denied that the state had the right to demand military service or to judge the validity of any matter of conscience. That the individual alone could decide. According to Adolf Arndt, the crown jurist of the SPD, if an individual stated his position as a conscientious objector, then it should be unnecessary for him to prove that "he was not a Schweinehund."[72]

Although the Social Democrats felt strongly about protecting the rights of conscientious objectors, their main concern was not to write a better conscription law. They wanted to prove that conscription was "unnecessary, inappropriate, and detrimental."[73] In the final readings they reread their catalogue of objections to the government's bill and underlined their belief that because the threat of a major war had greatly

171

diminished, the need for a German military contribution had been reduced proportionately. Adenauer responded by warning that, far from standing on the threshold of peace, the world was entering one of the most crucial phases of the Cold War. The Social Democrats rejected such talk as mere propaganda designed to scare the people so that the chancellor could have his army, and the West Germans could become the last "tin soldiers" of the Cold War. According to Fritz Erler, informed sources in the West considered a Soviet attack in Central Europe unlikely in the foreseeable future. If anything, the signs indicated a marked improvement in the international climate and a greater chance for agreement on disarmament among the powers.[74]

Kurt Georg Kiesinger, who had become the CDU's foreign-policy spokesman, responded by arguing that nothing fundamental had changed in the ongoing struggle between East and West.[75] Peaceful coexistence represented merely a tactical shift by the Kremlin, and in the face of a continuing military challenge the West must maintain a strong and diversified defense system. Kiesinger warned that NATO's comparative weakness in conventional forces left the West open to Soviet blackmail. If the Red Army marched now, the choice open to the Western powers would be an atomic response, with a global nuclear war as the end result, or capitulation. Kiesinger suggested that a German contribution of twelve divisions would help free the Western powers from this dilemma. They would no longer be dependent solely on atomic weapons, and the danger of a nuclear holocaust would be greatly reduced. Turning to the SPD, he said, "If this idea is not convincing, then I am open to new ones. So far I have heard nothing from the SPD."

The Social Democrats refused to debate with Kiesinger over military strategy. They claimed that in the nuclear age standing armies were an anachronism and war, should it come, would be a nuclear war. NATO had recognized that by adopting a strategy based on an automatic nuclear response to Soviet aggression. The Social Democrats, however, made no attempt to offer a more flexible strategy for Western defense. Either they accepted current NATO strategy as an immutable fact, or they ignored it because they wanted to wage the debate at the political rather than the military level. Karl Wienand, a young SPD deputy, even criticized the Christian Democrats for concentrating too much on the military question instead of dealing with the "purely human side of the problem."[76]

As for the Kremlin's new tactics, Erler considered them more dangerous, though not for the reasons that Kiesinger gave.[77] The Soviet Union had switched the focal point of its efforts to political, social, and economic areas, yet the Western powers fixed their gaze on the Red Army and in the process allowed the Soviets to go from one success to another. The Western powers were fighting communism "at the wrong place, at the wrong time, and with the wrong weapons." The government's conscription bill was just another example of this mistaken strategy.

Before the final vote on conscription Ollenhauer told Parliament that the SPD would continue its fight against the government's rearmament program with "full determination and undiminished strength."[78] He failed to say, however, what the SPD would offer in its place; in fact, throughout the debate the Social Democrats limited themselves to rejecting conscription without offering any alternative. True, Erler mentioned a volunteer army, but he could not present the idea to Parliament as SPD policy because no one knew whether the party, which was about to meet in Munich, would accept rearmament in this form.

The Munich Party Conference

On June 15, four weeks before the Munich conference, the editor of *Vorwärts* warned that the party barometer indicated a storm was brewing. Indeed, a number of issues troubled the party, including the leadership's gradual shift away from traditional Socialist ideas.[79] Rearmament, however, stirred the most controversy. No less a witness than Erich Ollenhauer conceded that in the months before the conference there had been "a lively intraparty discussion" about rearmament.[80] At local party meetings across the country disgruntled Social Democrats had debated SPD policy and drafted resolutions for the upcoming conference.

More than a fourth of the resolutions submitted to the Munich conference by local party organizations dealt with rearmament, and, significantly, almost all of them demanded a declaration from the leadership that if the SPD won the next election it would annul the government's conscription law.[81] One-third of the military resolutions rejected any form of rearmament whatsoever on the grounds that a German army could not provide security in the atomic age; it would only present a threat to democracy and to the chances for reunifying Germany. The party groups presenting these resolutions also demanded that the leadership use all parliamentary and extraparliamentary means, including a revival of the Paulskirche movement, to prevent Adenauer from going any further with rearmament. As for the Fraktion's work in the military debates, only two of the resolutions praised the SPD deputies for their efforts in securing parliamentary control of the armed forces and legal protection for the soldiers. Some organizations thought that the Fraktion was being overly optimistic in its belief that effective safeguards could be established against the misuse of the armed forces; many felt that the Fraktion had gone beyond the authority granted to it by the Berlin party conference and in the process had caused confusion within the party and with the general public about the SPD's position on rearmament. To clarify the situation, they insisted on a declaration of SPD opposition to either conscription or rearmament of any kind. Among all the resolutions only one called for a positive statement on the military question. The party in Coblenz seconded the security committee's proposal of a volunteer army to replace Adenauer's policy of conscription.

Security committee members realized how deeply the party disagreed with their recommendations. They believed, however, that the SPD needed an alternative to Adenauer's plans for conscription in order to be effective against the chancellor in Parliament and in public. In view of the party's response to SPD participation in the military legislation, however, and considering the tenor of the resolutions drafted by local party organizations, it seemed likely that any attempt to force acceptance of the recommendations would trigger the storm that was brewing.

Fritz Erler was particularly concerned about how the military question should be handled in Munich. He realized that a major debate on rearmament would be self-defeating and advised—as he had before the Berlin party conference—that the leadership limit the discussion. Speaking to a combined meeting of the security committee and the Fraktion's working group on security questions, Erler stated that, since the SPD had never established the concept of a people's army as a party principle, the conference had no need to make a decision about this or any other kind of military system. At Munich it would be sufficient for the party to pass a resolution acknowledging its support of national defense. Later, to implement the resolution, the leadership could simply state its preference for a volunteer army.[82]

Several weeks later the military adviser of the Fraktion, Friedrich Beermann, composed a memorandum on the problem of how—in terms of the upcoming election campaign—the party conference should deal with the military question.[83] Beermann stated bluntly that the SPD would pay a heavy penalty if the Munich conference failed to affirm the party's support of national defense (Landesverteidigung). First, the new army would be somewhat hostile toward any political party which ignored military affairs. Second, the voters in the 1957 general election would vote only for a party that had made a commitment to national defense. Even those voters who believed in the SPD's reunification policy would be reluctant to back a party that could not explain how it would defend a reunited Germany against militant communism. Third, if by some chance the SPD did enter the government after the election, SPD cabinet members would soon find themselves in opposition to their own Fraktion on defense questions unless the party changed its policy. Beermann recommended, therefore, that the SPD propose the creation of a volunteer army of 300,000 men and affirm its support for national defense at the Munich party conference. The SPD had to make a decision. It could base its policy on the antimilitary sentiments of the old Social Democrats, or it could draft a new course which would attract new voters to the party. "In the first case, we will lose the election for sure; in the other, we can win it."

Although Beermann received some encouragement from eminent Social Democrats, the leadership decided that the mood of the party dictated a more cautious treatment of the military question, more cautious than even Erler had recommended. As the conference approached, the SPD leaders moved toward the kind of compromise arrangement that had proved so successful for them two years before.

The Social Democrats opened their five-day conference in Munich on July 10. After the opening ceremonies, Ollenhauer delivered a long, carefully prepared address entitled "German Politics at the Crossroads."[84] He declared that it was time for a change in the direction of German policy, time for West Germany to "get out of the armed fortress of a one-sided policy of strength and venture into the broad field of international negotiations." There new possibilities had emerged because of changing attitudes toward the Cold War in both East and West. On the military question Ollenhauer spent considerable time defending the actions of the Fraktion while at the same time assuring the delegates that the SPD had not altered its opposition to the government's rearmament plans. In the coming months "the Social Democrats will fight for a shift in policy . . . such that, instead of a rigid adherence to a Western military alliance, the Federal Republic will promote a relaxation of international tension and further the prerequisites of reunification." He added in passing that a West German defense contribution "should remain subject to this supreme goal."

After Ollenhauer's address, the delegates heard the resolutions sponsored by the leadership.[85] The resolution on foreign affairs advocated a policy oriented toward reunification, one that would acknowledge the interlocking nature of the problems of European security and German unity and the dependence of both on the promotion of detente between East and West. The resolution also called for the normalization of relations with the Soviet Union and the establishment of diplomatic ties with the East European states—except East Germany. All the Social Democrats wanted from East Berlin was an agreement on the free movement of people and goods across the zonal border. The resolution stated further that under a new foreign policy West Germany would support all steps toward reducing international tension. The resolution proposed that, as a first step, the powers release the two German states from membership in the Warsaw Pact and NATO. The West German government could then work for the reduction of foreign troops on German soil and the establishment of a ceiling on the number of troops in the two German armies. To make the last proposal realistic, however, the Social Democrats needed a military policy. The security committee had recommended a policy which would have been appropriate for this kind of situation, but the party leaders set it aside and drafted a policy recommendation of their own.

In contrast to the resolution on reunification, which could be considered a contribution to the West German foreign-policy debate, the military resolution dealt less with establishing a new West German military policy than with satisfying the antimilitary sentiments of the party. The resolution failed to offer any clear alternative to Adenauer's

Munich party conference, July, 1956. Ollenhauer and Deputy Chairman Wilhelm Mellies sit in the center of the front row (bottom of photograph). Courtesy German Press Agency.

military program; it simply stated that the aim of the SPD was to repeal the conscription law and to revise West Germany's treaty obligations in agreement with its treaty partners. After appealing for popular support in the next general election, the resolution concluded by declaring that the SPD would exploit all the possibilities available in a parliamentary democracy to attain, "even in cooperation with others, a revision of the government's disastrous defense policy."

The military resolution was a statement of opposition, but not total opposition. Significantly, it spoke of revising rather than annulling the Paris Accords, and it referred to that part of the Berlin resolution which called on the Fraktion to work for a democratic military system and for civilian control of the armed forces. Furthermore, the resolution alluded to the possibility of SPD membership in a new coalition government. The SPD leaders realized that the Social Democrats could not realistically expect to win a parliamentary majority by themselves. They would have to find allies, and that would require a more flexible position on the military question. With this in mind they drafted a resolution that made no unconditional demands but spoke only of aims—aims which could be modified if political conditions made their fulfillment impossible.[86] Thus, while reaffirming SPD opposition to Adenauer's rearmament program, the Munich resolution still left the leadership some room to maneuver.

In the ensuing debate the opponents of the resolution complained about its calculated vagueness. Such phrases as "the aim of the SPD" sounded as though the party was establishing a long-term objective rather than recognizing an immediate and imperative duty. One Bavarian delegate suggested that the party should state its opposition to rearmament and stop worrying about whether or not it could find a coalition partner next year. Arno Beherish, one of the twenty Bundestag deputies who had voted against the constitutional amendments in March, urged the conference to adopt a policy of uncompromising opposition. He received a thunderous ovation from the delegates when he warned that there were "bugs in the Federal Republic, brown bugs out of the past."[87]

The defenders of the resolution responded by referring to the party's political ambitions and appealing to its sense of responsibility. Fritz Erler reminded the conference that if the SPD wanted to govern it would have to deal with all matters of state, including military policy. He saw no reason why the party should embrace a pacifist policy out of fear of the military. An SPD-led government could control the new armed forces. With even greater assurance Herbert Wehner swept aside criticism of the Fraktion's cooperative efforts in the military legislation and firmly denied that the constitutional amendments were mere "paper guarantees" against the misuse of the armed forces by antidemocratic forces. Those guarantees, he said, were worth only as much as the Social Democrats were "willing and able to put into them."[88]

The delegates responded favorably to the speeches of Erler and

Wehner. Although many retained their doubts and suspicions, it seemed certain that most would vote for the resolution. The only exceptions would be the radical antirearmers. To everyone's surprise, however, the military resolution passed without a dissenting vote.

The Munich party conference offered another great surprise during the elections for the Parteivorstand. As expected, party Chairman Ollenhauer and Deputy Chairman Mellies gained reelection, but some new names appeared on the Executive Committee's list. Erler, who had missed being elected to the party's highest-ranking committee two years before at Berlin, now won the support of an overwhelming majority of the delegates—an impressive showing for a man who represented not the party's opposition to rearmament but the conversion of that opposition into a constructive response to Adenauer's military policy. Some have suggested that Erler succeeded at Munich because he had become a better party politician; specifically, he treated the military question more discreetly than he had in 1954.[89] Perhaps; but at that time the SPD had still been debating the "if" of rearmament, whereas in 1956 a new German army already existed. What Erler said at Munich, therefore, sounded less shocking to the delegates. It certainly seemed relevant to the party's most immediate concern: the 1957 election. Furthermore, everyone recognized that Erler was an extremely capable individual. During the recent military debates in the Bundestag, which German radio and television had covered extensively, Erler had stood out as the most articulate and convincing spokesman for the SPD's position. At party meetings Erler gave the impression of knowing what he wanted. He was someone who could take charge, who could be trusted. Above all his self-confident assertion of the SPD's will to power naturally impressed a party that had been out of office since 1930.[90]

A number of other party reformers joined Erler at the top of the list. Of the twenty-three unpaid members of the Parteivorstand elected at Munich, the first eight could be considered advocates of a more pragmatic approach to West German politics than the party had previously taken. Significantly, they were all prominent at the state or federal level. A Munich paper commented that the leaders had convinced the conference that strong personalities counted more than a well-defined program.[91]

The most controversial member of the SPD leadership corps was Herbert Wehner, a former Communist who had joined the SPD in 1946. Working closely with Schumacher in the postwar years, he had established a position of influence at party headquarters, and in 1952, at the Dortmund conference, he won election to the Parteivorstand. In the following years Wehner amassed an extraordinary number of party offices. He displayed a flair for party politics and eventually gained the confidence of all factions within the party—the leftists, the reformers, and the large traditionalist bloc in the center. An American magazine referred to him as "an evil grey eminence in the SPD."[92] To his CDU opponents he was the SPD's resident Bolshevik, but Wehner always acted more from political than from ideological reasons. He agreed with much that the party reformers advocated, and at Munich he sided with Erler in efforts to swing the delegates behind the military resolution.

Before the conference opened, many observers had predicted a showdown between the pro- and the antirearmament forces. Instead, the Munich conference turned out to be little more than the usual "ceremonial march past of the SPD foot-soldiers (Fussvolk)."[93] This amazed observers, but by the skillfull use of traditional techniques the SPD leaders managed to avoid a bloody battle. Two days before the conference opened, the Parteivorstand met in joint session with the Parteiausschuss, a much larger committee composed of local party leaders and officials, to hammer out policy resolutions that the delegates would be certain to accept. After considerable bargaining behind closed doors the leadership corps finally found the right wording for the resolutions. The delegates were then informed, and the conference was conducted, according to Der Spiegel, in an atmosphere of "carefully prepared unanimity."[94]

The resolutions drafted by the SPD leaders represented a masterpiece in the art of political compromise. The military resolution, for example, contained something for everyone. By calling for the repeal of the conscription law and by subordinating rearmament to the higher task of reunification, it appeased the opponents of rearmament. By refraining from an outright rejection of rearmament and by leaving the party leaders room for maneuver, it became acceptable to the reformers as well. True, neither side was fully satisfied with the resolution, and both would have preferred a clearer statement, but they accepted a compromise because the feeling prevailed at Munich that the SPD's chances for electoral success in 1957 were greater than ever before. As a result, the SPD leaders could argue with considerable effect that now was the time to stand together; the party was big enough for everyone.

At Munich, therefore, the party's pacifists and leftists contented themselves with a public declaration of their views. They made no attempt to organize a countermovement,[95] and in retrospect it would have been difficult to do so given the tactics employed by the SPD leaders. The leaders could, furthermore, count on the support of the many local party officials who regularly attended the biennial conferences. They felt bound by a strong sense of loyalty and willingly left policy formation to the men at party headquarters.

Under the circumstances, then, why did the leadership feel so concerned about the Munich party conference? First, rearmament was a very sensitive issue, one which aroused the membership as no other issue did during these formative years of the Bonn Republic. Second, even if the party leaders decided to make a more positive declaration on the military question, they could not ignore the unrest that rearmament had caused within the party. Their authority rested on the trust of at least the active members of the party, and to maintain it they had to spend a considerable amount of time and energy explaining policy decisions to them.[96] Furthermore, although Ollenhauer increasingly shared the views of the party reformers, he was reluctant to abandon long-established party traditions too quickly. According to Wehner, Ollenhauer wanted to maintain continuity in the development of the SPD. He would move on a broad front, slowly and cautiously, with the party solidly behind him.[97] In that way he also hoped to prevent a split in the party through the alienation of a dissident left wing. A potential rallying point for those who felt that the SPD had abandoned traditional Marxist and antimilitary policies was *Das Andere Zeitung,* a newspaper edited by former Social Democrats for the noncommunist radical left. The SPD leaders showed signs of genuine concern.[98] Given the discontent in the party over rearmament, therefore, and the furor raised in 1954 over the demands of the reformers, the leadership decided that Munich was not the place to press the SPD onto a new course.

At Munich the SPD leaders prepared resolutions for the party rather than for the public, and in so doing they sacrificed clarity for the sake of party unity. After the conference no one knew what defense policy an SPD government would support. The question of West Germany's membership in NATO had been left unsettled, and although the SPD had declared its intention to repeal the conscription law, the conference had failed to adopt the alternative of a volunteer army. Thus the Social Democrats were poorly equipped to wage an election campaign against Adenauer or to reenter the fray against the coalition parties when Parliament convened in the fall. They set sail from Munich, as one reporter wrote, "without knowing exactly where they were going."[99]

Between June, 1955, and July, 1956, the Social Democrats tried to prevent the government from embarking on the path of rearmament. When their efforts failed, as they were bound to, the Social Democrats felt compelled to accompany Adenauer on the unpleasant journey. At times they threatened to boycott the legislative work, and on one occasion the SPD deputies marched out of the Bundestag, but on the whole the SPD met its responsibilities as an opposition party and contributed significantly to the new military legislation. The Social Democrats played a decisive role in creating the Personnel Review Board and in securing passage of several constitutional amendments needed to protect the democratic rights of the soldiers and to establish parliamentary control of the armed forces.

Even though the SPD traveled further along the road to rearmament than many expected, it remained, paradoxically, in the same place; that is, the party still opposed the creation of a West German army. Furthermore, although the SPD leaders had an opportunity to make a positive declaration by adopting the security committee's recommendation, they chose to maintain an opposition course out of respect for the strong antimilitary sentiments of the party. The leaders also acted on the basis of their estimation of political trends in West Germany, their evaluation of recent military developments, and above all their concern for reunification.

Immediately following the SPD conference in Munich, *Vorwärts* denied with great indignation that the military-policy resolution was the product of an intraparty compromise. According to the newspaper, the resolution stemmed from the SPD's continuing commitment to reunification as the primary task of West German foreign policy.[100] Indeed, the commitment remained strong, but now the leadership had a different perspective of the international situation. Whereas earlier the SPD leaders had maintained that detente would follow reunification, in 1956 they argued that disarmament and detente were the preconditions for reunification, with the understanding that a real detente—that is, an end to the Cold War—was possible only after the restoration of German unity. The Social Democrats believed that the Soviet Union wanted detente with the West and would agree to German reunification if its position as a world power remained secure. This would require that the Western powers abandon their attempt to incorporate a reunited Germany into NATO. According to the Social Democrats, they could work instead for the creation of a European security system.

The Social Democrats pushed this line of argument with renewed vigor through the first ten months of 1956. Without exaggerating the possibilities for a settlement, they claimed that since the Soviets had adopted a policy of peaceful coexistence the international situation had improved considerably. Now both the Western powers and the West German government had new opportunities for negotiation. The Social Democrats called on the government to take advantage of the diplomatic ties West Germany had recently established with Moscow to discover what could be done for reunification. They rejected the idea of a separate agreement with the Soviet Union, however, insisting that the Germans would have to work as closely as possible with the Western powers. It was up to the Bonn government to ensure that the German question remained on the international agenda. Unfortunately, Adenauer did nothing, they said, except cling to an outdated foreign policy.[101]

Adenauer drew heavy criticism for his reluctance to pursue a more active reunification policy, but the Social Democrats drew even more for failing to face the facts.[102] For example, when the Soviet Union declared after the Geneva Summit Conference that reunification was not a matter to be solved by the two German governments, the Social Democrats had claimed that the Russians would never let their East German agents handle such an important question, and when the Soviet note of October, 1956, failed to mention free elections, *Vorwärts* explained that this was only a temporary omission.[103] Unquestionably the SPD had a genuine commitment to reunification, but by making such assertions, the party left itself open to the charge of being naïve and irresponsible. It is ironic that the SPD, which as the main opposition party had the important task of compelling the government to defend and explain its policies in parliament, found itself on the witness stand more often than the CDU.

A second reason for opposing Adenauer's rearmament program, and specifically conscription, stemmed from recent developments in military technology and strategy. Ever since the Carte Blanche incident the Social Democrats had been arguing against a large standing army because NATO had decided on a nuclear response to Soviet aggression. They now pointed out, in the summer of 1956, that military planners in Britain and the United States had gone one step further and advocated a drastic reduction of ground forces. Chancellor Adenauer, who defended his conscription bill with the argument that conventional forces were still an essential part of Western defense, was embarrassed by the recommendations and warned publicly against any shift in Western strategy.[104] Erler commented that the chancellor was "tilting at windmills." NATO would maintain a nuclear strategy.[105]

The Social Democrats found NATO's nuclear strategy alarming. Erler warned that, once the shooting began, neither NATO forces nor the new German army would be able to protect the Federal Republic from annihilation because the nuclear weapons used to destroy the Red Army would destroy Germany as well. To have any value at all, he said, a policy of national defense had to assure at least the survival of the nation. Several of his colleagues concluded that since NATO could not give that assurance a military contribution to the Western Alliance was meaningless.[106]

Erler never went so far as to reject outright any West German tie with NATO; rather, he recommended that if West Germany became part of the Western defense system, it should be as an associate member with the connection limited to German representation at NATO Supreme Headquarters. Then if a chance arose to promote reunification, it would be possible to disengage German military forces without destroying the alliance. Erler never said, however, what contribution West Germany could make to Western defense, and during this period those Social Democrats who favored rearmament never justified the creation of a West German army in terms of its role in NATO. They viewed it as a counterweight to the East German army, especially during the period of reunification, when the democratic forces would face the threat of a Communist putsch.[107]

A third reason for opposing rearmament involved the SPD's assumptions about public opinion in West Germany. The Social Democrats believed that, although public opposition to rearmament had weakened somewhat, conscription remained a highly unpopular issue. Young Germans in particular opposed compulsory military service, and along with many independent voters they would probably support the party which promised to abolish conscription.[108] The Social Democrats hoped that they might be that party.

Looking ahead to the general election, the Social Democrats felt more confident than ever before, and, as it turned out, others shared their estimation of the political scene. In March, 1956, the *Economist* (London) wrote that "for the first time since the Federal Republic was founded in 1949, the possibility of a change in government has ceased to appear remote." Political observers noted a decline in Adenauer's prestige during the following months, and by the fall public-opinion polls were showing that the SPD's popularity either matched or slightly surpassed that of the CDU.[109]

Four state elections confirmed this trend as the SPD, focusing more on national than on local issues, continued to make impressive gains. Since even the CDU's executive committee admitted that the gains made by the Social Democrats were due largely to their rejection of conscription,[110] it seemed that the SPD had found an issue for the 1957 election campaign.

Finally, the antimilitary sentiments of the party rank and file greatly influenced the SPD's position on rearmament. Most Social Democrats opposed rearmament in any form, and while they accepted the Fraktion's tactics of cooperation, they did so grudgingly and with the understanding that the SPD would return to a policy of total opposition to Adenauer's rearmament policy and in particular to conscription. The SPD leaders offered no alternative. They even shelved the security committee's recommendation, which they knew the party would reject. After all, it made no sense to argue that a volunteer army would be a militarily more effective contribution when most Social Democrats questioned the possibility of gaining security by military means in the nuclear age. Furthermore, the party viewed West Germany's involvement in the Western defense system as a barrier to reunification. Wilhelm Mellies presented a more relevant argument. He suggested that if West Germany decided on a volunteer army it would facilitate a four-power agreement on disarmament and thus help open the road to reunification.[111] That did not appeal to the party either. During the communal elections of 1956 local party organizations demonstrated just how much they opposed rearmament. Their election slogans said nothing about a choice between a volunteer army and conscription, rather, they promised the voters "homes instead of barracks."[112] A Bundestag deputy said very simply, "If you do not want your son to become a soldier, then vote SPD."[113] Although the SPD leaders never approved of such statements, they seldom made any attempt to clarify the party's position, in fact, the Parteivorstand felt concerned enough about the party's antimilitary sentiments to avoid any positive declaration on rearmament.

The military experts and their supporters sought to counter the party's antimilitary sentiments by focusing on the political aspects of the question.[114] They pointed out that, even though the Federal Republic was only a Provisorium—a halfway house on the road to reunification—it was nonetheless a state which the SPD had helped build and which it hoped to govern. At Munich, Brandt and Erler told the delegates that the Social Democrats needed more than a comprehensive program of social and economic reform. They must deal with all the problems faced by a national government, including military problems. To those who wanted nothing to do with a new German army, Erler warned, "Unless the democrats in Germany learn to deal with power, ultimately power will deal with them."[115]

The party's military specialists expressed extraordinary confidence in the effectiveness of the new military legislation to prevent a revival of German militarism and, even more, in their own ability to handle military affairs. Helmut Schmidt told the Bundestag that one of the major reasons for the failure of the Reichstag to control the Reichswehr in Weimar was the inferiority complex of the politicians when face to face with the generals. He assured the deputies that the SPD was no longer troubled by such feelings, and he hoped that the government was not either.[116]

A party critic has charged that the SPD under the leadership of Ollenhauer and the military specialists pursued a policy which stemmed from an uncontrollable urge to draft the best possible legislation and to play the part of the government party. In cooperating with the coalition parties, the Social Democrats sacrificed their position as an opposition party without achieving their goal—stopping Adenauer—yet Ollenhauer attempted to convince the party that its "defeats and retreats were political successes."[117]

Certainly the party leaders claimed greater victories from their encounter with the government than they actually won, but there is no question that without SPD collaboration the parliamentary controls established over the armed forces would have been less extensive. Furthermore, what was the alternative to cooperating with the coalition parties? A policy of obstruction had been tried in the Paulskirche campaign without success, and a policy of abstention had been followed in Weimar with catastrophic results. The decision to cooperate was the only course open to a responsible political party. But by cooperating in the military legislation the SPD placed itself in a difficult position. How could the SPD avoid the mistakes of the past, in dealing with the military question, without destroying what chances remained for reunifying Germany? That was a dilemma which the party could not resolve.

CHAPTER 7

From Hungary to the General Election

From 1953 to 1956 the Cold War underwent a slow but perceptible thaw. There was a reduction of international tension and a good deal of talk about peaceful coexistence. In the fall of 1956, however, the international climate changed. In Central Europe the Hungarians revolted in an attempt to break free of Soviet domination, while in the Middle East the British and French sent troops to Suez to bolster their declining influence there. Both events sent a shock running through the Western Alliance. The Anglo-French action lacked NATO approval and failed in large measure because of American opposition. Even more alarming, the Soviet Union, after sending tanks into Hungary, threatened to intervene in Egypt—with nuclear weapons if necessary. For Western leaders the Hungarian revolt and the Suez crisis were forceful reminders that, despite the many signs of detente, the East-West conflict had not ended.

In Bonn, Chancellor Adenauer expressed grave concern about the impact of events on the Western Alliance. He believed that now more than ever the free world had to stand together. The chancellor had never been very optimistic about the chances for detente, and Soviet behavior in Hungary merely confirmed his view that the Kremlin's policy of peaceful coexistence was nothing more than a clever tactic to conceal its aggressive intentions. Addressing the Bundestag, he declared that the government's policy of military preparedness and close alliance with the West was "the only common-sense approach" in a dangerously tense world.[1]

Although the Social Democrats shared the chancellor's concern about the sharp rise in international tension, they disagreed with him on the course to pursue. They claimed that the time had arrived for West Germany to get beyond NATO and for the powers to think of something other than military-bloc building. Having been to the brink of war, Wehner said, the world needed a policy that could break down the barriers of fear and mistrust to establish the conditions for a stable peace.[2]

185

Beyond NATO

The Social Democrats wanted to prove that NATO membership held few benefits for the Germans. They argued that, in spite of the bold talk about an offensive policy to roll back communism, the Western Alliance could never serve as a vehicle for the liberation of those who lived under Soviet domination. Military intervention in Hungary would have led to World War III. In any case, the Western Alliance could hardly claim to speak for the cause of freedom—not after the Suez crisis. By sending troops to the Middle East, Britain and France destroyed the moral position of the West and shifted the focus of world opinion from the Hungarian tragedy to Suez. Furthermore, the Western Alliance could no longer view itself as a partnership because Britain and France had acted without informing their allies. By their actions they had threatened to involve everyone—including the Germans—in a global conflict.[3] Deputy Chairman Mellies predicted that NATO would never fully recover from the events of November, 1956. He urged the government to search for a radically new policy, one founded on the principle of collective security and manifested in a strengthened and universally respected United Nations.[4]

The Social Democrats showered praise on the United Nations for its prompt action in the Middle East. By sending an international peace-keeping force to the area, the UN had halted the immediate crisis before it could escalate into a third world war. According to the SPD's press service the UN had won "a new moral authority" which even the Soviets could not ignore.[5] Wehner and Erler pointed out more realistically that success had been achieved in the Middle East because the superpowers were willing to cooperate in ending the crisis. By contrast, however, the Soviet Union had refused to allow UN observers to enter Hungary.[6] The Social Democrats insisted, nonetheless, that the UN offered at least the hope of a new world order, whereas the policy of strength pursued by the power blocs meant a world filled with the ever-present danger of war.

By trying to portray NATO as a heavy liability for the Germans, the Social Democrats committed a serious tactical error. They emphasized the faults of the alliance and ignored its importance for West Germany. They treated the Soviet military threat as insignificant— *Vorwärts* called the possibility of an attack absurd as long as West Germany refrained from meddling behind the iron curtain.[7] For most West Germans, however, the sight of Russian tanks rumbling through the streets of Budapest brought back unpleasant memories of 1945 and 1953, and they were thankful for Adenauer's close ties with the Western powers. The Social Democrats, of course, admitted that the Western Alliance, or at least the American presence in Europe, offered a credible deterrent to Soviet aggression, but unfortunately neither NATO nor American military power could reunify Germany.

According to the SPD, only a policy of detente could bring the two parts of Germany together again. The Social Democrats insisted that recent events made the need for such a policy more necessary, and they warned the West to avoid making an already tense situation more serious by resorting to Cold-War rhetoric. It would only permit the Russians to tighten their hold on the Warsaw Pact nations at a time when events in Hungary, and those several months earlier in Poland, had already demonstrated the precarious nature of the Soviet position in Eastern Europe.[8] Ollenhauer recommended that, since both military blocs were experiencing serious internal difficulties, a four-power conference on European security and German reunification was "the only constructive alternative to the new situation." He added that the powers now appeared ready to discuss detente.[9]

On November 17, in a letter to President Eisenhower, the Soviet government proposed a comprehensive program of arms control and disarmament. What particularly interested the Social Democrats was the Soviet suggestion that during 1957 the former occupying powers reduce by one-third the armed forces stationed on German territory, thin out the military units in the territory of member countries of NATO and the Warsaw Pact and then close down all military bases on foreign soil within two years. The party's press service immediately announced that "whether the Soviets are serious or not, we must negotiate to find out."[10] The Social Democrats, who had proposed a troop reduction in the Munich foreign-policy resolution, believed strongly in a policy of disengagement. After all, the main task of German policy centered on getting the Red Army out of East Germany, and the Russians were offering this and more. With the Soviet plan, the Red Army would be back across the Russian border in two years. That would mean the liberation of Eastern Europe. As for the military feasibility of the plan —whether Europe would be secure—Wehner said that only the United States could give an answer, but he felt confident that military and political considerations could be brought into harmony.[11]

During the next two months the Social Democrats gave considerable attention to the idea of disengagement, believing that it could be used to promote reunification.[12] They admitted that the Soviet Union had as yet made no commitment to discuss the German question—only disarmament and arms control had been mentioned—but the Western powers would have ample opportunity to raise the matter. Furthermore, in spite of Soviet insistence that responsibility for reunification rested with the two German states, the Social Democrats claimed that ultimately the Soviet Union would demand four-power negotiations. In the meantime, they urged the Bonn government to turn from its rearmament program to a diplomatic offensive designed to bring the powers together in a discussion of European security and German reunification.

In the first foreign-policy debate of 1957 both the government and the opposition parties focused on reunification, but neither side made any new proposals. Foreign Minister Heinrich von Brentano claimed that, since the international situation showed few signs of improvement, the government saw no reason to alter its course. Everything possible had been done to achieve reunification, he said; in fact, "We have done more for reunification than those who now stand aside and toss out cheap election slogans."[13] The Social Democrats responded with a chorus of boos and catcalls. When their turn came to address the Bundestag, they presented a formidable list of errors and omissions which they claimed the government had made in dealing with the German question. According to Fritz Erler, the government made its greatest mistake in viewing NATO membership as the only possible way to guarantee the security of Germany. Such narrow-mindedness frustrated all efforts to negotiate with the Russians on reunification and resulted in the capitulation of politics to the demands of military strategy. Erler reminded the Bundestag that the Germans already had enough experience with such things—the Schlieffen Plan, for example—to convince them of the need for different priorities. Other "technical solutions" to the security question could be found without making Germany the "deployment area of any specific military coalition." Erler failed to explain what he meant by this. The only hint of an SPD security plan came from Erich Ollenhauer. The SPD leader resubmitted his party's earlier proposal of a European collective security system, guaranteed by the Soviet Union and the United States, in which a reunited Germany would join with other European states as a full partner, with equal rights and duties, in the task of maintaining peace in Europe. Ollenhauer advised the chancellor that he would never "master the situation by clinging to the old conceptions of security" because NATO and a policy of strength would never lead to reunification.[14]

The SPD always maintained that NATO's defense planning was a response to the division of Germany. If Germany was reunited, the strategic considerations which arose from the division would lose their significance, and a new security system could be created in place of the existing military blocs. This position was based on the assumptions that the division of Germany produced the tension in Europe, that the reunification of Germany could be attained at a reasonable price, and that a collective security system would be more reliable than a military alliance. The coalition parties considered these assumptions false and charged the SPD with confusing cause and effect in the development of its foreign policy.

In the January debate the coalition parties took the offensive against the SPD to prove, in that election year, that the foreign-policy position advocated by the SPD was untenable. They argued that the expansionist nature of communism, rather than the division of Germany, caused the high tension in Europe. Thus reunification would not automatically reduce European tension, as the Social Democrats suggested, because the restoration of German unity would have no effect on the foreign-policy objectives of the Soviet Union. Besides, the Russians showed no willingness to grant reunification in freedom. When Karl Mommer called out from the SPD benches, "You still have not asked them!" Kurt Georg Kiesinger responded that the Russians had made their demands perfectly clear.[15] They wanted to create a neutralized and defenseless Germany, to leave negotiations to Bonn and Pankow, to maintain the so-called democratic achievements in East Germany, and to force structural changes in the social and political system of the Federal Republic. Furthermore, the Russians had never said that West Germany's departure from NATO would lead to reunification. On the contrary, they had said that it would improve the atmosphere for a meeting between the two German states, who, Moscow maintained, would have to solve the German problem themselves. "Is that clear enough, Herr Mommer?" The SPD deputy called back: "Does that mean that reunification is a chimera?" No, said Kiesinger, but "the belief that we can have reunification in freedom with the Soviet Union and without the protection of the Western world is a chimera."

Throughout the debate coalition speakers stressed that Germany had to remain in the Western Alliance; otherwise, the Germans would fall under Soviet domination. The greatest threat would be the complete withdrawal of the Americans from the Continent, as envisaged in the recent Soviet note. The Social Democrats saw no reason for alarm; in fact, Erler quoted President Eisenhower to prove that American protection would be granted even to countries not militarily allied with the United States. Defense Minister Franz Josef Strauss, however, who had replaced Theodor Blank, doubted that the Americans would unleash their strategic nuclear force every time the Red Army ventured across the Russian border. He warned that for the security of Germany "we need Americans on German soil."[16] To the Social Democrats such a demand amounted to a declaration of bankruptcy, a sign that the government had no reunification policy whatsoever.

The SPD Proposes a Volunteer Army

Before the Hungarian and Suez crises gave the Social Democrats a chance to put the spotlight back on the German question, the Social Democratic party had been preparing for another parliamentary debate on the government's military legislation. They had fought unsuccessfully in July against the conscription bill. Since no decision had been made, however, on the service period required of those drafted into the new army, the Bundeswehr, the Social Democrats knew that the battle would be resumed in the fall.

The government presented a service-period bill to Parliament soon after the summer recess. It surprised the Social Democrats because, instead of the eighteen months which Blank had insisted on earlier, the bill called for a service period of only twelve months. The change had been made for both military and political reasons.[17] By September, Adenauer had to admit that NATO was committed to a nuclear strategy and that, since the allies were reducing their ground forces, it made little sense for the Germans to build a half-million-man army. Equally important, the government found itself under pressure from its own supporters to reduce the proposed service period. The coalition parties, especially the CSU, thought conscription to be exceedingly unpopular in West Germany, and they hoped that a shorter service period would appease an electorate which some observers felt had grown disenchanted with the government.

A radio interviewer asked Erler what he thought of the proposed twelve-month service period.[18] The SPD deputy replied that it would be better than spending eighteen months in uniform but the government "should be satisfied with the recruitment of volunteers." His colleagues, on the other hand, wasted little time in announcing that they would reject any military-service bill. They opposed conscription as well as the hectic pace of the government's rearmament program. Mellies claimed that Adenauer sought to build a German army faster than Adolf Hitler had. Such haste, he warned, would increase the confusion in an already chaotic rearmament program and hamper efforts to instill a democratic spirit in the Bundeswehr, West Germany's new army.[19] Although the government altered its recruitment plans in October by reducing the proposed schedule of men under arms from 96,000 to 75,000 by the end of 1956 and from 250,000 to 120,000 by the end of 1957, Adenauer and Defense Minister Strauss refused to postpone the first reading of the service-period bill, scheduled for early November. Ollenhauer complained that no reason existed for presenting the bill then or even discussing such a bill until after the general election. If the government wanted more military legislation, he said, then it could begin by introducing a bill on such outstanding matters as the duties of the defense commissioner, the organization of the Defense Ministry, the pay and maintenance of the soldiers, or the regulation of discipline and grievances in the armed forces.[20]

In the first reading of the service-period bill on November 8, the defense minister informed the Bundestag that the government needed the authority promptly in order to begin the draft on April 1, 1957. According to Helmut Schmidt, who presented the SPD's case against the bill, the Bundeswehr would never be ready in the spring to handle a massive influx of soldiers.[21] There were not enough trained instructors or sufficient weapons, uniforms, schools, and barracks for the men who had already enlisted, let alone for those who were to be drafted. Under these conditions, and without specific legislation on military pay, living conditions, and fringe benefits, the Defense Ministry would be unable to attract qualified officers, in particular noncommissioned officers, for the Bundeswehr. The only ones to enlist would be those who had failed to achieve in civilian life. How would it be possible, Schmidt asked, to establish a proper relationship between officers and men if those drafted into the Bundeswehr had no respect for their superiors? The government, he said, faced the prospect of placing "unwilling conscripts under the command of discontented officers." The young SPD deputy recommended that since plenty of volunteers were available the government could postpone the draft for the time being.

The Social Democrats realized that the government controlled enough Bundestag votes to pass the service-period bill, but they hoped to delay matters long enough that Adenauer would find it politically inexpedient to begin conscription so close to the general election. The coalition parties, however, had no intention of letting the Social Democrats drag out the proceedings. Following a brief first reading, the government's bill spent less than a month in committee and completed its final reading on December 5.

Even though the SPD failed to prevent, or even delay, Adenauer's rearmament program, the service-period debate was important because it compelled the Social Democrats to take a closer look at their position on West German rearmament. Those most closely concerned with military affairs recognized the SPD's vulnerability to attacks from the coalition parties. During the final reading of the bill, for example, Erler found himself in the embarrassing position of having to avoid a debate on the kind of army that was best suited to West Germany.[22] A CDU deputy asked him if an SPD government would keep West Germany in NATO and maintain at least a volunteer army until Germany was reunified and integrated into a new security system. Since neither the Munich party conference nor the newly elected Executive Committee had dealt specifically with these matters, Erler could only reply that a Social Democratic government would "never tear up treaties in a Hitlerian manner." He added that it would be the responsibility of the new Bundestag, elected in September, to decide what kind of army West Germany needed to meet its treaty obligations.

Erler realized that such evasive remarks would hardly suffice in the upcoming election campaign, and after the debate he tried to push the party into making a positive declaration. When asked by the press about SPD military policy, he stated that if the Social Democrats came into office in the fall not the Bundeswehr but conscription would be abolished. The army could be raised by voluntary enlistments. Furthermore, an SPD government would negotiate with the NATO powers to revise the Paris Accords or, more specifically, those treaty stipulations "which have turned out to be barriers on the road to reunification." Erler recommended again that for the sake of reunification the Bundeswehr should establish some form of loose association with NATO and undertake limited military tasks such as counterbalancing the East German military forces.[23]

Erler's remarks angered some sections of the party. A few members of the Fraktion complained to Ollenhauer about "the private declarations of comrade Erler," while the Frankfurt Young Socialists informed the chairman that the SPD military expert should stop trying to make party policy and start carrying out the party's directives by opposing rearmament.[24] Ollenhauer also had to deal with inquiring reporters who wanted a clear statement on SPD military policy. At a press conference in mid-January, 1957, he explained that for the SPD the issue was not West German membership in NATO but whether a reunited Germany could belong to the Western Alliance. Obviously, if the Germans wanted reunification, they would have to leave NATO because the Russians would never accept a settlement which tied Germany militarily to the West. However, he said, the SPD was neither advocating immediate withdrawal from NATO nor suggesting that withdrawal was a prerequisite for four-power talks—it would be a result of successful negotiations on a new European security system. Would the SPD support NATO membership for West Germany in case four-power negotiations should fail? The SPD leader tried to evade the question, stating only that unsuccessful negotiations would create an entirely new situation. Another reporter asked him what would happen to the Bundeswehr if the SPD formed a new government in September and carried out its promise to abolish conscription. Ollenhauer responded that since the situation could have changed completely by next fall it made no sense to discuss the details of SPD military policy now. The following day the press reported that the SPD's position remained as cloudy as ever.[25]

Ollenhauer's badly managed press conference finally convinced the SPD leaders that something had to be done. Urged on by proponents of rearmament in the Fraktion, the Parteivorstand decided to adopt the policy recommendation advanced earlier by the security committee. It fell to Ollenhauer to inform local party leaders. At a meeting in Bonn on January 24 he told them that on the question of reunification and NATO membership the SPD would maintain the position adopted at Munich. If the Russians refused to allow any progress toward reunification in freedom, however, an SPD government must loyally meet the country's treaty commitments and seek to fulfill its military obligations "on the basis of a volunteer army."

Ollenhauer had made an important policy statement, but it remained incomplete. He said nothing about the defense tasks of the army or the nature of its commitment to NATO, and while the party's military experts suggested force goals of from 100,000 to 200,000 men, Ollenhauer declared that it was unnecessary, and even inexpedient, to become involved in a "game of numbers."[26] His reasons were obvious. The SPD leader knew how firmly the party still opposed rearmament, and having made the difficult decision in favor of a volunteer army, he wanted to avoid further trouble by ending the discussions quickly. Yet he described the Parteivorstand's declaration as appropriate, claiming that if used correctly it would contribute a great deal to the party's success in the election campaign which lay ahead.

The SPD leaders made the decision in favor of a volunteer army primarily for domestic political purposes. They wanted to fill a gap in the party's program and thus deny the CDU a point of attack during the campaign. By itself, however, such a tentative declaration could hardly be expected to impress the West German public or to help the party deal with an increasingly serious problem—its relations with the new West German army.

The Bundeswehr: An Unwanted Child

During the budget debate in February, 1957, Defense Minister Strauss asked why relations between the Bundeswehr and the SPD were already so strained. Part of the explanation was the traditional antipathy with which soldiers and Socialists viewed each other, and even Strauss admitted that the SPD had had good reason to be suspicious in the past. According to the Defense Minister, however, the SPD had done much to create the present situation. After all, it was the Social Democrats who had described the Bundeswehr as "dangerous, detrimental, and superfluous" and had declared that the very existence of a West German army aggravated the political situation, increased the danger of war, and provoked the Russians into taking measures which deepened the division of Germany. Was there any wonder that a problem existed![27]

Fritz Erler conceded that his party viewed the Bundeswehr as an unwanted child but maintained that "some people do care about its upbringing."[28] In the SPD the concerned people included mainly military specialists. Those in the Fraktion continued their work in the Bundestag Defense Committee by helping shape further legislation, including laws on such matters as military discipline, justice, pay, and maintenance. They also expanded their earlier contacts with army officers and visited army barracks in order to convince the soldiers that the SPD had regard for their welfare. They failed to persuade the party, however, to take an interest in the Bundeswehr. At a meeting of the party's security committee in April, 1956, Erler had expressed concern about the fate of those Social Democrats who, out of a sense of responsibility, would take a commission voluntarily. He wanted the SPD to give these men public assurance that the party still stood behind them,[29] but at the Munich party conference the SPD leaders decided against raising such a sensitive issue. The attitude of most party members toward the officer corps remained one of deep suspicion, and they refused to understand the need for cooperating with men who had served Adolf Hitler, much less for supporting those comrades who chose to enlist in the new army. The party's military experts tried, nonetheless, to bring Social Democrats and soldiers together, and early the following year a breakthrough occurred.

In late January, 1957, fifteen members of the Young Socialists (Jungsozialisten or Jusos) invited fifteen young Bundeswehr officers to Bad

Godesberg to see whether the gap between Socialists and soldiers could be bridged. Their efforts met with some skepticism in the Young Socialist movement itself and with outright opposition from the teenage Socialists, the Falcons, who refused even to accept rearmament as an accomplished fact. One Socialist youth group threatened to cancel the membership of any Falcon who joined the Bundeswehr.[30] Mellies stated later that the SPD disapproved of such radical action, and the Jusos gave no indication that they would follow the Falcons' lead; in fact, those who participated in the Bad Godesberg meeting considered it a success because the Bundeswehr officers at least recognized that SPD opposition "to Adenauer's hectic rearmament policy was based on a sense of responsibility toward German democracy and unity."[31] That alone justified further meetings. *Vorwärts,* however, questioned their significance. Could these young officers resist the grinding pressure of the military machine? The paper assumed that they would fall victim to the "militaristic forces that controlled the Defense Ministry."[32]

Long before rearmament began, the Social Democrats had expressed concern about the reactionary tendencies of the men who worked in the Blank Office. When Theodor Blank became defense minister in 1955, they warned of his "almost total reliance" on former Nazi generals and complained of the growing influence of certain right-wing organizations at the Defense Ministry.[33] One of them, the Arbeitsgemeinschaft Demokratischer Kreise (Work Group of Democratic Circles, ADK), so provoked the SPD that in February, 1957, Helmut Schmidt asked the Bundestag to undertake a full investigation of the organization's activities. Schmidt charged that the ADK had used funds from the government's Press and Information Office to carry out a propaganda campaign in defense of Adenauer's policies. At a seminar held earlier in Hamburg, he said, ADK speakers had told young Bundeswehr officers that "only fools can still talk about negotiations with the Russians over reunification; the Soviet Union understands only the language of force." This represented an attempt by the government to propagate its policy of strength and was, to say the least, politically dangerous. Schmidt also complained about the political activities of certain senior Bundeswehr officers. He quoted a general who said that if the Social Democrats came to power they could not expect the soldiers to fight for them. Under shouts of protest from the coalition parties and loud applause from the SPD benches, Schmidt told the Bundestag, "That is the seed which is being sown" by the government in the ranks of the Bundeswehr.[34]

Although concerned about political opinion in the Bundeswehr, especially the officer corps, the SPD military experts were far from pessimistic about the chances of creating reliable armed forces. They remained confident of the effectiveness of the new military legislation and of their own ability to deal with the military. They rejected, furthermore, the rank and file's blanket condemnation of the military establishment; in fact, very early in the rearmament debate they discovered military men in the Defense Ministry like Colonel Wolf von Baudissin who shared their ideas on how to create a new German army. As early as 1953, Erler and his colleagues in the Bundestag Committee for European Security Questions had discussed and approved Baudissin's ideas — specifically, the principle of Innere Führung (self-direction) and the citizen in uniform.[35]

The military reformers in the political parties and the Defense Ministry believed that because of recent political and technological developments they would have to produce a new kind of fighting man. War at midcentury had become an extension of a much greater ideological conflict, and the modern soldier had to be armed with firm political convictions. "The days are over when it was of no concern to the citizen how the soldier conducted a war," said Baudissin. "But the days are over too, when the soldier need not concern himself with the daily problems of his people."[36] This meant that, instead of standing in opposition to each other as before, the soldier and the citizen had to become one. The soldier had to be a citizen in uniform, that is, a politically conscious soldier who knew why he was fighting and thus could resist the threats and temptations of the enemy's propaganda. According to Baudissin, the modern soldier would have to be the very epitome of the active citizen of a modern democratic state.

To assure that the modern soldier remained a citizen in uniform, the military reformers insisted that he would have to possess all the rights and duties of an ordinary citizen—the right to vote, to join a political party, and to participate freely in political activities insofar as he did so outside the normal routine of military life. The reformers disagreed, however, over the question of how active the soldiers could be. The Social Democrats wanted to grant the soldiers the maximum of political freedom, including the right of association and assembly. The coalition parties objected to the latter, as well as the right to present collective petitions, because of the opportunities created for political subversion within the armed forces. Concerned with the immediate Communist threat, the coalition parties feared that too much freedom could undermine the morale of the armed forces and upset the stability of the democratic order. The Social Democrats, on the other hand, looked to the past. They felt that without greater freedom the soldiers would be unable to resist attempts from above to use the army against the republic.[37]

The Social Democrats believed, therefore, that the soldier's political consciousness had to be "awakened, maintained, and aided."[38] A problem arose in trying to determine the responsibilities of the Bundeswehr in this area. While the Social Democrats agreed that the army, through its new academies for Innere Führung, could help in teaching young Germans the lessons of citizenship, they warned against trying to make the Bundeswehr the "school of the nation," as conservatives had viewed the army in imperial Germany.[39]

As for the military side of the reform program, the reformers believed that to meet the demands of modern warfare the soldier had to be trained and commanded differently from in the past. There could be no senseless drill, because parade ground maneuvers had nothing to do with military tactics or with the use of highly sophisticated military equipment. Nor could there be cadaver-like obedience; the modern soldier had to be a thinking individual capable of independent action. Finally, there could be no attempt by petty martinets to break the will of the new recruits, because the man in uniform had to accept authority and discipline from inner conviction rather than blind obedience. Training should be designed, therefore, to strengthen the soldier's individuality so that he possessed the sense of responsibility needed to meet his obligations to society, the self-confidence necessary to accept authority without servility, and the self-discipline to take the initiative and make decisions without relying on his superiors. He would then possess Innere Führung, which was nothing more than the leadership qualities of a democratic society applied to the military.[40] The Social Democrats expressed concern, however, that the concept would be used simply to produce a more efficient fighting man. In their eyes the military reform program was primarily a means of integrating the army into the democratic structure of the state, the by-product of which would be a first-class soldier.

Although it had its supporters, the reform program also had a number of influential critics. When the discussions began in 1952, the military reformers in the Blank Office came under heavy criticism from political conservatives and tradition-minded military men who viewed the proposed changes as a deadly threat to the cohesion of the armed forces. The critics called it a mistake to believe that an army could be organized without discipline and motivated by nothing more substantial than civic pride. While he was in the Defense Ministry, Colonel von Bonin had openly opposed Baudissin and argued that the spartan code of the old Prussian army represented the only possible basis for building an effective army. Werner Picht, a military publicist and one of the most persistent critics of the reform program, emphasized the need for a sense of military professionalism. He ridiculed the idea that a soldier was someone who performed military work from eight to five like a civilian. The development of an efficient military force, he said, would require a group of men who were totally committed to a military life, with an ethos, identity, and tradition of its own.[41]

The SPD's military experts immediately came to Baudissin's defense, praising his efforts to create a democratic army and complaining that neither Defense Minister Blank nor his successor, Franz Josef Strauss, properly understood the need for military reforms. Early in 1956, when the first volunteers joined the Bundeswehr, the Social Democrats noted that Blank had totally ignored a Bundestag committee report in support of Baudissin's reform program. A year later they charged Strauss with failing to protect the colonel from the vicious attacks of the right-wing *Deutsche Soldaten Zeitung,* or even to end "the guerrilla war" being waged against Baudissin by militarists in the Defense Ministry.[42] According to the Social Democrats, this negligent and at times negative attitude toward the reform program stemmed from the government's primary concern with getting an army as quickly as possible, whatever the cost.

Early in 1957 the Social Democrats fumed over Strauss's decision to begin conscription on April 1 because in their eyes the Defense Ministry still lacked the means to put the Bundeswehr on a solid, democratic foundation. They would have agreed with the English journalist who commented after a visit to the Defense Ministry that one "still gets a decided impression of having called on moving-in day."[43] When draft notices went out as scheduled, the Social Democrats charged that, while conscription was the product of a "stubborn and thoughtless" policy, the draftees were the unfortunate victims of the confusion pervading the government's rearmament program.[44] In June disaster struck. At a training base in Bavaria, fifteen young soldiers drowned when their platoon leader ordered them to wade across the flood-swollen Iller River. Only two weeks later a corporal accidently exploded a tank grenade, killing one soldier and seriously wounding another. The Social Democrats wasted no time claiming that their charges against the government had been tragically substantiated.

Defense Minister Strauss rejected the charge that the government had shown precipitate haste in its rearmament program. He pointed out that during the period from October, 1956, when he became defense minister, to June, 1957, when the Iller incident occurred, the Bundeswehr had recruited only 32,000 men—clearly a manageable number.[45] The Social Democrats responded that perhaps this constituted a reasonable increase for an established military force but the Bundeswehr still lacked qualified instructors. Acting under intense pressure, the Defense Ministry had recruited noncommissioned officers who were too young and too inexperienced to be entrusted with the lives of those drafted into the army. Helmut Schmidt referred to them as the "Achilles' heel" of the Bundeswehr. As for the Iller incident, the Social Democrats said that it would be unfair to make the officers involved bear the blame for all that had happened. On the contrary, responsibility rested mainly with those politicians who supported the government's rearmament program and ultimately with the man who had originated this "mistaken military policy"—Chancellor Konrad Adenauer.[46] In response, Defense Minister Strauss accused the Social Democrats not only of grossly exaggerating conditions within the Bundeswehr but also of trying to exploit the training accident for political profit in the upcoming general election.[47]

The Social Democrats were enraged by such accusations, especially coming from Strauss. Ever since his appointment, eight months before, they had expressed anxiety about the new defense minister. They considered Strauss a man of "unbridled dynamism and boundless ambition," a staunch supporter of the policy of strength, and, even more alarming to the SPD, a strong advocate of an atomic arming of the Bundeswehr.[48]

Atomic Weapons Again

On March 22, 1957, *Vorwärts* carried a front-page headline: "Atom Bombs Among Us!" Although the Social Democrats had known for several years that American forces in Germany possessed atomic weapons, they had said nothing about it.[49] Their silence stemmed, in part, from their preoccupation with the domestic battle over rearmament—at least until the military legislation passed. They had also remained silent out of a desire not to upset the military balance by challenging the Americans' reliance on atomic weapons. In 1957, however, because of technological developments in rocketry and diplomatic initiatives from the East, they considered it safe to tackle the sensitive subject. The *Vorwärts* article signaled the opening of a new round in the military debate between the government and the opposition.

Four weeks later the SPD newspaper carried another front-page story on atomic weapons. This time, in bigger and bolder type, the headline read: "Black Lion Devours Germany!" Black Lion was the code name for a NATO exercise in which the Allies explored the use of tactical atomic weapons against a Soviet attack on Western Europe. From the reaction of the West German public, it appeared as though this latest exercise—which left Germany "hacked, torn, and blown to pieces" by one hundred atomic bombs—would have greater repercussions and provide more political profit for the SPD than Carte Blanche. It was, after all, an election year.

Initially, however, the Social Democrats had to take a back seat to eighteen nuclear scientists at Göttingen University who captured the public's attention with a statement on the horrors of atomic warfare. The scientists pointed out that a single tactical weapon would have "an effect similar to that of the first atom bomb which destroyed Hiroshima." As for so-called strategic weapons, one hydrogen bomb could make the Ruhr district uninhabitable, and the radiation from a series of these bombs could wipe out the population of the Federal Republic. The scientists advised the government to "voluntarily renounce the possession of all types of atomic weapons."

The government reacted sharply to the Göttingen declaration by charging the scientists with needlessly arousing public fears of an atomic war. What they had done with their "meddling in politics," Adenauer said, was weaken popular support of NATO and encourage the Russians to believe that something could be gained by applying diplomatic pressure on a divided West.[50] That was a gross exaggeration, as he knew, but the chancellor had been publicly embarrassed in an election year. He knew that the Social Democrats would take full advantage of the outcry to attack the government's defense policy.

The Social Democrats applauded the scientists for their courageous "act of conscience" and defended them against what Ollenhauer called the "arrogant and overbearing" attitude of the government.[51] During the following weeks the SPD press carried a series of articles on the atomic danger. In a sensational two-page story *Vorwärts* concluded that if war broke out in Central Europe the Germans would be annihilated. The cost of building air-raid shelters for the entire population was prohibitive, and mass evacuation would be physically impossible. The only hope was general disarmament.[52]

On May 10 the Social Democrats presented their views on atomic weapons to the Bundestag in the form of a motion. They called on the government to relinquish the idea of acquiring atomic weapons for the Bundeswehr and to request that all atomic weapons be removed from West Germany. In addition they asked the other political parties to join them in appealing to the great powers for immediate action in dealing with the atomic danger. Erler, who delivered the party's main address, told the Bundestag that because of the threat to mankind from the development and deployment of atomic weapons the time had come for the great powers to work for a relaxation of tension in the world.[53] The first step would have to be the cessation of nuclear test explosions, followed by a general agreement on disarmament in stages under international controls. Turning to the government benches, Erler warned that the presence of atomic weapons on German soil was preventing the emergence of a favorable climate for disarmament talks and increasing the danger that a border incident would escalate into a global conflict.

Throughout the debate, which at times became heated, the Social Democrats charged the government with pursuing the old dream of making Germany a great military power. For Adenauer and Strauss, Erler said, "atomic weapons are the mark of a world power, as battleships were for Tirpitz and the Kaiser." It would be a disaster, however, if they obtained them, because "the time bomb of German division [is] already dangerous enough without giving it an atomic warhead."

In May, 1957, the West German government wanted atomic weapons for the Bundeswehr. Whereas only the summer before Adenauer had argued in favor of a large standing army, he now brought his policy into line with Western Alliance strategy and informed NATO that West Germany would accept tactical atomic weapons for its armed forces. At the NATO conference in December, 1956, the Allies had discussed the question of distributing tactical atomic weapons among the member forces, and four months later the United States agreed in principle to share these weapons as long as custody of the atomic warheads remained in American hands. The Social Democrats immediately expressed opposition to the idea.[54] Although Strauss stated in early April that the entire matter was only at the discussion stage, Adenauer explained that West Germany would demand equal treatment so that the Bundeswehr would not be equipped with inferior weapons.[55]

Although a champion of equal rights for the Federal Republic, the SPD argued this time that the Bundeswehr could perform its defense tasks without atomic weapons. German troops played "a completely subordinate role" in NATO, said Erler.[56] No one expected them to rush in and hold the line in the event of a Soviet attack. If the Red Army marched, it would unleash World War III and a nuclear strike from the United States. On the other hand, the Bundeswehr could effectively counterbalance a non-Russian attack and do so with conventional forces because the satellite armies were still without atomic weapons.

The Social Democrats also argued against stationing atomic weapons in West Germany, "on the territory of the most dangerously exposed member of NATO." According to Carlo Schmid, the Americans could move the weapons a hundred kilometers back from the zonal border. In that way Germany would no longer automatically be an atomic battlefield. Of course, that meant shifting them to France, and, as one coalition deputy pointed out, the French would be upset to know that they were now the target of Soviet bombs and missiles. Schmid, however, brushed aside the problem of where to station tactical atomic weapons because, he told the Bundestag, the strategic weapons which would deter a Soviet attack were stationed outside Europe, "in the United States or Greenland, or some other place."[57]

Except for the military specialists, most Social Democrats shared this conception of Western defense. They paid little attention to the question of credibility in the atomic age or to the relationship between deterrence and defense. They cared even less about the direction of recent military thinking, which now focused on the need for a graduated deterrent and a limited-war strategy.[58] Military writers in Britain and the United States warned that with the approach of nuclear parity between the super powers the Americans would be reluctant to use atomic weapons against the Soviet Union to defend Frankfurt, Hamburg, or Berlin if they knew that the Russians could retaliate by annihilating New York, Chicago, or Washington. Some military men argued that with tactical weapons on the Continent NATO would have a better chance of deterring Soviet aggression in Central Europe and would be in an even stronger position if the alliance had significant conventional forces. With a more flexible defense capability, NATO would no longer have to invoke massive retaliation against every challenge from the East. In the event of a border conflict, the Western powers would not have to choose between a local defeat and a thermonuclear war. The Social Democrats, however, wanted neither to build a large standing army nor to let the Americans station tactical atomic weapons at the front. They argued that a limited-war strategy would never work because any con-

SPD poster used in 1957 against the atomic-arms race. It reads: "Enough of that! Therefore SPD." Courtesy Friedrich Ebert Stiftung.

flict in Central Europe between the United States and the Soviet Union would automatically escalate into a global war. As for a graduated deterrent, the Social Democrats refused to believe that peace had to rest on something so terrifying as a balance of terror. According to Ollenhauer, the path to peace was through detente, disarmament, and reunification. It could all begin with the removal of atomic weapons from Germany.[59]

As expected, the coalition parties rejected the SPD motion on atomic weapons. They argued that if the Germans were going to rely on the Americans to provide a security guarantee against the threat of Soviet aggression, then "we must be prepared to give them the opportunity to make this guarantee effective." Since that required atomic weapons, the Federal Republic would have to give its approval or face the loss of American protection and the eventual disintegration of NATO.[60] At the end of the debate Defense Minister Strauss assured the Bundestag that the government had no atomic ambitions and would support all efforts to promote a disarmament agreement. The Social Democrats were unimpressed. They concluded that the government, rather than trying to call a halt to "the macabre race with Atomtod [atomic death]," was more determined than ever to equip the Bundeswehr with atomic weapons.[61]

The bitterness along the line separating the government and the opposition, already apparent in the January, 1957, foreign-policy debate, deepened during the parliamentary encounter on atomic weapons. With the general elections approaching, both sides wanted to establish their respective positions on what promised to be a major campaign issue. For the Social Democrats it meant showing the nation that atomic weapons, in the hands of American forces or the Bundeswehr, offered no security for the Germans. They neglected, however, to suggest an alternative to the government's defense policy.

In an interview with the press one week after the Bundestag debate, Ollenhauer added to the confusion about his party's position by stating that the SPD wanted atomic weapons out of West Germany, despite "all the possible consequences that could result from the American reaction to this demand." Under further questioning Ollenhauer conceded that such a demand would be a matter of negotiation; "that is obvious." When asked, however, what the SPD would do if the United States made its security guarantee contingent on the continued maintenance of atomic weapons in West Germany, the SPD leader refused to discuss the matter.[62] Several days later, after the coalition parties had pounced on Ollenhauer's ill-considered remarks, Erler explained that the SPD had no intention of asking the Americans to remove all atomic weapons from West Germany irrespective of what the Russians were doing in East Germany. The question was, however, whether the government would discuss with the United States "a mutual withdrawal of atomic weapons from Germany." By removing atomic weapons from both parts of Germany, and from neighboring areas if possible, the powers could greatly reduce the chances of an atomic war in Central Europe.[63]

Erler realized, of course, that even after the removal of atomic weapons from the area Germany could still be converted into an atomic battleground if the powers became involved in a major war, but this danger existed as long as Europe was divided into two armed camps. That was the key. To the Social Democrats the atomic arms race demonstrated more clearly than ever that military alliances could provide no real security.[64] The time had come, therefore, to move beyond NATO to a European collective security system and the reunification of Germany.

The Ollenhauer Plan

Near the end of the parliamentary debate on atomic weapons Ollenhauer complained bitterly that government speakers hardly mentioned the subject of reunification. He found that especially deplorable because, in his view, the international climate had improved in recent months, as had the chances for "a positive development" in four-power negotiations. Ollenhauer believed that the powers wanted a relaxation of international tension, but he feared that they would seek detente on the basis of the status quo. After traveling to London in May to take a firsthand look at the disarmament talks going on there, Ollenhauer advised the government to draft a German proposal for the conference. He considered it imperative that any international agreement on arms control be treated in conjunction with the related question of European security and German reunification.[65] This was the basis of the so-called Ollenhauer Plan.

In presenting the Ollenhauer Plan to its readers, *Vorwärts* pointed out that, whereas the Western powers wanted free elections to come first and the Russians insisted that the security question be given priority, the Social Democrats had placed the two demands side by side. They accomplished this by proposing that a Germany reunited on the basis of free elections join with its neighbors to form a European collective security system. The essential aspects of the security system included a nonaggression pact between the member states; an arbitration agreement for the settlement of disputes by peaceful means; a military contribution from each member-state, based on its respective strength; a system of arms control and limitation within the area; an automatic obligation of military assistance to all member states; and a guarantee for the security system from the United States and the Soviet Union. The Social Democrats admitted that the establishment of such a system would be difficult, but the alternative was the status quo and the continuation of a period of uncertainty and insecurity for the people of Europe.[66]

The coalition parties promptly rejected the Ollenhauer Plan as nothing more than a collection of familiar SPD projects, all proceeding from a continuing failure to appreciate the importance of German membership in NATO.[67] The Ollenhauer Plan, however, attempted to show the Germans that there could be security without NATO. In a newspaper article Erler commented that if the United States would mobilize the Sixth Fleet for the King of Jordan then it would certainly do more to prevent the Ruhr from falling into Soviet hands.[68] How would the Americans defend their interests in Central Europe? Since the Russians wanted the Americans to withdraw from the European continent, and the Social Democrats would concede that much to get the Red Army out of Central Europe, an American guarantee would have to be based on the threat of nuclear retaliation against the Soviet Union from bases outside of Europe.[69] Ignoring for the moment the question of credibility, how could this reliance on American nuclear power be reconciled with the party's demand for a ban on nuclear weapons? Erler answered that atomic disarmament would have to be carried out in association with an agreement on the limitation of conventional forces so that a "reasonable balance" of Western and Soviet forces would be established.[70] If achieved, such an agreement would mean that not American nuclear power but European conventional strength would have to balance the military potential of the Soviet Union.[71] To the West Germans that was unthinkable. Before they would travel the road to reunification, the security question would have to be resolved, and the Ollenhauer Plan failed to provide a safe answer.

The Social Democrats ignored public skepticism about the Ollenhauer Plan. In the following weeks they gave more and more attention to their program for German reunification; in fact, they made reunification the focal point of their election campaign. In Ollenhauer's words, "There was no more pressing task than to restore the national unity of our country."[72] The Social Democrats, however, had little cause for optimism. Between February and September, West Germany and the Soviet Union exchanged views on matters of mutual interest, including reunification, and from the beginning the Russians emphasized that the German question could be solved only through a rapprochement between the two German governments. While visiting East Berlin in August, Khrushchev underlined this by giving his support to the idea of a German confederation. Walter Ulbricht had earlier suggested the creation of an all-German council with equal representation from the two Germanys in order to prepare the final stages of the reunification process. He now added, however, that, to assure genuinely free elections for an all-German parliament, West Germany would have to undergo a number of important political and social changes. One week before the West German elections the Russians sent a note to Bonn reiterating their support for the confederation plan and reminding the government that progress toward reunification could be made only with the cooperation of the Pankow regime.[73] Although this was a devastating blow to the Social Democrats, they never gave up hope.

The Social Democrats tried to ignore the Russian reference to Pankow. They insisted that the German question remained a four-power responsibility and that neither the Russians nor the Western powers could divest themselves of the obligation to restore German unity.[74] In late July the Western powers had issued a declaration from Berlin in which they reaffirmed their support for reunification through free elections, but Ollenhauer called it "thoroughly disappointing" because they had said nothing new. They had merely repeated their earlier demand that a reunited Germany should be granted freedom of choice, which meant freedom to join NATO. The Social Democrats warned again that the Soviet Union would never agree to reunification until a satisfactory solution had been found to the question of Germany's military status, and this, they insisted, could be done on the basis of the Ollenhauer Plan.[75]

By continuing to ignore Russian demands and to insist, in spite of them, on the validity of the Ollenhauer Plan, the Social Democrats made themselves vulnerable to attack by the coalition parties. At the opening of the election campaign Adenauer had already warned that an SPD victory in September would mean "the downfall of Germany."[76] The chancellor never described the Social Democrats as willing helpers of the Soviet Union—though he always mentioned Wehner's Communist background—rather, he treated them as unwitting dupes of the Kremlin who would deliver Germany over to the Bolshevik dictators. He told an election audience that Ollenhauer in negotiations with Khrushchev would be like "Little Red Riding Hood standing face to face with the wolf."[77] Unfortunately for the Social Democrats, their single-minded attachment to the cause of German reunification made the image which government propaganda painted seem plausible.

In January, 1957, Ollenhauer declared that the party's main objective in the upcoming general election was "to end the Adenauer era and the predominance of the CDU in parliament." Its slogan was security for all, by which the Social Democrats meant security through peaceful reunification and social reforms. At a meeting in Bonn he told the party leadership that the SPD had an excellent chance to reach the many West Germans who wanted to overcome "the insecurity of the present situation." He estimated that four to five million voters had yet to decide how they would vote in September, and they would determine the outcome of the election.[78]

In the following months the Social Democrats watched the public opinion polls very closely. They discovered to their satisfaction that the two major parties stood only a few percentage points apart, with one or the other leading in popularity depending on the poll. As the campaign unfolded, however, it became obvious that the CDU would remain the largest party in the Bundestag. The Social Democrats, none-theless, felt confident down to election day that they would break Ade-nauer's parliamentary majority, thus opening the possibility of a coalition with the Free Democrats. No one suffered a greater shock than the SPD over the election results of September 15, 1957. Although the Social Democrats received a million and a half more votes than they had won in 1953, they won less than 32 percent of the popular vote. The CDU received two and a half million more votes and increased its share of the vote to slightly over 50 percent. For the first time in Ger-man parliamentary history one party had won an absolute majority.

Four weeks before the election a prominent German weekly news-paper commented that, if the SPD lost the election, it would be be-cause the CDU knew what it wanted and the SPD did not.[79] During the campaign the Christian Democrats focused public attention on the government's success in achieving prosperity at home and security abroad. They reminded the voters that West Germany had gone from rags to riches in only eight years and from a pariah among the nations to an equal partner in the Western Alliance. If the West Germans wanted to continue the present course, CDU posters explained, then they should vote for the man who had made West Germany prosperous and secure — Konrad Adenauer. In effect the Christian Democrats made the elec-tion a plebiscite for or against the chancellor, and the CDU victory can be interpreted above all as an expression of the voters' confidence in the leadership of Adenauer.

The Social Democrats treated the chancellor's victory as a sign of the German people's continued political immaturity and warned of a new "Führer cult to which the majority of the people has still not become immune, despite the experiences of the past."[80] The SPD had enhanced Adenauer's appeal in the eyes of the electorate, however, by failing to select an attractive candidate for chancellor. Erich Ollenhauer can be described as a genuinely decent and respectable man, factual in his treatment of the issues, and fair in his references to the other political parties, but he lacked the will to power and combativeness of either his predecessor, Kurt Schumacher, or his adversary, Konrad Adenauer. Even his own colleagues found his approach too gentle, and they en-couraged him to take the offensive against the chancellor. That would have been out of character for the mild-mannered and conciliatory Ollenhauer, who continued to rely on the good sense of the electorate to produce an SPD victory at the polls.[81]

Adenauer's strong personality and immense prestige contributed greatly to the CDU victory, but some have argued that even with Ollenhauer at the helm the Social Democrats could have made it a close race if only they had presented their case in a convincing manner. After all, Clement Attlee had defeated Winston Churchill by speaking effectively to the issues that troubled the British nation after the war, and Churchill had reached a much higher peak of public renown than Konrad Adenauer. By contrast, in 1957 the Social Democrats appeared uncertain on most issues. In no way did they recommend themselves to the electorate as a government party.[82]

In dealing with domestic policy, the SPD drew on the set of principles enunciated by Ollenhauer in the so-called Dortmund Manifesto of June, 1957.[83] In it the SPD promised to protect private property, to guarantee free competition, and to prevent the misuse of economic power. There was no mention of nationalization; in fact, the SPD adopted the fundamental concepts of Ludwig Erhard's social market economy. The party leadership decided to take this important step in order to reach more middle-class voters, as well as to open the way to a coalition with the FDP, but the tactic failed to work. Many voters wondered with good reason whether the party had actually developed a new economic policy. Parteivorstand member Willi Eichler and union chief Otto Brenner still advocated nationalization; even Ollenhauer talked of some form of public control over the major industries.[84] Exploiting the confusion over SPD economic policy, Adenauer offered to pay a hundred marks to anyone who could tell him what the SPD wanted. What many saw, or thought they saw, in SPD economic policy was a socialization program under a different guise; at best they were uncertain about what the Social Democrats might do.[85]

At the outset the Social Democrats wanted to center their campaign on social and economic issues, but foreign policy became the main battleground. The Christian Democrats took the offensive early, claiming that the election would determine whether Germany "would remain Christian or become Communist." Although the Social Democrats mounted a counteroffensive, attacking Adenauer's commitment to NATO and a defense policy based on atomic weapons and conscription, they spent most of the campaign on the defensive.[86]

One of the SPD's major campaign promises was to abolish conscription. The party insisted on it at the Munich party conference; the leadership reaffirmed it at a meeting in January, 1957, and SPD candidates on the hustings pledged themselves to end the draft. Yet although it became clear very early in the campaign that conscription no longer stirred great public interest, the Social Democrats stood fast; in fact, during the last days of the campaign, Ollenhauer made a special effort to assure his audiences that an SPD government would abolish conscription.[87] For the Social Democrats opposition to conscription was necessary for the sake of reunification, which, as they reminded the voters, remained the primary task of a German government. This was a reasonable argument and one that West Germans could acknowledge, if the Social Democrats would provide an alternative to conscription. In January, 1957, the SPD leaders advocated the creation of a volunteer army and made isolated references to it during the campaign, but out of respect for the antimilitary sentiments of the party rank and file they emphasized the abolition of conscription. As a result the electorate became more conscious of what the SPD opposed than what it favored.

In atomic weapons the Social Democrats also thought that they had a vote-getting issue, though in this case a far more powerful one. In April, at the time of the Göttingen declaration, the public appeared to be genuinely alarmed by the dangers facing West Germany because of the atomic arms race. By the time the election campaign got under way, however, the sense of alarm had diminished considerably, and by August, one reporter noted, Ollenhauer's warning that the government's atomic-weapons policy would lead to the destruction of Germany hardly impressed the "well-dressed and well-fed German burghers" who sat in the summer sun listening to the election speeches.[88] A greater concern than the danger of having atomic weapons on German soil was the question of what would happen if an SPD government demanded their removal. Some feared that the Americans would leave. Since only the United States had the military power to deter Soviet aggression, the West Germans agreed with Adenauer that everything had to be done to keep American forces in Germany.

Obviously the SPD made a grave mistake in campaigning against Adenauer's security policy, but only ten months before the election the Social Democrats seemed to be on the right track. Public-opinion polls recorded a significant drop in the chancellor's popularity, and in several state elections the SPD made impressive gains campaigning on national issues, including rearmament. It seemed logical to assume that a similar tactic would bring even greater rewards in the upcoming federal elections. The Soviet intervention in Hungary undermined the SPD position, however, and reversed the trend which had appeared to be running so strongly in favor of the SPD. In the following months security became a more pressing issue than ever before. West Germans wanted assurance that the NATO connection remained firm, and Adenauer's rearmament policy, which had been so unpopular the previous summer, became more acceptable.[89] For the Social Democrats, therefore, success in the election would depend on their ability to convince the West Germans that the SPD possessed a more effective security policy than the CDU.

According to the Social Democrats, the Germans would find real security only after the country had been reunified.[90] In the meantime, Germany would be protected by the balance of military power that existed between East and West. This would deter Soviet aggression and reduce the chances of a third world war. Since peace under these conditions would be maintained by a balance of terror, however, mankind would never be freed from the nightmare of an atomic holocaust. Real security, therefore, would be achieved when the powers decided to end the arms race and remove the greatest source of international tension—the division of Germany. How could German unity be restored?

Two weeks before the election the director of the SPD's eastern bureau wrote an article describing the transformation the Soviet Union had undergone since the death of Stalin. He implied that the Soviet policy of peaceful coexistence had a firm domestic basis.[91] To most West Germans, however, Russia still posed an enormous threat to Germany. Thus they viewed reunification as a risky venture, and rather than gamble with an unknown and potentially dangerous future they preferred to hold on to what they had. Their vote for Adenauer was a vote against experiments, especially in foreign policy.[92]

The Social Democrats acknowledged the risks involved in reunifying Germany and in accepting a disarmament or disengagement agreement with the Russians, but the greatest risk was in doing nothing in the face of a threatening situation. Only two days before the election *Vorwärts* commented that some observers now believed that war, if it came, would begin as a clash between two German armies and would be fought with conventional weapons. "What a choice—a civil war or an atomic war!"[93] The Social Democrats concluded that the only sound guarantee for security was the reunification of Germany within the framework of a European security system. Even at that late date, however, they made no attempt to explain how the system would work, even though it had been part of SPD policy since 1954, or to indicate what would happen to the NATO connection in the meantime.[94]

Throughout the campaign Adenauer exploited the continued lack of clarity that surrounded SPD policy by warning that if the Social Democrats came to power they would take the Federal Republic out of NATO. Although the SPD issued a firm denial, uncertainty about the party's position remained. A journalist who followed Ollenhauer through northern Germany in mid-August reported that at every press conference the SPD leader faced a question on NATO membership. In every instance Ollenhauer replied courteously that the Social Democrats had not called for a unilateral withdrawal of the Federal Republic from the alliance; rather, they had proposed a renegotiation of the Paris Accords in order to promote the chances for reunification.[95] He never said what West German's new relationship with NATO would be, however.

Furthermore, in spite of periodic affirmations by its leaders, the SPD never passed a resolution stating its readiness to support a defense of the Federal Republic. The rank-and-file members gave no indication that they even saw the need for a West German army. During the campaign, local party groups displayed a poster showing an amputee on crutches standing before a bombed-out city, with the words: "Never Again! Therefore Negotiate!" Even Ollenhauer could still remind his audiences that "social and cultural concerns [are] more important than army divisions and barracks."[96] By default, therefore, the Social Democrats left it to Adenauer to satisfy the needs of security-conscious West Germans.

Ten months before the election *Vorwärts* announced that an SPD election victory in September would mean that the majority of the population wanted a decisive change in West German foreign policy, specifically, "an active policy of peace and reunification through the re-

Antirearmament poster used by the SPD in 1957. It reads: "Never again!
Therefore negotiate." Courtesy Friedrich Ebert Stiftung.

nunciation of military alliances and the regulation of security problems through negotiation." Soon after the election, however, Carlo Schmid told a radio audience that he saw no reason to alter SPD foreign policy. "I think this policy is correct, and a party has to support what it thinks is right even if it knows that the voters do not agree. It is unworthy of a responsible party to advocate only those ideas which it knows the voters will support."[97] Many other Socialist leaders, shared this view, but they also realized that the SPD could not live by principles alone. The Social Democrats wanted to be the government party, and they had nothing to look forward to except four more years on the opposition benches. In the following months, therefore, the leadership gradually conceded that unless the Social Democrats made an effort to bring themselves more into line with majority opinion in West Germany, especially on foreign-policy and security matters, they would be condemned to play the role of the eternal opposition party.

CHAPTER 8

Kampf dem Atomtod

The Social Democrats were deeply disappointed by their performance in the 1957 election. They had expected a victory; instead, they suffered their third and most crushing defeat at the hands of Konrad Adenauer. A bitter intraparty battle seemed inevitable. Some observers predicted that trouble lay ahead for the SPD leaders, but that, as had happened after the 1953 election, the storm would soon pass, and the party would settle back into a mood of easy self-satisfaction. Others, however, believed that the SPD would experience something more serious and warned that before it was over party unity would be severely tested.[1]

Demands for a reexamination of the party's position were heard immediately. Three days after the election the local party group in Bonn requested that the Parteivorstand take immediate action by convening a special conference to deal with the question of party reform. During the following week other local organizations, as well as prominent party politicians at the state and federal levels, submitted proposals on how to make the SPD a more effective political force.[2]

The Reform Movement

The call for reform angered the people at party headquarters. Press secretary Fritz Heine, who had been managing SPD elections campaigns since 1928, snapped back furiously at those well-meaning "outsiders" who gave "dumb advice" without concern for the consequences.[3] Ollenhauer was equally defensive, though more patient with his critics. In a speech to the Parteivorstand on September 18, he argued that the election represented "a great success" for the party. With 9.5 million voters, 600,000 members, and 169 Bundestag deputies, the SPD had a great deal of political capital. Ollenhauer conceded that the SPD had failed to achieve its main goal, to deny the CDU an absolute majority, but that was the result of "essentially objective" factors: (1) the intervention of big business, the Catholic church, and the Western powers on the side of the CDU; (2) the impact of international events, especially the Soviet action in Hungary and the lack of progress in the disarmament talks; and (3) the effect of the voters' frame of mind, which in September, 1957, was dominated by a feeling of "relative security and prosperity" and by the desire not to risk anything through a change in government.

One week later Ollenhauer informed the party leadership that some people were urging the SPD to overcome the differences between the party and the government on foreign policy. "Why not accept NATO and conscription?" they asked. After all, a policy of opposition had achieved nothing. Ollenhauer replied that if the Social Democrats accepted this line of argument it "would mean the beginning of the end of the SPD and of democracy in this country." He saw no cause for panic. The SPD had lost a battle, nothing more, and to prepare for the next campaign the party needed only to reexamine its position. Ollenhauer viewed this mainly as a question of political style and electoral tactics rather than as a step toward fundamental reform.[4]

In the following weeks *Vorwärts* opened its columns to those Social Democrats who wanted to discuss the party's performance in the September election. Most correspondents agreed with Ollenhauer that the party's failure to defeat Adenauer was caused primarily by factors beyond SPD control and to a lesser extent by weaknesses in the SPD campaign. In the latter case few questioned the correctness of SPD policy or believed that it should be changed simply because a majority had voted for Adenauer. In spite of this broad support, however, the leaders came under sharp criticism, especially from the activists on the right and left wings of the party.

The left viewed the SPD as a workers' party with the task of demolishing the class structure of West Germany by a thoroughgoing Socialist policy. Professor Wolfgang Abendroth, a prominent leftist, stated that the SPD lost the 1953 and 1957 elections because the ruling class used its enormous financial resources to control the mass media and "hire" political parties like the FDP and the CDU.[5] The response of the SPD should be to arouse the class consciousness of the exploited masses. Abendroth suggested protest movements, and he referred in particular to the opportunities for political mass action afforded by the current public unrest over atomic weapons. As an example, he mentioned that in the election campaign the SPD could have countered the CDU's tactic of emphasizing the threat of bolshevism by concentrating more effectively on the even greater threat of an atomic war. The one SPD candidate who did so, Karl Bechert, won a seat for the party. Abendroth thought that the party leaders had underestimated the extent to which the rearmament question could be used as a means of mobilizing the masses. In dealing with reunification, the leftists expressed strong interest in establishing contacts with the East German regime. They were impressed by the changes the Soviet bloc had undergone since the death of Stalin, and although they were critical of Soviet intervention in Hungary, they saved their harshest words for the "imperialist actions" of the Western powers. They considered Adenauer's policy of strength extremely provocative. Their recommendation, therefore, was not only to increase the party's opposition to the domestic and foreign policy of the government but also to give it a more radical expression in order to create a Socialist majority in West Germany.

The reformers believed that the SPD should become a party for all the people (Volkspartei). In practice this meant an opening to the right by the SPD rather than a shift to the left by middle-class voters. The reformers emphasized a social-welfare policy and a shift from nationalization to less radical economic measures for controlling large industrial and financial enterprises. Furthermore, they opposed the kind of extra-parliamentary action favored by the left and rejected a policy of obstruction, insisting that parliament be used for constructive work—even in cooperation with the bourgeois parties. On foreign-policy questions the reformers still believed in the primacy of reunification, but they would not deal with Pankow. They showed greater concern about Soviet intentions than that shown by the left and insisted on security guarantees for a reunited Germany, as well as a German military contribution. In dealing with West German security, the reformers recognized the need to accept the Bundeswehr and the NATO connection, both of which they would limit rather than abolish. Their recommendation, therefore, was to present a clear alternative to Adenauer's policies by drawing closer to the majority view in West Germany without abandoning the fundamental goals of the SPD.[6]

There could be no decision on what course the SPD would follow until May, 1958, when the party met in its biennial conference, but as early as October there were indications of what the results might be. At the first caucus of the new SPD Fraktion a conflict arose over who should serve as assistant to parliamentary leader Erich Ollenhauer. He recommended Mellies and Schoettle, the incumbent deputy chairmen, but after a particularly tense meeting at the Bundeshaus (Parliament Building) the delegation voted for Erler, Schmid, and Wehner.[7] According to *Die Welt* the three men had already formed an alliance with the intention of setting the party on a new course.[8]

At first glance Erler, Schmid, and Wehner seemed an unlikely trio to be united on a common front. While Erler and Schmid stood on the right, Wehner gave the appearance of being a militant Marxist. On most issues, however, he aligned himself with the moderates because of his fundamentally pragmatic approach to politics. On one thing they all agreed: something substantial had to be done to improve the party's chances in the next general election.

The Fraktion elections indicated that most SPD deputies considered it essential to shake up the party after the disastrous defeat of September 15.

Ollenhauer at the Stuttgart party conference, May, 1958, with Deputy Chairmen Herbert Wehner (left) and Waldemar von Knoeringen (right). Courtesy German Press Agency.

By voting for Erler, Schmid, and Wehner, the deputies were declaring their support for the reform movement, as well as signaling the party to turn to new leaders. Mellies and Schoettle had contributed to the party's many achievements in Parliament since 1949, but like Ollenhauer they had achieved their positions of leadership mainly as a result of loyal service to the party. Erler, Schmid, and Wehner, on the other hand, were successful politicians who the Fraktion believed could lead the party to victory at election time. By electing the trio, the SPD deputies also hoped to surround Ollenhauer with men who were more clearly aware of the political situation than those guiding the party from headquarters in Bonn.

The party reformers had long complained that party bureaucrats— especially those at the highest level—exercised too much influence in shaping the spirit and policy of the SPD. During his term Schumacher had consulted men of ability, without regard for their position in the party. Ollenhauer, however, relied mainly on the advice of Deputy Chairman Mellies and the five permanent members of the Parteivorstand who worked with him at party headquarters. These men at the Baracke (the barracks on the Friedrich Ebert Allee), which one critic described as "a kind of refuge camp for bureaucrats who had fled reality," tended to be inward-looking, concerned primarily with the party organization, lacking the sharp political sense needed to interpret events outside the party.[9] To reduce their influence, the reformers wanted to restrict their activity to purely administrative matters. In that way, policy making would be in the hands of the politicians, and power within the party would shift from the Baracke to the Bundeshaus.[10]

Initially, therefore, the debate centered less on the differences between left and right than on the struggle between the politicians and the bureaucrats; in fact, men of the left like Kühn and Birkelbach supported Erler and Schmid in their attempt to carry out major organizational changes.[11] Ollenhauer and Mellies defended the bureaucrats, arguing that the party functioned as well as ever. If the SPD needed to sharpen its image and clarify its policy, that could be done through more intensive educational work within the party and among its supporters, a task traditionally performed by the bureaucrats. The reformers quickly pointed out that the party wanted to convince more than its circle of friends and that the existing party structure, which dated from the Weimar period and the emergencies of the postwar years, lacked the flexibility needed to reach a wider audience. The party had to reorganize and use what one reformer called "the outstanding variety of men the SPD has at its disposal" to build a new corps of leaders.[12]

The first important victory of the reformers over party traditionalists came in Berlin rather than Bonn. There, on September 30, Willy Brandt, the popular and energetic president of the Berlin House of Deputies, received his party's nomination to succeed the late Otto Suhr as mayor of the city.

Brandt's nomination had been strongly opposed by the head of the Berlin party organization, Franz Neumann. A party man steeped in the tradition of the old SPD, Neumann had been the local leader since 1946. He had supported Schumacher and Ollenhauer against rivals in Berlin such as Ernst Reuter and had remained a loyal defender of the policies laid down by the Parteivorstand. Brandt had followed Reuter, and after the mayor's death in 1953 he had upheld the Reuter tradition, continuing to offer policies which differed, at times markedly, from those advocated by party headquarters in Bonn. This in large part explains why he failed to win a place on the Parteivorstand at the Berlin and Munich party conferences, while Neumann succeeded on both occasions.

The two men represented different political and ideological viewpoints. While Neumann still believed in the validity of Socialist theories, in the correctness of the party's foreign policy (especially its antimilitary posture), and in the need to strengthen the party bureaucracy, Brandt argued that a rigid attachment to traditional points of view would only confirm the SPD in its role as the opposition party in Bonn. For Brandt and the other reformers practical political considerations were more important than the preservation of party traditions, especially when those traditions no longer corresponded to the realities of the German situation. It was this political realism, as well as his attractiveness as a political candidate, that carried him to the mayor's office.[13]

In spite of the victory in Berlin and an equally impressive showing in Hamburg, where Max Brauer, a prominent reformer, led the SPD to victory in the city elections, the Bonn reformers moved cautiously. They preferred to save their heavy ammunition for the biennial conference and in the meantime concentrate on convincing the rank and file of the need for party reform. In so doing, they hoped to prevent a repetition of the Berlin party conference, where they had been outmaneuvered by the bureaucrats and traditionalists. The reformers also tried to win Ollenhauer for the reform movement because of his ability to hold the party together while it underwent dramatic change.[14]

In the fall of 1957 it was still uncertain what Ollenhauer would do. He had supported certain changes in party policy at the Berlin and Munich party conferences, even those dealing with the military question, but he would not push too hard in the face of resistance from the ranks. Ollenhauer, one observer wrote, "would march with whatever side had the biggest battalions."[15] Thus it fell to Erler, Schmid, and Wehner to educate the party before the SPD met at Stuttgart in May. In the meantime, with the Bundestag reconvening, the reformers had to turn their attention from the struggle within the party to the renewal of the conflict with Adenauer and the CDU.

The Rapacki Plan

On October 29, West Germany's Third Parliament convened in Bonn to hear Chancellor Adenauer read a policy statement by the new government. It contained no surprises. In the area of foreign policy Adenauer offered nothing more than the simple slogans which had characterized his speeches during the preceding seven years. He warned of hard times ahead for the German nation. East-West tension remained high, and the threat of Soviet totalitarianism still loomed ominously in the east. Adenauer felt confident, however, that as long as they worked together the free nations could resist any political or military pressure from the Soviet Union. On the vital question of German reunification the chancellor offered little hope of an immediate solution. He told the Bundestag that, once the Soviet Union overcame "its completely unfounded mistrust of the West" and saw that "its attempt to rule the world" was unrealistic, then the nation could advance toward unity in freedom. In the meantime, the West had no alternative but to pursue a policy of strength.[16]

One week later the Bundestag met to discuss the government's declaration. The Social Democrats accused Adenauer of advocating a policy that seriously endangered peace and ruined the chances for restoring German unity. Instead of continuing an ill-fated course, Ollenhauer said, the government should encourage the Western powers to hold a summit conference with the Russians "as soon as possible and in any case before final decisions are made by the West on further military strategy." An agreement on disarmament would lead to a relaxation of international tension and ultimately to a more favorable situation for promoting German reunification. Ollenhauer conceded that serious obstacles stood in the way of any comprehensive agreement and admitted frankly that the SPD had "no magic formula for reunification," but as long as the government clung to NATO, he said, there could be no hope of successful negotiations with Moscow.[17]

The debate took place under the impact of a startling scientific achievement. On October 4 the Soviet Union launched Sputnik, the first man-made satellite. The news shocked the United States because it meant that the Russians had the capability to build an intercontinental ballistic missile (ICBM).[18] In response, the United States immediately accelerated its own ICBM program, while relying for the moment on an arsenal of intermediate-range ballistic missiles (IRBM) to maintain the nuclear balance between East and West. The American government also discussed again the possibility of sharing tactical nuclear weapons with its NATO allies, this time as a means of obtaining permission to station IRBMs on European soil. These questions, along with a review of the general military situation, would be subjects of discussion when NATO members met at Paris in December.

Before NATO met, the Eastern bloc had another surprise. Polish Foreign Minister Adam Rapacki proposed the creation of a zone in Central Europe, including Poland, Czechoslovakia, and the two Germanys, which would be free of atomic weapons. In a series of lectures given at Oxford University in November, 1957, George Kennan, former American ambassador to the Soviet Union, expanded on the idea. He argued that a stable peace could be achieved in Europe if there was a "general withdrawal of American, British, and Russian armed power from the heart of the continent." The physical separation of the powers would reduce the threat of war and permit the states of Central Europe to "accept a higher level of responsibility for the defense of the continent." Kennan proposed that a reunited Germany, along with Poland, Czechoslovakia, and perhaps Hungary, withdraw from the existing alliance systems. They could then establish their own security pact for mutual defense, which in turn could be guaranteed by the great powers. Kennan's disengagement plan, along with Rapacki's proposal of an atomic-weapons-free zone, immediately aroused the interest of the SPD.[19]

The Social Democrats responded by calling on the government to support disengagement as a means of "reducing tension, increasing our security, and . . . smoothing the path to the solution of our political problems."[20] Adenauer, however, viewed disengagement as a high security risk with the added disadvantage that it would mean the loss of political stature for West Germany and the disruption of Western integration. He had no intention of deviating from his established Western course. With reference to the Rapacki Plan, he said that West Germany would remain a loyal ally. If NATO decided to implement its nuclear strategy by stationing IRBMs in Europe and distributing atomic weapons among the Allied armies, the chancellor would insist that the Bundeswehr also receive the most modern weapons.[21]

The Social Democrats criticized Adenauer and the Allies for thinking in terms of the arms race. Since the Russians and the Americans could wipe out the entire human race several times over with the weapons they already possessed, it made no sense to continue building more powerful missiles with more deadly warheads. The powers should work for a political solution, specifically, a disarmament agreement. The choice, according to a *Vorwärts* headline, was "Disarmament or Atomic Anarchy."[22]

The SPD pointed out that the Russians had endorsed the Rapacki Plan and applauded certain aspects of the Kennan Plan. They had even offered to discuss "an end to the Cold War and the arms race" at a summit conference.[23] The Western powers, doubting Soviet good will and feeling somewhat at a disadvantage because of Sputnik, showed little interest in taking up the offer. Much to the chagrin of the SPD, they continued to focus their attention on the upcoming NATO meeting.

Early in December the Social Democrats tried to force a Bundestag debate before Adenauer went to Paris. They drafted a resolution calling for the creation of an atomic-weapons-free zone in Central Europe and the removal of all foreign troops from the area, as in the Kennan and Rapacki plans. They demanded also that the Allies neither equip the Bundeswehr with atomic weapons nor station medium- or long-range missiles in West Germany. Although the Social Democrats said nothing about tactical atomic weapons already stationed there, Erler had implied several weeks earlier that all atomic weapons could be removed safely with or without a general arms agreement. Finally, the resolution warned against integrating the Bundeswehr so tightly into the NATO command structure that it would prevent any changes in the military status of both parts of Germany.[24] With this resolution the Social Democrats hoped to bind Adenauer's hands. The chancellor, however, countered by instructing the CDU to use its majority to delay a foreign-policy debate until after the NATO meeting.

Although the SPD was anxious about the mid-December NATO meeting in Paris, very little happened. Only Britain and Turkey agreed to the installation of missile bases on their territory. Denmark and Norway refused to have them, while the remaining NATO members decided to delay a decision on the missile bases and on the proposal to arm NATO forces with tactical atomic weapons.[25] Ollenhauer deplored Adenauer's failure to join the Danes and Norwegians in rejecting atomic weapons and missile bases, and he expressed dismay over NATO's preoccupation with military matters. He noted with approval, however, that the NATO powers had agreed to investigate the possibility of renewing disarmament talks with the Soviet Union, and during the following weeks he urged them to use the Rapacki Plan as a basis for discussion.[26]

On January 23 the Bundestag held its long-awaited foreign-policy debate. At the center of discussion was the Rapacki Plan, which the coalition opposed and the opposition parties (SPD and FDP) favored. According to the Social Democrats, by rejecting the plan, the government demonstrated that it cared more about an atomic arming of the Bundeswehr than the reunification of Germany. Since the government could neither deny its interest in atomic weapons nor offer anything more than the old arguments about a policy of strength, the coalition parties found themselves continuously on the defensive. The press thought that the Social Democrats outshone the coalition speakers.[27] Later the SPD press service proudly proclaimed that Adenauer and his cabinet, "sitting in the dock," were condemned before the millions of Germans who heard the entire debate on radio.[28] Whatever satisfaction the Social Democrats received from their performance in the debate, however, they still faced the coalition's firm opposition to the Rapacki Plan.

In the debate the Social Democrats emphasized two points: first, the need for negotiations between the great powers and, second, the value of the Rapacki Plan as a starting point for those negotiations. Ollenhauer admitted that it would be difficult to bring the two sides together, because Cold War attitudes had hardened, and the Soviet Union had strengthened its power position. But later in the debate Carlo Schmid offered a different view. History had demonstrated, he said, that the Russians were easiest to deal with when they had a feeling of strength. Schmid gave the example of Czar Alexander's generous attitude toward the French after the allies had defeated Napoleon at the Battle of Leipzig in 1813. Kurt Kiesinger called out from the CDU side of the house, "There are not only Russians in Moscow, but Communists!" Schmid replied smoothly, "Qui gratte le communiste, trouvera le Russe." Underneath the ideological coating, the Soviets shared with the czars a common desire: security against the West. The Social Democrats assumed that if this desire was satisfied the Russians would evacuate Central Europe, and the vehicle for their evacuation could be the Rapacki Plan. Since the Kremlin had shown an interest in the plan, Ollenhauer asked why the Western powers had not discussed it with the Russians. A CDU deputy called out, "We have just finished talking to them in London." The London disarmament talks had failed to produce an agreement, Ollenhauer responded. What the West needed was a proposal to break the deadlock in the negotiations. He suggested the Rapacki Plan.[29]

The coalition parties viewed the Rapacki Plan as a device of Soviet diplomacy designed to consolidate the status quo by forcing West Germany to recognize the Pankow regime. They also feared that if the Americans had to remove their atomic weapons from Germany they would soon withdraw their troops rather than leave them to face superior Soviet conventional forces. Kurt Kiesinger, the CDU's foreign-policy expert, reminded the Social Democrats of the Soviet commitment to a policy of expansion. He urged them to show greater realism in foreign affairs and to stop advocating a policy that would benefit only the Soviets.[30]

In response Ollenhauer asked how the Rapacki Plan could strengthen the Soviet military position if, along with the creation of an atomic-weapons-free zone, the powers carried out a mutual withdrawal of their conventional forces. This would mean a barrier of 800 to 1,200 kilometers between the military forces of East and West. Erler added that once the Red Army had withdrawn from East Germany and the other satellite states the political situation would change because the Communist regimes, including that of East Germany's Walter Ulbricht, would fall without Soviet military protection. A CDU deputy asked Erler whether the overthrow of Ulbricht would not bring the Red Army back into East Germany, as had happened in Hungary in 1956. Erler thought that the question of political change in Germany would have to be discussed with the Russians, presumably during the negotiations on troop withdrawals, but he had no clear answer. To the deputy who challenged him, he demanded, "Tell me, how are you going to bring about reunification with Soviet troops in the zone?"[31] He assumed that they would leave if the powers could agree to end the arms race and thus reduce world tension. The Germans, therefore, had to do everything possible to promote a disarmament agreement.

Through the early months of 1958 the four powers exchanged diplomatic notes and made a series of public declarations about the possibility of a summit conference, but nothing developed.[32] Neither side could agree even on an agenda. While the Americans, and to a lesser extent the British and French, wanted the German question to be an integral part of the negotiations, the Russians insisted that the powers deal only with disarmament and leave reunification to the two German states. Although the Social Democrats rejected the Russian view of reunification, they would accept a summit conference limited to disarmament talks as a means of getting the negotiations started. As a result, when no meeting occurred, they accused the Americans of clinging to the same mistaken concepts that had led to failure at Geneva in 1955.

Of even greater concern to the Social Democrats was the attitude of the West German government. In February, 1958, Defense Minister Strauss went to Washington to discuss German purchase of the Matador, a medium-range missile which could be fitted with either a conventional or an atomic warhead. The Social Democrats immediately protested the purpose of the trip, claiming that the Matador would be used only as an atomic weapon.[33] They also denounced the timing of the trip because Rapacki had just offered a more detailed statement of his disengagement plan. To the government the plan still lacked the semblance of a security system.

In an official statement Strauss declared that to be effective an atomic-weapon-free zone would have to include all the satellite states of Eastern Europe. This, the SPD responded, would only cause the Russians to demand that Western Europe be cleared of atomic weapons as well, thus destroying the purpose of the Rapacki Plan, which was to promote disarmament in a restricted area.[34] The Social Democrats agreed that the plan needed revisions, but they viewed the concept of working from a limited to a comprehensive disarmament agreement as basically correct. In the past the attempt to achieve global agreements leading to total disarmament had failed because the powers refused to take such a gigantic step. The Rapacki Plan, however, gave the powers an opportunity to test disarmament in a limited zone without sacrificing the established alliance systems or the existing balance of power. But to make it work, the Adenauer government would have to refrain from entering the atomic-arms race.[35]

Adenauer had no intention of voluntarily relinquishing West Germany's chance to obtain atomic weapons. On March 20, in a major foreign-policy address to the Bundestag, he announced that the government was prepared to arm the Bundeswehr with tactical atomic weapons if the powers failed to agree on a comprehensive disarmament scheme.[36] Since the powers seemed unlikely to reach such an agreement, West Germany would gain atomic weapons if NATO decided to implement the proposals for weapons sharing made at the Paris conference in December.

Adenauer received the full support of the coalition parties. They presented a resolution in support of his atomic weapons policy which the Social Democrats fought but could not defeat. By the end of the debate, the most acrimonious of the republic's short history, the government and opposition were farther apart than at any time since the Schumacher era. The Social Democrats refused to accept the majority's decision as final. They intended to find a way to block Adenauer's path—if it could not be done in Parliament, then they would go to the people.

Kampf dem Atomtod ("Fight Atomic Death")

On several occasions during the rearmament debate the Social Democrats turned to the public for support against the government. They had tried to mobilize the population in 1952, at the time of EDC, and again in 1955 with the Paulskirche campaign. Two years later the Social Democrats attempted to make atomic weapons an election issue by exploiting the wave of public concern which followed the publication of the Göttingen Declaration, but without success. By voting day the sense of alarm had greatly diminished, and most West Germans were no longer concerned about West Germany's entry into the atomic-arms race. Later in the year, however, atomic weapons again became an issue. In December scientists and scholars issued warnings about the dangers of atomic warfare, and in several state parliaments the SPD delegations expressed opposition to the idea of having American IRBM bases in their areas.[37] In Bonn, after accusing the government of failing to inform the public about what was involved for West Germany in NATO's new defense plans, Fritz Erler concluded that it was time "to give public opinion a jolt." Deputy Chairman Wilhelm Mellies went one step further, proposing a national movement against the "arms madness."[38] One month later the Parteivorstand adopted the idea.

At a meeting in Bonn on January 20 the SPD leaders called on all party members to make "Kampf dem Atomtod" ("Fight Atomic Death") the center of their political activities and to demand (1) that all test explosions with atomic weapons be stopped, (2) that no other armies, including the Bundeswehr, be equipped with atomic weapons, (3) that German researchers be excluded from atomic-weapons development, and (4) that atomic weapons and missile bases be kept out of Germany. With this campaign the SPD leaders hoped to unleash "a wave of resistance to atomic death" which would compel Adenauer and Strauss to abandon their attempt to join the atomic-arms race and to undertake instead an active policy of political negotiations leading to disarmament, detente, and eventually reunification.[39]

Others joined in the protest against the government's defense policy, and, as in Great Britain, ban-the-bomb committees sprang up across the country. Scientists, writers, theologians, trade unionists, and politicians— the same lineup of forces as those in the Paulskirche movement—now combined to form a Kampf dem Atomtod committee.

On March 10, in its first public statement, the committee declared that "the goal of German policy must be detente between East and West. Only such a policy serves the security of the German nation and the national existence of a free democratic Germany. We call upon the government and the Bundestag not to participate in the atomic arms race but to support all efforts to create in Europe a zone free of atomic weapons as a contribution to detente."[40] Walter Menzel, the SPD parlia mentary whip, and chairman of the committee, told the press that the declaration was the work of concerned citizens speaking out on an issue of great national importance. The Christian Democrats, however, promptly labeled Kampf dem Atomtod an SPD affair. They accused the Social Democrats of trying not only to exploit a highly emotional issue for political gain but also, by supporting this new campaign, to avoid the conflict which would result within the party from an attempt to formulate a clear defense program.[41] Ignoring the charges, the SPD went ahead with plans for a series of mass demonstrations and continued preparing pamphlets, films, and brochures to make the public aware of the atomic threat.

One of the pamphlets distributed by the Kampf dem Atomtod committee came from Karl Bechert, a physicist at Mainz University and an SPD Bundestag deputy. Bechert described in great detail the destructive force of a hydrogen bomb, as well as the dangers to mankind from the radioactive fallout of such a blast. He concluded that the only hope for Germany's survival was a policy of massive public resistance to the government's insane attempt to join the atomic-arms race. "Everyone among us can influence the policy of atomic armament. Local governments can refuse to provide the land. The workers can refuse to build the [missile] sites. And the physicists can refuse to participate in nuclear research" for military purposes.[42]

Bechert's call to resistance was by no means an isolated expression of party opinion. The SPD press carried many articles on Kampf dem Atomtod, and leading Social Democrats sounded the alarm that Germany had been plunged into a state of national emergency by the fatal policy of the "rocket Christians."[43] When the March foreign-policy debate ended with a majority in favor of the government's policy, the SPD joined with the FDP in calling for Adenauer's resignation and the formation of a government which would take Germany out of the atomic-arms race. According to Karl Mommer, a party moderate, "extraordinary situations require the use of extraordinary means."[44] Since the opposition parties lacked the strength to force a governmental change, however, the SPD quickly abandoned the idea of a frontal assault on the chancellor in favor of a more indirect approach.

At the close of the March foreign-policy debate, Ollenhauer had announced that the SPD planned to introduce a bill calling for a national poll (Volksbefragung) to ask the people whether they wanted German armed forces equipped with atomic weapons and missile sites built in Germany. On April 24 the Social Democrats presented it to the Bundestag, where before being sent to the parliamentary committees for further study, the bill came under sharp attack from the government parties. They accused the Social Democrats of trying to manipulate the constitution for party purposes and charged that the SPD proposal would lead Germany back to the kind of demagogic democracy that had killed the Weimar Republic.[45]

The Social Democrats responded that their proposal had nothing to do with a plebiscite, which constituted a direct legislative act by the people. They simply wanted to give Parliament a chance to see whether its decisions were in accord with the will of the people. Since the constitution did not specifically prohibit opinion surveys, Carlo Schmid argued that the constitution makers, though opposing the use of plebiscites, had no intention of muzzling the people until election day.[46] The people had a right to be heard when the very existence of the German nation was at

Ollenhauer and Adolf Arndt before a giant "Kampf dem Atomtod" poster, March, 1958. Courtesy Friedrich Ebert Stiftung.

stake. During the last election, moreover, the chancellor had assured the voters that a decision on atomic weapons would not be made any time soon, and the majority had responded by voting for a government which promised "no experiments." The government, therefore, had no mandate for its atomic-weapons policy. It should wait until the people had been given a chance to express an opinion through a national poll.[47]

The Social Democrats realized they had little chance of getting Bundestag approval for a national survey. With everything to lose and nothing to gain, the coalition parties would vote against the SPD bill in its final readings. As a result, the leadership in Bonn decided to open a new front by encouraging SPD parties in the eleven state parliaments to demand local surveys on the atomic-weapons question.[48] Although the Social Democrats held a much stronger position at the state level, they still faced serious difficulties. In states where the party sat in opposition — in Bavaria, for example — the government majority promptly voted against a state-conducted poll. In North Rhine-Westphalia, where the SPD was in the government, the state organization decided against a poll for fear of alienating their coalition partners. Only in Bremen and Hamburg, where the SPD had an absolute majority, was legislation passed for conducting surveys. Even there, however, the Social Democrats found themselves blocked. In early May the CDU, which had the power to prevent a federal survey, moved to close the other avenues open to the SPD by appealing to the Federal Constitutional Court.

The Christian Democrats labeled the opinion polls illegal because the states lacked competence in the disputed area. Atomic weapons related to defense matters, and defense was a federal, not a state, responsibility.[49] Furthermore, the whole notion of opinion polls ran contrary to the spirit of the Basic Law, which rested on the concept of representative government. The government won an initial victory when the court, which waited until late July to deliver a final ruling, granted an immediate injunction preventing state and local authorities from conducting opinion polls.

At this point the Kampf dem Atomtod movement began to lose some of its momentum. For almost two months, however, the ears of the public rang with the cry "Fight Atomic Death!" Beginning on March 23 with a rally in Frankfurt, where Ollenhauer and six other prominent personalities addressed an audience of 2500 invited guests, the movement grew rapidly.[50] During the following days, in response to the call from Frankfurt — "never to rest as long as an atomic death threatens the nation" — thousands of workers laid down their tools in support of the Kampf dem Atomtod movement, and several trade unions joined the protest by calling for a general strike. On March 28 the executive committee of the Trade Union Federation met in an emergency session to discuss union strategy. The committee passed a resolution denouncing the atomic-arms race and urging the six million members of the federation to participate in protest demonstrations, but it refrained for the

226

moment from calling a general strike.[51] The movement also found support on university campuses and among some Protestant theologians. A delegation from the Council of Protestant Churches visited the chancellor to express the council's concern about the effect of the atomic-arms race on the chances for German reunification.

Through the month of April, Kampf dem Atomtod committees organized protest marches and rallies in cities and towns across the country. On April 17 more than 100,000 people gathered before the city hall in Hamburg to hear a battery of speakers, led by SPD Mayor Max Brauer, blast away at Strauss and Adenauer. The demonstrations reached their climax in the May Day celebrations conducted by the SPD and the unions.[52] Thereafter the movement gradually ran out of steam.

The Kampf dem Atomtod movement far surpassed the SPD's earlier attempts to use extraparliamentary means against the government. In comparison with the Paulskirche movement, the party mobilized more manpower and resources. In fact, up to this point in the life of the Bonn Republic no other campaign had evoked a greater sense of involvement from the party rank and file than the call to fight atomic death. Naturally some party groups became extremely active, while others felt compelled to show restraint because of local political conditions—as in Berlin, for example.

On April 19 the Berlin SPD held a special conference on the issue. Willy Brandt, who had been elected party chairman only three months before, wanted to avoid a confrontation, but his opponents within the Berlin organization—mainly party traditionalists and militant leftists—demanded that the Berliners give unconditional support to the Kampf dem Atomtod movement. Led by Franz Neumann, the former party chairman, they proposed that the Berlin SPD organize a massive demonstration followed by a plebiscite, which the West Berlin constitution would allow. Brandt and his supporters argued strenuously against this course of action. First of all, they said, street demonstrations could too easily be exploited by the Communists. Second, an antiatomic-weapons policy, unless coordinated with a program for general disarmament, would lead to a one-sided weakening of the West and therefore could be construed as an anti-Western policy.[53] This possibility concerned Brandt. He wanted to maintain the good relations the Berlin SPD had enjoyed with the Western powers since the blockade. At the same time, however, he wished to avoid a conflict with the SPD leaders in Bonn and tried to be as conciliatory as possible, especially on foreign-policy matters. He shared their interest in disengagement, which he had been cautiously advocating for several years, and on a recent trip to the United States he had proved to be a very able spokesman for a more active reunification policy.[54] On the atomic-weapons question he spoke out against the atomic arming of the Bundeswehr, as the Parteivorstand had done, but he refused to support Kampf dem Atomtod. At the special Berlin party conference in April, Brandt's policy prevailed. By a margin of only eight votes the conference decided against sponsoring either a plebiscite or a mass demonstration.[55]

Some influential Social Democrats in Bonn also opposed an all-out fight against the government's atomic-weapons policy. Fritz Erler, for example, supported the idea of using protest rallies and opinion polls as a means of bringing public pressure to bear on the government. When Adenauer obtained an injunction from the Federal Constitutional Court, however, Erler encouraged the party to shift its propaganda efforts to the upcoming state elections and away from any possible radicalization of the campaign, such as a general strike.[56] Erler also expressed concern about the effect of the Kampf dem Atomtod movement on the Stuttgart party conference. He feared that the party's emotional involvement in the fight against atomic weapons would blind it to the need for a meaningful security policy. Furthermore, the party's military experts realized that sooner or later the SPD would have to deal with the atomic-weapons question in a positive way. In concrete terms this meant that at least American troops, though not necessarily the Bundeswehr, would have to be equipped with atomic weapons. The most dramatic presentation of this view was given in the so-called Beermann memorandum, which exploded on the scene at the very moment the Kampf dem Atomtod movement began to unfold.

The Beermann Memorandum

Six months before the Stuttgart party conference, the SPD's security committee began making preparations by commissioning a five-man study group to draft an advisory report on West German defense policy. Friedrich Beermann, the military adviser of the Fraktion, belonged to the study group and composed a memorandum on the subject. In the following months the memorandum underwent a series of revisions that changed it beyond recognition, but it remained the focal point of an intense party debate and a source of considerable embarrassment to the SPD leaders.

The Beermann memorandum dealt with the question of how to defend West Germany under existing conditions, as well as within a Central European zone free of atomic weapons and foreign troops. At the outset Beermann stated that security for the German people could best be achieved by reunifying Germany within the framework of a European security system and a general disarmament agreement. He considered the creation of an atomic-weapons-free zone a step in this direction, but he saw little reason to believe that the powers would soon agree on disengagement or reunification.

Beermann began with the assumption that under existing conditions "the only security for those living in the free part of Germany was a military balance between East and West." He argued that the West

228

Germans had an obligation to make a military contribution, and he felt confident that it would strengthen Western defenses. At present, he said, the Red Army could move quickly to the Rhine, but with German units at the front Beermann thought that NATO would be able to repulse the initial Soviet thrust. An effective Western defense assumed, of course, a Soviet attack with conventional forces. If it came to nuclear warfare, then "we can forget about military considerations." Yet the existence of these weapons of mass destruction did not make military measures senseless. Because of the strategic nuclear balance between the United States and the Soviet Union, the superpowers could decide to use only certain weapons in their arsenal. They could fire only tactical nuclear weapons, or, given the danger of escalation, they could avoid the use of even those weapons. Under such conditions a limited war fought solely with conventional forces and weapons became a distinct possibility. Beermann admitted that it all rested on speculation, but he warned the party against thinking that war in the nuclear age had to be a nuclear war.

Beermann advocated a small, mobile, heavily armed professional army supported by a militia as the best means of meeting both the military needs and the international obligations of the Federal Republic. The army would operate at the front with other NATO forces, while the militia would serve as a home guard protecting military installations and the communications system, as well as certain border areas and the flanks of the main Western defense force. Thoroughly civilian, the militia would have its own officers and a general service obligation for young men between twenty and thirty. The basic training period would be four months, with an annual refresher course of about three weeks.

The most controversial aspect of the memorandum was Beermann's suggestion that the SPD drop its blanket opposition to atomic weapons. He argued that for deterrence intermediate-range ballistic missiles had to be stationed in Continental Europe, though not necessarily in West Germany. Shorter-range missiles, on the other hand, played an important part in the Western air-defense system, and the Bundeswehr, as an equal partner in NATO, had a right to share in their use.

Beermann had some reservations on the question of West German security in the event the four powers agreed on disengagement without immediate reunification. He pointed out that, should the Warsaw Pact and NATO remain intact after the occupying powers had returned home, then the West would have a better ratio of military forces in Central Europe than it had before disengagement. If, however, the Russians decided to intervene to prevent political change in East Germany, as they had in Hungary, the military picture would be drastically altered, and the West would be faced with the problem of how to bring American forces back into Germany. Militarily Beermann saw an easy solution: the United States could airlift troops to Europe. The political problems associated with reengagement could be more difficult to handle. Furthermore, disengagement could make the Berlin problem more acute, unless Western forces remained in the divided city. It could also increase the danger of a German civil war if foreign troops no longer stood between the two German armies.

The Beermann memorandum was discussed by the study group and then redrafted in the form of a sixteen-page advisory report before it was submitted to the security committee. The main difference between the report and the memorandum was the greater emphasis given to political considerations by the study group. The group still advocated the creation of a small professional army which would fulfill its defense tasks in association with other NATO forces and with the help of a militia recruited on the Swiss model. The report stated, however, that, although the Bundeswehr played a vital role in the Western defense system, a defense contribution should not be so great as to threaten the nation's standard of living or destroy the chances for a general disarmament agreement. The study group had a very favorable view of disengagement, arguing that the Rapacki Plan offered real political gains without upsetting the military situation. In dealing with atomic weapons, the study group showed greater caution than Beermann, though without denying the advantages of an atomic arming of the Bundeswehr at least for air defense. There were modifications, therefore, even shifts of emphasis, but the report maintained the radical nature of the Beermann memorandum.

At the beginning of February the party's security committee met to discuss the formulation of an SPD defense policy. According to the press, which as yet knew nothing of an advisory report, the committee wanted to develop a national defense program with no atomic weapons.[57] Several days later a copy of the report fell into the hands of a reporter in Bonn, and excerpts soon appeared in all the major German newspapers. Naturally, it embarrassed the SPD leaders. At a time when they were organizing a public campaign against the government's atomic-weapons policy, evidence emerged that some Social Democrats favored an atomic arming of the Bundeswehr. The leadership promptly denied that either the Parteivorstand or its security committee was responsible for the report. Several days later a spokesman for the Fraktion labeled the report "a sheer falsification," adding that the opposition party had made no report on military questions—a damning admission in itself.[58]

Beermann immediately came under suspicion as the one responsible for leaking the report to the press. Not only did he strongly oppose the party's involvement in a Kampf dem Atomtod campaign, but he had also made use of the press on previous occasions to promote his ideas when the SPD leaders refused to listen.[59] Beermann, however, could respond in his own defense that much of the memorandum was based on what the party leadership had already acknowledged. To begin with, the Parteivorstand had announced before the September election that an SPD government would meet West Germany's military commitments with a volunteer army, and in the November Bundestag debate Ollen-hauer had asked the government about a home defense force, a subject which three SPD deputies discussed with Defense Minister Strauss a week later.[60] Furthermore, in November, Erler had admitted that missiles could be used against enemy tanks and planes, though he warned that, because missiles with a range of over one thousand kilometers would have to be equipped with atomic warheads, the Bundeswehr could do without them.[61] Of course, Beermann had gone further, recommending atomic weapons for West German defense, and this the party would resist. To some members of the Parteivorstand, the Beermann memoran-dum appeared in most ways indistinguishable from the defense policy advocated by Strauss and Adenauer. They demanded, therefore, that the security committee reexamine the defense question and develop an alternative to the government's mistaken policy.

In mid-February the security committee commissioned five of its mem-bers to prepare a new report on SPD defense policy. Headed by Fritz Erler, the new subcommittee included Beermann and Helmut Schmidt from the original study group, as well as two SPD deputies, Hermann Schmitt and Karl Wienand. In less than two weeks the committee filed a report which differed considerably from the original Beermann memo-randum.[62] To begin with, the Erler committee recommended the use of missiles for air defense but emphasized that under no circumstances could they be equipped with atomic warheads. It also advocated a volunteer army supported by a militia with a short-term service obli-gation, as Beermann had. Unlike Beermann, however, the committee wanted the Bundeswehr to be loosely associated with NATO. In that way the Federal Republic would be in a position to take advantage of whatever opportunities arose to promote reunification, such as the Rapacki or Kennan plans. This concern for the political aspects of the defense question dominated the thinking of the Erler committee.

Ever since the 1957 election defeat Erler had campaigned for a realistic statement on national defense. He realized that the West German voters would never rally to the SPD unless the party developed a West German defense policy of its own, and, therefore, he urged his colleagues to deal decisively with the question at the upcoming party conference. Writing in the Socialist journal *Die Neue Gesellschaft* in January, 1958, Erler said that SPD policy statements had given rise to a great deal of mis-understanding.[63] While the military resolution of the Munich conference looked perfectly clear to all Social Democrats, the public still remained in doubt about the party's position on national defense in a divided Germany. These doubts had to be removed at the Stuttgart party con-ference in May. This was so important, Erler said, that if the unanimous support of the delegates for a new policy statement proved unattainable then majority approval would have to do.

In early March the Parteivorstand accepted the Erler committee report as the basis for discussion in drafting a resolution for the Stuttgart party conference. For this purpose the party leaders organized an editorial committee, composed of Erler, Wienand, and Parteivorstand members Erwin Welke, Willi Birkelbach, and Herbert Wehner. Welke was a party official who reflected the antimilitary sentiments of the SPD bureaucracy. Birkelbach, who had been elected to the party leadership at the Berlin party conference on an antirearmament platform, was a man of the left and an opponent of an active SPD role in military affairs. Wehner, on the other hand, agreed with Erler that the SPD needed a West German defense policy, but he worried about the effect of such a policy on the chances for reunification, as well as its reception by the party.

Plenty of evidence existed to show that the Social Democrats were not yet ready to deal with West German rearmament. On the atomic-weapons question most party members shared the opinion of Gustav Heinemann, a prominent neutralist who had joined the SPD in 1957. Heinemann considered atomic weapons immoral and rejected the notion that the Western world could find security under the existing balance of terror. The party's military experts, on the other hand, considered them a necessary evil—until the powers had reached a general disarmament agreement.[64] As for the Bundeswehr, whose existence the Social Democrats could no longer ignore, most party members viewed it as militarily "superfluous and useless." Except for the Young Socialists and a few parliamentary deputies, the Social Democrats avoided contact with the soldiers. They wanted nothing to do with the Bundeswehr because, as a Social Democrat from Kassel stated, "it's Adenauer's army, not ours."[65] The SPD leaders felt the impact of such remarks, but they also recognized the need to deal more realistically with the military question, as the resolution offered by the Parteivorstand showed.

On May 4 the Parteivorstand voted unanimously to accept the military-policy resolution that its five-man editorial committee had prepared for the Stuttgart conference.[66] The resolution began with an appeal to the nation for help in the struggle against the atomic-arms race. Without a ban on atomic weapons, without a general and controlled disarmament, without the reunification of Germany there could be "no security for our people and no lasting peace in the world." The resolution criticized the government for pursuing a policy which "sharpened international tension and deepened the division of our country." By contrast, the SPD proposed a policy which would secure peaceful relations in Europe, based on "the incorporation of a reunited Germany in a European security system."

Up to this point the resolution contained nothing more than a repetition of old SPD slogans on foreign policy, with the emphasis on security for a reunited Germany. Entirely new was the section on defense in a divided Germany, in which for the first time the Bonn SPD committed itself officially to a military defense of the Federal Republic—though with certain qualifications. According to the resolution, a meaningful West German defense could be established only when the government adopted a policy "directed toward detente and reunification." This meant that the Bundeswehr would receive neither atomic weapons nor guided missiles, which the Parteivorstand feared could too easily be equipped with atomic warheads.[67] It would be an associate member of NATO and be kept as small as possible. The resolution spoke of a small professional army supported by a militia. The Parteivorstand, however, dropped the recommendation of a short-term service obligation for the militia. Without question the party rank and file would be unreceptive to a military-service obligation in whatever form, so the party leaders decided to skirt the issue. They offered instead the ingenious argument that a service obligation was unnecessary because an SPD government would have no trouble finding volunteers for a home defense force.[68] The resolution stated, finally, that any meaningful defense would include the attempt to promote a four-power agreement on the creation of a zone in Central Europe free of all foreign troops and atomic weapons.

The resolution never clearly established what the role of the Bundeswehr would be in Western defense. According to the resolution, the army could serve as a counterbalance to the military forces of the neighboring satellite states, especially East Germany, and could be used to resist local attacks. This, however, contradicted the line of argument advanced by the SPD ever since the conscription debate of 1956 that a limited war would automatically escalate into a total war. The only justification for the defense policy advocated by the SPD leaders was disengagement. If the great powers agreed to withdraw their troops and remove atomic weapons from Central Europe, then West Germany would have to have military forces of its own in the event of aggression by its Communist neighbors. What the West German connection with NATO would be under these circumstances was never made clear.[69] The resolution also rested on the assumption that disengagement would lead in time to reunification and a new political situation in Europe. This hardly corresponded with the views of most West Germans, who remained skeptical about the chances for reunification and even more so about the validity of disengagement. They preferred to see West Germany in NATO rather than on the rim of the alliance, as the SPD advocated.

In spite of the continued lack of clarity, the resolution represented a considerable advance beyond the military-policy position adopted by the SPD at the Munich party conference in 1956. It did, after all, present a positive statement on national defense. If little remained of the Beermann memorandum, the SPD leaders had accepted some of the advice offered by the military experts. Could the leaders now persuade the delegates at the Stuttgart party conference to accept the resolution?

The Stuttgart Party Conference

Most observers assumed that the upcoming SPD conference would deal mainly with party reform. The party had debated the subject intensely, but in May, 1958, when the conference opened, it became clear immediately that Kampf dem Atomtod had become more important. For several months the rank and file had been involved in ban-the-bomb demonstrations, and in preparation for the Stuttgart conference local party organizations had armed their delegates with resolutions calling for a halt to the atomic arms race.

Erich Ollenhauer opened the conference with an hour-long speech.[70] At previous party conferences his address had served as an introduction to the policies proposed by the party leadership on a wide range of issues. This time, however, the SPD leader concentrated almost exclusively on one subject—Kampf dem Atomtod. Given the mood of the party, Ollenhauer could expect a highly receptive audience, but he began by telling the delegates that the question of atomic weapons had not been pushed to the forefront as a means of diverting attention from the difficult problem of party reform, "as our opponents have asserted." Kampf dem Atomtod was "a question of life and death. . . . Every sensible individual must do all in his power to end the madness of the atomic arms race." The delegates applauded loudly. When Ollenhauer announced that the SPD would strive even harder than before to prevent the atomic arming of the Bundeswehr, he received a thunderous ovation. Ollenhauer continued in this vein, promising support for the Kampf dem Atomtod committee and confessing to the conference that it had been a long time since the SPD had "gone into the streets for such a good cause and in such good company." He concluded by calling on the party to play its part as "the defender of the democratic order in the Federal Republic" in order to prevent the government from embarking on "the dangerous path of new militaristic and nationalistic adventures."

Although radical in tone, Ollenhauer's keynote address failed to satisfy some delegates. In the discussion which followed, they criticized him for, among other things, failing to outline a second offensive for the Kampf dem Atomtod campaign. One speaker wanted to know what the leadership proposed to do if the courts declared referenda on the atomic-weapons question to be unconstitutional. Would the Social Democrats go into the streets? In Weimar the workers had defeated the Kapp Putsch with a general strike, and today, because of the threat to mankind, the party would similarly be justified in using the most far-reaching means against the atomic danger. The SPD, another speaker declared, should mobilize the nation now, before it was too late.[71]

At the conclusion of the debate Ollenhauer responded to the criticism from the floor.[72] He appeared sobered by the call for radical action and tried to dispel the notion that the SPD could employ more aggressive tactics in combating the government's atomic-weapons policy. While "it is easy to talk about so-called extraparliamentary actions", he said, "it is very difficult to carry them out." Besides, it would be a mistake to prescribe a specific course of action beforehand because events would determine what could actually be done. What the leaders needed from the conference at this point, Ollenhauer said, was a mandate to act.

The Parteivorstand asked the delegates to vote on a general policy statement which condemned the government for its participation in the atomic-arms race and committed the party to a policy based on earnest negotiations toward disarmament and detente. This meant that at home the SPD would work both inside and outside Parliament, "using all available constitutional means," to prevent the government from carrying out its atomic-weapons policy. The resolution, with a pledge of continued SPD support for Kampf dem Atomtod, won unanimous approval.

Next on the agenda came the military-policy resolution. It was presented to the conference in two major addresses by Erler and Wehner.[73] Neither dealt with the technical details of rearmament or the strategy of Western defense, and little was said about relations with the Bundeswehr; rather, both men focused on the foreign-policy aspects of a defense contribution, specifically, its effect on the problem of German reunification.

Erler spoke to the conference first. After presenting the party's case for a policy based on disarmament and detente, including the promotion of current disengagement schemes, he discussed the question of an SPD defense policy for West Germany. Erler began by reminding the delegates that the SPD would have to accept German membership in NATO because it had been confirmed by the voters in the last election. The party could, however, work for a renegotiation of the Western treaties, to make those changes which were "absolutely essential for the reunification of Germany." But why was a West German defense contribution necessary? Erler responded by referring neither to military necessities nor to moral obligations but to the party's political priorities. According to Erler's equation, there could be no advance toward reunification until the SPD came to power in Bonn, and, by implication, there could be no SPD government until the party officially acknowledged its support for a policy of national defense.

In his address Wehner told the delegates that it had become fashionable to reproach the SPD for either avoiding or confusing the problem of national defense. What the party's critics failed to realize, however, was that defense could "not be an end in itself." In a divided Germany "military security measures have to be brought into line with reunification efforts." Unfortunately, the government with its policy of strength had led the nation down a dead-end street without hope of unity or security. The only way to achieve these goals "is the path which Kennan has shown us." Wehner said that the ideal solution would be disengagement with simultaneous progress toward reunification, but if this was impossible, he would accept a situation which left East and West Germany face to face in a zone cleared of foreign troops and atomic weapons. Wehner devoted most of his address to the question of how the Germans on both sides of the demarcation line could draw closer together and eventually break down the barriers between them. He proposed the establishment of social and economic contacts. This involved certain dangers, including Communist attempts at subversion, but Wehner felt that something had to be done to find new approaches to the reunification problem.

In the discussion which followed, eighteen speakers paraded to the podium to state their views on the military question. As at previous party conferences, opinion on this controversial subject varied, but opposition to a positive statement on national defense had weakened. There were the usual statements in favor of neutrality and pacifism and the expected warnings about the threat of militarism and the danger of being too closely identified with the government's military policy.[74] Most of those who joined in the debate, however, spoke in favor of the resolution, its emphasis on the primacy of reunification, and its rejection of an atomic arming of the Bundeswehr, which was the demand raised most often in the resolutions passed by local party organizations. Only a few speakers referred to the positive aspects of the resolution or mentioned the need to establish close contact with the men in the Bundeswehr.[75] Only one speaker demanded a stronger statement on national defense than the one proposed by the Parteivorstand. Kurt Mattick of Berlin declared that security and unity were possible only in cooperation with the Western powers, which "is surely the opinion of Erler and Wehner."[76]

Before the debate ended, Erler and Wehner returned to the speakers' platform to rebut the arguments of their critics and call upon the delegates to stand behind the party leaders.[77] Surprisingly, they rejected the proffered support from Kurt Mattick, arguing that a closer attachment to NATO would not provide greater security and, more important, would not increase the chances for reunification because the consent of all four powers was needed to restore German unity. On the other hand, Erler and Wehner argued that the conference could accept nothing less than what the resolution contained. It represented a clear alternative to the government's defense policy and a means of attracting those West Germans "who until now have been unwilling to vote SPD."

The resolution passed with only eight negative votes and six abstentions. It represented a remarkable victory for the reformers, especially when one considers the amount of antimilitary sentiment generated by the Kampf dem Atomtod movement, and it can be explained only in part by the compelling political arguments presented by Erler. Equally important, the resolution, though acknowledging SPD support for national defense, maintained the party's opposition course so that the rank-and-file members could continue to concentrate their efforts on opposing the government's military policy, which they did.

The next controversial item on the agenda was the first draft of a new party program. Prepared by a thirty-four-man commission under the chairmanship of Willi Eichler, the program further modified the party's Marxian philosophy and liberalized its economic policy. This had been the line of development going back to the Schumacher era, but the party raised a number of objections.

In resolutions prepared by local party organizations for the Stuttgart conference, and in discussions at the conference itself, leftists and traditionalists warned against what they saw as an attempt to attract middle-class voters to the SPD at the expense of the party's working-class followers. They criticized the program commission for no longer treating nationalization as a central demand of the SPD and, above all, for diluting the party's Marxian base.[78] Eichler responded that the commission had no intention of throwing Marxism overboard. If the party clung dogmatically to every Marxist word and insight, however, it would find itself "in hopeless conflict" with reality. Heinrich Deist, who presented the economic section of the program, pointed out that the program commission agreed with the demand for some form of public ownership, as well as for public control of "the commanding heights" of the economy, to prevent the misuse of economic power by the industrial giants.[79] This hardly satisfied the left or removed the doubts of many traditionalists about the program. Since the Parteivorstand promised to take into consideration the criticisms made at Stuttgart, however, the delegates voted by an overwhelming majority to let the leadership go ahead with the final draft of the new program and present it to a special party conference sometime within the next two years.

The last major piece of business on the agenda was the election of new leaders. For the Social Democrats this was the most important party election since the Dortmund conference. At that time they had to elect a successor to Schumacher; now they had to find someone who could lead them to victory. Although Ollenhauer came under considerable criticism, he still retained the loyalty of most party members. They believed that in his opposition to Adenauer's foreign policy and in his attachment to traditional Socialist views he represented the party. Ollenhauer, however, had led the SPD to defeat twice. Obviously to win the next election the party would need a more attractive political personality. For the moment, though, the SPD had no one else and the delegates reelected him chairman with the tacit understanding that he would not be the party's candidate for chancellor in 1961.[80] More important, they surrounded him with men who would rejuvenate the party.

As his deputies the conference elected Waldemar von Knoeringen and Herbert Wehner. Knoeringen, the leader of the Bavarian party organization, was a reformer and a very popular figure. Neither he nor Ollenhauer, however, could match the dynamic and aggressive personality of Wehner.

The emergence of Wehner raised questions about the course of the SPD. Would it mean a shift to the left? Some observers spoke of a new radicalism in the SPD, and Wehner gave some credence to this view by his use of harsh class slogans and his suggestion of talks with Pankow. Rather than representing a leftward trend, however, his election indicated that the party had finally become aware of the need for decisive leadership. Wehner, of course, could never be the party's candidate for chancellor. Because of his Communist past, Wehner frightened most middle-class Germans, and Adenauer exploited their fears at election time. Yet he could still provide the direction and the drive for the party by operating behind the scenes. As one Social Democrat commented, Wehner could "fill our party with new life" and "at the right time, produce a chancellor candidate with whom we can win."[81]

The Parteivorstand elections clearly reflected this desire to pump new life into the party. Of the twenty-nine selected, fourteen appeared on the committee for the first time. This represented by far the largest turnover since the first postwar election in 1946. At the top of the list stood such national political figures as Arndt, Menzel, Schmid, and Erler, along with Länder leaders Zinn (Hessen), Brauer (Hamburg), and Steinhoff (North Rhine-Westphalia)—all prominent reformers. The election also produced a dramatic shift in party influence from the bureaucrats to the politicians. This the conference confirmed by creating a presidium (Parteipräsidium) from within the Parteivorstand to serve as a kind of general staff directing the daily operations of the party. Significantly, six of the presidium's nine members belonged to the executive committee of the Bundestag Fraktion.[82]

Some have suggested that, other than certain changes in personnel, not a great deal happened at Stuttgart.[83] The Social Democrats made no clear-cut decisions on domestic policy, though the victory of the reformers indicated that the new program would certainly push Marxism further into the background and bring SPD economic policy more into line with the social market economy of the CDU. In dealing with foreign policy and defense, they had with one important exception—their acceptance of the principle of national defense—maintained the established course. Reunification continued to be the party's primary objective, and the military policy of the Adenauer government remained totally unacceptable to the Social Democrats. Although the party had made few decisive policy changes at Stuttgart, however, it had elected men who could and, under the pressure of events, would carry out a reform program. The importance of the Stuttgart party conference in the political development of the SPD, therefore, rests less on what the party achieved there than on the possibilities it established for more fundamental change in the near future.

In the eight months between the general election and the Stuttgart party conference, two major issues occupied the attention of the Social Democrats—party reform and Kampf dem Atomtod. Without question the latter predominated. Although the reform movement regained some momentum at Stuttgart, the atomic-weapons question remained uppermost in the minds of most Social Democrats, and not until the Kampf dem Atomtod campaign had run its course did the reformers begin to test their ideas.

The atomic-weapons issue was a highly emotional one for the Social Democrats, but throughout the period they never lost sight of their main objective—the restoration of German unity. They spoke of a fluid international situation and of the opportunities for promoting reunification, for example, through Russian interest in the Rapacki Plan.[84] They believed, furthermore, that the West Germans still considered reunification the primary goal of German foreign policy. In April, 1958, Erler cautioned foreign observers against misinterpreting the results of the September, 1957 election. "Prosperity and the Hungarian Revolt led the electorate to confirm the Adenauer administration, but by no means did the nation, by its votes, accept partition."[85] Thus the SPD could feel justified in maintaining its opposition course.

To promote the chances for reunification, the Social Democrats called for a renegotiation of West Germany's treaties with the NATO powers. Although the military experts tried to devise a new role for the Bundeswehr in NATO, they never succeeded in creating a relationship with the alliance that would satisfy the party's interest in reunification and the country's concern for security. Most Social Democrats considered NATO to have limited value, both militarily and politically, and recommended that West Germany maintain the loosest possible connection with the Western Alliance.[86]

In contrast to their treatment of West German defense, the Social Democrats spoke with enthusiasm about disengagement. Since the announcement of the Kennan and Rapacki plans, the Social Democrats had been among the most ardent supporters of disengagement. It offered a chance to promote reunification and, with the Rapacki Plan, to limit the atomic arms race in Central Europe. At a rally in Frankfurt to open the Kampf dem Atomtod campaign, Ollenhauer conceded that, although the Rapacki Plan would work no miracles, it could serve as a means of "bridging the gap between East and West, reducing the tension, and bringing the nations together—not in fear, but in hope. It is all so simple, and yet apparently so difficult."[87] The Social Democrats never gave up hope. At Stuttgart they made the creation of an atomic-weapons-free zone an immediate aim of their foreign policy and based their defense policy on the possibility of a four-power agreement on disengagement.

Three weeks after the Stuttgart party conference the Social Democrats became engaged in a hard-fought Bundestag debate. The occasion was the second reading of their request for a national referendum on the atomic-weapons question. Although expecting defeat, the Social Democrats had gone ahead, hoping to keep this sensitive subject before the public. On the other side, the government parties welcomed a Bundestag debate on the bill because they planned to use it as a launching pad for their state election campaign in North Rhine-Westphalia. They called the SPD proposal unconstitutional and extraordinarily dangerous. When Interior Minister Schröder warned the Social Democrats that by promoting the Kampf dem Atomtod campaign they were aiding the Communist cause, the SPD deputies walked out of the Bundestag.[88] The bill died soon thereafter.

After the debate the party directed its efforts at the July 6 election in North Rhine-Westphalia, the largest state in the Federal Republic. Neither the Social Democrats nor the Christian Democrats made any pretense of conducting their campaign on state and local matters. As Carlo Schmid pointed out, this was a Bundestag by-election, and national issues took precedence. The Christian Democrats emphasized the Soviet threat and thus the importance of West Germany's close ties with NATO, while the Social Democrats tried to direct the electorate's attention to the dangers of the atomic-arms race. The basis of the campaign was, as one reporter noted, an appeal to the fears and anxieties of those who stood in the front lines of the Cold War.[89]

An election victory for the SPD in North Rhine-Westphalia would have represented a great triumph for Kampf dem Atomtod, but by July the momentum of the campaign had faded, and so had the public's interest in the atomic-weapons question; in fact, the protests that grew after the atomic debates of January and March, 1958, ebbed very quickly, even more quickly than had the earlier public protests against rearmament and conscription. This became clear in the North Rhine-Westphalian election, where the CDU won over 50 percent of the vote. More important for the SPD's Kampf dem Atomtod campaign, over one-third of the West German voters went to the polls in this state contest, and they "demonstrated that their confidence in Adenauer was greater than their fear of a misuse of atomic weapons."[90]

The North Rhine-Westphalia election made it clear that Adenauer's rearmament program could no longer be used against him. If the SPD wanted to become the government party, therefore, it would have to come to terms with the military and foreign policy which the chancellor had established for West Germany. The Social Democrats, however, refused to abandon their opposition course. They insisted that the CDU had won its majority at the expense of the FDP, not the SPD, which gained more votes in the Rhine-Ruhr area than it had in September, 1957. Furthermore, many in the party believed that the SPD should maintain its Kampf dem Atomtod policy because it was correct and necessary.[91] Speaking to the party leadership one week after the election, Ollenhauer declared that the SPD would continue to warn the nation of the dangers of the atomic-arms race and to use every legal means to combat the government's attempt to arm the Bundeswehr with atomic weapons.[92] The path of legality, of course, led the Social Democrats to Karlsruhe.

On July 30 the Federal Constitutional Court handed down its decision on Adenauer's appeal against state referenda on the atomic weapons question. Not surprisingly, the high court declared in favor of the government.[93] The Social Democrats accepted the verdict with a mild protest and a vow to continue the campaign. In reality the court's decision spelled the end of any major party effort to use Kampf dem Atomtod against the government.

From the beginning the SPD received severe criticism for promoting the Kampf dem Atomtod campaign.[94] The party was accused of threatening the very basis of parliamentary democracy, of using scare tactics, and of resorting to sheer opportunism. The Social Democrats responded that their campaign grew out of a concern to alert the nation. The party's press service pointed out that since 1945 the party had been criticized for failing to do anything of consequence to prevent Adolf Hitler from coming to power. "Today, all Social Democrats are agreed that a similar reproach will not be made again."[95] The Social Democrats, however, disagreed among themselves on what should be done. Whereas Erler, Schmid, and Wehner played a minor role in the campaign and avoided the major rallies and public demonstrations, Menzel, Brauer, and Knoeringen not only played a prominent role in the campaign but also remained active in the Kampf dem Atomtod movement for several more years. For Ollenhauer the campaign represented a commitment to a great cause, and he could abandon it only with difficulty. The leaders, however, had to agree with Erler, Schmid, and Wehner that Kampf dem Atomtod was merely one weapon to use against Adenauer, a weapon which had proved ineffective and, therefore, must be replaced by another.

In January, 1958, Erler had written in a Socialist journal that before there could be an SPD government, and thus an active reunification policy, the West Germans would have to be convinced that the Social Democrats were ready to defend the Federal Republic. "Ostpolitik and defense go together."[96] Four months later, at Stuttgart, the party made a declaration in favor of national defense. The party's press service proudly proclaimed that the SPD had taken "a very clear position on defense and security matters." But already in July, Wehner was complaining that people still questioned the party's commitment to national defense.[97] After its deep involvement in the Kampf dem Atomtod campaign that should have come as no surprise. The campaign had ended, however, and the party rested in the hands of men who could create a new image for the SPD.

CHAPTER 9

The End of Opposition

In late August, 1958, the readers of *Vorwärts* witnessed the opening of another debate by mail on the military question, a debate much like the 1955 exchange over the Stampfer article. What sparked the controversy this time was the appearance of a Bundeswehr recruiting advertisement in the party newspaper. The following week the paper carried letters from three disgruntled Social Democrats who warned about the dangers of serving in an army commanded by reactionaries and militarists. Friedrich Beermann responded in the next edition that a policy of abstinence would benefit neither the party nor the democratic state. A similar, though more emphatic, warning came from the pen of Helmut Schmidt. Despite these warnings the letters published by *Vorwärts* through September and October ran about three to one against the idea of Social Democrats joining the army.[1]

In the midst of the uproar over the recruiting notices, Defense Minister Strauss appealed to the SPD at a press conference to join the government in sponsoring a common defense policy. Strauss conceded that agreement on every issue was unlikely, but the Socialists had to accept three basic aspects of West German policy: (1) the immunization of the army and nation against the threat of Communist infiltration through a process of "psychological defense," (2) the recognition of the citizen's military service obligation, and (3) the creation of an effective air-defense system through the use of "modern weapons," by which Strauss meant atomic weapons.[2]

Responding immediately, Erler charged that Strauss wanted to create the impression of seeking the lowest common denominator for agreement between the government and the opposition on defense questions when in fact he expected the SPD to accept the government's entire program. With reference to Strauss's three basic demands, Erler reemphasized his party's opposition to conscription and atomic arming of the Bundeswehr. The former was unnecessary for West German defense; the latter was undesirable because atomic weapons were means of self-destruction, not self-defense. As for the concept of psychological defense, Erler agreed that something had to be done to counter Communist propaganda, but he suggested that the task of educating the troops should be left to the free forces in society—the political parties, the schools, the churches, the trade unions—not to the state, least of all the Defense Ministry. Helmut Schmidt spoke of the danger of Strauss's converting the Bundeswehr into a "crusade army" which would be used against the Communists abroad and the enemies of the government at home, the Social Democrats.[3]

Since the founding of the Bundeswehr, the Social Democrats had expressed concern about the danger that the new German army would become a CDU army. They had done very little to avert the danger, however, and now the military experts exhorted the party to establish better relations with the armed forces.

The Social Democrats and the Bundeswehr

On October 14, in response to an initiative by Fritz Erler, the Bundestag Fraktion passed a resolution advocating that greater efforts be made to promote contacts between the SPD and the Bundeswehr.[4] Only 14 of the 181 deputies opposed the resolution or abstained, an indication of how broadly based the feeling was in the Fraktion that something had to be done to prevent a repetition of the Weimar situation, in which soldiers and Socialists had stood in opposition to each other. The resolution called on the deputies to meet with military personnel in their electoral districts and asked the Parteivorstand to investigate how party groups could achieve better relations with local Bundeswehr units. In presenting the resolution to the Fraktion, Erler explained that, while the SPD still opposed the government's military policy, the existence of the Bundeswehr could no longer be ignored. At the Stuttgart conference the party had passed a resolution demanding "a relationship of trust between the soldiers and the democratic forces of the nation; now is the time to carry it out."

The resolution also suggested that it would be advantageous, in trying to strengthen relations between the party and the army, for Social Democrats to volunteer for military service. Schmidt had already informed Ollenhauer in July that he intended to become a reserve army officer because SPD participation in the Bundeswehr was now "a political necessity." It would be an impossible situation, he said, if only CDU deputies could tell the Bundestag about their military experiences, while the Social Democrats had to rely on secondhand information. It would, furthermore, have a negative psychological effect on the soldiers if no SPD politicians were in uniform.[5] Schmidt and fellow SPD Deputy Karl Berkhan joined the Bundeswehr reserve in October, shortly before the Fraktion passed the resolution.

In *Vorwärts,* letters to the editor ran more than two to one against the resolution, with correspondents questioning the logic of a policy that called for opposition to the government's military policy and at the same time urged Social Democrats to join Strauss's army.[6] The leadership committees of both the Falcons and the German Socialist Students Union (SDS) criticized the resolution as a violation of past commitments in the struggle against rearmament. A left-wing Social Democrat accused the SPD leaders of capitulating to Strauss and the generals.[7]

Ollenhauer acted promptly to calm his critics. Ten days after the Fraktion meeting he assured the Party Council (Parteirat)—a miniature party conference composed of national and state leaders—that the SPD would maintain its opposition course and its support for the work of the Kampf dem Atomtod committee. As for the idea of Social Democrats joining the Bundeswehr, Ollenhauer explained that the Fraktion did not say that party members should join, but that they could if they wished. Several council members who strongly opposed the resolution pointed out that on the basis of the party statute the Fraktion had no right to act before the Parteirat had discussed the matter. Ollenhauer eventually worked out a compromise whereby the Parteirat, while neither confirming nor rejecting what the deputies had done, would let Erler explain the resolution to the party and the public in a *Vorwärts* article.[8]

Appearing on October 31, Erler's article revealed all the evidence of party compromise. On the one hand, it contained a full restatement of the party's opposition to conscription, atomic weapons, and West German integration into NATO; on the other, it argued convincingly that what the Fraktion had done represented nothing more than an attempt to put into practice the principles enunciated at Stuttgart. This impressed observers outside the party, who applauded Erler's efforts to gain the SPD's acceptance of the new German army,[9] but the article failed to satisfy critics within the SPD.

During the following months criticism of the resolution continued to pour into party headquarters, especially from the leftist party organizations.[10] The SPD leaders, however, failed to take a strong stand. They preferred to leave the task of reeducating the party to the military experts. Erler campaigned at the local level, and, although he always got a hearing, the audiences applauded loudest those local speakers who rejected the resolution.[11] This obviously impressed the leadership because as late as July, 1959, the security committee of the Parteivorstand was still urging the party leaders to recognize the importance of close contact with the Bundeswehr and the value of having Social Democrats in uniform.[12]

Just before the Fraktion drafted the resolution, a reporter had asked Erler about the situation in the Bundeswehr. Erler responded, "Not rosy, but not all that bad either."[13] In spite of the precipitous pace set by the government for its rearmament program, the Bundeswehr had a relatively normal development, and the efforts of Parliament to prevent the revival of the old militaristic forms had succeeded. Erler expressed satisfaction that the Bundestag parties, after much wrangling, had appointed a parliamentary defense commissioner—"the single most important SPD contribution to the concept of civilian control of the Bundeswehr," he said.[14] As for the principles of Innere Führung, they were being applied, though resistance still existed, and some conservative officers emphasized only the military aspects of the training program. Vorwärts reminded its readers that German democrats would have to give the Bundeswehr constant attention; otherwise, the entire reform program could become meaningless.[15]

The party's military experts maintained a constant vigil over the Bundeswehr. But as Erler told a Hannover gathering, the new military legislation would remain just so much paper until men with a democratic spirit gave life and meaning to what the legislators had done. Social Democrats who volunteered for military service, he said, could provide that democratic spirit.[16] Before the Social Democrats would take an interest in the Bundeswehr, however, they would have to accept the primacy of West German defense, and that would be possible only after the SPD had altered its foreign-policy goals. For the Social Democrats reunification was still an immediate and primary goal—as the Berlin crisis demonstrated.

The Berlin Crisis

In November, 1958, Berlin once again became the focal point of a major confrontation between East and West. What provoked the crisis was a Soviet note to the Western powers and West Germany demanding an end to the occupation of Berlin and the conversion of West Berlin into a demilitarized free city. The Russians threatened to sign a separate treaty with East Germany and transfer Soviet rights in Germany to the Pankow regime if the powers failed to reach an agreement within six months. The immediate purpose of the Soviet ultimatum was to isolate West Berlin, a city that greatly embarrassed the East Germans. Ultimately, however, it was to be a means of forcing the West to abandon the idea of four-power responsibility for Germany and to accept the existence of two German states.[17]

The Soviet note culminated almost a year of diplomatic activity by the Kremlin in an attempt to gain Western recognition of the status quo in Europe. Although East and West had exchanged a series of notes, nothing concrete developed. The Russians had accelerated their efforts in September, 1958, when they encouraged the East Germans to initiate a discussion of the German question. In a note to the four powers East Germany had proposed the formation of two commissions: the first, composed of representatives of the four powers, would discuss the drafting of a German peace treaty; the second, composed of delegates from the two German states, would participate in the negotiations and "also concern itself with such questions as are exclusively the affair of the two German states"—reunification. Five days later the West German government, acting on a resolution passed unanimously by the Bundestag, had sent a note to the four powers urging them to establish a four-power group "with a mandate to prepare joint proposals for the solution of the German problem." The powers had responded during the next three weeks, but there seemed little chance that they would get together.[18] The Western powers insisted that the first step would have to be free elections and the formation of an all-German government, which would then negotiate a peace treaty with the four powers. The Russians declined to negotiate on that basis.

The West German government identified with the Western position. At a special Bundestag meeting in Berlin on October 1, coalition speakers stressed the primacy of free elections and argued that there could be no negotiations between Bonn and Pankow because the East German regime had been imposed on the people. Besides, as Johann Gradl of the CDU pointed out, negotiations with Ulbricht would lead nowhere, since the Socialist Unity party leaders feared reunification. Urging patience, Gradl advised the Bundestag to maintain the principle of four-power responsibility for the restoration of German unity.[19]

The Social Democrats had a different view of the situation. Although they agreed that four-power responsibility had to be maintained, they complained that the government offered nothing more than a rigid adherence to a policy that had failed to move Germany one step closer to reunification. They themselves showed little optimism about the chances for healing the division of Germany. With a few exceptions they spoke mainly of opportunities for improving the international climate preparatory to direct talks on the German question. Ollenhauer, for example, commented on the Kremlin's interest in detente and mentioned specifically the upcoming meeting of the three nuclear powers in Geneva to discuss a cessation of test explosions. He spoke with even greater enthusiasm in early November, when Rapacki offered a new version of his plan, one that would include a reduction of conventional forces as well as the removal of atomic weapons from Central Europe.[20] A *Vorwärts* writer called the new plan the most realistic and least objectionable offer ever made to the West by the other side.[21]

As it turned out, the other side had demands as well as offers to make. On November 27, after a threatening speech by Nikita Khrushchev, the Soviet Union formally demanded the transformation of West Berlin into a free city. The Social Democrats promptly rejected the demand, warning that such a step would seal the division of Germany. They insisted, however, that the Soviet note be investigated because it contained certain points that could be used to open discussions on the entire German question, including security relations in Central Europe. They therefore urged the West to negotiate.[22] Yet behind their call for negotiations lay the fear that the Russians would carry out their threat to hand over authority to the East Germans, just as they had carried out earlier threats to block reunification if West Germany joined NATO.

The Social Democrats agreed on the need for negotiations, but differences existed within the party over the procedure for handling the current crisis. The Brandt group in West Berlin disagreed with the leadership's view that the Berlin crisis offered a chance to negotiate; to Brandt, and to the Adenauer government, it represented a threat. As Brandt said later, he feared that the Soviets believed that they could squeeze the Western powers out of Berlin without serious risk.[23] Thus the West needed to assert its rights in Berlin in order to clear up this misunderstanding and then to inform the Soviets that there could be no negotiations on the basis of a Berlin ultimatum. For that matter, there could be no negotiations on Berlin alone. "Without a European solution, there is no solution to the German problem," Brandt said, "and without a German solution, there is no solution to the Berlin problem."[24]

Brandt's concern for the safety of West Berlin stemmed from the city's frontline position in the Cold War and, more immediately, from the demands of an impending election. The West Berliners were to go to the polls on December 7, and Brandt assured them that the Berlin SPD would maintain the closest possible relations with the Western powers. As a precaution he kept Ollenhauer away from the campaign for fear the SPD leader would alienate the voters. Brandt wanted the SPD to adopt the image of a moderate reform party with a safe foreign policy, and to a large extent he succeeded. The SPD won over 50 percent of the vote, while the SED garnered less than 2 percent.[25]

The election victory brought Brandt considerable international acclaim and dramatically increased his standing within the SPD. He was a winner, something the party lacked. He was young and ambitious, a politician rather than a party manager, but a skilled tactician who had learned from experience how to handle his party colleagues as well as the political opposition. In Bonn, where some at headquarters resented his independent stance and his advocacy of policies that sounded too much like those of Adenauer, he extracted a firmer statement from SPD leaders on the Berlin question.[26] Serious differences remained, however, between Brandt and the Bonn leaders. The latter wanted to press ahead with negotiations on the German question, whereas the mayor urged patience and unity with the West in trying to promote reunification.

On December 31, supported by a declaration from the NATO Council, the Western powers answered the Soviet note of November 27.[27] According to their reply, they would neither accept the unilateral repudiation of Soviet obligations with respect to Berlin nor hold talks with the Soviet Union under any threat or ultimatum. They would discuss Berlin, however, on a friendly basis and within the wider context of "negotiations for a solution to the German question as well as that of European security." Ten days later the Soviet Union responded to the Western powers in a considerably milder tone than its November ultimatum. The Russians agreed to accept counterproposals from the West on how to end the occupation regime in Berlin. They refused, however, to discuss reunification, which remained "an internal German problem"; instead, they proposed negotiations on a German peace treaty and they included a draft treaty in their note. The treaty was much harsher than earlier Soviet drafts in terms of what the Germans would have to surrender. Furthermore it could be signed by the two German states pending reunification or, if a German confederation had been created, by "representatives of the confederation and also of both German states."[28] One way or another, therefore, the Soviets would gain recognition of East Germany by the Western powers.

As they had done so many times before, the Social Democrats rejected the contents of the Soviet note but insisted that a chance to negotiate still existed if the West would make new counterproposals. Who knows, said Wehner, perhaps the preliminary discussions of a peace treaty could be the threshold which, once crossed by the four powers, would open the way to a solution of the entire German problem.[29] In private Ollenhauer conceded that the Russians wanted to discuss only the peace treaty, not reunification. He demanded, however, that the West negotiate and, in the process, uphold the principle of four-power responsibility for the solution of the German question. Without negotiations, Ollenhauer warned, the Russians would probably sign a separate treaty with East Germany.[30] The Social Democrats expressed great concern about the six-month deadline Khrushchev had set, and they encouraged the Western powers to use what could be "the last possible chance" to prevent the current status of Germany from becoming permanent.[31]

In trying to promote reunification, the Social Democrats had always appealed to the Western powers while avoiding direct contact with the Soviet Union. In early March, 1959, however, Ollenhauer decided to accept an invitation from the Russians to meet with Khrushchev in East Berlin during the Soviet leader's visit to East Germany. Ollenhauer could explain SPD policy on German reunification and hear Khrushchev's views on the subject firsthand.

The trip, which took place on March 9, proved to be an embarrassment for the party. Khrushchev skillfully exploited the joint communiqué issued by Ollenhauer and him after their hour-long meeting as evidence that the SPD shared the Soviet position on the Berlin crisis. This Ollenhauer denied, adding that he had left the meeting with no illusions about Soviet intentions. Yet when asked by reporters what he had gained from his conversation with Khrushchev, the SPD leader responded that he had seen a readiness on the other side to negotiate. He conceded that the Soviets were primarily concerned at this moment with the question of security and military detente; nevertheless, a new initiative by the West could open up discussions on a whole range of problems, including the German question.[32] The SPD had a new proposal, called the Deutschlandplan, for the West to try.

Ollenhauer with Nikita Khrushchev, March, 1959. Their meeting, in East Berlin, caused Ollenhauer and the SPD considerable embarrassment. Courtesy German Press Agency.

The Deutschlandplan

In late January, 1959, the party leaders commissioned seven SPD Bundestag deputies—Herbert Wehner, Ernst-Wilhelm Meyer, Gustav Heinemann, Ernst Paul, Fritz Erler, Helmut Schmidt, and Kurt Mattick—to draft a foreign-policy statement on the related questions of disengagement and reunification. Under Wehner's guiding hand the committee completed its work within a month and passed the so-called Deutschlandplan on to the leadership for approval. On March 3 the Parteivorstand and the executive committee of the Bundestag Fraktion unanimously approved the plan. Two weeks later Ollenhauer presented it to the public at a press conference in Bonn.[33]

The Deutschlandplan was an elaborate scheme for promoting reunification, first, through disengagement, which would create "more favorable conditions" for the solution of outstanding political problems, and, second through "a gradual, step-by-step rapprochement" of the two German states. The authors of the plan denied that this would make reunification a German affair, as the Russians were demanding; rather, deliberations between East and West Germany would be conducted "within the framework of a four-power settlement on European security and the German question."

To begin negotiations the Social Democrats called for the creation of a four-power commission to work out proposals for a European security system and to draft a German peace treaty in consultation with representatives of the two German states. The first task facing the commission would be to establish a "zone of relaxed tension," composed of East and West Germany, Poland, Czechoslovakia, and Hungary. All foreign troops would be withdrawn, and strength limitations set for national forces within the designated zone. These forces would have no atomic weapons, of course. After the military thinning-out of the area had been achieved, "in definite stages of time and space" and with adequate air and ground controls, all interested states—including the United States and the Soviet Union—would guarantee the inviolability of the zone by a collective security agreement. This agreement would also allow the states in the zone to withdraw from either NATO or the Warsaw pact and to make a suitable contribution to European security within the framework of a European security system.

As for the German question, the plan called for reunification to be carried out in four stages. In the first stage the two German governments would send envoys on the basis of equal representation to an all-German conference, which would be charged with negotiating a settlement on internal German affairs. In the second stage an equal number of representatives would be elected in both parts of Germany and sent to an all-German parliamentary council, which would be authorized to handle legislation concerned with the communications network, the transportation system, and the economy. In the third stage the all-German parliamentary council would prepare further legislation on fiscal matters (taxation, currency, and tariffs) and social policies, as well as approve a law for electing a national assembly to draft an all-German constitution; it was assumed that by this stage basic human rights would be respected in both parts of Germany under a guarantee from the four powers. In the final stage, once the constitution had come into force, free elections would be held for an all-German parliament, which in turn would choose an all-German government.

In presenting the Deutschlandplan to the press on March 18, Ollenhauer claimed that the SPD had made a sober evaluation of the facts. The government parties, however, saw the plan as exceedingly dangerous.[34] To begin with, it failed to establish any direct connection between disengagement and reunification whereby a step-by-step withdrawal of foreign troops from Central Europe would be synchronized with a step-by-step restoration of German unity. Moreover, the plan made no provision for automatic progress from one stage to the next in the reunification process. As a result, the final decision on restoring German unity would be in Ulbricht's hands.

Some coalition deputies warned of a sinister design in the SPD plan, a readiness by the Social Democrats to make a deal with the Communists for a Socialist reconstruction of Germany. This, they claimed, was Wehner's goal.[35] The deputy leader of the SPD gave them reason for concern by leading the charge against "the profiteers of Germany's division." No one expected Adenauer and Ulbricht to strive for reunification, he said. The workers must lead the way. Wehner called on them to support social democracy as a third force operating between the rival forces of capitalism and communism. The SPD would build a social-democratic Germany, one that would be "neither a Communist dictatorship nor a state controlled by the Grossbesitz (big property owners)"[36] Naturally, Wehner's rhetoric increased public apprehension of the plan, and coalition deputies cleverly played on these fears by labeling the Deutschlandplan the "Wehner Plan." Later, when the SED gave its approval to the SPD proposal, critics reminded the West Germans of Wehner's Communist past.[37]

To those less critical of the SPD, the Deutschlandplan could hardly be called a dangerous plot. Some saw it as merely a reflection of the party's continued naïveté in foreign-policy matters; most simply expressed astonishment that the Social Democrats would publish the plan after Ollenhauer's encounter with Khrushchev and, even more, after Erler and Schmid returned from a Kremlin visit with a highly pessimistic report of Soviet intentions.[38]

On March 11, Erler and Schmid flew to Moscow to discuss the German question with Soviet leaders. They returned six days later sobered by the experience. At a press conference in Bonn the two Social Democrats discussed their impressions of the trip and in particular their conversation of nearly three hours with Khrushchev.[39] They reported that the Soviets wanted to sign a peace treaty with the Western powers and the two German states in order to gain de jure recognition of a divided Germany. If the West refused, the USSR would conclude a separate treaty with East Germany. Erler and Schmid believed, however, that Khrushchev wanted to negotiate, and they emphasized to reporters that the Soviet leader had assured them that the USSR would do nothing to Berlin while negotiations were in progress. Yet Khrushchev offered them nothing. He clung to his free-city plan for Berlin, and he flatly rejected their proposal that a peace treaty contain stipulations for a step-by-step restoration of German unity in line with a step-by-step withdrawal of foreign troops from Central Europe. The Soviet leader expressed strong interest in disengagement, however, adding that as long as there was no outside interference the Soviets would stand aside if the East Germans chose a different form of government once the Red Army had left. The two Social Democrats viewed this as a hopeful sign, though Erler conceded that Khrushchev himself would decide whether there had been interference. On the subject of free elections Khrushchev told Erler and Schmid that, with fifty million people in the Federal Republic and only seventeen million in the German Democratic Republic, "the majority would win, not the truth." He added that no one really wanted reunification anyway, "not even in the West."

In spite of the depressing report that Erler and Schmid brought back from Moscow, the Social Democrats went ahead and published the Deutschlandplan. The decision is difficult to explain. Broadly speaking, it stemmed from their commitment to reunification as the primary task of German policy and their sense of frustration in trying to convince the Adenauer government of the need for a new approach to the German question. It was also a response to what the Social Democrats hoped would be a change in the attitude of the Western powers toward a European settlement. Before releasing the plan, the leadership sent party representatives to various Western capitals, and they returned with the impression that at least London and Washington favored a more flexible approach to four-power negotiations.[40] Ultimately, however, publication of the Deutschlandplan could be described as an act of desperation in the face of Khrushchev's Berlin ultimatum.

More than ever before, the Social Democrats saw this as the last chance to promote reunification. It was a very slim chance, but they refused to give up hope. According to Wehner, Western diplomats now faced the task of making proposals which the other side would have to discuss. After all, the Russians wanted to negotiate and had asked again and again for concrete proposals from the West. On his return from Moscow, Carlo Schmid warned the Western powers to act quickly because the international situation would only get worse.[41]

In such a threatening situation the Social Democrats submitted the Deutschlandplan to establish a basis for negotiations. They insisted that the plan constituted neither a change in their German policy nor a weakening of their attitude toward the East, though clearly they had made extensive concessions to the Russians for the sake of reunification. Previously SPD leaders had demanded a strict timetable for the stages of reunification, as well as a binding connection between military and political measures,[42] but they dropped these demands after talking to Khrushchev. They had also rejected the idea of negotiations between the two German states. Now the leadership agreed to political talks with the people Schumacher had once called the "Pankow marionettes."[43] According to the SPD leaders, these concessions had to be made; otherwise, the Communists would have refused to discuss the German question. The important thing was to get negotiations started.

The Social Democrats pointed out that, because of Russian interest in the subject, disengagement could provide a starting point. Besides, disengagement offered the West a number of advantages. Militarily, it would provide greater security because the Red Army would move back inside the Soviet frontier. Politically, it would reduce international tension and thus improve the climate for a settlement. More immediately, disengagement would produce a new political situation in East Germany. With Soviet troops on German soil, political change would be "as good as impossible," Wehner explained. Once they had left, however, certain changes would be unavoidable.[44] Ulbricht would suddenly find himself under strong pressure to liberalize the regime and work for closer ties with West Germany. Here was a chance, "the only chance," to alter the situation in Germany and open the path to reunification.[45]

The Social Democrats claimed that there was nothing to fear in standing alone in Germany face to face with Ulbricht. In an open competition between the forces of democracy and communism, the democrats would win.[46] The coalition parties found it hard to believe that Ulbricht would ever surrender his position of power voluntarily. More likely, he would attempt a coup, as had been done in Prague, to place all of Germany under Communist rule. Baron zu Guttenberg, a member of the CSU and a severe critic of the SPD, questioned the readiness of the Social Democrats to defend German democracy. Based on the performance of the SPD in Weimar and of other Social Democratic parties in Eastern Europe after the war, he found no reason to believe that they could stand up to the Communist challenge. Guttenberg doubted, moreover, that Khrushchev would remain a spectator of these events in Germany and elsewhere. He would certainly intervene to prevent the emergence of anti-Communist regimes in Eastern Europe, and upon the removal of American troops from the Continent—which the government claimed would inevitably follow an American withdrawal from Germany—the Kremlin leaders would be tempted to conquer Western Europe.[47]

The Social Democrats rejected such criticism coming from a party that, as Ollenhauer put it, "did not have a reunification plan of its own." In their eyes the plan contained the necessary safeguards against a Communist coup or a Soviet military threat. Wehner said he failed to see why NATO, even after American troops had been withdrawn from Germany, could not continue to protect the Germans until a European security system came into existence. As for the problem of relocating NATO forces in France, Wehner commented that, if one accepted the French view that "American soldiers are beautiful as long as they are on German soil," then progress would probably be impossible.[48] This the Social Democrats refused to admit because they based their Deutschlandplan on the assumption that both East and West possessed "the will to achieve reunification."[49] That will, as Khrushchev had warned them, did not exist.

From Geneva to Camp David

After a further exchange of notes the four powers agreed to hold a foreign ministers' conference in Geneva. The conference opened on May 11 and lasted, with one interruption, until August 5.[50] In spite of its length, however, the conference achieved nothing more than a postponement of the threatening confrontation over Berlin. It made no progress in dealing with the German question because neither side proved willing to make any fundamental concessions in order to open the way to a four-power agreement.

Although disappointed, the Social Democrats were less critical than usual. They conceded that the Western powers had shown themselves more flexible in negotiations than ever before—for example, by submitting a four-stage plan for reunification—but claimed that the West had also raised "insurmountable obstacles" to a four-power agreement. To overcome those obstacles the SPD recommended its Deutschland-plan, the only proposal offering "a chance for success at Geneva."[51]

Although the party leadership held firmly to this view, some Social Democrats had doubts about the feasibility of the plan. Mayor Willy Brandt viewed it skeptically and expressed concern about a growing tendency among Social Democrats toward wishful thinking in dealing with the Communists, a luxury the Berlin party could scarcely afford.[52]

Brandt's skepticism about the plan provoked a sharp encounter with the left wing of the Berlin SPD. The left called him "a cold warrior" in the style of Chancellor Adenauer and demanded that he follow the party line by supporting the Deutschlandplan.[53] At the Berlin party's annual conference in May, Brandt conceded that it could be useful as a basis of discussion, but he refused to endorse the plan. Later he claimed that his differences with the Bonn leaders over the plan consisted of nuances rather than sharply contrasting points of view. Brandt had no intention of provoking the Parteivorstand as Ernst Reuter had done. He preferred to let the plan die on its own, as it certainly would.[54]

Less tactful in expressing his differences with the leadership was Karl Mommer, the talented but temperamental whip of the SPD Bundestag Fraktion. Like many other party reformers, Mommer worried about the SPD's image; in particular, he feared that the party, which under Schumacher had drawn a very firm line between itself and the SED, now gave the impression of being soft on communism. As an example Mommer pointed to the Deutschlandplan. He considered the plan badly conceived, and in April, when the authors of the plan published a forty-seven-page commentary to clarify the party's position, Mommer responded with a number of amendments. Among other things he proposed the synchronization of military and political measures and the establishment of free elections as part of the second rather than the fourth and final step of the plan. Although as many as one-third of the SPD deputies criticized similar aspects of the plan, the Fraktion accepted the commentary with only one abstention—Mommer.[55] One month later Mommer and the leadership clashed again. This time the incident involved Mommer's criticism of a group of SPD journalists and his warnings about trends within the German Socialist Students Union (SDS).

The SDS was an independent organization operating at the university level in affiliation with the SPD. Although not large—under two thousand members—it attracted considerable attention because of its increasingly radical views on ideological matters and above all on such major issues as reunification and rearmament. In January, 1959, in West Berlin, an SDS-sponsored students' congress passed a resolution calling for direct

Karl Mommer caused an uproar in the party because of his criticism of the Deutschlandplan in 1959. Bundestag Archives.

negotiations with Pankow in order to sketch out a peace treaty and examine the possible form of an interim confederation. Four months later, led by student radicals from Hamburg and Hessen, the SDS organized a conference in Frankfurt carrying the banner: "For Democracy—Against the Restoration and Militarism." What caught the public's attention— and Mommer's—was a resolution demanding negotiations between East and West Germany, as well as a ban on atomic weapons in the Federal

Republic, the abolition of conscription, the purging of the old officer corps from the Bundeswehr, and a reduction in the current armaments level in West Germany. The resolution clearly reflected the views of most of those in attendance: when one student suggested the inclusion of a statement condemning militarism in East Germany, he received "little applause and much laughter." Even Wolfgang Abendroth, an orthodox Marxist from Marburg, failed to persuade the conference to bring its views of reunification into line with the party's Deutschland-plan, specifically, to call for negotiations between Bonn and Pankow only within the framework of a four-power agreement.[56]

Speaking in Bonn several days after the conference, Mommer warned that the Communists had obviously infiltrated the SDS, and he advised those Socialist students "who did not want to be used as a Trojan ass for Pankow" to leave the SDS. He also recommended that the Parteivorstand take action against the student group.[57] The leaders needed little coaxing. They demanded that the SDS disavow the Frank-furt resolution or face a severance of all connections with the SPD. Although the SDS drafted a more acceptable policy statement, the tie between the student group and the SPD remained fragile. It broke less than a year later.[58]

While sounding the alarm on the SDS, Mommer also upbraided nine SPD journalists who during a visit to the Soviet Union had used the term "Genosse" (comrade) in addressing Khrushchev. It sounded as though they were all fellow Socialists, he said. Furthermore, they had failed to defend Brandt when Khrushchev called the mayor a provocateur who, in his defense of Western interests, had become "more Catholic than the Pope." By their behavior, Mommer said, they had identified the SPD with the Soviet point of view.[59]

Mommer found strong support of his criticism among members of the Bundestag Fraktion. At a meeting of the parliamentary party on June 2 the deputies sided with Mommer in expressing concern about the party's image. They agreed that the Deutschlandplan represented a major source of confusion for the public about the SPD's attitude toward communism,[60] but since they had nothing to offer in its place, they went along with the leadership knowing that the party supported the plan. Most Social Democrats saw the Deutschlandplan as a necessary measure in the struggle for reunification and agreed with the leaders that under the circumstances it represented the only way to bring the two Germanys together. As the summer passed, they became more convinced that the party had judged correctly.

In early August, President Eisenhower announced that Khrushchev had accepted an invitation to visit the United States the following month. The Social Democrats viewed this as a new and more hopeful phase in the negotiations; in fact, before the end of August they were talking of "a new dynamism" in the world situation. Deputy leader Waldemar von Knoeringen reported that the rigid fronts which had been so in evidence at Geneva had apparently been broken by the Soviet Union's decision to adopt more flexible tactics in dealing with the West and by the United States' readiness to meet the challenge of personal diplomacy.[61]

With these new opportunities for promoting detente, the Social Democrats offered many suggestions on how it could be achieved. On August 21 a spokesman for the Parteivorstand described to the press a four-point program that Adenauer could present to President Eisenhower.[62] First, the West German government should renounce the idea of acquiring atomic weapons for the Bundeswehr. The Social Democrats continued to accuse Defense Minister Strauss of trying to make West Germany "the dominant military power on the Continent" by obtaining atomic weapons from the Americans and, when that failed, by offering German financial and technical assistance to the French in their A-bomb testing.[63] Second, since the four powers were unable to deal with reunification, negotiations should start with the formation of an all-German committee on the basis proposed in the SPD's Deutschlandplan. As Carlo Schmid explained, "If one cannot move along the international path, then one ought to try the national route."[64] Third, the government should abandon its policy of nonrecognition of the East European states. Without friendly relations with the East there could be no detente, and without detente there could be no progress toward reunification. Karl Mommer, who had visited Poland in late August, said that the Poles sincerely wanted detente—as demonstrated by their initiation of the Rapacki Plan—but they still feared a revanchist Germany.[65] Finally, steps should be taken to improve West German-Soviet relations. Ernst-Wilhelm Meyer, co-author of the Deutschlandplan, recommended that in foreign policy the Germans think less in ideological terms. They could pursue friendly relations with the Russians even while fighting communism at home. Quoting American diplomat Charles Bohlen, Meyer described the Soviet Union as a power whose expansionist drive had been satiated and whose goals were now basically defensive. He suggested, therefore, a nonintervention treaty between Bonn and Moscow as a means of promoting goodwill.[66]

The Social Democrats realized that, while closer West German-Soviet ties could help improve the international climate, only in better American-Soviet relations could a solution to the German question be found. For that reason they followed Khrushchev's visit to the United States with great interest. Ollenhauer conceded that the powers still had a long way to go in removing their differences.[67] At Camp David, Khrushchev and Eisenhower merely restated their positions so that it would be a matter of determining in the upcoming series of meetings what possibilities existed for promoting reunification. Ollenhauer believed, however, that the powers were about to enter a long period of negotiations, and he wanted the Germans to be ready with their own set of proposals.

Throughout the Geneva foreign ministers' conference the Social Democrats had charged that the West German government was doing everything possible to block progress in the direction recommended by the SPD. After the Camp David meeting, when the American and Soviet leaders agreed to meet again soon, the Social Democrats accused Adenauer of trying to prevent further high-level talks. The ice was melting, *Vorwärts* reported, but Bonn remained frozen in a cold-war position.[68]

The Social Democrats had solid grounds for making their accusations. Adenauer very much wanted to avoid an early summit meeting. He feared that negotiations now would lead to Western concessions because the British and American governments were ready to work for an interim agreement on the Berlin question to lessen tension in Central Europe. According to Adenauer, that would lead to a total collapse of the Western position. As a result, when French President Charles de Gaulle expressed his opposition to an early summit meeting and to an isolated Berlin settlement, Adenauer believed that he had found an ally. Of course, de Gaulle's intervention at this point stemmed not from a concern for German reunification but from a desire to assert French rights as a great power. Nonetheless, Adenauer looked to Paris for help in preventing what he feared might be an agreement between East and West at German expense.[69] As a further precaution Adenauer suggested in a late-October CDU meeting in Baden-Baden that a summit conference should concentrate on general disarmament and avoid the German problem and Berlin for the time being. Since Khrushchev had initiated the call for general disarmament at a UN meeting in September, this would be a way to test the Soviet leader's good faith without the West having to make dangerous concessions.[70] It was in the aftermath of Adenauer's Baden-Baden pronouncement that the Bundestag held a full-scale foreign-policy debate—its first in nineteen months.

The debate was a disappointing affair. Both the government and the opposition adopted defensive positions—the former trying to prove that its foreign policy had not failed even though Germany remained divided, the latter trying to justify its Deutschlandplan in the face of heavy criticism. They agreed, however, that detente would eventually lead to reunification and that disarmament would promote detente. Here agreement ended. The Christian Democrats called for general disarmament while the Social Democrats insisted, as they had in earlier debates, that it would have to begin with a regional agreement. When the debate concluded, government and opposition were as far apart as ever.

The only high point in the debate for the Social Democrats was the address by Helmut Schmidt. He embarked on a clear, comprehensive discussion of disengagement that immediately caught the attention of coalition deputies. Even Adenauer listened attentively to the young deputy.[71] Schmidt argued that to be acceptable a disengagement scheme had to maintain the existing military balance between East and West. After surveying the power position of the five states included in the zone and taking into account the nuclear capability of the superpowers,

Helmut Schmidt during the November, 1959, foreign-policy debate.
Courtesy Friedrich Ebert Stiftung.

Schmidt concluded that "an equilibrium of the total tactical and stra-
tegical situation" could be maintained both now and later. As for Adenauer's major concern that disengagement would lead to West German
withdrawal from NATO and the collapse of the alliance, Schmidt responded that the SPD had no intention of taking *West* Germany out of
the alliance. Furthermore, other countries—Denmark and Norway, for
example—had already secured a special position for themselves without
hurting NATO's effectiveness as a defense system. What Schmidt ig-

nored, however, was the emerging French problem. Advocates of disengagement had assumed that NATO troops stationed in West Germany could be transferred across the border to France; but France, under de Gaulle, would have none of it—as the Social Democrats well knew.

Four months before Schmidt's Bundestag address, *Vorwärts* carried a major story entitled, "Increased Danger for the Federal Republic."[72] Two hundred planes and six thousand members of the United States Air Force had been moved from France to West Germany because de Gaulle objected to having them on French soil. The author of the article questioned, therefore, the current value of NATO as an instrument for the common defense of the West and suggested that the Germans "consider what consequences French action might have for the Federal Republic." If de Gaulle could ignore France's treaty obligations to chase dreams of national glory, then the Germans had every right to pursue their interests—that is, to promote disengagement in order to open the way to reunification. Disengagement was what Schmidt proposed and what the Social Democrats enshrined in their new party program.

Bad Godesberg

From November 13 to 15 the SPD met at Bad Godesberg for the purpose of establishing a new party program to replace the one adopted thirty-four years earlier at Heidelberg. The demand for a restatement of party principles had been heard ever since the SPD had reorganized in 1945, but for one reason or another Schumacher had always postponed a discussion. He would agree to nothing more than an Aktionsprogramm, a formal declaration of party policy. After the SPD's defeat in the 1953 election, the cry for a new program became louder. Both reformers and traditionalists felt a need for such a program; the former wanted to reshape the party's image in the light of recent social and economic developments, the latter to provide a Marxian analysis of the contemporary scene. At the Berlin party conference the leaders agreed to organize a program commission and later appointed Willi Eichler to serve as chairman. The sense of urgency had by then diminished, and the commission worked at a leisurely pace. Three years later, at the Stuttgart party conference, Eichler revealed the first draft of a new program. Under the impact of the SPD's crushing defeat in the recent election, however, and in anticipation of the next general election, early in 1959 the leaders decided to have the party adopt the new program at a special conference in November. The program commission worked quickly, reducing the original draft from sixty-four pages to eighteen and reshaping it as the reformers wanted.[73]

At Bad Godesberg the Social Democrats bade farewell to Karl Marx. The program, which the Parteivorstand approved and the conference accepted with only minor revisions, mentioned neither Marx nor Marxism and made no attempt to provide a comprehensive analysis of current conditions. The program also discarded the notion of socialism as a final goal—the classless society emerging from the ashes of a burned-out capitalist society—instead, it defined socialism as a "continuing task" to create and preserve a democratic society for all. The SPD became thereby "a party of the people" (Volkspartei), ready to act as a broker for diverse interests rather than to represent only the workers.[74]

In the economic-policy section the Social Democrats adopted the essentials of Erhard's social market economy. To begin with, they no longer advocated the transference of the means of production to common ownership, and the words "nationalization" and "socialization" appeared nowhere in the program. The Social Democrats promised to protect "private ownership of the means of production . . . insofar as it does not hinder the building of a just social order." The party also abandoned the idea of central planning, because "totalitarian control of the economy destroys freedom." It advocated instead a free-market economy with public controls as a last resort. The formula read: "As much competition as possible—as much planning as necessary."

The military policy section began with a simple declaration. The SPD "advocates the defense of the free democratic order. It affirms the defense of the country." This some critics found insufficient because it made no reference to the Federal Republic. Others suggested that the second sentence be deleted because defense of the country and defense of the free democratic order were not necessarily the same. Walter Möller, a Frankfurt delegate, gave the example of Hitler's Germany or Ulbricht's Germany—and, some felt, even Adenauer's Germany.[75]

Werner Stein, a Berlin delegate and a leftist opponent of Brandt, pointed to a lack of clarity in the military-policy section. For example, he said, the idea that "defense must be adapted to the political and geographical position of Germany" was truism, but what did it mean?[76] To clarify matters the editorial committee agreed to add that a defense program would have to observe the limitations necessary "to create the conditions for an international detente, and effectively controlled disarmament, and the reunification of Germany."

The section also referred to the need for maintaining civilian control of the military, assuring confidence between the soldiers and the democratic forces in the nation and preserving the civic rights and duties of the citizen in uniform. The Social Democrats stressed, as they had since the rearmament debate began, that the armed forces could be employed only for military purposes. In addition, the program contained a statement affirming the right of every citizen to refuse, for reasons of conscience, to take up arms or to use "means of mass destruction." This latter point had been added at Bad Godesberg in response to the party's insistence on action against the atomic danger.

In the draft presented by the Parteivorstand the only reference to atomic weapons was the general demand that they "should be neither produced nor used." Many delegates considered this inadequate, and a motion demanding that atomic weapons be removed from West Germany received considerable support from the floor.[77] This greatly alarmed the party leaders because, as Erler explained, it amounted to a demand for the withdrawal of American forces from West Germany without any counterconcessions by the Soviets. He recommended, therefore, that the draft be amended to include a general demand for a worldwide ban on atomic weapons and a more specific demand relating to Germany which would state (1) that the Federal Republic could not use or produce weapons of mass destruction and (2) that the removal of atomic weapons from German soil would not be a unilateral act but would result from the creation of a Central European arms-control area in which these weapons could not be produced, stationed, or used.[78] The conference accepted this compromise proposal.

A further point of dispute was whether the program should mention the party's opposition to conscription. Several delegates, supported by motions from local party groups, spoke in favor of an anticonscription amendment, but Wehner rejected the idea, pointing out that the SPD had already rejected conscription at the Stuttgart party conference and that "nothing in our Stuttgart resolution will change so long as we live under the horrible burden of a partitioned Germany."[79] This caused one of the anticonscription advocates to respond that if the program was designed for the SPD in West Germany, as Ollenhauer had already underlined in his keynote address, and the SPD was opposed to conscription in West Germany, then it should say so in the program. Erler, who desperately wanted to avoid any reference to it in the program, answered that with conscription "we are not dealing with a universally binding principle of Socialist thinking." He urged the party to keep its options open.[80] The implication was obvious: the SPD could be faced with a situation in which it would have to accept conscription in West Germany. Even then the delegates proved willing to accept the leadership's position, and only 52 of the 354 delegates voted in favor of an anticonscription amendment.

In general, antimilitary sentiment never reached the level of previous SPD conferences. The antirearmers offered their usual warnings about the danger of militarism in the Federal Republic, the threatening nature of the government's military policy, and the advisability of doing away with the Bundeswehr for the sake of democracy in Germany and peace in Europe. Not surprisingly, the Frankfurt group took the lead in rejecting the idea that the SPD should support national defense. Wehner, however, warned the conference against taking a position that would place the SPD in opposition to the men in uniform or that would give the government something to use against the party. Furthermore, he said, it would make little sense to approach the nation saying, "If you elect us, we can do much for you with reference to the legal order, school questions, home construction, and the regulation of social matters, but on one question—

national defense—you must stick with the others." Erler placed an even greater emphasis on this point. He reminded the delegates that as a political party they were fighting for political power. They were fighting, first, for the chance to reshape the Federal Republic, "not some state in the distant future." The Social Democrats could realize many of their goals without waiting for reunification. To become the government party in Bonn, however, the SPD would have to win the confidence of the nation, and that would "require us to show we are able to handle even the problem of national defense so that the people could without fear place their fate in our hands."[81]

On the final day of the conference the delegates gathered to vote on the slightly amended program presented by the Parteivorstand. Voting section by section, they cast only twenty-three ballots against the statement on national defense and forty-two against the economic policy section. The program as a whole received the approval of all but 16 of the 354 delegates.

Although the program passed with relative ease at Bad Godesberg, observers wondered how the local party organizations would respond. One young leftist at the conference told a reporter that he thought "all hell would break loose."[82] That never happened. The leadership had laid the foundation at Stuttgart, where the decisive step toward reform had been taken, and the party now accepted the new program with little opposition—but with little enthusiasm either. Most Social Democrats agreed with the leadership that the party had to get in step with the times to become a more effective political force.[83] Among delegates of the older generation there were skeptics who questioned the need to abandon long-established party traditions to make the SPD more attractive to the voters. More open opposition appeared among a group of young radicals drawn mainly from the ranks of the Falcons, the SDS, and the Jusos. They considered the program an act of capitulation to "the Bonn ideology" and more specifically to the military policy of Franz-Josef Strauss. To one leftist critic it was "electoral opportunism" of the worse kind.[84] For the moment, however, neither the radicals nor the skeptics represented a threat to the party leaders.

The man mainly responsible for the passage and subsequent adoption of the Bad Godesberg program was Herbert Wehner. More than Ollenhauer or Erler, he commanded the attention of the party. At Bad Godesberg he intervened decisively in crucial debates by, for example, arguing the need for greater realism in dealing with the defense question or by referring to his own experience with an exclusive ideology to counter the arguments of the Marxists. Naturally his attempt to play the role of a party moderate surprised many inside and outside the SPD; however, once Wehner had convinced himself—probably late in the summer of 1959—that the Stuttgart draft would need further revision to produce the desired results, he shifted his considerable energies to a more drastic restatement of party principles. The goal was political power, without which the SPD could not create a Social Democratic society;[85] and the moment was now, so that the party would have plenty of time to prepare for the next election.

The Bad Godesberg program served as the first step toward making the SPD more politically competitive, but before the party could win greater electoral support, it had to present policies that would correspond to the needs of West Germans and find a candidate for chancellor who could rival Adenauer. Four months before the SPD met at Bad Godesberg, Ollenhauer announced that he had decided not to run as the party's candidate in 1961. Everyone agreed that the party would benefit from his decision; even with a new program Ollenhauer was no match for Adenauer.[86] After Ollenhauer's resignation the leadership organized a seven-man commission to begin the search for a new candidate for chancellor. The most likely choice was Carlo Schmid, a man with statesmanlike qualities who had represented the SPD in the recent presidential election. On the horizon, however, was a more popular political figure: Berlin's Mayor Willy Brandt. As for the political platform of the party's new candidate, the Bad Godesberg program left some questions unanswered; the most pressing continued to be the party's attitude toward NATO.

Death of the Deutschlandplan

In December, 1959, *Vorwärts* ran several articles on the "death of NATO." The author of the articles accepted NATO's demise philosophically. NATO was a purely military alliance with no common purpose, and it died because the member states preferred to pursue their own national interests. Remembering earlier episodes that had strained the bonds of the alliance—the Anglo-French involvement in Suez in 1956 and the American intervention in Lebanon in 1958—the author now saw de Gaulle's attempts to make France less dependent on NATO as the last blow to the alliance.[87] Even Erler, who saw the importance of NATO, spoke of fateful changes in the structure of the alliance. He mentioned the possibility of the United States considerably reducing its forces in Europe in response to financial stringencies and recent advances in military technology. What concerned him was less the threat that Europe would have to bear a greater share of the defense burden—because he still trusted in the deterrent effect of American nuclear power—than the fear that "the Americans would withdraw, while the Soviets stayed where they were." He urged the government, therefore, to emphasize in Washington the need to seek counterconcessions from the Soviet Union before removing American forces from Germany. The line of negotiation could be toward a mutual withdrawal of foreign troops and the creation of a zone of detente in Central Europe.[88]

During the following months the Social Democrats continued to advocate disengagement as a realistic contribution to detente, but the government still showed no interest in the idea. In a New Year's message Ollenhauer warned that the great powers might strike a bargain without the Germans and on the basis of the continued division of Germany unless the government took the initiative. He reminded his listeners of the SPD's efforts to get negotiations started through the Deutschlandplan and of the reception the plan had received in Bonn. "Criticism is cheap, but where are the government's ideas and proposals?" There were none, because the chancellor was committed to a defense of the status quo. Speaking in Nuremberg a couple of weeks later, Ollenhauer told an audience that "whoever insists on the current defense policy accepts the division of Germany."[89]

The party's criticism of the government mounted as Adenauer drew closer to de Gaulle, a resolute foe of German reunification, and reached a high point in February, 1960, when the SPD discovered that Defense Minister Strauss had discussed with the Spanish government the possibility of obtaining supply bases and training sites for the Bundeswehr in Spain. To Helmut Schmidt the attempt to make West German defense policy dependent on a connection with Spain was "not only politically and morally intolerable, but also militarily senseless." West Germany could never be supplied in wartime from bases 1,500 to 2,000 kilometers away, he said. It would, furthermore, hardly benefit NATO's credibility in the worldwide struggle against communism if the alliance, dedicated to the defense of freedom and democracy, joined forces with a Fascist power—"a vestige of the Hitler era."[90] The party's press service described Madrid as a place where Bonn's authoritarian element could go to gain "courage and inspiration." Ever since the founding of the Federal Republic, the SPD had been warning about the reemergence of antidemocratic forces in West Germany, and as a measure of its concern *Vorwärts* devoted seven pages of its Christmas, 1959, issue to the restoration in business, law, education, the army, and government. Erler gave as an example Parliament, where, instead of expressing the will of the people, the majority obediently followed the commands of a government which rested in the hands of one man—Adenauer. In the light of the Spanish affair the Social Democrats conjured up visions of an authoritarian quartet—Adenauer and de Gaulle along with the "Iberian dictators," Franco and Salazar.[91]

While sounding the alarm about the emergence of "neo-Fascist forces" in Europe, the Social Democrats also warned of the threat from the left. On January 30 the leadership approved a set of party guidelines which severely restricted contacts with the SED and Communist-front organizations.[92] Two days later the SPD published a pamphlet entitled *The Alternative of Our Time: Social Democracy's Clash with Communism.*

The pamphlet opened with an expanded discussion of the difference between communism and social democracy as outlined in the Bad Godesberg program and then went on to deal with the recent Communist challenge. According to the pamphlet, the Soviet Union desired "not the peaceful coexistence of states and differing governmental systems but the undermining and weakening of Western power and the expansion and consolidation of Soviet power." Significantly, the Russians relied mainly on a combination of political, social, ideological, and economic factors to achieve their goals. Meeting the challenge, therefore, would require something more than the government's present policy, which amounted to nothing more than "a primitive anti-Bolshevik crusade" and a reliance on military factors alone. West Germany needed to focus on the creation of a genuinely democratic society, one founded on social-democratic principles.[93]

After reading the pamphlet, the government parties commented on the SPD's "sudden discovery of the threat of communism," but SPD Chairman Ollenhauer declared that the Social Democrats had said nothing new. They had been in the front ranks of the struggle against communism since 1945 and had nothing to learn from the CDU.[94] Why, then, did the party choose this particular moment to publish a major policy statement on the differences between communism and social democracy?

First, the pamphlet and the guidelines were designed to remind party members of the line drawn between Socialists and Communists. In the early postwar years Schumacher had made sure that no one crossed the line, but as time passed and the division of Germany deepened, some leftists began to talk of contact with the SED to promote reunification and find allies against "the reactionary policies" of Adenauer, Erhard, and Strauss. The leadership resisted their appeals and eventually forced a few obstinate leftists to leave the party. In the late 1950s the SDS had caused the party leaders some embarrassment by talking favorably of East Germany. It was in response to their activities that Mommer expressed concern about dangerous trends within the Socialist movement. Several months later the Parteivorstand warned the SDS to get into step with the party, but nothing changed. When the young radicals rejected the Bad Godesberg program, the party leaders encouraged the moderates to form a new student organization, which they did in May, 1960.[95]

Second, the pamphlet and guidelines were designed to help the party's electoral chances in 1961. In earlier campaigns Adenauer had exploited the common ideological base of Socialists and Communists to warn West Germans that all forms of Marxism led to Moscow. He had implied as well that an SPD government, dominated by its left wing, would make a deal with East Germany. Now, with the guidelines to restrict contact with the East and the pamphlet to show the differences between democratic socialism and totalitarian communism, the SPD leaders believed that they had removed a powerful weapon from the chancellor's hands.

Finally, the two documents reflected a slowly emerging shift in the party leaders' view of foreign policy. The pamphlet, for example, made reference to the expansionist tendencies of the Soviet Union, whereas previously the Social Democrats had tended to focus on the changes that had occurred in Moscow since the death of Stalin, specifically on the trend toward a policy of peaceful coexistence. They had based their Deutschlandplan on the hope that the Kremlin's desire for detente with the West would open the way to negotiations on the German question. Now, in early 1960, as Soviet propaganda attacks on "militaristic and imperialistic" West Germany increased and Khrushchev continued to talk of "two German nations in two states,"[96] the Social Democrats showed their disappointment by adopting a more critical view of Soviet behavior. Erler told the Bundestag in February that if Khrushchev carried out his threats against Berlin responsibility for an increase of international tension and "the destruction of all hopes for detente would lie, in the eyes of our nation and world opinion, with the Soviet Union." A *Vorwärts* writer commented somewhat more pessimistically that after the great disappointments suffered in recent years "only small hopes" remained of achieving reunification.[97] There could be no clearer indication that a major shift in party policy was on the way.

On March 17, Wehner announced the death of the Deutschlandplan. It came as no great surprise. Ever since the Bundestag debate on November 5 the Social Democrats had cautiously refrained from advocating the plan as the path to reunification. In recent weeks leading Social Democrats had been hinting at its demise,[98] but the only one who could lay it to rest was Wehner, the man whom everyone outside the party viewed as the author of the plan.

In an article for the party press Wehner explained that the Deutschlandplan was merely a link in the chain of attempts made by the SPD to get four-power negotiations on the German question under way. "Unfortunately, it had been just as unsuccessful as earlier attempts. This makes it a thing of the past." The Christian Democrats immediately interpreted Wehner's article as a public confession by the SPD that its Deutschlandplan had failed, but a party spokesman declared that the plan could hardly be described as a failure when it had never been tested by the powers.[99]

Although SPD leaders realized that the party had to abandon the Deutschlandplan, they balked at the idea of scrapping it entirely. They insisted that certain aspects of the plan remained valid, in particular those relating to the need for prior agreement on the military status of a reunited Germany, for regional as well as general disarmament agreements in promoting reunification, and for progress in stages toward a restoration of German unity. These ideas made up the core of a new set of proposals which the Social Democrats asked Adenauer to use as a German contribution to the upcoming summit conference, scheduled to open in Paris on May 16.[100]

The Thirtieth of June

Unlike previous four-power meetings, the Social Democrats showed few signs this time of their usual hopefulness. Even Ollenhauer found it difficult to be optimistic. After watching the Communists tighten their control over East Germany, he concluded that "the chances of the two German states coming together step-by-step were worse than in 1959 when the Deutschlandplan was announced."[101] The Social Democrats expected the Russians to raise the Berlin question at the conference, but the West could be counted on to defend its rights in the city. As for the German question, Erler feared that it would "hardly be more than the subject of a propaganda battle."[102] The most the Social Democrats hoped for was a discussion of the arms race, leading to a further round of talks, but even that failed to materialize.

The Paris summit conference ended the day it opened. In a dramatic gesture Khrushchev left the conference when he failed to obtain an apology from President Eisenhower for the violation of Soviet air space by an American U-2 reconnaisance plane. The plane had been shot down a thousand miles inside Russia by a Soviet missile, but the U-2 incident served mainly as a pretext for Khrushchev's actions. Realizing that the Western powers would never accept his Berlin policy, he decided to leave matters as they were eighteen months before when the crisis started. During the intervening period there had been times when Khrushchev thought that concessions would be forthcoming. At Camp David, Eisenhower had agreed that something had to be done about "the abnormal situation" in Berlin; but after Adenauer, aided by de Gaulle, had expressed concern about a Western retreat at the summit, the Americans clarified their position by tying a Berlin settlement to the German question. In a sense, therefore, the U-2 incident gave a spectacular ending to what would have been a very uneventful conference.[103]

For the Social Democrats the Paris summit conference marked the end of a chapter of German history. Since the 1955 Geneva summit conference they had been trying to ignore, and then to overcome, Soviet talk of a two-Germanys solution. Now they had to admit that Germany would remain divided for a long time. That was no easy task for the Social Democrats, but considering the international situation and the party's political ambitions, they could no longer maintain the course set by Schumacher. Instead of opposing West Germany's military ties with the West, they would have to accept NATO and pursue reunification from within the framework of the alliance. Thus reunification could no longer be treated as an immediate task, though the Social Democrats would insist that it be considered the highest goal of German policy. This was Adenauer's view. The Social Democrats could not, however, simply announce that they would adopt what the chancellor had been telling them all along was the only course open to the Federal Republic. There had to be a compromise. They claimed, therefore, that both the government and the opposition had something to learn from recent events, and they called on all responsible political forces "to take stock calmly and soberly" of the new situation in order to develop a new policy for West Germany.[104]

On May 24, Ollenhauer told the Bundestag that the SPD was ready to sit down with the other parties and work out a common foreign policy.[105] He received a favorable response from the Free Democrats, but the Christian Democrats declared that the only basis for a common foreign policy could be the government's policy, specifically its defense policy.[106]

This was no easy task for the Social Democrats. As late as March 1960, Erler was still speaking of the need to renegotiate the Paris Accords in order to facilitate a more active reunification policy.[107] After the Paris conference, however, the Social Democrats began stressing the security advantages of West German membership in NATO. Schmidt declared, without reference to the unity question, that the SPD supported NATO because it "guarantees our security," and Erler now reminded a party gathering that, until Germany was reunified and the powers had negotiated a disarmament agreement, West Germany should belong to NATO.[108] This change of emphasis posed no serious problem for the military experts. They had long ago recognized the importance of NATO, but others—like Ollenhauer and Knoeringen—found it difficult to refrain from attacking "the madness of the arms race."[109]

Accepting NATO, however reluctantly, came easier for the Social Democrats than abandoning certain other aspects of their opposition course—disengagement, for example. After the collapse of the Paris conference an SPD spokesman renewed the argument that in a very tense international situation the Germans would be safer, and peace more secure, if Soviet and American troops no longer stood face to face across the zonal border. Furthermore, Ollenhauer asserted early in June, that the only way to get the powers talking about the German question was to open negotiations on the creation of a zone of reduced armaments in Central Europe. According to the SPD leader, "If the government adheres to its earlier view in this matter, and thus to the status quo, then there is no possibility for a common foreign policy."[110]

As for their attitude toward conscription and an atomic arming of the Bundeswehr, the Social Democrats yielded somewhat on the former[111] but remained adamant on the latter. In a letter to Adenauer shortly before the Paris conference, Ollenhauer urged the government to relinquish its drive for atomic weapons and work instead for a nonproliferation treaty. The Social Democrats clung to this line even after the sudden breakup of the conference. When asked by a reporter if the SPD's continued opposition to an atomic arming of the Bundeswehr conflicted with its affirmation of support for NATO, since the alliance expected its members to support a common strategy, Wehner replied that Denmark and Norway had refused to have atomic weapons and no one questioned their commitment to NATO.[112] The government held a different view, and the SPD leaders knew that Adenauer and Strauss would make atomic weapons the ultimate test of SPD loyalty to the Western alliance.

Finally, the government demanded that the SPD vote for the defense budget. This the Social Democrats refused to do, Ollenhauer said, because "we oppose the policy pursued by Strauss."[113] The Social Democrats argued that differences between the government and the opposition over the details of a policy were normal in any democratic parliamentary system. Since the SPD supported the main lines of the government's defense policy—security in alliance with the West—the coalition parties had no reason to treat the budget debate as a test of the opposition party's loyalty. It should be enough to go on from this shared adherence to the Western connection to a discussion of what the SPD and the CDU had in common in the foreign-policy area.

The Christian Democrats disagreed. They referred to important differences over aspects of the defense question and wondered how the Social Democrats could so suddenly change their foreign-policy priorities. There were also electoral considerations. Adenauer had no reason to build "golden bridges for the SPD to cross over before election time." He realized, as the Social Democrats did, that foreign policy had been the decisive weapon in defeating the SPD in 1953 and 1957, and he had no intention of relinquishing that weapon now by letting them off the hook.[114] Adenauer also saw an opportunity to exploit the factional differences which had been revealed at Bad Godesberg. Certainly left-wing Social Democrats would resist the leadership's efforts to make common cause with the government on foreign policy. For that reason the SPD leaders wanted time to explain to the party why a change in course was necessary. They proposed to the CDU, therefore, that the foreign-policy discussion be opened at the committee level, far from the glare of public lights, but the Christian Democrats rejected the idea. More than that, they organized a full-scale parliamentary debate to prove that a common foreign policy was unnecessary and, as CDU Deputy Ernst Majonica told his colleagues, to make the Social Democrats say it was impossible.[115]

On June 30 the Bundestag held one of its most important foreign-policy debates. The main speaker for the SPD was Herbert Wehner.[116] At first glance it was a surprising choice because as a speaker Wehner lacked the intellectual brilliance of a Carlo Schmid or the debating skills of a Fritz Erler. Furthermore, he tended to be antagonistic at the podium, which made it unlikely that he could ever convince the CDU of the SPD's sincerity in asking for an understanding with the government on foreign policy. Ollenhauer would have been a more likely choice because of his reputation as a conciliator, and, moreover, he was the leader of the SPD. In the eyes of the coalition parties, however, Wehner pulled the strings, and thus he was the only one who could speak authoritatively for the SPD.

Wehner mounted the podium not as a repentant sinner but as a confident suitor who with proper modesty and restraint explained why it would be a suitable match. He began by appealing to the coalition parties to forget about past disputes and look to the future. After what had happened in Paris, the democratic forces in the Federal Republic needed

Herbert Wehner, with Adenauer and Ludwig Erhard looking on, addresses the Bundestag during the June, 1960, foreign-policy debate. Courtesy German Press Agency.

to stand together in an effort to keep the German question on the international agenda.

To demonstrate to the coalition parties how close the two sides were in their views, Wehner presented a list of four conditions laid down by Defense Minister Strauss for a common foreign policy. Strauss had demanded from the Social Democrats that they (1) accept NATO as the necessary prerequisite for maintaining peace and attaining reunification; (2) reject all disengagement schemes; (3) share the defense burden with the coalition parties; and (4) acknowledge free elections as the only path to reunification. Without hesitating Wehner accepted all four conditions. He told the coalition parties that the SPD had made "the European and Atlantic treaty systems the basis and the framework of West Germany's foreign and reunification policy." The party had buried the Deutschlandplan. As for SPD support of national defense, Wehner declared that the Social Democrats were committed in both word and deed to the defense of the free democratic order. He conceded that there were "different conceptions of what was appropriate in this area" but in a democratic state differences over policy matters were normal. Taking the offensive, Wehner asked the coalition parties why they insisted on questioning the readiness of the SPD to be a loyal treaty partner of the West. Was there any doubt? Look at the behavior of the Berlin Social Democrats in the current crisis, or look at Kurt Schumacher, who had left his imprint on the party. To loud applause from the SPD benches Wehner declared that the country had a democratic alternative to the present government. The decisive question, Wehner said in conclusion, was the willingness of the democratic forces in West Germany, irrespective of their differences, to cooperate with one another in meeting their responsibilities "to the entire nation in our divided Fatherland."

Wehner's Bundestag address was a masterful performance. He abandoned the party's foreign-policy course without making it appear as though the Social Democrats had capitulated to Adenauer. More than that, he denied the Christian Democrats the tactical victory they sought: an admission by the Social Democrats that a common foreign policy was impossible. Instead, he appealed to them to bury past differences for the sake of Germany. In the ensuing debate coalition speakers conceded that what Wehner said he said well but his speech contained nothing more than generalities. He said nothing about defense policy, including such vital issues as atomic weapons, conscription, and the defense budget. Furthermore, serious doubts existed that the party shared Wehner's point of view; in fact, in recent days leading Social Democrats had made less than a full commitment to NATO. It seemed to Baron zu Guttenberg that the Social Democrats, like democratic Socialists elsewhere, were still searching for a place in modern society. Since the government already knew where it stood, there was no reason to join the SPD in taking stock of German policy.[117]

At the end of the debate the coalition parties introduced a resolution calling on the members of the house to confirm the government's foreign policy. In the past the Social Democrats would have responded by voting no, but this time they abstained and in so doing gave formal notice to Parliament and the public that a political era was coming to an end. For a decade the primary issue had been whether reunification or security should take priority in West German foreign policy. Now, motivated by political ambition and convinced by Khrushchev of the hopelessness of the German situation, the Social Democrats changed course.

Commenting on the debate, a reporter marveled at how the SPD Fraktion had maintained discipline in spite of a sudden change in course by the leaders. The SPD deputies had even refused to be provoked by taunts and catcalls from the CDU benches about the party's long-standing criticism of NATO. They responded to Wehner's commands, one writer said, with the cadaver-like obedience of an old Prussian regiment.[118] This was an overstatement, though true to the extent that after being briefed by Wehner during the preceding week the deputies had agreed to follow.[119] That proved true even of those backbenchers who opposed the Bad Godesberg program and abhorred the idea of a common policy with the government. Most deputies, however, had no trouble accepting Wehner's lead because since the Stuttgart party conference they had become increasingly convinced of the need to change course.

Outside the Fraktion, however, the reaction was different. An immediate outcry arose over Wehner's "solo decisions" in foreign policy. The party organizations in Frankfurt and Munich passed resolutions expressing their opposition to the new course and criticizing the leadership for arbitrarily changing party policy without consulting the rank and file. They demanded a full discussion of the matter when the SPD met at Hannover in November for its biennial conference.[120]

Troubled by what had happened in Bonn, one local leader claimed that the party had been plunged into one of the greatest crises in its history. He feared a split similar to the great schism the SPD had undergone in 1917, but he exaggerated the danger. Less than two weeks after the Bundestag debate Wehner met with district party secretaries from across the country to present the leadership's case, which he did in a very persuasive address, and to hear the secretaries describe the mood of the SPD. These officials, with a hand on the pulse of the party, reported that, while there was "grumbling among the crew, there would be no mutiny."[121]

In the following months the SPD leaders set out to pacify the party and, one suspects, remove any final doubts they themselves had. Although some could still talk enthusiastically about the prospects for new East-West talks, realists like Wehner and Erler remained skeptical about the possibility of achieving any kind of satisfactory agreement with Khrushchev.[122] *Vorwärts* reflected the change as well by focusing not on the chances for detente, or even the need for detente, but on the need to stand up to a renewed East German challenge over Berlin. For the SPD leaders, Khrushchev's decision to put Ulbricht "on a long leash" merely served to confirm the correctness of the new course.[123] Under the circumstances the rank and file agreed that something had to be done, but emotionally most Social Democrats found it difficult to accept a change in the party's priorities. In their eyes the SPD could change course only by sacrificing principles honored since the rearmament debate began. Besides, it embarrassed party members to have to talk of NATO as the basis of an active German policy when all along they had viewed the alliance as an obstacle to reunification and, even worse, to praise the Bundeswehr as the defender of the democratic order when most Social Democrats still viewed the military with deep distrust. Nonetheless, the leaders felt confident that the policy change would be accepted without a major struggle at the upcoming party conference.

For the conference the Parteivorstand approved a series of resolutions, including one on foreign policy and another on security. The foreign-policy resolution attempted to justify the new course by arguing that international problems in the 1960s would be more difficult than those of the previous decade. "On a whole series of important questions" the Germans had only one course of action open to them. There were no alternatives.[124]

At Hannover, Wehner and Erler ardently defended the resolution and called on the party to face the facts.[125] The more favorable conditions of 1952 had gone forever, and now, after the debacle at Paris, the Germans had no choice but to pursue their goals in alliance with the West. Thus if the Social Democrats wanted to do more than write "mere proclamations and declarations," Wehner said, they could not stand outside NATO waiting for it to become a Social Democratic citadel. They would have to help the Federal Republic gain a more influential voice in the alliance. This was an interesting reversal of the statement Carlo Schmid had made during the debate on West German membership in the Council of Europe ten years before, when he told the party to wage its campaign outside the walls of Strasbourg.

Erler carried Wehner's argument one step further. He argued that there had to be a stable military balance between East and West to guarantee the security of the West Germans and establish a basis for negotiations with the Russians. It came as no surprise to hear Erler talk of power politics, but even Ollenhauer warned the party that a weakening of NATO would hurt the West's chances in future negotiations with the Soviet Union.[126] The leadership had proclaimed its adherence to a policy of strength.

The SPD leaders also based their call for a more realistic approach to foreign policy on the party's legitimate political ambitions. If it wanted to be the government party, Erler said, then the SPD would have to make it clear to the nation that it would be a reliable treaty partner of the West. Without this clarification Adenauer would base his 1961 election campaign on the slogan: "With the CDU in NATO—or—With the SPD Against NATO."

The leadership's line of argument was irrefutable, but many delegates had reservations about the new foreign-policy course. One speaker from Frankfurt, whose party organization still described West Germany's entry into NATO as "false and dangerous," stated that the Western world and the Atlantic Alliance were not identical. The West meant humanity and freedom; NATO meant Salazar, Franco, de Gaulle, and the Pentagon. Another speaker asked whether the party had really searched for an alternative to Adenauer's foreign policy. It seemed to him that the SPD had accepted too readily the conditions set by the chancellor.[127] The leaders assured the delegates that, rather than one side giving in to the other, both sides would sit down together in a joint review of the foreign-policy situation to work out a policy that all democratic parties could accept. There would be no capitulation.

In the end the resolution passed with only one abstention. The party gave its stamp of approval to the new foreign-policy course, though, as *Der Spiegel* noted, the rank and file accepted the new course "on intellectual grounds and without deep conviction."[128]

Now the SPD leaders had to persuade the delegates to pass an appropriate defense statement. They realized that, to remove the last barrier to a common foreign policy with the government, the SPD would have to accept more than NATO membership. It would have to accept NATO strategy as well. That meant conscription, which the security-policy resolution covered by stating that national defense required "the cooperation of all citizens," and it meant atomic weapons. According to the CDU, if the Social Democrats wanted to maintain West Germany's status as a loyal ally, they would have to agree to the atomic arming of the Bundeswehr.[129] The party, however, would never approve such an idea—not after all that had been said and done in the past two years—and the CDU would accept nothing less as the basis for a common foreign policy. What the leadership wanted—more specifically, what the new triumvirate Wehner, Erler, and Brandt wanted—was to strike a balance between these conflicting points of view. They believed that the SPD could no longer cling to its unconditional no to atomic weapons if it wanted to remove all doubts about the party's loyalty to NATO, and thus the triumvirate fashioned a resolution that would satisfy the ban-the-bomb group without denying the new leaders some room to maneuver.[130]

The last thing the advocates of the new course wanted to do, of course, was provoke a confrontation over the atomic-weapons question, but on this issue they could hardly jump from one position to another without causing a stir. The resolution was certain to be challenged on the floor of the convention. Amazingly, the challenge came from, of all people, Erich Ollenhauer.

In his opening address to the conference Ollenhauer revealed that he had some doubts about the new course. After expressing his confidence in the Western powers and his readiness to embark on a common stock-taking of the foreign-policy situation with the government, he went on to assure the delegates that the SPD would never stop working for reunification or for a policy of disarmament and detente. Turning to the subject of atomic weapons, which obviously troubled him deeply, he said that every effort had to be made to abolish these instruments of mass destruction. Nothing could justify an enlargement of the atomic club. To shouts of "bravo" from the floor Ollenhauer declared that the SPD still stood by its Bad Godesberg resolution that West Germany "must neither produce nor use atomic weapons and other means of mass destruction." Nothing has happened since then, he said, to make us change our point of view. "We reject the atomic arming of the Bundeswehr." The delegates responded with cheers and a thunderous ovation.[131]

In taking such a strong stand against atomic weapons, Ollenhauer gave expression to what weighed on the minds of most delegates. It contradicted the sense of the security resolution, however, a resolution that Ollenhauer himself had accepted only the day before at a special meeting of the party leaders. Now, before the conference, he stated flatly that the SPD rejected atomic weapons; the resolution stated only that the Germans should not *strive* for atomic weapons, which could be interpreted to mean that they could accept them if the initiative came from NATO. Following a suggestion from the United States, the alliance had already begun to discuss the idea of making NATO an atomic power by creating a special integrated force equipped with atomic weapons. Supporters of the idea pointed out that it would keep people like de Gaulle from trying to develop an independent deterrent and, in Germany, keep atomic weapons out of Strauss's hands. The triumvirate felt that if NATO planned to move in this direction the Social Democrats had to go along.[132] Now, however, the delegates were aroused, and they apparently had a spokesman in Ollenhauer.

When the security resolution came up for debate, an atmosphere of anxious anticipation existed on both sides. Those who shared Ollenhauer's emotional reaction to the atomic-weapons question urged the party to declare its opposition by drafting a thoroughly unambiguous resolution. This, they claimed, had to be done if the party wanted to remain true to its convictions. "The applause for Ollenhauer's rejection of atomic weapons in yesterday's session was so overwhelming," a Hamburg delegate said, that there could be no doubt about where the conference stood on the matter.[133] Carlo Schmid, who spoke next in the debate, responded that the party could not be guided in its political actions by how much applause a measure received. In the military question the conference had to grant its leaders the flexibility they needed to meet the demands of a rapidly changing situation.[134]

Fritz Erler, in what many considered the best party speech of his career, assured the delegates that the leaders were abandoning neither their opposition to an atomic arming of the Bundeswehr nor their Bad Godesberg commitment to work for an end to the atomic-arms race. They simply wanted to make the SPD more competitive in the next election. He reminded the conference that a ban-the-bomb resolution from the SPD would change nothing. The atomic-arms race would end when the great powers changed their policies. "If we want to influence the great powers, we must be in the government and not at the wailing wall." He demanded that the delegates not bind the leaders' hands in the election campaign by means of a strictly worded resolution. "Every word that blocks our path to the government contributes to the atomic-arms race, because the others [the Christian Democrats] will pursue it." However difficult the path, therefore—even if it meant accepting NATO as an atomic power—the Social Democrats had to gain office to assure a German contribution to arms control and disarmament.[135]

Erler's arguments helped neutralize the emotional appeal of Ollenhauer's unexpected declaration against atomic weapons, and, with the aid of pointed comments in favor of the resolution by Wehner and Brandt, they opened the way for the leadership's victory. What assured the victory, however, was a statement by Ollenhauer. The chairman's keynote address had triggered the crisis at Hannover, and members of the Parteivorstand prevailed upon him to do what he could to repair the damage before a serious split emerged. Moved by a strong sense of party loyalty, Ollenhauer agreed. He told the delegates that his remarks of the previous day in no way conflicted with the main objective of the security resolution, which was to promote arms control. They should, therefore, support the leadership.[136]

Without Ollenhauer to lead the cause, the opposition forces had no one to rally around. They tried to gather signatures for an amendment which would limit the leaders' freedom of maneuver, but with little success. When it came to the final vote, the resolution proposed by the Parteivorstand passed with only 17 negative votes and 20 abstentions. Most delegates responded to the call for party discipline in view of the upcoming election and took refuge—as Ollenhauer had—in that part of the resolution which declared the party's continued opposition to the proliferation of atomic weapons. Whatever their reservations, however, they granted the new leaders the flexibility they wanted in the 1961 election campaign.

The last major piece of business before the conference was the acknowledgement of the leadership's choice for chancellor candidate, Willy Brandt. Brandt's rise to national prominence had been meteoric. Following an unsuccessful bid in 1956 to gain election to the Parteivorstand, he had moved on the next year to become mayor of Berlin and to establish himself there as an extraordinarily capable politician. His victory in the December, 1958, Berlin elections had enhanced his reputation, but the Berlin crisis did even more, catapulting him to the center of the world stage. He traveled abroad—to London, Paris, Wash-

Willy Brandt, the SPD's candidate for chancellor, congratulates Ollen-hauer on his reelection as party chairman at the Hannover party con-ference, November, 1960. Courtesy German Press Agency.

ington, even to the Geneva foreign ministers' conference—as a spokes-man for a beleaguered Berlin. He visited Bonn to talk to Chancellor Adenauer and to address Parliament on the Berlin situation. By 1960, when the party selected him as its candidate for chancellor, Brandt had received enough public exposure to have gained recognition as both politician and statesman.[137]

Brandt was an ideal candidate for the SPD. A proven vote-getter, he could appeal beyond the party's regular supporters to those dissatisfied with the old chancellor. He had a practical approach to domestic policy, now confirmed in the Bad Godesberg program, and a keen awareness of the security interests of the West German population. Wehner's address to the Bundestag on June 30 had corresponded to his own well-established views on the importance of NATO. With Brandt as the party's candidate, therefore, Adenauer would be unable to use the foreign-policy card against the SPD or frighten the electorate with the old slogan about the Social Democrats being soft on communism. In Wehner's words, by selecting Brandt, "we converted our previously uncovered flank—in foreign policy—into a protected flank."[138]

Looking back, the party had traveled a long way since the Stuttgart party conference in May, 1959. It had a new program, one that placed emphasis on pragmatic considerations rather than ideological precepts; it had a new image, one that cast the SPD as a party for all Germans; it had a new chancellor candidate to head its election campaign in 1961; and it had a new set of policies in all areas, including national defense. At Hannover the Social Democrats affirmed West Germany's membership in NATO and announced that they could live with conscription and even atomic weapons. Although the Christian Democrats tried to keep the issue alive, the rearmament debate was over. The political battles of the 1960s would be fought on a different front.

Conclusion

In 1960 the decade-long debate over rearmament in West Germany came to an end. Certainly no one expected a debate of such intensity and duration because initially the differences between the government and the main opposition party, the SPD, did not appear to be that great. Yet before long the two sides stood face to face across a seemingly unbridgeable chasm. The government refused to alter or delay its Western course; the SPD, with equal determination, refused to accept it. What sustained SPD opposition to Adenauer's rearmament policy was a combination of three distinct but related factors: the party's pacifist and antimilitary sentiments, its fervent hostility to an Adenauer-led government, and its deep commitment to German reunification.

Throughout its long history the SPD had always expressed the greatest suspicion about the intentions of the military establishment. The Social Democrats had disliked the imperial army, distrusted the Reichswehr, and argued against the idea of building a new German army in the postwar years. In their eyes it posed a deadly threat to peace and freedom.

When the rearmament debate began, the Social Democrats immediately foresaw the danger of military interference in politics such as had happened under the empire and in the last days of the Weimar Republic. Although the party's military experts had great confidence in their ability to assure democratic control of the military, most Social Democrats felt that nothing could prevent the new army from falling into the hands of militarists and reactionaries. In 1956 a survey showed that 80 percent of the Social Democrats interviewed believed that the Bundeswehr would soon revert to the old ways.[1] During the following four years the military experts tried to promote a relationship of mutual confidence between the SPD and the Bundeswehr, but with limited success. Only the Young Socialists and some concerned SPD politicians made contact with the soldiers. They received little support from the leadership until 1960, when the Parteivorstand appointed liaison officers (Kontakt Leute) to coordinate party contacts with the Bundeswehr at the district level. Thereafter the original mistrust in the party began to diminish but was not replaced by a feeling of confidence toward the military.[2]

Most Social Democrats also found it difficult to deal realistically with the power factor in international affairs. When Adenauer talked of achieving reunification through negotiations from strength—Western military strength supplemented by a German military contribution—they criticized the chancellor for making diplomacy a function of the arms race. They condemned, as well, his argument that rearmament in alliance with the West would increase West German security. According to the Social Democrats, membership in the Western Alliance would only increase tension and heighten the danger of war in Europe. They proposed instead a collective security system and, later, a disengagement scheme. Critics viewed both proposals as a reflection of the party's "naïve internationalism"[3] and its inability to grasp the true nature of world politics. Unlike Adenauer, who viewed the Cold War as the normal state of affairs in the postwar world, the Social Democrats saw it as an abnormal condition which mankind was striving to overcome.

The Social Democrats had one further reason for rejecting Adenauer's policy of strength; they considered communism to be primarily a political, social, or ideological challenge. As a result, from the outbreak of the Korean War to the collapse of the Paris summit conference, the average party member treated new houses and schools as more important to the defense of democracy than barracks and tanks. Such sentiments extended beyond the rank and file to idealists in the Parteivorstand like Waldemar von Knoeringen. In the late fifties, while criticizing the government's policy of strength, Erler warned against seeking military solutions to political problems, and even Schmidt talked of the primacy of social tasks over military ones, but these realists did so without denying the need for a defense policy and a stable balance of power.

One of the major tasks facing the reformers was to convince the SPD of its responsibilities in the military area. The mood of the party was *ohne mich,* preferring abstinence to active participation, regardless of what the leaders said. In November, 1950, after Schumacher had called for a forward strategy, local party organizations in state elections campaigned on the slogan that a vote for the SPD was a vote against rearmament. Certainly this, rather than Schumacher's extravagant military demands, represented the position that the party wanted to take. In 1955 the Paulskirche movement reflected more clearly the feelings of the party toward rearmament than the Fraktion's constructive labors in military legislation, just as three years later the Kampf dem Atomtod campaign offered a more authentic expression of party sentiment than the reference to West German defense contained in the Stuttgart security resolution. Even then it took the reformers another two years before they could neutralize, without entirely overcoming, the party's pacifist and antimilitary sentiments.

The party's bitter rivalry with the CDU compounded even further its fundamental opposition to rearmament. Under Schumacher the SPD viewed itself as the principle agent for a democratic renewal of Germany and the CDU as the vehicle by which right-wing forces planned to subvert German democracy. The party accepted, as well, Schumacher's view that the SPD should join only a government the party could dominate. As a result, when the CDU emerged as the strongest party in the 1949 elections and Adenauer expressed his preference for an alliance with the bourgeois parties, the Social Democrats went into opposition.

When the rearmament debate opened, therefore, a clear line separated the government and the SPD on most issues. On the military question, however, both Adenauer and Schumacher accepted the need for a defense contribution. They differed over the conditions under which the West Germans would rearm. Adenauer assumed that West Germany would receive sovereignty and equality in return for rearming; Schumacher made those conditions a prerequisite for rearmament. Neither side made any attempt to find a common position. Schumacher clung to his opposition course and to the proposition that only the SPD could provide the Germans with the government they needed, while Adenauer preferred to have the SPD as an adversary rather than a loyal opposition party. He could point to an uncompromising Schumacher waiting in the wings as a threat to extract better terms from the Western powers. Later he also found it advantageous to use the Socialist bogeyman to frighten the West Germans at election time. He offered them the choice: freedom or slavery, the CDU or the SPD.

The SPD responded in kind. After Schumacher's death the Social Democrats continued to attack the CDU as a front for capitalist and clericalist interests in West Germany and portrayed their own party as the only hope for democracy and peace. Even a disappointing defeat in 1953 failed to persuade the leaders to change course. Ollenhauer declared then and again after the 1957 election that nothing had happened at home or abroad to cause the SPD to abandon its campaign promises.

The party's decision to maintain an opposition course came as no surprise; Ollenhauer and his colleagues considered themselves loyal trustees of the Schumacher legacy. Opposition to rearmament, however, stemmed from more than a sense of moral obligation to a revered leader. It also rested on an emotional factor (the party's antimilitary sentiments) and a party principle (the creation of a Social Democratic Germany). Thus, if Adenauer represented a threat to democracy, there could be no compromise with the man or his policy.[4]

After 1952 the Social Democrats treated rearmament as Adenauer's policy. To accept rearmament, therefore, meant to aid in the restoration of antidemocratic forces in West Germany. To cooperate in the military legislation, as the parliamentary party did in 1955, meant to abandon the struggle against what Ollenhauer called a regime with clerico-Fascist tendencies, a regime which also appeared willing to exploit the division of Germany for its own selfish purposes. The latter issue, reunification, became the focal point of SPD opposition to the government's rearmament policy. Before long opposition to rearmament for the sake of reunification became a party principle—a myth, Klaus-Peter Schulz called it[5]—to inspire and sustain the party's opposition course.

Before the rearmament debate began, the Social Democrats warned that any attempt to create a West German military force would deepen the division of Germany. In August, 1950, however, Schumacher failed to mention reunification when he stated his conditions for a military contribution, and during the following year, while Adenauer and the Allies discussed German participation in an integrated European army, he said nothing about a possible conflict between the pursuit of reunification and the acceptance of rearmament. Of course, Schumacher never saw rearmament as an immediate task. He insisted first on social reforms to create living conditions in West Germany that would act as a magnet on the Soviet-zone population, and he demanded a military buildup by the Allies that would guarantee German security and give the West an opportunity to negotiate with the Soviet Union from a position of strength. By late 1951, however, Schumacher had to admit that the Western powers were not going to meet the conditions he had set for West German rearmament. They turned instead to the European Defense Community and the Coal and Steel Community (ECSC), both of which Schumacher considered to be grossly discriminatory toward the Germans. He warned that these schemes of Western integration represented a threat to the chances for reunification because they robbed West Germany of its attractive power on the East. Even more alarming, they indicated that the Western powers—along with the chancellor—no longer considered reunification a primary task. In early 1952, therefore, Schumacher sounded the alarm. He demanded that reunification be treated as an immediate, not a distant, goal of German policy, and his colleagues warned increasingly as the parliamentary debate on EDC progressed that the choice was rearmament or reunification. By the time of Schumacher's death, in August, 1952, party policy had hardened along those lines.

In taking this position, the Social Democrats assumed that a chance to restore German unity with security and freedom did exist and that an offer from the Western powers to renounce West German rearmament for the sake of free elections in Germany would receive a favorable response from the Russians. Yet initially, at least, the Social Democrats were far from optimistic about the chances for successful negotiations. When the Soviet Union suggested a four-power conference in late 1950, Schumacher told the party that he doubted that the Russians were ready to grant free elections. He demanded a meeting, nonetheless, to clarify the situation and see what the Russians really wanted. Not until Stalin's note of March, 1952, and the subsequent diplomatic exchange between East and West did the Social Democrats begin to display a certain cautious optimism about four-power talks. They now implied that the thrust of Soviet foreign policy was toward security rather than expansion. Therefore, to gain Soviet consent to free elections there would have to be a prior agreement on the military status of a reunited Germany. The Social Democrats rejected the neutralization of Germany, which the Soviets had called for in 1952, and proposed instead that a reunited Germany join the world security system of the United Nations.

After the 1953 election the Social Democrats made this proposal the heart of their reunification policy. They urged the Western powers to treat German unity and European security as two sides of the same coin and to seek negotiations with the Soviet Union on that basis. The foreign ministers' conference in Berlin in 1954 afforded an opportunity for negotiations, but according to the Social Democrats the West failed to test the Russians to see whether they would exchange reunification for a renunciation of German membership in EDC. When EDC died later in the year, the Social Democrats pressed the Western powers to go to the conference table before settling on a new scheme for rearming the West Germans. They grew alarmed when Adenauer and the Allies concentrated on bringing West Germany into NATO and the Russians issued a warning that Germany would remain divided if the Federal Republic joined the Western Alliance. But the choice was still rearmament or reunification.

The Social Democrats faced a new situation during the remainder of the decade. After the 1955 Geneva summit conference and the entry of West Germany into NATO, the Russians announced that they could live with a two-Germanys solution. Although the Social Democrats recognized the change in the Soviet position, they refused to accept it. They clung to the hope that the Russians would discuss the German question if the Western powers would relinquish the notion that a reunified Germany should be free to join NATO. According to Ollenhauer, much would be gained by clarifying the situation through negotiations, that is, by compelling the Russians to give an unambiguous answer to the question of what they considered an acceptable military status for Germany.

After the summit meeting no major conference on the German question occurred until May, 1959, yet the Social Democrats maintained the priority of reunification. They conceded, however, that before there could be successful negotiations there would have to be a considerable reduction in international tension. Detente was the first step, and the means to detente was disarmament, or, as the Social Democrats claimed, disengagement. Although the Kennan and Rapacki plans stirred considerable interest within the SPD, they failed to promote four-power negotiations; instead, the powers came together over the Berlin crisis of November, 1958. For the Social Democrats this was the moment of decision. They feared that the door to reunification would be slammed shut, and in an act of desperation they produced the Deutschlandplan.

The stalemate at Geneva and the fiasco at Paris a year later, however, finally convinced the SPD leaders that the Russians had no intention of altering the status quo in Central Europe. Wehner's speech of June 30 served as a formal announcement that the SPD had abandoned its demand for reunification first.

Why did it take the Social Democrats so long to admit that there was no chance of achieving reunification on acceptable terms? To re-unify Germany, there had to be agreement among the four powers, but at every meeting and in every diplomatic exchange since 1945 the Soviets had raised demands that even the Social Democrats had re-jected. For that matter, the Western powers had always insisted on conditions that the Soviet Union found unacceptable. There was a stale-mate, and the Social Democrats knew it. They nonetheless adhered to their demand for reunification first.

The Social Democrats stated on many occasions that the West had to determine beyond the shadow of a doubt that the Russians barred the way to reunification in freedom; otherwise, the Bonn Republic could face the same kind of nationalist reaction that had destroyed the Weimar Republic. Clarification of the situation would also show the Germans living behind the iron curtain that everything possible had been done to free them from Soviet domination. Without question the Social Demo-crats had a genuine concern for the fate of the eighteen million Ger-mans in the Soviet zone, a concern they claimed the government did not share, but they also had a very practical interest in reunification. The Social Democrats believed that with reunification they would gain access to traditional Socialist strongholds in East Germany and in na-tional elections become the largest party in Parliament.

It is difficult to say which motive predominated because the party combined a pursuit of political profit with a sincere devotion to prin-ciples.[6] To the extent that tactical considerations prevailed, however, the party erred greatly. After the rearmament debate had ended, Erler explained that the party's foreign-policy position had been a source of spiritual strength for the SPD;[7] unfortunately, it had also been a source of electoral weakness. The West Germans preferred Adenauer's alliance with the West.

What further complicates the attempt to unravel the party's motives for insisting on the primacy of reunification is that the party's idealism was intertwined not only with its political ambitions but also with its antimilitary sentiments. For many Social Democrats reunification was an alternative to rearmament. They did not want a German army, much less a West German army, and they realized that if the party deempha-sized reunification it would have to accept West German rearmament. When the SPD leaders called for "one more conference," therefore, they did so to convince the Germans *and* their own members that every-thing possible was being done to reunify Germany. In this sense the Deutschlandplan represented more than a desperate gamble to promote reunification; it was a necessary step in the intraparty battle to make rearmament acceptable to the rank and file.[8]

The extent to which the party's commitment to reunification was bound up with its antimilitary sentiments can be measured by comparing the SPD's response to the various schemes for Western integration. Initially the Social Democrats fought both EDC and ECSC, but gradually SPD opposition to the idea of an economic union began to abate. By 1954 they were working actively to "democratize" ECSE and to promote the economic prosperity of its members. As a measure of their acceptance of the European Coal and Steel Community, an SPD delegate to the ECSC parliament commented that, in contrast to EDC, this form of Western integration posed no threat to reunification.[9] In the following year the SPD fought West German membership in NATO, primarily on the grounds that it would destroy what chances remained for reunifying Germany; yet less than a month after the Bundestag ratified the Paris Accords, the Social Democrats welcomed the proposal to create the European Economic Community (EEC). Although they had certain reservations about the so-called Common Market, fear that it would deepen the division of Germany was not one of them.

As a Marxist party, the SPD should have known that the Soviet Union would react adversely to West Germany's economic merger with the West. By joining the Common Market, West Germany was increasing the economic power base and thus the military potential of the Western Alliance. The Social Democrats felt, however, that German economic cooperation with the West would serve as a demonstration of the Federal Republic's peaceful intentions. Ever since the postwar period, moreover, the Social Democrats had assumed that a reunited Germany would have the closest possible ties with the West, politically, culturally, and economically—but not militarily. They believed that by removing the military factor from the equation the Western Alliance could convince the Soviets that the German problem could be solved.

How difficult it was for the SPD to deal with military policy can also be illustrated by comparing it with other areas in which the party made changes. There was, for example, less friction over revising economic policy or abandoning Marxism than there was over accepting rearmament;[10] in fact, rearmament sparked greater emotional resistance from the rank and file than did any other single issue. Throughout the 1950s, during election campaigns and at party conferences, the SPD moved progressively away from an economic program of nationalization and central planning without provoking more than a few brief if heated skirmishes. On ideological matters as well there was no uproar over abandoning Marxism comparable to the confrontations at the Berlin and Munich conferences on the military question, or those at Stuttgart, where Kampf dem Atomtod caused greater excitement than Eichler's first draft of the new program. Furthermore, in adopting a new program at Bad Godesberg, the Social Democrats accepted the argument that the party had to get into step with recent social and economic developments. It was another full year, however, before they conceded that to win in West Germany the SPD would have to accept NATO.

When the party finally declared an end to the rearmament debate at the Hannover conference in November, 1960, it came under severe attack from critics. Leftist dissidents, already upset by the Bad Godesberg program, labeled the SPD's acceptance of NATO an act of capitulation which spelled the final surrender of the party to the Adenauer state.[11] Yet far from capitulating to Adenauer, the SPD leaders had acknowledged only the basic premises of the chancellor's foreign-policy position, without relinquishing their highest goals. As Brandt told the Hannover conference, it was no longer a question of changing the course of West German foreign policy but one of "changing the accent here and there, offering fresh impulses, and testing new methods."[12] The SPD would continue to search for a path to reunification.

Critics also charged that the party had abandoned its principles in the vain hope of winning more votes. Indeed, political ambition did play an important part in persuading party members to accept the changes proposed by the leadership at Bad Godesberg and Hannover. The Social Democrats wanted to get off the opposition benches, and they knew that by adhering to the same policy line they faced certain defeat in the 1961 election.[13]

The decision to end the rearmament debate has been interpreted by some observers as an admission by the Social Democrats that they had been wrong and Adenauer had been right all along.[14] On the contrary, the Social Democrats never admitted to being wrong. As Fritz Erler told an interviewer in 1966, "One cannot say today whether or not negotiations would have led to reunification because no one really tried." According to the Social Democrats, there was plenty of time between Stalin's note of March, 1952, and the Geneva Summit Conference in 1955 to test the sincerity of the Soviets; the West missed its chance. Thereafter the Soviets insisted on direct negotiations between Bonn and Pankow. Even worse, after the Soviet Union launched Sputnik, the men in the Kremlin became so intoxicated with a sense of power that a compromise settlement became exceedingly difficult to obtain. Finally, in 1960, Khrushchev closed the door to an immediate solution of the German question. Recognizing the realities of the new situation, Erler explained, the Social Democrats adjusted their policy accordingly.[15]

In the early years of the Bonn Republic the Social Democrats argued that the West German state was a provisorium, a halfway house on the road to reunification. As the chances for reunification diminished, however, and the party became more involved in West German political life—at the federal, state, and local levels—they became reconciled to their role as a West German party. In 1960 they formally acknowledged this by accepting the primacy of West German security. They realized that the time had arrived to bring their policies into line with the views and desires of the people among whom they lived and worked. Theirs was the politics of accommodation in a belated response to the international situation and the political climate in West Germany.

The SPD in Opposition

Looking back on the confrontation between the governing coalition and the Social Democrats in the 1950s, observers have tended to emphasize the way in which the struggle ended rather than the manner in which the contending parties fought. Led by Otto Kirchheimer, political scientists studying the role of opposition parties in parliamentary regimes have noted that the SPD, after trying initially to play the role of the loyal opposition, soon began removing its differences with the government and eventually buried all traces of opposition in order to gain access to the governing coalition.[16] The starting point of the party's transformation has been set as early as 1953, when the SPD decided to relegate the socialization aspect of its domestic program "to an inconspicuous place," or 1955, when the SPD participated in the legislative work of building a new German army.[17] Most observers, however, date the waning of SPD opposition from the 1957 election. Using Kirchheimer's original observations on West German politics, furthermore, scholars have treated the transformation as a unilinear process, the assumption being that the desire to make policy gradually overcame the party's original commitment to play the role of the opposition party.[18] The problem is, however, that viewing the confrontation between the government and the opposition in this light oversimplifies the process of change the SPD underwent and misrepresents the nature of the confrontation itself.

In September, 1949, responding to the policy declaration of the first Adenauer government, Kurt Schumacher outlined what he viewed as the role of the opposition party in a parliamentary democracy. According to Schumacher, the opposition should neither content itself with merely affirming the actions of the government nor exhaust itself in pure negation; rather, the essence of opposition "is the permanent attempt to impress on the government and its parties the positive creative will of the opposition through concrete proposals based on concrete evidence."[19] During the following decade the Social Democrats never became a passive or purely negative force in Parliament, but only with difficulty could they adhere to Schumacher's code of behavior for a constructive opposition party.

The root of the problem lay in Schumacher's attempt to set the tasks of the party in response to the political system and to what he envisaged as the class structure of West Germany. Schumacher believed that in a parliamentary system the opposition should serve as a constructive critic of the government because, as he told the party, "governing and opposing are almost equally important factors." At the same time he expected the SPD to protect the German workers and to resist the demands of "a government which represented the propertied classes."[20] Obviously the two roles could not be harmonized because they rested on conflicting assumptions: the first on a measure of cooperation between the government and the opposition, the second on a policy of confrontation between two class-conscious rivals. Naturally the latter prevailed.

The emergence of a policy of confrontation also followed directly from his Socialist beliefs, his Weimar experience, and his antagonistic nature. Schumacher seemed more suited to the role of a political opponent than that of a legislative partner, and he tended naturally toward confrontation rather than cooperation. Beyond the personality and predilections of the party leader, the issues shaped the role of the SPD in opposition. Initially Schumacher wanted to focus on domestic matters, but Germany's frontline position in the Cold War made foreign policy the dominant issue. It was there that the major disputes arose and the lines between the two sides hardened.

From the start the Social Democrats were severe critics of the government's foreign policy, but they directed the brunt of their criticism at the methods rather than the goals of the Adenauer regime. They questioned the chancellor's manner of dealing with the Western powers in the Petersberg Agreement of November, 1949, which introduced minor revisions of the Occupation Statute. According to Schumacher, the conciliatory approach used by Adenauer led him to sacrifice vital German interests, including the Saar and the Ruhr. The SPD leader also criticized the Schuman and Pleven plans, though without rejecting the idea of economic integration or a military contribution. When Adenauer went ahead with negotiations to create ECSC and EDC, however, ignoring the party's grave warnings about German participation in these integration schemes, the SPD's criticism became more bitter, and its opposition to the chancellor's Western course became more intransigent. By the first months of 1952 at the latest, it appeared that the Social Democrats stood in opposition to the goals, not simply the methods, of Adenauer's foreign policy.

As the foreign-policy debate continued and the differences between the governing coalition and the SPD deepened, it became obvious that, however the Social Democrats may have viewed the role of the opposition party originally, they could no longer play the part. During the ratification debates on the EDC treaties few traces remained of what Schumacher called the "essence of opposition"; instead, SPD policies appeared to most political observers purely negative, stemming from the party's traditional antimilitary sentiments and its emerging anti-Adenauer complex. The party gradually acquired the image of being uncompromising and uncooperative. By 1953, when the election campaign began, the public viewed the SPD as the opposition party, one radically opposed to the Adenauer regime.

Certainly the Social Democrats contributed greatly to the popularization of this belligerent image by stressing in public the inflexible nature of their policy. A close look at the first legislative period, however, shows that, far from being in total opposition, the Social Democrats behaved as responsible members of Parliament. During that four-year period they voted for more than 80 percent of the measures introduced in Parliament. Of course, agreement was greatest on domestic legislation, which made up most parliamentary business; nonetheless, the Social Democrats worked closely with coalition deputies in the Bundestag committees to amend government bills and in the plenary sessions voted for all but the most controversial.[21] On foreign policy the coalition and the SPD found less room for agreement, but even here the Social Democrats were neither entirely uncompromising nor uncooperative. They sat on the Bundestag's EDC committee, reviewing plans for a new German army, and they sent delegates to the EDC advisory meetings in Paris before the project collapsed. Although initially the Social Democrats were reluctant participants, in time they became among the most European of the parliamentarians at these international gatherings.

The Social Democrats gave little publicity to their involvement in parliamentary committees and European assemblies. They preferred to emphasize their continued enmity to the Adenauer government and said very little about their political contribution. In truth, however, during the first legislative period the SPD played a more constructive role than its public image would suggest.

In the second legislative period the pattern of SPD opposition remained the same. The party was generally cooperative in Parliament and overwhelmingly antagonistic in public, and again foreign policy served as the major area of controversy between the government and the opposition.

Clinging to their belief in the primacy of reunification, the Social Democrats demanded four-power negotiations on the German question before the government began its rearmament program. They fought the Paris Accords and organized the Paulskirche movement, trying to persuade the chancellor to wait. When Adenauer went ahead with rearmament anyway, the Social Democrats continued to argue against the creation of a West German army, disputing even the need for a military contribution to Western defense. In spite of their vehemence, however, the Social Democrats never adopted a policy of complete negation. They accepted the Paris Accords as legally binding once the treaties were ratified, and the Paulskirche movement was followed by SPD cooperation in the military legislation. Nonetheless, the party's negative image prevailed. Most West Germans remembered the party's firm no to a West German army and a close connection with the Western Alliance. They knew little of the SPD's accomplishments in Parliament; in fact, few West Germans were ready to concede that the SPD had played the role of a loyal and constructive opposition party and thus served as a potential governing party. For this the Social Democrats had no one to blame but themselves.

After the 1957 election the reformers tried to change the party's image, style, and program. During the first half of the third legislative period, however, SPD opposition increased rather than diminished in intensity. Rejection of the Adenauer course became more determined, as evidenced by the Kampf dem Atomtod campaign, and alternatives proposed by the Social Democrats became more radical. The Deutschlandplan is a prime example. In proposing the plan, Wehner gave greater emphasis to the idea of social democracy as a third force between capitalism and communism. He promised a new Germany with a political and social system vastly different from that prevailing in either German state. Thus, as the SPD marched for Kampf dem Atomtod and fought for the Deutschlandplan, there seemed to be even less room for compromise between the government and the opposition on foreign-policy matters than ever before.

On the basis of the facts presented to the public, this was a reasonable observation. Since the founding of the Bonn Republic there had been talk of a common foreign policy, but until Wehner's historic speech in June, 1960, neither side made a serious effort to bridge the gap. No doubt in the early years of the republic it would have been very difficult to bring Schumacher and Adenauer together. Both men were intent on dominating any coalition they joined, and since Adenauer was in office, he governed alone. He steadfastly refused, as one writer put it, "to accede to the Socialist demand for systematic, advanced consultation in the formulation of foreign policy measures." Of course, members of the coalition received the same treatment,[22] but it infuriated the Social Democrats. As late as September, 1959, an SPD spokesman complained that "ten years after the foundation of the Federal Republic, government and opposition have become estranged to a degree which leaves little to be expected for the future. The government makes use of its majority in parliament with complete disregard for the opposition."[23]

The picture painted by the Social Democrats of relations between the government and the opposition was accurate in its broad outlines. Adenauer was uncooperative, and the coalition parties were willing only in exceptional circumstances to challenge openly the government's policies.[24] Even then the Social Democrats still found plenty of room for effective cooperation with coalition deputies, especially on defense questions.[25] SPD deputies like Erler, Schmidt, and Merten took advantage of the opportunities presented by the Bundestag committee system to gain a voice in building and maintaining the Bundeswehr.

During the early phases of the rearmament debate critics charged that SPD policy amounted to nothing more than sterile negation. That obviously was untrue, as the party's behavior behind committee doors clearly demonstrated, but it is no easy task to assess the role of the SPD in opposition. As the main opposition party the SPD attempted to "criticize, control, and change" the conduct of the government, though with varying degrees of success.[26] On the issue of rearmament Adenauer planned to build a West German army with or without the support of the SPD. But the Social Democrats did influence aspects of the government's military policy, such as the question of parliamentary control of the armed forces. They also served as constant critics of the government, and by their efforts to mobilize public opinion against rearmament, they gave the chancellor a clear indication of what the traffic would bear. Furthermore, SPD opposition was constructive in that during the early years of the debate the party diverted the *ohne mich* group into responsible, or at least less harmful, channels. By playing the role of the defender of Germany's national rights and by appealing to various dissident groups such as refugees and veterans, the SPD also made it less likely that an antidemocratic right-wing party would emerge to gain a mass following, as had happened in the Weimar period. The Social Democrats recognized the dangers. Writing in 1951, Carlo Schmid warned that for a parliamentary democracy to survive a strong democratic party had to man the opposition benches.[27] This the Social Democrats did. They acted as a state-supporting opposition (Staatserhaltende Opposition), and, by shunning radical antiparliamentary activities themselves, they served as a guarantee that the rearmament debate would remain within the limits set by the constitution.

As the opposition party, the SPD also had the task of offering the voters a clear choice on election day. In the 1950s, however, the Social Democrats were unable to convince the electorate that they should replace the Christian Democrats as the party in power. The problem did not lie in the failure of the SPD to provide policy alternatives; on the contrary, the SPD provided clear alternatives to the government's domestic and foreign policies, offering socialism instead of capitalism and German reunification instead of West German rearmament. Most West Germans, however, considered these alternatives either unacceptable or unrealistic.

The changes carried out at Bad Godesberg and Hannover represented a belated recognition by the SPD leaders that to gain acceptance by the electorate as a potential government party the SPD would have to accept Erhard's social market economy and the Western Alliance as the framework within which West German policy would have to be developed. In retrospect, the changes came as no great surprise. Throughout the period after 1945 the Social Democrats—like Socialists in other European countries—were diluting their Socialist principles. Even on foreign-policy matters the Social Democrats had accompanied Adenauer on his Western course by contributing to the military legislation and supporting efforts at economic integration in the mid-1950s. Thus, in Kirchheimer's sense, there had been "a waning of opposition" in West Germany. For most West Germans, however, the trend of SPD opposition from 1949 to 1960 showed few signs of growing moderation; if anything, it became more belligerent and inflexible in the late 1950s than it had been in the Schumacher era. The question is why SPD opposition should have remained so antagonistic, if not intensified, over the years, while the substance of its opposition policy was being eroded away by its cooperative behavior in Parliament.

The conflicting tendencies of SPD opposition policy, being both accommodating and antagonistic,[28] stemmed from the conjunction of four major factors. First, the SPD was an ideologically bound party with a program to fulfill. The Fraktion, therefore, felt compelled to go into combat for sacred party principles; yet at the same time the deputies had to secure what they could for their constituents through political bargaining. Second, the party's readiness to work with the government parties in the various parliamentary committees was counterbalanced by its unwillingness to compromise with Adenauer in public. Relations with the chancellor were never good, and the Social Democrats made no effort to improve them. Adenauer embittered the conflict by his refusal to take the opposition leader into his confidence on major policy matters and by his opportunistic use at election time of propaganda slogans designed to identify social democracy with bolshevism. Third, the issues themselves provoked a variety of responses from the party. Whereas the Social Democrats willingly shared in the task of domestic reconstruction and gradually warmed to the cause of European economic integration, they found it very difficult to abandon their opposition to rearmament without feeling that they had sacrificed their principles. Finally, the conflicting tendencies of SPD opposition policy can be explained as the result of a struggle within the party between traditionalists and Marxists on one side and the reformers on the other. The former group tended naturally toward an antagonistic opposition— the traditionalists because of an ingrained ghetto mentality, the Marxists because of their firm ideological beliefs. Both groups insisted that the SPD remain true to its past by taking an uncompromising stance against the "class policies" of the bourgeois parties. By contrast, the reformers thought less about the past than about the current political situation. They concerned themselves with achieving political power and pursuing attainable goals. At the Stuttgart party conference the reformers gained control of the party leadership and from there they moved with determination to prepare the way for the dramatic changes at Bad Godesberg and Hannover.

Political Leadership and Party Democracy

The rearmament debate also provides an opportunity to investigate the internal operations of a political party—specifically, the problem of political leadership and party democracy. Scholars have shown considerable interest in the roles and styles of political leadership. They want to know how political leaders obtain control of a party organization, how they exercise their authority, and what impact their actions have on party members.[29] Of no less importance is the role the average member plays in the party. Does he have a voice in selecting the leaders and determining party policy, or do men at the top act without regard for the rank and file? Do parties which profess democratic principles actually adhere to them in managing their own affairs?

In a pioneering study written in 1911, Robert Michels claimed that any mass party would succumb to an "iron law of oligarchy."[30] According to Michels, two primary factors promote oligarchic conditions: one is technical, relating to the size of the organization and the need for a professional staff to perform a variety of functions; the other is psychological, from the lack of any substantial interest in political matters on the part of most party members and a corresponding readiness to leave decisionmaking to the handful of people seeking a leadership role. The validity of Michels's work on political parties has generally been accepted by scholars. In the history of West German politics there is plenty of evidence attesting to the soundness of his conclusion.

During the period under investigation here, 1949 to 1960, the SPD gave the appearance of being firmly under the control of the party leadership. From Schumacher to Ollenhauer to the Wehner-Erler-Brandt triumvirate, the style of leadership varied, but the results remained the same—the leaders led the party.

In the postwar era no one doubted that Schumacher led the SPD. Lewis Edinger describes him as a "monocratic leader" whose special position rested on a favorable combination of organizational, traditional, and personal factors,[31] that is, the authority of his office as party chairman, the respect which the rank and file had always shown for decisions handed down by the leadership, and the sense of loyalty which he inspired among party members because of his forceful personality, sharp intellect, and raw courage.

Though not an inspiring leader, Ollenhauer led the SPD by serving as guardian of the Schumacher legacy and by managing the party bureaucracy with the aid of resident officials at the Baracke in Bonn. Lacking Schumacher's enormous personal authority, Ollenhauer could never settle the many policy disputes which arose in the mid-1950s by imposing a solution; rather, he had to employ the tactics of conciliation. He proved adept at finding compromise solutions that would satisfy the competing factions within the SPD.

After the Stuttgart party conference Ollenhauer gradually surrendered control to the triumvirate led by Wehner. Before long the press began referring to Wehner as the new party boss, and indeed he wielded considerable power. He held a firm rein on the party apparatus, but he never became a leader in the style of Kurt Schumacher or "a general secretary" with a Stalinlike grip on the party, as some critics charged.[32] Wehner had to share decision-making power with members of the Presidium. More than anyone else, however, he served as the driving force of the new leadership, ensuring that the party would be led forcefully and decisively, as it had been in the Schumacher era. Finally, the victory of the triumvirate meant that control of the party passed from the bureaucrats, who supported Ollenhauer, to the politicians.

Several indicators mark the rise of the SPD politicians and the progressive domination of the parliamentary party over the party organization.[33] To begin with, the interlocking membership of the Fraktionvorstand and the Parteivorstand (the executive committees of the parliamentary party and of the national organization) increased significantly from 1949 to 1960. As positions on the Parteivorstand became available at each succeeding party conference, the delegates elected prominent politicians rather than party officials. Second, politicians predominated on the various advisory committees created by the leadership to deal with specific policy areas (for example, the security committee which the party leaders formed in 1954). Most often it was these very same politicians who sat on the work groups (Arbeitskreise) organized by the Fraktion and represented the party in the corresponding Bundestag committee. Fritz Erler chaired the work group on security policy and served as deputy chairman on the Bundestag Defense Committee. He and other party experts often determined the position taken by the SPD in their area of specialization.[34]

The influence of the politicians also grew because of their role and responsibility in the political struggle. They had to make day-to-day decisions on policy matters in response to government initiatives. While Parliament was in session, they were in constant contact with each other at work-group sessions, Bundestag committee meetings, or parliamentary party caucuses. The Parteivorstand, on the other hand, generally met only once a month; the party conference, the party's highest organ, convened every two years. This meant that the party could only approve what the Fraktion had already done, as happened at the 1956 Munich conference on the question of SPD participation in the military legislation. Theoretically the party conference set the guidelines for the leadership and the parliamentary party to follow. That was the purpose of the military resolution passed two years before at Berlin. In the heat of the parliamentary battle, however, the Fraktion had to interpret these guidelines and often took the broadest interpretation possible. Furthermore, rather than being passive recipients of the party's will as expressed in conference resolutions, the deputies actually played a major role in shaping those resolutions. At party conferences they spoke more often and with greater effectiveness than did any other group because of their closer acquaintance with the issues. Gradually on policy matters conference delegates began to defer more and more often to the growing expertise and greater self-confidence of the parliamentary deputies.[35]

As the politicians came to dominate the Executive Committee itself, their impact on the outcome of the biennial meetings increased accordingly, because the leadership conducted affairs at an SPD party conference.[36] The leaders set the agenda and named the presiding chairman of the conference and its policy committees. There was little chance, therefore, of matters getting out of hand. When it came time to elect a new Parteivorstand, the party leaders proposed the list of candidates. On policy matters the conference debated and then adopted a slightly amended version of the resolution prepared by the leadership. In every case the leaders made the important decision, and the delegates accepted with more or less enthusiasm what had already been decided. As a result, an SPD party conference tended to take on "a demonstrative character," presenting a show of solidarity to the outside world.[37]

During the period between party congresses, the Parteivorstand had the responsibility of conducting the party's business and controlling the party organization, which it did with little interference from below. Most Social Democrats became involved only when the Fraktion tackled a highly controversial issue, like NATO membership or atomic weapons. At best, no more than a quarter of the members participated regularly in party affairs. As a result local party organizations tended to fall under the control of long-serving officials, most of whom adhered to the party line and preferred to leave the direction of the party to the men in Bonn.[38]

Based on the evidence, therefore, most critics believe that the SPD —like the other major parties in the Federal Republic—failed to meet the standards of intraparty democracy set by the constitution and further elaborated in the party law of 1967.[39] The criticism is valid, though it can be overstated in terms of what can realistically be expected from the members of any democratic party. To begin with, Michels was obviously correct when he pointed out that any large organization, even one organized on democratic principles, has tendencies toward oligarchy. While the leaders develop a strong desire to hold onto the reins of power, the members find it difficult to maintain a high level of interest in party affairs. These developments, as Philip Cook has pointed out, are real, but "they are not in themselves fatal to democracy."[40] As long as the policies pursued by the leadership correspond in general with the wishes of the party members, and as long as the "upward flow of ideas and policy views is not completely dominated by the downward flow of views and decisions by party leaders," then intraparty democracy does exist.[41] This certainly was the case in the SPD, at least with regard to the question of rearmament.

Before the rearmament debate opened in midsummer, 1950, the Social Democrats had already made their views known. A resolution passed at the Hamburg conference expressed the party's opposition to rearmament, as well as its general agreement on this particular issue. Differences emerged when Schumacher announced in August, 1950, the SPD's conditional acceptance of a defense contribution. Since Schumacher began to stress more and more in the following years the reasons why the SPD opposed rearmament, however, the party gained the impression that its views were being heard.

If under Schumacher the party followed the leadership on the assumption that leaders and followers were marching in step, under Ollenhauer the members showed that they could speak out vigorously if the men at the top deviated from the established course. This became obvious at the Berlin and Munich party conferences, where a majority of the delegates wanted the party to continue its fight against rearmament. To the extent that neither party conference issued a positive declaration on national defense, the rank and file got its way. Critics point out, however, that fundamental decisions on party policy are not made at the biennial conference. If a dispute arises, the party's leading committees (Parteivorstand and Parteirat) settle the matter before the conference convenes. The delegates merely give their approval, after a long discussion, to a resolution which follows in essence a draft proposed by the Executive Committee. Thus the leaders remain in control. The point is, however, that even if the leaders had their recommendations approved, they made those recommendations in response to pressure from below, pressure that members of the Parteivorstand felt as they traveled around the country visiting local party organizations. On the basis of their findings, they drafted proposals that they knew would gain acceptance, but even then — as happened at Berlin — they had to accept further restrictions on their freedom of action.

The Berlin and Munich party conferences also demonstrated the party's influence on personnel selection, particularly its preference for men who would maintain the established course and preserve cherished party traditions. At Berlin such rising political stars as Brandt and Erler failed to be elected to the Parteivorstand because their reformist views and compromising attitude toward rearmament made them suspect in the eyes of many party members. The delegates voted instead for anti-rearmers like Birkelbach, Kühn, and Wenzel. Two years later at Munich the delegates passed over Brandt in favor of his rival, Neumann. After the 1957 election, however, the party conceded that something had to be done to improve the SPD's sagging political fortunes. At Stuttgart the delegates turned to new men with new ideas.

In studying the rearmament debate, there can be little doubt that the rank and file made itself heard and that policy views flowed upward as well as downward in the party organization. Too often, all that the members really accomplished was to delay action on the military question. Given the Soviet Union's attitude toward reunification and the government's readiness to go ahead with rearmament, however, the SPD had to make a decision. At this point the party needed leadership.

The question of leadership can be treated in various ways. Viewed from the top down, it can be defined as the leader's ability "to guide and structure the collective behavior of the group members in a direction dictated by his personal values." This the party's first postwar chairman accomplished. During the Schumacher years no one in the party questioned his right to be chairman, and no one outside the party doubted that, when he spoke, he spoke for the SPD. From the members' point of view, a leader should represent "the norms and aspirations of the group."[42] The party never really accepted Schumacher's conception of the SPD's role as a Volkspartei and never fully understood his offensive strategy for Western defense. Ollenhauer, on the other hand, shared the antimilitary sentiments of most other party members, as well as their traditionalism and their loyalty to the party as an end in itself. In that sense he established a closer identification between leaders and followers than Schumacher had achieved.

Besides looking at the leadership from the inside, in terms of party expectations, however, it is also necessary to look at it from the outside and take into consideration the party's political role. In a parliamentary democracy leadership includes the task of making party members face their responsibilities within the political system and acknowledge the realities of the political situation. A major criticism of SPD leaders is that they did very little to convince the party of the need for a more realistic attitude toward the military question. Even Schumacher avoided this unpleasant task. Although he warned the party against trying to adopt a pacifist policy or cater to the *ohne mich* crowd, he avoided any detailed explication of his policy of strength. He allowed Erler and the military specialists to become involved in the parliamentary committee work on rearmament, realizing that if the SPD came into office it would be responsible for military affairs. Out of appreciation for the party's strong antimilitary sentiments, however, he preferred to wait on events—concessions from the Allies or new elections leading to the defeat of Adenauer—before challenging the party to rethink its position on the military question. Events worked against Schumacher. After December, 1951, failing health forced him to rely on party officials who shared to a great extent the views of the rank and file, and since neither Adenauer nor the Allies would accept his conditions for a West German defense contribution, he saw no reason to confront the party.

Indeed, Ollenhauer proved even more reluctant than Schumacher to confront the party on the military question. Of course, at first there seemed no need to do so because all agreed that the SPD should continue Schumacher's opposition policy. As Adenauer moved closer to realizing his rearmament plans, disagreement arose over how the Social Democrats should respond. Ollenhauer's major concern was to maintain party unity and prevent a bitter struggle within the party over rearmament. This he achieved at Berlin and Munich by sponsoring compromise resolutions. If the SPD wanted to win at the polls, however, it had to satisfy the public's desire for security against the Soviet threat, and that would require a clear statement of the party's unequivocal support of national defense. Given the strength of antimilitary sentiment in the party, the members could hardly be expected to take the lead. Leadership had to come from above. Unfortunately, Ollenhauer allowed himself to be pulled one way by the rank and file and another by the military specialists. In the end the latter prevailed, with Ollenhauer as a reluctant partner.

The military specialists acted as the main driving force in changing the party's position on rearmament. Since at first they could not extract a positive statement from the party, they concentrated on securing enough freedom of maneuver to deal with rearmament. This much Ollenhauer was willing to provide. With the aid of flexible resolutions, and by persuading Ollenhauer to take executive action on certain pressing matters, they participated in the legislative debates. Certainly the military specialists carried the party further than it wanted to go,[43] but except for pacifists and a few radical leftists the Social Democrats recognized the need to pursue something more than a policy of negation. Finally, at Stuttgart, they accepted a positive statement on national defense. During the next two years the new leaders persuaded the party to accept a good deal more. The pressure of events—the Berlin crisis, the abortive Paris summit conference, the harsher conditions in East Germany—made their task easier, but even then it required determined leadership and a clear sense of direction from those holding the reins of power.

Soon after the Stuttgart party conference, a West German reporter commented that the problem facing the Social Democrats in dealing with military policy was "a leadership problem of the first order."[44] Neither Schumacher nor Ollenhauer had confronted the party with its responsibilities in the military area; rather, they had merely confirmed the party's oppositionist tendencies by either ignoring or appeasing the rank and file's antimilitary sentiments. Between Stuttgart and Hannover, however, the triumvirate Brandt, Erler, and Wehner challenged the party to create a positive image and to think of governing instead of opposing. That they persuaded the party to abandon policies and traditions deeply rooted in the SPD's long history can only be described as a triumph of political leadership. The result was the emergence of a party better able to compete in the West German political arena because it could offer the electorate an acceptable alternative to the governing coalition. By abandoning the party's Marxist heritage and ending the futile struggle against rearmament and the NATO connection, the new leaders laid the foundation for the SPD's political success in the following decade.

Notes

Introduction

1. For example Robert Michels, *Zur Soziologie des Parteiwesens in der modernen Demokratie;* Harold K. Schellenger, *The SPD in the Bonn Republic: A Socialist Party Modernizes;* A. Joseph Berlau, *The German Social Democratic Party, 1914-1921;* Klaus Epstein, "Three American Studies of German Socialism," *World Politics* 11 (July, 1959):629-51.

2. For a discussion of recent views, see Arthur B. Gunlicks, "Intraparty Democracy in West Germany," *Comparative Politics* 2 (January, 1970):229-32.

3. Otto Kirchheimer, "The Waning of Opposition in Parliamentary Regimes," *Social Research* 24 (Summer, 1957):127-56; Otto Kirchheimer, "Germany: The Vanishing Opposition," in R. A. Dahl, ed., *Political Opposition in Western Democracies,* pp. 237-59.

4. See, for example, Roger B. Tilford, "Grand Coalition: Not So Grand for the Parliamentarians," *Parliamentary Affairs* 20 (Spring, 1967):136-43; Gordon Smith, "West Germany and the Politics of Centrality," *Government and Opposition* 11 (Autumn, 1976):387-407. Others have argued, however, that once the SPD improved its competitive position, as it did in the sixties, alternating party governments became a real possibility. See Lewis J. Edinger, "Political Change in West Germany: The Federal Republic After the 1969 Election," *Comparative Politics* 2 (July, 1970):549-78; David P. Conradt, "The 1976 Campaign and Election," in K. H. Cerny, ed., *Germany at the Polls: The Bundestag Election of 1976,* pp. 29-56.

5. Seymour M. Lipset, "The Changing Class Structure and Contemporary European Politics," *Daedalus* 93 (Winter, 1964):271-303. Although some argued that socioeconomic developments in postwar Western Europe were leading to an end of ideology, others have more realistically pointed out that there has been only a decline or watering down of ideological commitments. See Jeff Fishel, "On the Transformation of Ideology in European Political Systems," *Comparative Political Studies* 4 (January, 1972):406-37.

6. Dolf Sternberger, "Der Wille des Bundeskanzlers," *Die Gegenwart* 8 (August 1, 1953):489; Klaus von Schubert, *Wiederbewaffnung und Westintegration,* p. 7.

7. This was true for theoreticians such as Karl Kautsky and Rudolf Hilfer-

ding but not for party radicals like Rosa Luxemburg and Karl Liebknecht. See Carl E. Schorske, *German Social Democracy, 1905-1917,* pp. 243-46; Milorad M. Drachkovitch, *Les Sozialismes Francais et Allemand et le Probleme de la Guerre, 1870-1920,* pp. 281-86.

8. Quoted in Berlau, *German Social Democratic Party,* p. 373.

9. Gustav A. Caspar, *Die SPD und das Deutsche Wehrproblem in Jahren der Weimarer Republik,* p. 11. On SPD foreign policy during the Weimar period, see Reimund Klinckhammer, "Die Aussenpolitik der Sozialdemokratischen Partei Deutschlands in der Zeit der Weimarer Republik" (Ph.D. diss., Freiburg University, 1955).

10. For SPD treatment of the military question in imperial Germany, see Reinhard Höhn, *Sozialismus und Heer;* Albrecht Lothholz, "Die Haltung der Sozialdemokratie in den Heeres-, Flotten-, und Weltmachtsfragen, 1890-1914," (Ph.D. diss., Freiburg University, 1966).

11. On relations between the Socialists and the army during the revolution, see Wolfgang Sauer, "Das Bündnis Ebert-Groener," (Ph.D. diss., Free University, Berlin, 1956); Hermann Heidegger, *Die Deutsche Sozialdemokratie und der Nationale Staat, 1870-1920,* pp. 277-302.

12. Harold J. Gordon, *The Reichswehr and the German Republic, 1919-1926,* p. 392.

13. On the SPD and the Reichswehr, see ibid., pp. 374-95; Caspar, *Die SPD und das Deutsche Wehrproblem,* pp. 47-50.

14. Drachkovitch, *Les Socialismes Francais et Allemand,* p. 262; Schorske, *Social Democracy,* pp. 59-87; Hedwig Wachenheim, *Die deutsche Arbeiterbewegung,* pp. 428-45.

15. The SPD's decision to support the war effort was directly influenced by (1) the fear of government reprisals, which was well founded, since the Defense Ministry did make plans to dissolve the party in case it went into opposition; (2) the fear of losing the backing of their working-class supporters, who had also been caught up in the wave of patriotism that had swept Germany; and (3) the fear of seeing Germany defeated by Czarist Russia, which the Social Democrats viewed as a threat to Western freedom and civilization. See Wachenheim, *Die deutsche Arbeiterbewegung,* pp. 584-99; Schorske, *Social Democracy,* pp. 286-91.

16. On the national-defense question and the Magdeburg resolution, see Caspar, *Die SPD und das Deutsche Wehrproblem,* pp. 5-20.

17. Drachkovitch, *Les Socialismes Francais et Allemand,* pp. 259-61; Schorske, *Social Democracy,* pp. 69-75.

18. Caspar, *Die SPD und das Deutsche Wehrproblem,* pp. 89-96; Gordon, *The Reichswehr,* pp. 378-83.

Chapter 1

1. For studies of Schumacher's life, see Lewis J. Edinger, *Kurt Schumacher: A Study in Personality and Political Behavior;* Friedrich Heine, *Kurt Schumacher: Ein demokratischer Sozialist europäischer Prägung;* Arno Scholz and Walther Oschilewski, *Turmwächter der Demokratie: Ein Lebensbild von Kurt Schumacher;* Fried Wesemann, *Kurt Schumacher: Ein Leben für Deutschland.*

2. Flora Lewis, "The Hard-Bitten Herr Schumacher," *New York Times Magazine,* July 31, 1949, p. 33; Wesemann, *Schumacher,* p. 44.

3. Scholz, *Turmwächter,* 1:124, 467.

4. Ibid., 2:23-24.

5. Edinger, *Schumacher,* p. 65.

6. "Tiger Burning Bright," *Time Magazine,* June 9, 1952, p. 33.

7. Schumacher was once quoted as saying, "I am wedded to politics and that would not make a wife very happy." See Joachim Joesten, "Kurt Schumacher: Politician on a Tightrope," *Tomorrow* 7 (July, 1947):28; Ernest O. Hauser, "The German Russia Hates Most," *Saturday Evening Post,* November 15, 1947, pp. 24-26.

8. From the titles of two laudatory biographies. His opponents variously described him as another Hugenberg, Vishinsky, or Hitler. See Waldemar Ritter, *Kurt Schumacher: Eine Untersuchung seiner politische Konzeption,* p. 105. One reporter, reflecting the ambiguous feeling of many, wrote: "He is dogmatic to the point of fanaticism and an authoritarian who does not accept criticism or opposition. Even when conversing with him in a relaxed atmosphere I could detect in him no human warmth. . . . But I could not help being deeply impressed by his integrity, his sharp logic, and by his devotion to a cause." Leo Lania, "Schumacher: Violent Martyr," *United Nations World* 6 (May, 1952):15.

9. On the rebirth of the party see Albrecht Kaden, *Einheit oder Freiheit: Die Wiedergründung der SPD, 1945-46;* Klaus Schütz, "Die Sozialdemokratie im Nachkriegsdeutschland," in Max G. Lange et al., *Parteien in der Bundesrepublik.*

10. "Tiger Burning Bright," p. 34. Schumacher made anticommunism a social-democratic principle, and it was maintained by his successors. They did so not only because they shared his view of communism but also because of West German politics. The other parties never missed an opportunity to point out the common Marxist heritage of both the SPD and the SED and to suggest that the path of all Marxists leads eventually to Moscow. Although unfair, the tactic was effective at election time and compelled the party to enforce the rigidity of its anti-Communist line. As a result, there could be no flexibility on the left. The only option open to the party was to move toward the right. Wolf-Dieter Narr, *CDU-SPD: Programm und Praxis seit 1945,* p. 120; Richard Petry, "Die SPD und der Sozialismus," *Frankfurter Hefte* 9 (September, 1954):663.

11. Lewis, "Hard-Bitten Herr Schumacher," p. 10.

12. Erich Ollenhauer to the chairman of the Dutch Socialist party in April, 1946, quoted in Hans Peter Schwarz, *Vom Reich zur Bundesrepublik: Deutschland im Widerstreit der aussenpolitischen Konzeptionen in den Jahren der Besatzungsherrschaft 1945-49,* p. 499; article by Schumacher in *Die Neue Zeitung,* March 22, 1946.

13. Schutz, *Parteien,* p. 157; Kaden, *Einheit,* p. 281.

14. For example, Schumacher brought to the top people who were outside the SPD before 1945—Carlo Schmid, Adolf Arndt, Herbert Wehner, Karl Schiller—or people who held views which conflicted with those of the Weimar party—Willy Brandt, Waldemar von Knoeringen, Erwin Schoettle, Willi Eichler. See Suzanne Miller, *Die SPD vor und nach Godesberg,* p. 15.

15. Edinger, *Schumacher,* p. 109. In 1950 about 68 percent of the members were over forty-five, whereas only 46 percent of the West German population was in that age group. See Schütz, *Parteien,* p. 205. On the disillusionment of young party members, see Sidney Lens, "Social Democracy and Labor in Germany," *Foreign Policy Reports* 26 (November, 15, 1950):145.

16. Narr, *CDU-SPD,* p. 105.

17. Carlo Schmid, quoted in "Tiger Burning Bright," p. 33. Those who worked closely with Schumacher believed that it was his party. Erich Ollenhauer described him as the man who shaped "the practical policy and the goals of the reemerging SPD." See Scholz, *Turmwächter,* 2:7. Herbert Wehner said that the SPD "at that time was Kurt Schumacher." See Günther Gaus, *Staatserhaltende Opposition oder Hat die SPD kapituliert: Gespräche mit Herbert Wehner,* p. 11.

18. Edinger, *Schumacher,* p. 78; see Schumacher's comments in SPD, *Protokoll der Verhandlungen des Parteitages der SPD vom 9 bis 11 Mai 1946 in Hannover,* p. 26 (hereafter cited as *Hannover Protocols*).

19. Speech in Hamburg, September 4, 1946, in Scholz, *Turmwächter,* 2:328; "Aufruf, Sommer 1945," in ibid., 2:26-27.

20. Ibid., 2:42. SPD, *Protokoll der Verhandlungen des Parteitages der SPD 29 Juni-2 Juli 1947 in Nürnberg,* pp. 34, 41 (hereafter cited as *Nuremberg Protocols*).

21. Scholz, *Turmwächter,* 2:32, 37; *Der Telegraf,* October 19, 1946.

22. Speech in Berlin, October 18, 1946, in Scholz, *Turmwächter,* 2:308.

23. Conscious of how the Nazis had controlled the middle-class vote, Schumacher pointed out that the campaign for their support was a "central problem" for the party. Schumacher, *Nach Dem Zusammenbruch,* p. 53.

24. Wesemann, *Schumacher,* pp. 234-35; see also a speech in Koblenz, July 28, 1949, in "Schumacher Reden, 1949," file Q 10, SPD Archives.

25. Gaus, *Staatserhaltende Opposition,* p. 11.

26. *Hannover Protocols,* p. 54.

27. Scholz, *Turmwächter,* 2:30-33; *Hannover Protocols,* p. 39. He called the Social Democrats the "elite troops of democracy" and the "vanguard of humanity and internationalism on German soil." *Jahrbuch der SPD, 1947,* p. iii.

28. *Jahrbuch der SPD, 1946,* p. 7; *Die Zeit,* April, 1946, quoted in Scholz, *Turmwächter,* 2:419.

29. *Nuremberg Protocols,* p. 56; Edinger, *Schumacher,* pp. 80-82.

30. Unpublished manuscript of summer 1951, in Scholz, *Turmwächter,* 2:407; speech in Berlin, June 20, 1946, quoted in ibid., 1:69.

31. *Hannover Protocols,* pp. 34, 45-46.

32. Scholz, *Turmwächter,* 2:105. Fritz Sternberg, in "The Cancer Spot of Europe," *Nation* 164 (February 8, 1947):148, described the German people as "sullen and despairing" and Germany as a "stagnant slum."

33. Hauser, "The German Russia Hates Most," p. 25; speeches in Husum, July 7, 1946, and in Nürnberg, February 10, 1946, quoted in John A. Maxwell, *"Social Democracy in a Divided Germany 1945-1952"* (Ph.D. diss., West Virginia, 1969), p. 124.

34. For a discussion of Schumacher's view of the nation and the state see V. Stanley Vardys, "Germany's Postwar Socialism: Nationalism and Kurt Schumacher," *Review of Politics* 27 (April, 1965):220-244; Narr, *CDU-SPD,* pp. 106-12; Edinger, *Schumacher,* pp. 146-52.

35. Edinger, *Schumacher,* p. 91. Alfred Grosser, in *Western Germany: From Defeat to Rearmament,* p. 154, says that Schumacher adopted "a sort of preventive nationalism."

36. Speech in Frankfurt, June 1, 1947, in Scholz, *Turmwächter,* 2:427; "Aufruf, Sommer 1945," in ibid., 2:33.

37. *Pravda,* quoted in Joesten, "Kurt Schumacher," p. 28. Willy Brandt, *My Road to Berlin,* p. 159.

38. T. H. White, "Kurt Schumacher: The Will to Power," *Reporter* 5 (Decem-

ber 11, 1951):14. *Time* called him the "gospel preacher of a revived German nationalism" and said that he seems to be "the reincarnation of the rabble rousers . . . who led Germany down to catastrophe." *Time,* June 9, 1952, pp. 33-34.

39. Scholz, *Turmwächter,* 1:257.

40. Adenauer, *Verhandlungen des Deutschen Bundestages,* January 10, 1952, 10:7816 (hereafter cited as *Verhandlungen*). Delbert Clark, *Again the Goose Step,* p. 113.

41. *Hannover Protocols,* pp. 44-47; Schumacher, *Verhandlungen,* November 15, 1949, 1:407.

42. Schumacher, *Verhandlungen,* November 8, 1950, 5:3574.

43. Speech of April, 1946, quoted in SPD, *Dokumentation, Acht Jahre sozial-demokratischer Kampf um Einheit, Frieden, und Freiheit,* p. 10.

44. Excerpts from Wennigsen conference in Wesemann, *Schumacher,* pp. 89-92.

45. SPD, *Protokoll der Verhandlungen des Parteitages der SPD vom 11 bis 14 September 1948 in Düsseldorf,* pp. 41-42 (hereafter cited as *Düsseldorf Protocols*). A reporter quoted him as saying: "Simple minded people may think it is merely the future of Germany itself (which is at stake). Actually, it is the relationship among the victors which is now clarified on German soil." See Hauser, "The German Russia Hates Most," p. 170.

46. A commentary on a party resolution written January, 1946, in Scholz, *Turmwächter,* 2:60.

47. Scholz, *Turmwächter,* 1:211; *Nuremberg Protocols,* p. 56.

48. Article, "Deutschland und das Ruhrgebiet," May 31, 1946, quoted in Maxwell, *Social Democracy,* p. 247; see also a speech to the SPD Executive Committee in Hannover, April 20, 1949, and a public address in Gelsenkirchen, June 19, 1949, in "Schumacher Reden, 1949."

49. Scholz, *Turmwächter,* 2:48-50, 58-63; Wesemann, *Schumacher,* pp. 90-92.

50. Schumacher, *Hannover Protocols,* p. 44; Schumacher, *Zusammenbruch,* p. 173.

51. Schumacher, *Zusammenbruch,* p. 97.

52. *Düsseldorf Protocols,* p. 45. On European Socialists and a third force, see Adolf Sturmthal, "Democratic Socialism in Europe," *World Politics* 3 (October, 1950):112. For the SPD, see Schwarz, *Vom Reich,* pp. 574f.

53. Schumacher, *Düsseldorf Protocols,* p. 37. Ernst Reuter warned the Western powers: "Don't go to Munich again"; ibid., p. 53.

54. Scholz, *Turmwächter,* 2:48-49; *Hannover Protocols,* p. 32.

55. Schumacher referred to the so-called magnet thesis continuously from 1947 to 1952. See, for example, a speech in Frankfurt, May 31, 1947, in *Acht Jahre,* p. 26; and a radio address on the Bavarian Radio Network, June 11, 1952, published as a brochure: *Die Staatsgewalt geht von den Besatzungsmachten aus,* p. 12. For a discussion of the magnet thesis, see Ulrich Buczylowski, *Kurt Schumacher und die deutsche Frage,* pp. 41-47.

56. Edinger, *Schumacher,* p. 193.

57. Adenauer, *Verhandlungen,* March 19, 1953, 15:12300; Edgar Alexander, *Adenauer and the New Germany,* p. 17.

58. For Schumacher's views on European integration and the Schuman Plan, see *Protokoll der Verhandlungen des Parteitages der SPD vom 21 bis 25 Mai 1950 in Hamburg,* pp. 67-75 (hereafter cited as *Hamburg Protocols*). Speech to SPD members in Gelsenkirchen, May 24, 1951, in Scholz, *Turmwächter,* 2:363-86; Carlo Schmid, *Verhandlungen,* July 12, 1951, 7:6510-20.

59. The last interview before his death in August, 1952; Wesemann, *Schumacher,* p. 251; similarly, Adolf Arndt, *Verhandlungen,* November 24, 1949, 1:478; Carlo Schmid, "Die Politik der Deutschen Sozialdemokratie," *Die Zukunft,* November, 1951, p. 302.

60. Ollenhauer, *Verhandlungen,* October 28, 1953, 18:48. A good discussion of the reunification question appears in Klaus Erdmenger, *Das Folgenschwere Missverständnis,* pp. 33-43.

61. *News from Germany,* January, 1952; Carlo Schmid, "Germany and Europe: The SPD Program," *Foreign Affairs* 30 (July, 1952):533. The Provisorium idea is discussed in Schwarz, *Vom Reich,* pp. 512-18.

62. Schumacher in December, 1948; see Scholz, *Turmwächter,* 1:192.

63. On the Council of Europe debate, see Schumacher, *Hamburg Protocols,* pp. 62-84; Schmid, ibid., pp. 113-14; Schumacher, *Verhandlungen,* June 13, 1950, 4:2472-74. Two weeks after the Bundestag voted to join the Council of Europe, the SPD decided to send delegates to Strasbourg as well. The reason given by an SPD spokesman was that Germany could not be represented by Adenauer's supporters alone. See William E. Patterson, *The SPD and European Integration,* pp. 34-42.

64. Konrad Adenauer, *Memoirs, 1945-53,* p. 194.

65. Schumacher, *Verhandlungen,* June 13, 1950, 4:2474; speeches in Gelsenkirchen, May 24, 1951, and in Hannover, January 23, 1950, in Scholz, *Turmwächter,* 2:386, 394.

66. *Münchner Merkur,* December 6, 1949; *Die Welt,* May 24, 1950; *Frankfurter Allgemeine Zeitung,* July 13, 1951 (hereafter cited as *FAZ*).

67. Ollenhauer, *Verhandlungen,* January 11, 1952, 10:7819.

68. Edinger, *Schumacher,* p. 142.

69. Brauer, *Hamburg Protocols,* p. 101; Kaisen, quoted in Edinger, *Schumacher,* p. 130.

70. Wesemann, *Schumacher,* p. 162; Heine, *Schumacher,* p. 110; Edinger, *Schumacher,* p. 110.

71. Fritz René Allemann, *Bonn ist nicht Weimar,* p. 149.

72. Speech in Hamburg, July 30, 1949, in "Schumacher Reden, 1949."

73. Bad Durkheim program in *Neuer Vorwärts,* September 3, 1949. There was a lively discussion within the SPD in 1947 and 1949 over the question of a Grand Coalition, but Schumacher's views prevailed. He did hold open the possibility of a coalition with the left wing of the CDU, if the entire SPD program was accepted, but with Adenauer there could be no compromise.

74. Ibid., January 13, 1950. Walter Dirks wrote that Schumacher, in preparation for the next general election, was attempting to bind together the national opposition (to Adenauer and the Allies) and the social opposition (to capitalist exploitation). Dirks, "Das Jahr der Wahl-Strategie?" *Frankfurter Hefte* 7 (January, 1952):5.

75. Klaus Boelling, *Republic in Suspense,* trans. J. Steinberg, p. 10.

76. Quoted in Eugene Davidson, *The Death and Life of Germany,* p. 158.

77. Reported in *New Republic* 125 (July 16, 1951):7. On social conditions see Karl Wilhelm Böttcher, "Die Neuen Reichen und die Neureichen in Deutschland," *Frankfurter Hefte* 6 (May, 1951):331-38; Thomas Wellman, "Die soziologische Lage der Bundesrepublik," *Deutsche Rundschau* 79 (June, 1953):591-600.

78. Hans Meyerhoff, "Parties and Classes in Postwar Germany," *South Atlantic Quarterly* 46 (January, 1947):19. Wellmann, "Die soziologische Lage," p. 594.

79. Otto Kirchheimer, "Notes on the Political Scene in West Germany,"

World Politics 6 (April, 1954):314.

80. Schumacher's supporters claim that his intransigent nature stemmed from a moral strictness which barred all compromise on matters of principle. See Ritter, *Schumacher*, p. 244. Edinger, on the other hand, believes that Schumacher was psychologically incapable of taking a flexible position not only because he was "a man of principle" but also because he was a man suffering from extreme internal tensions. He had to remain consistent to his personal beliefs, even at the expense of his political goals, to maintain the equilibrium of his personality. Edinger, *Schumacher*, p. 279. Whereas Ritter emphasizes Schumacher's philosophical views to explain his actions, Edinger stresses psychological factors.

Chapter 2

1. U.S., Department of State, *Foreign Relations of the United States: Diplomatic Papers: The Conferences at Malta and Yalta, 1945*, p. 970.

2. Thomas M. Forster, *The East German Army*, trans. A. Buzek, pp. 17-24; Institut für Staatslehre und Politik, *Der deutsche Soldat in der Armee von Morgen*, pp. 17-20.

3. Institut für Staatslehre und Politik, *Der deutsche Soldat*, p. 23; Norbert Tönnies, *Der Weg zu den Waffen*, p. 20.

4. Institut für Staatslehre und Politik, *Der deutsche Soldat*, pp. 20-25; Gerhard Wettig, *Entmilitarisierung und Wiederbewaffnung in Deutschland 1943-1955*, pp. 230-32; Laurence W. Martin, "The American Decision to Rearm Germany," in Harold Stein, ed., *American Civil-Military Decisions*, p. 646.

5. W. Martini, *Süddeutsche Zeitung*, July 24, 1948 (hereafter cited as *SDZ*); Jens Daniel, *Der Spiegel*, October 2, 1948. For a more positive view, see F. A. Kramer, *Rheinischer Merkur*, November 6, 1948.

6. Kogon interview and public reaction in Institut für Staatslehre und Politik, *Der deutsche Soldat*, pp. 26-33.

7. *Jahrbuch der SPD, 1948-49*, pp. 135-36.

8. Carlo Schmid, *Die Forderung des Tages*, p. 75.

9. Walter Menzel, *Nuremberg Protocols*, p. 136.

10. Schumacher, *Hannover Protocols*, p. 34; Viktor Agartz, ibid., p. 86.

11. Schmid in Parlamentarischer Rat, *Verhandlungen des Plenums*, September 8, 1948, p. 17; also *Verhandlungen des Hauptausschusses*, November 19, 1948, p. 72; *Die Welt*, December 14, 1948.

12. *Neue Züricher Zeitung*, December 13, 1948.

13. *Neuer Vorwärts*, January 1, 1949.

14. Speech in Hannover to party leaders, April 20, 1949, "Schumacher Reden, 1949."

15. On the November rumors see Peter Calvocoressi, *Survey of International Affairs, 1949-50*, p. 151; see Wettig, *Entmilitarisierung*, pp. 273-81, for comments by General Lucius D. Clay, General Jean de Lattre de Tassigny, and Field Marshal Montgomery in favor of German rearmament.

16. For the *Plain Dealer* interview see Wallace C. Magathan, "The Politics of German Rearmament, 1949-53," (Ph.D. diss., Princeton University, 1962), pp. 8-20; Wettig, *Entmilitarisierung*, pp. 282-89.

17. Beate Ruhm von Oppen, ed., *Documents on Germany Under Occupation, 1945-54*, p. 440.

18. Ollenhauer, *Verhandlungen des Deutschen Bundestages*, December 16,

1949, 2:735-36 (hereafter cited as *Verhandlungen*). Ollenhauer was interrupted eighteen times by applause from the SPD benches during his brief address. The Social Democrats applauded loudest when Ollenhauer expressed opposition to any kind of rearmament and mentioned that responsibility for German security rested with the occupying powers.

19. *Neuer Vorwärts*, May 14, 1949. A year later he said that the Vopos have the task of waging civil war, of terrorizing the Germans in the Soviet zone, and finally of suppressing a conquered West Germany. Scholz, *Turmwächter der Demokratie*, 1:327.

20. *Neuer Vorwärts*, January 13, 1950.

21. Ibid., March 14 and April 6, 1950.

22. Ibid., January 13 and March 17, 1950.

23. SPD, *Sicherheit und Ruhrkontrolle*. According to Ulrich Buczylowski, the author of the memorandum was Fritz Baade, an SPD member and a Kiel University professor. *Schumacher*, p. 188.

24. *Verhandlungen*, November 15, 1949, 1:402.

25. *Neuer Vorwärts*, January 13, 1950.

26. SPD, *Sicherheit und Ruhrkontrolle*, p. 23.

27. Martin, "American Decision," p. 645.

28. Alfred Vagts, *Defence and Diplomacy*, p. 158. On NATO's military strength and planning, see Robert E. Osgood, *NATO: The Entangling Alliance*, pp. 28-68; Roger Hilsman, "NATO: The Developing Strategic Context," in Klaus Knorr, ed., *NATO and American Security*, pp. 11-22.

29. *New York Times*, July 4, 1950.

30. *Sozialdemokratischer Pressedienst*, June 30, 1950 (hereafter cited as *Pressedienst*).

31. Speeches in Bonn and Hannover, see *Neuer Vorwärts*, July 28 and August 4, 1950; *Sopade: Sozialdemokratische Parteikorrespondenz* 901 (September, 1950): 7-9 (hereafter cited as *Sopade*).

32. Royal Institute of International Affairs, *Documents on International Affairs, 1949-50*, pp. 322-26 (hereafter cited as *Documents*).

33. Willi Eichler, who was a member of the SPD delegation, reported from Strasbourg that if the Germans accept rearmament they are accused of being militarists, but if they refuse to rearm then the charge is that they lack sufficient interest in Germany's power position in Europe. *Neuer Vorwärts*, August 18, 1950.

34. Tönnies, *Der Weg*, pp. 51-54; Wettig, *Entmilitarisierung*, pp. 330-37.

35. Adenauer, *Memoirs*, pp. 267-83. For the primacy of the political aspects of rearmament in Adenauer's thinking, see Waldemar Besson, *Die Aussenpolitik der Bundesrepublik*, pp. 90-96; Arnulf Baring, *Aussenpolitik in Adenauers Kanzlerdemokratie*, pp. 81-90.

36. Jack Raymond, *New York Times*, August 23, 1950.

37. The interview was later published as a pamphlet. Kurt Schumacher, *Die deutsche Sicherheit;* see also his address in Stuttgart, September 17, 1950, published under the title *Deutschlands Beitrag für Frieden und Freiheit;* a foreign-policy debate in *Verhandlungen*, November 8, 1950, 5:3567-76; speech to SPD officials in Hannover, December 19, 1950, in *Sopade* 905 (January, 1951):4-9.

38. Schumacher, *Die deutsche Sicherheit*, p. 5; Schumacher, *Deutschlands Beitrag*, p. 17.

39. Interview with Fritz Sternberg, September 5, 1950, "Schumacher Interviews," file Q 7; *Neuer Vorwärts*, September 15, 1950.

40. *Neuer Vorwärts,* December 8, 1950.

41. Schumacher, *Deutschlands Beitrag,* p. 18.

42. Schmid, quoted in *Neue Züricher Zeitung,* October 23, 1950.

43. Schumacher, *Neuer Vorwärts,* September 22, 1950.

44. Schumacher, *Die deutsche Sicherheit,* p. 7; *Neuer Vorwärts,* December 8, 1950.

45. *Neuer Vorwärts,* December 22, 1950; Kurt Schumacher, *Deutschlands Forderung: Gleiches Risiko, gleiches Opfer, gleiche Chancen.*

46. *Frankfurter Allgemeine Zeitung,* December 13, 1950 (hereafter cited as *FAZ*).

47. Schumacher, *Deutschlands Beitrag für Frieden und Freiheit.*

48. Theo Pirker, *Die SPD nach Hitler,* p. 134; Allemann, *Bonn,* p. 204.

49. On the New York meeting and negotiations among NATO members on German rearmament from September to December 1950, see Wettig, *Entmilitarisierung,* pp. 341–42; Martin, "American Decision," pp. 645–46; Robert McGeehan, *The German Rearmament Question,* pp. 39–62.

50. Lewis Edinger, *West German Armament,* p. 13.

51. *New York Times,* October 26, 1950. For Adenauer's comments, see *Verhandlungen,* November 8, 1950, 5:3565–66; Paul Weymar, *Adenauer,* trans. Peter DeMendelssohn, p. 353.

52. For Schumacher's initial response to the Pleven Plan, see *Sopade* 903 (November, 1950):4–9; *Verhandlungen,* November 8, 1950, 5:3567.

53. *New York Times,* November 25, 1950; Weymar, *Adenauer,* pp. 361–65.

54. *Neuer Vorwärts,* December 15, 1950.

55. Interview in Heidelberg, January 29, 1951, in "Schumacher Interviews"; see also a speech in Bonn, March 31, 1951, published as a brochure: *Macht Europa Stark.*

56. Schumacher to Adenauer, February 6, 1951, "Schumacher Korrespondenz *A-C,*" file Q 21.

57. Eisenhower before the U.S. Congress, February 1, 1951, *Documents, 1951,* p. 12.

58. Speech in Hannover, February 24, 1951, "Schumacher Reden 1951-52," file Q 12.

59. For the Prague proposals and the Russian and Western notes on a four-power conference, which never was held, see *Documents, 1949-50,* pp. 167–78.

60. *Neuer Vorwärts,* March 16 and 23, 1951.

61. *Sopade* 905 (January, 1951):11; *Neuer Vorwärts,* January 26 and February 2, 1951; *Verhandlungen,* March 9, 1951, 6:4763.

62. From a speech to the students of the University of Kiel in February, 1951, republished as Fritz Baade, "Wie kann Deutschland verteidigt werden," *Aussenpolitik* 2 (July, 1951):254–62.

63. SPD, *Parlamentarische Politische Presse,* February 14, 1951 (hereafter cited as *PPP*); *Neuer Vorwärts,* February 16, 1951; see also a pamphlet published by the party: *Es geht um die Freiheit,* pp. 5–8.

64. Speech in Kaiserslautern, *Die Freiheit,* February 18, 1951; address on the Bavarian Radio Network in *PPP,* August 30, 1951; unpublished manuscript, summer, 1951, in Scholz, *Turmwächter,* 2:400–18.

65. Communiqué from Washington, September 14, 1951, in *Documents, 1951,* 133–35; Adenauer's response in *FAZ,* September 19, 1951.

66. *Pressedienst,* September 22, 1951.

67. On Schumacher's reaction to the Washington resolutions, see *Sopade* 914

(October, 1951):3-6, for excerpts from several speeches.

68. *Verhandlungen,* November 8, 1950, 5:3566.

69. Quoted in *New York Times,* December 12, 1950. According to a survey conducted by the Institut für Demoskopie in the fall of 1950, over 50% of the people feared that war might break out in the following year and that the Western powers would withdraw their forces if the Red Army did march. Elizabeth Noelle and Erich Peter Neumann, *Jahrbuch der öffentlichen Meinung, 1947-55* (Allensbach, 1956), pp. 350-55.

70. *Neue Züricher Zeitung,* October 23, 1950.

71. Quoted by Basil Liddell-Hart, "Should We Rearm Germany?" *New Republic* 121 (September 25, 1950):15.

72. For a discussion of the attitude of veterans' organizations, trade unions, youth groups, and the churches, see Institut für Staatslehre und Politik, *Der deutsche Soldat,* pp. 59-60.

73. *Neuer Vorwärts,* November 3, 1950; Alain Clement, "Voices of Germany: A Pastor and a Socialist," *Reporter* 4 (January 9, 1951):9-12. Niemoeller and Schumacher shared common fears about Adenauer's support for West European integration, the one that it would be a Catholic-dominated union, the other that it would be a reactionary capitalist structure.

74. Executive committee meeting in Bonn, November 1, 1950, "Schumacher Reden, 1950"; file Q 11. Hans Manthey, *Neuer Vorwärts,* December 9, 1950.

75. Paul Sethe, *FAZ,* November 13, 1950; Schumacher, *Macht Europa Stark,* p. 32.

76. Adenauer, *Verhandlungen,* November 8, 1950, 5:3565.

77. *Neuer Vorwärts,* May 4, 1951; Schumacher, quoted in *Die Freiheit,* May 15, 1951.

78. *Neuer Vorwärts,* May 25, 1951.

79. Edinger writes that "right up to his death, Schumacher insisted on following with unswerving determination the grand strategic design that he had adopted after the election." It seemed to Schumacher that the chancellor's majority rested "on a brittle alliance of basically hostile groups, and on an electoral fluke that was unlikely to recur if those who had voted for the CDU could be shown that they had been duped." Edinger, *Schumacher,* p. 212.

80. In Heidelberg, January 29, 1951, "Schumacher Interviews."

81. *New York Times,* October 12, 1950.

82. Executive Committee meeting, summer, 1951, "Schumacher Reden 1951-52."

83. Paul Sethe, *FAZ,* November 13, 1950.

84. Criticism of the SPD's opposition course, and especially of its demand for new elections, increased from the fall of 1950. *Die Welt,* October 25, 1950; *Deutsche Zeitung und Wirtschaftszeitung,* October 28, 1950; *FAZ,* April 21, 1951; *Die Zeit,* January 26, 1952.

85. His warning against an *ohne mich* attitude appeared in *Neuer Vorwärts,* October 5, 1951; his rejection of an alliance with the Communists, in *Bremer Nachrichten,* January 30, 1951.

86. Schumacher, *Verhandlungen,* November 8, 1950, 5:3569; *New York Times,* November 21, 1950.

87. Hartmut Soell refers to an Executive Committee meeting in late 1950 or early 1951 in which Schumacher had to exert considerable energy to defeat a resolution proposing that the SPD reject rearmament. One writer claims that Schumacher even threatened to resign if the resolution was accepted. Soell,

Fritz Erler: Eine politische Biographie, 1:571.

88. Schumacher, *Verhandlungen,* November 8, 1950, 5:3572.

89. *FAZ,* November 21, 1950.

90. In a speech to the SPD *Fraktion,* November 1, 1950, "Schumacher Reden, 1950." Udo Löwke refers to a memorandum which SPD press secretary Fritz Heine sent to local party leaders on February 8, 1951, stating Schumacher's preference for a democratic people's army. Löwke, *Für den Fall dass,* p. 79.

91. *News from Germany,* March, 1951; *Neuer Vorwärts,* February 9, 1951.

92. *FAZ,* October 1, 1951.

93. Edinger, *Schumacher,* pp. 232, 249-51; Buczylowski, *Schumacher,* pp. 119-21.

94. Schumacher, *Verhandlungen,* November 8, 1950, 5:3569.

95. Hans Speier, *German Rearmament and Atomic War,* p. 155.

96. Schumacher, *Deutschlands Beitrag,* p. 20; SPD, *Es Geht um die Freiheit,* p. 12.

97. Speier, *Rearmament,* p. 154; Edinger, *Schumacher,* p. 231.

98. Schmid, August 10, 1950; *Documents, 1949-50,* p. 322.

99. Adenauer, *Memoirs 1945 53,* pp. 323 28; Schumacher to Adenauer, February 6, 1951, "Schumacher Korrespondenz, A-C."

100. Löwke, *Für den Fall,* p. 69; Manfred Dormann, *Demokratische Militärpolitik: Die alliierte Militärstrategie als Thema deutscher Politik, 1949-68,* pp. 168-71; but see Schumacher, *Verhandlungen,* November 8, 1950, 5:3571. A month later he said in Hannover that the West "is in a position to give us protection." *Neuer Vorwärts,* December 22, 1950.

101. *New York Times,* March 12, 1951. According to Adenauer, Schumacher told John McCloy that sixty to seventy British and American divisions should be sent to Germany immediately. Adenauer, *Verhandlungen,* February 8, 1952, 10:8258.

102. For a thorough discussion of this view, see Buczylowski, *Schumacher,* pp. 78-141. Others have not seen this aspect of Schumacher's policy; see Erdmenger, *Das Folgenschwere Missverständnis,* p. 75; Edinger, *Schumacher,* p. 154. Even some of his colleagues failed to make the connection between his demand for a forward strategy and his concern for reunification, but in a report on Schumacher's August, 1950 press conference, Arno Scholz interpreted his demands to mean that "the restoration of German unity must be the main goal of any possible remilitarization," *Turmwächter,* 1:349; see also Carlo Schmid, *Vorwärts,* August 22, 1962; Herbert Wehner, "Vis-a-vis Konrad Adenauer," *Der Monat* 19 (June, 1967):13.

103. *Verhandlungen,* November 8, 1950, 5:3567. Adenauer's policy of strength is discussed in Schubert, *Wiederbewaffnung und Westintegration,* pp. 170-77.

104. Klaus Peter Schulz, *Vor der schwersten Entscheidung,* p. 15; Schumacher, *Deutschlands Beitrag,* p. 21.

105. Schumacher, *Deutschlands Beitrag,* p. 19; Scholz, *Turmwächter,* 2:525.

106. Schumacher, *Deutschlands Beitrag,* p. 11.

107. Broadcast on Radio Munich, February 14, 1951, *Sopade* 907 (March, 1951):5-7; speech in Kaiserslautern, April 16, 1951, "Schumacher Reden 1951-52."

108. Schumacher, *Macht Europa Stark,* p. 11.

109. Schumacher to Adenauer, February 6, 1951, "Schumacher Korrespondenz, A-C."

110. A speech on the Hessen Radio Network, October 5, 1951, republished as

a brochure: *Ein Winter der Entscheidungen;* speech in Hamburg, October 9, 1951, in Wesemann, *Schumacher,* pp. 215-16.

Chapter 3

1. For the negotiations, see: Wettig, *Entmilitarisierung und Wiederbewaff-nung,* pp. 450-87. Royal Institute of International Affairs, *Survey of International Affairs 1952,* pp. 55-109 (hereafter cited as *Survey*).

2. *Economist,* April 19, 1952, p. 143. The French position was registered in a nine-point resolution accepted by the national assembly in February, 1952; see Clarence C. Walton, "Background for the European Defense Community," *Political Science Quarterly* 68 (March, 1953):64-65.

3. Adenauer, *Verhandlungen des Deutschen Bundestages,* February 7, 1952, 10:8095-8108 (hereafter cited as *Verhandlungen*).

4. Ollenhauer, ibid., pp. 8108-8111.

5. *Frankfurter Allgemeine Zeitung,* February 25, 1952 (hereafter cited as *FAZ*). Adolf Arndt, quoted in *Lübecker Freie Presse,* March 24, 1952, said that in this situation "social accomplishments should be the German contribution to the defense of the West."

6. See the criticisms of Heinrich von Brentano, *Verhandlungen,* February 8, 1952, 10:8232; Richard Jaeger, ibid., p. 8177; Gerhard Schroeder, ibid., p. 8209.

7. Ollenhauer, ibid., February 7, 1952, 10:8110-11, 8238. In a seven-page memorandum on the party's strategy for the debate, the Executive Committee emphasized that in attacking the government's policy the SPD should concentrate on political questions rather than moral or military issues. *Debatte um den Wehrbeitrag,* file J 106, SPD Archives.

8. For the text of the treaties, see *Documents, 1952,* pp. 105-16. For commentaries, see Josef L. Kunz, "The Contractual Agreements with the Federal Republic of Germany," *American Journal of International Law* 47 (January, 1953):106-114; Elmer Plischke, "The Contractual Agreements and Changing Allied-West German Relations," *Political Science Quarterly* 69 (June, 1954): 241-65.

9. On the reaction of the coalition parties to the treaties, see Wallace Magathan, *The Politics of German Rearmament, 1949-53,* pp. 154-93; Baring, *Aussenpolitik in Adenaurs Kanzlerdemokratie,* pp. 151-62.

10. *Sozialdemokratischer Pressedienst,* May 25, 1952 (hereafter cited as *Pressedienst*); Arndt, *Verhandlungen,* May 23, 1952, 12:9415.

11. From an interview with United Press, May 22, 1952, in *Sopade* 922 (June, 1952):3-4.

12. Adenauer, *Verhandlungen,* December 5, 1952, 14:11458. For similar statements on the treaties by Carlo Schmid and Adolf Arndt, see *FAZ,* July 15 and December 5, 1952.

13. The exchange of letters was published along with other material relating to rearmament and sent out to local party organizations, see: "Information für Funktionäre und Referenten zum Thema: Verteidigungsbeitrag und Sozialdemokratie," *Debatte um den Wehrbeitrag,* file J 37, SPD Archives.

14. Willi Birkelbach of South Hesse advocated extraparliamentary action at the Fraktion meeting on February 5, 1952. William Patterson, *SPD and European Integration,* p. 82. A five-man committee, headed by Ollenhauer, was organized several weeks later to study the question. KA., *Deutsche Zeitung und Wirtschafts-*

zeitung, March 5, 1952.

15. From a resolution passed by the Hamburg-Nordwest party conference, *Neuer Vorwärts,* May 30, 1952; see also the resolutions of the Süd-Hessen party conference, ibid., July 11, 1952.

16. See Schumacher's interviews with the press, *Neuer Vorwärts,* June 6 and 27, 1952. For the attitude of the parliamentary party, see reports on the May 21, 1952, meeting in Patterson, *SPD and European Integration,* p. 87.

17. Ollenhauer, *Verhandlungen,* February 7, 1952, 10:8116. A resolution demanding new elections was passed by the Parteivorstand and Parteiausschuss on January 20, 1952. *Jahrbuch der SPD, 1952-53,* p. 282.

18. *Pressedienst,* March 6, 1952.

19. On the election and the formation of the Maier government, see *FAZ,* March 4 and April 26, 1952.

20. *Neuer Vorwärts,* October 27, 1950.

21. Adenauer, *Verhandlungen,* February 7, 1952, 10:8095. For the views of the coalition parties, see Wahl, ibid., December 3, 1952, 14:11196-201.

22. See earlier statements by Hans Manthey, *Neuer Vorwärts,* December 8, 1950; Schmid, ibid., January 25, 1952. A comprehensive statement of the SPD position by Arndt, *Verhandlungen,* December 3, 1952, 14:11201-13.

23. Fritz Erler, *Soll Deutschland rüsten?* pp. 36-38.

24. For the petition and the subsequent legal battle over the treaties, see: Freiherr von der Heydte, ed., *Der Kampf um den Wehrbeitrag,* 3 vols.; Karl Loewenstein, "The Bonn Constitution and the EDC Treaties," *Yale Law Review* 64 (1955):805-39; Edward McWhinney, "Judicial Restraint and the West German Constitutional Court," *Harvard Law Review* 75 (November, 1961):5-25.

25. Erler, *Neuer Vorwärts,* May 23, 1952.

26. *FAZ,* July 31, 1952.

27. For a discussion of the chancellor's tactics, see Magathan, *German Rearmament,* pp. 305-56; Baring, *Aussenpolitik,* pp. 235-61.

28. Wilhelm Mellies, *Verhandlungen,* December 5, 1951, 14:11623-24.

29. For the press conference, see "Ollenhauer Reden, 1952"; also a letter from Ollenhauer to Adenauer, January 7, 1953, in *Sopade* 930 (February, 1953): 4-6.

30. Alfred Grosser, *Die Bonner Demokratie,* p. 113. Narr speaks of a remarkable juridification of politics by the SPD; Narr, *CDU-SPD,* p. 285. According to the Social Democrats, the case against EDC was only one of five political suits that the SPD had before the BVG. *Jahrbuch der SPD, 1950-51,* p. 11; see also the criticism of Walter Dirks, *Frankfurter Hefte* 7 (January, 1952):2; R. Strobel, *Die Zeit,* January 24, 1952.

31. *FAZ,* May 27, 1952.

32. Schmid, "Die Aussenpolitik des Machtlosen." *Aussenpolitik* 3 (January, 1952):17; Schmid, *Verhandlungen,* July 9, 1952, 12:9811.

33. Schumacher on the Hessen Radio Network, October 5, 1951, republished as: *Ein Winter der Entscheidungen;* radio address to the Soviet zone in *News from Germany* 6 (January, 1952):1; preface to the *Dortmund Action Program,* p. 6.

34. Luetkens, *Verhandlungen,* October 16, 1951, 9:6930. Baring writes that following this incident Luetkens quickly lost influence in the formation of the party's foreign policy position. Luetkens claimed, however, that he was only echoing the views of Schumacher. Baring, *Aussenpolitik,* p. 142.

35. Ollenhauer, *Verhandlungen,* October 16, 1951, 9:6945.

36. Carlo Schmid, "Germany and Europe," *Foreign Affairs* 30 (July, 1952): 535; Wehner, *Verhandlungen,* July 10, 1952, 12:9874; Ollenhauer in a speech to the Lower Saxon party conference, in *Sopade* 923 (July, 1952):14.

37. Adenauer, *Verhandlungen,* February 7, 1952, 10:8106. Ibid., April 3, 1952, 11:8761; Adenauer, *Memoirs 1945-53,* pp. 415-27.

38. Ollenhauer, *Verhandlungen,* February 7, 1952, 10:8113.

39. Interview with United Press, May 22, 1952, in *Sopade* 922 (June, 1952):3.

40. Buczylowski, *Schumacher,* p. 151.

41. Erwin Schoettle, *Parlamentarische Politische Presse,* January 24, 1952 (hereafter cited as *PPP*); Ollenhauer, *News from Germany,* January, 1952.

42. Osgood, *NATO,* pp. 87-91; Hilsman, "NATO: The Developing Strategic Context," pp. 14-16.

43. Ollenhauer, *Verhandlungen,* February 7, 1952, 10:8109; Erler, *Pressedienst,* March 5, 1952; Willi Eichler, "Ein Verteidigungsbeitrag für die Freiheit," *Geist und Tat* 7 (March, 1952):71.

44. *Neuer Vorwärts,* February 29 and August 15, 1952; SPD, *Dortmund Action Program,* p. 12.

45. Republished in *Sopade* 922 (June, 1952):3-4; similar warnings by Schmid in ibid., pp. 5-6; Wehner, *Verhandlungen,* July 10, 1952, 12:9874; Ollenhauer, ibid., December 5, 1952, 14:11450.

46. Erler, *Verhandlungen,* July 10, 1952, 12:9902.

47. On the Communist offensive from September, 1951 to February, 1952, see *Survey, 1951,* pp. 144-53; *Survey, 1952,* pp. 59-61.

48. For the exchange of notes between East and West, see *Documents, 1952,* p. 85-86.

49. Wolfram Hanrieder, *West German Foreign Policy, 1949-63,* p. 71; Wettig, *Entmilitarisierung,* pp. 439-522; Werner Feld, *Reunification and West German-Soviet Relations,* pp. 97-98.

50. Quoted in Schubert, *Wiederbewaffnung,* p. 169.

51. *Times* (London), March 17, 1952; Adenauer, *Verhandlungen,* April 3, 1952, 11:8751-53.

52. *FAZ,* March 31, 1952; *Manchester Guardian,* June 12, 1952.

53. *Neuer Vorwärts,* October 1, 1951.

54. Radio address September 18, 1951, in *Europa Archiv* 6 (October 5, 1951): 4407.

55. *Neuer Vorwärts,* December 28, 1951.

56. Ollenhauer, *Verhandlungen,* April 3, 1952, 11:8765-66; Wehner, ibid., pp. 8753-57. The Parteivorstand and Parteiausschuss passed a resolution on German reunification, April 9, 1952, in *Jahrbuch der SPD, 1952-53,* pp. 284-85.

57. Ollenhauer on radio, April 25, 1952, in *Sopade* 921 (May, 1952):7-9; *Pressedienst,* July 11, 1952.

58. From a speech in Stuttgart, June 8, 1952, by Erich Ollenhauer, *Vor Entscheidungen für Jahrzehnte,* pp. 7-8; Gerhard Gleissberg, *Zukunft,* September, 1952, p. 253.

59. Wehner, *Verhandlungen,* July 10, 1952, 12:9875. Ollenhauer, *Neuer Vorwärts,* June 27, 1952.

60. Schmid, "Germany and Europe," p. 543.

61. Erler, *Deutsche Zeitung und Wirtschaftszeitung,* July 19, 1952.

62. Ollenhauer, *Verhandlungen,* January 11, 1952, 10:7802; Schmid, ibid., April 3, 1952, 11:8775.

63. Erler at Bonn University in *FAZ,* June 25, 1952. For a discussion of

Erler's views on the subject, see Soell, *Erler,* 1:147-55.

64. Schmid, "Germany and Europe," p. 543; Soell, *Erler,* 1:154; Rudolf Hrbek, *Die SPD—Deutschland und Europa,* pp. 166-68.

65. Wehner, *Verhandlungen,* July 10, 1952, 12:9876; Fritz Baade, "Entscheidung zwischen drei Deutschlandkonzeptionen," *Aussenpolitik* 3 (September, 1952):558-62.

66. Ollenhauer, *Vor Entscheidungen,* p. 19.

67. Ollenhauer, *Neuer Vorwärts,* January 25, 1952; *FAZ,* April 29, 1952; Mellies, *Times* (London), December 30, 1952.

68. Schmid, *Verhandlungen,* April 3, 1952, 11:8772; ibid., July 9, 1952, 12: 9818.

69. For a summary of the EDC Treaty, see "An European Army," *Current History* 23 (July, 1952):38-42; Josef L. Kunz, "The Treaty Establishing the European Defense Community," *American Journal of International Law* 47 (April, 1953):275-78.

70. Arndt, *Verhandlungen,* December 4, 1952, 14:11366.

71. Erler, *Soll Deutschland,* pp. 31-32. The SPD expressed the same concern about an "authoritarian manager's regime" in the European Coal and Steel Community. Ollenhauer, *Verhandlungen,* July 12, 1951, 8:6511.

72. Erler to Menzel, February 25, 1954, "Walter Menzel Wehrfragen," SPD Archives.

73. Ollenhauer, *FAZ,* May 15, 1952. On the SPD views of the economic aspects of EDC, see Fritz Baade, *Stuttgarter Zeitung,* March 18, 1952; Erwin Schoettle, *Verhandlungen,* July 9, 1952, 11:9834; Joachim Schoene, ibid., December 5, 1952, 14:11410.

74. Erler, *Vorwärts,* May 26, 1965; Soell, *Erler,* 1:143-47.

75. See also Erler, *Pressedienst,* June 30 and July 30, 1952; *Verhandlungen,* December 5, 1952, 14:11474-78. Erler had discussed the question of the internal structure of a new defense force earlier in the year on the North West German Radio Network. *Berliner Stimme,* January 25, 1952.

76. Erler, *Verhandlungen,* January 21, 1953, 14:11674-75; Mellies, *Neuer Vorwärts,* July 25, 1952; Ollenhauer, ibid, November 21, 1952. On the Blank Office and parliamentary control of its activities, see Arthur B. Boenau, "Civilian Control of the Military by the West German Government, 1949-57," (Ph.D. diss., Columbia University, 1964).

77. Ollenhauer, *Verhandlungen,* December 5, 1952, 14:11455.

78. Adenauer, ibid., July 9, 1952, 12:9801.

79. Ollenhauer, *PPP,* November 30, 1952.

80. Erler, *Verhandlungen,* December 5, 1952, 14:11478; Schmid, ibid., July 9, 1952, 12:9813; Schumacher, *Times* (London), November 27, 1951.

81. Schmid, *Verhandlungen,* February 8, 1952, 10:8185; Ollenhauer, *Vor Entscheidungen,* pp. 13-14; Schumacher, *Die Staatsgewalt,* pp. 5-6.

82. Mellies quoted in *FAZ,* January 16, 1953.

83. Adenauer, *Memoirs 1945-53,* p. 406; Allemann, *Bonn ist nicht Weimar,* p. 198.

84. Schmid, "Germany and Europe," pp. 532-34; Ollenhauer, *Neuer Vorwärts,* March 28, 1952.

85. Adenauer, *Verhandlungen,* December 3, 1952, 14:11144; ibid., July 9, 1952, 12:9789-9801.

86. Ollenhauer, ibid., December 3, 1952, 14:11448.

87. Ollenhauer, *Neuer Vorwärts,* September 5, 1952; Gleissberg, ibid., De-

cember 19, 1952; Brandt, *Pressedienst,* February 4, 1952.

88. Arndt, *Verhandlungen,* February 8, 1952, 10:8155.

89. Alistair Horne, *Return to Power,* p. 34. The lack of a clear and acceptable alternative was the most consistent criticism of the SPD's position in 1952. See *Christ und Welt,* February 14, 1952; *Die Zeit,* May 29, 1952; *FAZ,* September 4, 1952.

90. Wehner, *Neuer Vorwärts,* October 31, 1952.

91. Erler, *Verhandlungen,* December 5, 1952, 14:11483. Eichler warned that there would be no chance for reasonable conversations once both sides faced each other with heavy artillery. Willi Eichler, "Kanonen und Vernunft," *Geist und Tat* 7 (April, 1952):98.

92. Kurt Schumacher, "Peace Contract Brings No Peace," *Newsweek,* June 30, 1952, p. 36; Schmid at Rüsselsheim, *Die Freiheit,* July 7, 1952; Ollenhauer, *Verhandlungen,* December 5, 1952, 14:11454.

93. Ollenhauer in Hannover, *Neuer Vorwärts,* November 7, 1952.

94. Ollenhauer in Bonn, June 11, 1952, and in Vienna, July 7, 1952, "Ollenhauer Reden, 1952."

95. It is difficult to say whether Adenauer actually believed that his policy of strength would lead to reunification and force the Russians not only to withdraw from Eastern Europe, but also to let Germany join the Western alliance with its 1937 frontiers. For critical views of the chancellor, see Baring, *Aussenpolitik,* p. 138; James L. Richardson, *Germany and the Atlantic Alliance,* p. 29.

96. Schumacher in an interview with United Press, May 15, 1952, in *Sopade* 922 (June, 1952):3-4; Schmid, "Germany and Europe," p. 544.

97. Erler, *Neuer Vorwärts,* August 29, 1952; Erler, *Soll Deutschland,* p. 49.

98. Narr, *CDU-SPD,* p. 118; Speier, *German Rearmament,* p. 75.

99. Schumacher, *Die Staatsgewalt,* p. 11; Schmid, *Verhandlungen,* July 9, 1952, 12:9818.

100. *Pressedienst,* June 27, 1952; Ollenhauer, *Neue Zeitung,* May 13, 1952; Magathan, *German Rearmament,* pp. 36, 348.

101. Wolfgang Kralewski and Karl Heinz Neunreither, *Oppositionelles Verhalten in Ersten Deutschen Bundestag, 1949-53,* pp. 97-99.

102. Schoettle, *Verhandlungen,* February 8, 1952, 10:8241. The committee, called the Ausschuss zur Mitberatung des EVG-Vertrags, and, later, the Ausschuss für Fragen der europäischen Sicherheit, sat from July 19, 1952 to August 4, 1953. Session reports are kept by the secretary of the Bundestag Defense Committee in Bonn.

Chapter 4

1. For laudatory accounts of Ollenhauer's career, see Walther G. Oschilewski et. al., *Erich Ollenhauer: Der Führer der Opposition;* Dieter Schröder, *Erich Ollenhauer.* For critical comments, see Walter Theimer, *Von Bebel zu Ollenhauer,* pp. 103-108; Pirker, *SPD nach Hitler,* pp. 165-66.

2. *Der Spiegel* 6 (October 1, 1952):6; Drew Middleton, *New York Times,* August 22, 1952.

3. Edinger, *Schumacher,* p. 134; Wesemann, *Schumacher,* p. 243.

4. *FAZ,* August 28, 1952.

5. Walter Henkels, *FAZ,* February 26, 1953; Hans Schuster, *SDZ,* May 20, 1958.

6. Schellenger, *The SPD in the Bonn Republic*, pp. 40-42, 72-75; Douglas A. Chalmers, *The Social Democratic Party of Germany*, pp. 55-60.

7. Ollenhauer, *Protokoll der Verhandlungen des Parteitages der SPD vom 24 bis 28 September 1952 in Dortmund*, p. 33 (hereafter cited as *Dortmund Protocols*).

8. The original draft was printed in *Neuer Vorwärts*, August 1, 1952. The Dortmund Program was published as a pamphlet: *Aktionsprogramm der SPD*.

9. Resolutions passed by local party organizations for the Dortmund conference were published in *Neuer Vorwärts*, August 29, 1952.

10. Brandt, *Dortmund Protocols*, p. 161. The Berlin party was divided between the supporters of Ernst Reuter and the traditionalists, led by Franz Neumann, who adhered to the party line set by the Bonn leaders. Abraham Ashkenasi, *Reformpartei und Aussenpolitik*, pp. 60-97.

11. Speaking in Bonn, June 11, 1952, "Ollenhauer Reden, 1952."

12. Eichler, *Dortmund Protocols*, p. 246.

13. *Sozialdemokratischer Pressedienst*, September 29, 1952 (hereafter cited as *Pressedienst*).

14. *London Times*, October 28, 1952.

15. Brandt, *Verhandlungen des Deutschen Bundestages*, December 3, 1952, 14:1111-16 (hereafter cited as *Verhandlungen*); Arndt, ibid., p. 11201; Ollenhauer, ibid., December 4, 1952, 11445-56; press conference in Bonn, December 12, 1952, "Ollenhauer Reden, 1952."

16. Hans Baumgarten, *FAZ*, March 10, 1953.

17. Eichler, "Kanonen und Vernunft," p. 98.

18. Baade, "Entscheidung zwischen drei Deutschlandkonzeptionen," p. 558; *Dortmund Protocols*, p. 55.

19. Erler, *Neuer Vorwärts*, March 27, 1953; Brandt, quoted in Ashkenasi, *Reformpartei und Aussenpolitik*, p. 97.

20. Brauer, quoted in *FAZ*, May 17, 1953. For Reuter's views on rearmament, see Willy Brandt and Richard Löwenthal, *Ernst Reuter*, pp. 638-62.

21. Memorandum from Herbert Wehner, January 17, 1953, "Ollenhauer Aussenpolitik, 1951-55," file J 34, SPD Archives.

22. *Die Welt*, February 9, 1953.

23. Gerhart Luetkens, "Betrachtungen zu einem Deutschlandvertrag," *Aussenpolitik* 4 (March 1953):141-51. Speaking in London, Adolf Arndt proposed that West German armed forces be coordinated within the framework of an all-European pact of friendship and mutual assistance. *FAZ*, January 14, 1953. Ollenhauer told a radio audience that the SPD favored a grand coalition, including Britain, Norway, and Denmark, as the organization for Western defense. *New York Times*, January 24, 1953.

24. *FAZ*, February 4, 1953. Two weeks earlier Ollenhauer told the press that Eisenhower did not view the existing treaties as the only possible solution. *FAZ*, January 17, 1953. Willy Brandt added that most of the other European states were amenable to new negotiations. *Die Freiheit*, February 6, 1953.

25. *FAZ*, February 7, 1953; *Der Spiegel*, 7 (February 11, 1953):6-8. According to Dulles, the SPD did not have an alternative to EDC. The party's proposals, he said, were "extremely feeble and unsubstantial."

26. Ollenhauer, *Verhandlungen*, March 19, 1953, 15:12324; Adenauer, ibid., p. 12302; also Adenauer's interview with *Le Monde*, quoted in *FAZ*, March 21, 1953.

27. Ollenhauer, *Verhandlungen*, pp. 12327-28. Erler explained Ollenhauer's

security proposal to SPD readers in *Neuer Vorwärts,* March 27, 1953.

28. Paul Sethe, *FAZ,* March 21, 1953. For a critical view, see Walter Dirks, "Sozialdemokratische Alternativen," *Frankfurter Hefte* 8 (April, 1953):249; Werner Friedman, *SDZ,* March 21, 1953.

29. Ollenhauer in Paris, *SDZ,* April 16, 1953.

30. For Maier's role in the Bundesrat and the ultimate passage of the treaties, see Baring, *Aussenpolitik in Adenauers Kanzlerdemokratie,* pp. 271-91; Magathan, *The Politics of German Rearmament,* pp. 379-436.

31. Pirker, *SPD nach Hitler,* p. 177. For the differences between Bonn and Stuttgart, see *FAZ,* May 16 and 19, 1953; *SDZ,* May 18 and 23, 1953.

32. *Neuer Vorwärts,* March 13, 1953.

33. See Drew Middleton, *New York Times,* May 11, 1953 and Hans Ulrich Kempski, *SDZ,* May 12, 1953. Ollenhauer's speech was published as a brochure: *1953: Das Jahr der Entscheidung.*

34. Wolfgang Hirsch-Weber & Klaus Schütz, *Wähler und Gewählte: Eine Untersuchung der Bundestagswahlen 1953,* p. 20.

35. Ollenhauer in Dortmund, *Neuer Vorwärts,* May 22, 1953; on the North German Radio Network, June 9, 1953, and to the SPD Fraktion, August 2, 1953, "Ollenhauer Reden, 1953."

36. *New York Times,* June 25, 1953. Ollenhauer told the parliamentary party on August 2 that because the Russians were conscious of what effect a second East German uprising would have on the other satellite states, there was now a chance for "promising talks." "Ollenhauer Reden, 1953."

37. Ollenhauer, *Neuer Vorwärts,* July 3, 1953; Gleissberg, ibid., June 5, 1953.

38. For example, Ollenhauer at the Socialist International Convention in Stockholm, *New York Times,* July 16, 1953.

39. Erler, *Neuer Vorwärts,* July 10, 1953; Ollenhauer, ibid., August 14, 1953.

40. Willi Eichler, "Sie stimmten mit den Füssen ab," *Geist und Tat* 8 (July, 1953):195-99. The Parteivorstand protested against "the chancellor's efforts to prevent the convening of a four-power conference"; see its resolution of June 4, 1953, *Jahrbuch der SPD, 1952-53,* p. 292.

41. An article by Ollenhauer in *SDZ,* September 5, 1953; see also his comments in *Neuer Vorwärts,* July 3, 1953; *Die Freiheit,* August 10, 1953.

42. Hirsch-Weber, *Wähler und Gewählte,* pp. 118-22; the SPD's answer in *Pressedienst,* August 4, 1953.

43. *Die Neue Zeitung,* August 29, 1953. Erler summarized his view in *Pressedienst,* September 1, 1953; similar statements by the party's press secretary, Fritz Heine, quoted in *New York Times,* August 31, 1953.

44. Hirsch-Weber, *Wähler und Gewählte,* pp. 123-24; Ollenhauer responded in Hamburg, *New York Times,* September 1, 1953; in Minden, *FAZ,* September 4, 1953; and in *SDZ,* September 5, 1953.

45. *London Times,* August 31, 1953; *Manchester Guardian,* September 3, 1953.

46. *New York Times,* September 2, 1953.

47. Brandt and Löwenthal, *Reuter,* pp. 690-91.

48. *New York Times,* September 6, 1953.

49. Hirsch-Weber, *Wähler und Gewählte,* pp. 19-22, 396-402.

50. Norbert Muhlen, "The Victory of Konrad Adenauer," *The New Leader* 36 (October 19, 1953):16.

51. Ollenhauer quoted in the *New York Times,* August 13, 1953. Erdmenger points out that in West Germany the Soviet Union was not viewed as a state with interests corresponding to those of a state in the free world, but as the

center of a world-conquering communism. Erdmenger, *Folgenschwere Missverständnis*, p. 97.

52. Erler's letter to Fritz Sänger, October 13, 1953, and to Kurt Mattick, September 26, 1953, "Erler Veröffentlichungen, 1953-54."

53. Quoted in Horne, *Return to Power*, p. 222.

54. Hirsch-Weber, *Wähler und Gewählte*, p. 122; Frank Tollman, "Wuerzburg goes to the Polls," *New Republic* 129 (September 21, 1953):5; Edgar Schranz, "Deutschland nach der Wahl," *Zukunft*, October, 1953, p. 275.

55. *Pressedienst*, September 8, 1953; *Westfälische Rundschau* (SPD Dortmund), September 9, 1953; *Neue Ruhr Zeitung* (SPD Essen), September 8, 1953; *Die Freiheit* (SPD Mainz), September 7, 1953; *Neuer Vorwärts*, September 11, 1953.

56. Willi Eichler, "Das schwarze Sonntag," *Geist und Tat* 8 (September, 1953):257-62; Ollenhauer, *Neuer Vorwärts*, September 11, 1953.

57. Published as a pamphlet: Erich Ollenhauer, *Nach der Entscheidung*. Also, Ollenhauer on the Bavarian Radio Network the evening before the conference, *Neuer Vorwärts*, September 18, 1953.

58. Criticisms expressed publicly by Paul Löbe, *Berliner Stimme*, September 13, 1953; Heinrich Albertz, quoted in *Der Spiegel* 7 (September 16, 1953); see the discussion of party critics in *FAZ*, September 18 and 19, 1953.

59. Brandt and Löwenthal, *Reuter*, pp. 700-702.

60. *News from Germany*, September/October, 1953.

61. A resolution drafted September 17 by the party's three main committees sitting in joint session with the Fraktion. *Jahrbuch der SPD, 1952-53*, p. 296.

62. Ollenhauer, *Verhandlungen*, October 28, 1953, 18:35.

63. *Basler Nationalzeitung, Neue Züricher Zeitung*, and *Die Tat*, October 29, 1953.

64. Ollenhauer, *Verhandlungen*, October 28, 1953, 18:48-50.

65. Quoted in *SDZ*, October 30, 1953.

66. For example *Pressedienst*, October 30, 1953; *Neuer Vorwärts*, November 13, 1953; Erler, "Es geht auch anders," *Links*, November, 1953, pp. 9-11.

67. *Neuer Vorwärts*, November 13, 1953.

68. Luetkens in Strasbourg, *Neuer Vorwärts*, September 25, 1953; Erler, *Pressedienst*, October 13, 1953; Luetkens in Washington, *New York Times*, October 16, 1953.

69. Eichler, *Pressedienst*, October 19, 1953; Ollenhauer in Hannover, November 15, 1953, "Ollenhauer Reden, 1953."

70. *FAZ*, December 11, 1953.

71. Gleissberg, *Neuer Vorwärts*, January 8, 1954; Erler, *Pressedienst*, January 21, 1954; Ollenhauer, quoted in *SDZ*, January 23/24, 1954.

72. On the conference, see *Survey, 1954*, pp. 130-37; United States Senate Committee on Foreign Relations, *Documents on Germany, 1944-61*, pp. 146-55; Walter Bodigheimer, "Die Verhandlungen über das Sicherheitsproblem auf der Berliner Konferenz von 1954," *Europa Archiv* 9 (1954):6496-6513.

73. Hanrieder, *West German Foreign Policy*, p. 73.

74. United States Senate, *Documents on Germany*, p. 154.

75. Adenauer, *Verhandlungen*, February 25, 1953, 18:518-22.

76. Ollenhauer, ibid., pp. 522-28; also, Ollenhauer to the Parteivorstand, Parteiausschuss, and Kontrollkommission, February 19, 1954, "Ollenhauer Reden, Januar-Juni 1954."

77. Ollenhauer in Berlin, *SDZ*, March 3, 1954; also, Gerhard Gleissberg

and Eberhard Zachmann, *Neuer Vorwärts,* February 19, 1954.

78. Richard Tungel, *Die Zeit,* February 25, 1954; Georg Schröder, *Die Welt,* February 25, 1954; Hans Baumgarten, *FAZ,* February 26, 1954; Dehler quoted in *FAZ,* March 10, 1954.

79. Ollenhauer to Adenauer, February 20, quoted in *SDZ,* February 22, 1954; also, the declaration by the Parteivorstand, Parteiausschuss, and Kontrollkommission in Bonn, February 20, 1954, in *Jahrbuch der SPD, 1954-55,* pp. 318-20.

80. Quoted in *Die Welt,* February 24, 1954.

81. Ollenhauer, *Neuer Vorwärts,* February 26, 1954.

82. Kaisen quoted in a *SDZ,* February 22, 1954 and *Die Welt,* March 4, 1954; Karl Schiller, ibid., February, 25, 1954.

83. *Jahrbuch der SPD, 1954-55,* pp. 318-20.

84. On the formation of the committee and a report on its first meeting, see *Neuer Vorwärts,* November 20, 1953 and January 22, 1954.

85. Ollenhauer, *Verhandlungen,* February 25, 1954, 18:527; Schmid, ibid., February 26, 1954, p. 572.

Chapter 5

1. Statement by the Hamm party organization in *Der Spiegel* 7 (November 11, 1953):6; Erler, quoted in *SDZ,* November 5, 1953.

2. Schmid, *Neue Ruhr Zeitung,* December 19, 1953. On the inner party debate, see Hans Ulrich Kempski, *SDZ,* December 5, 1953; Johannes Gaitanides, *FAZ,* March 9, 17, and 25, 1954; Conrad Ahlers, *Die Welt,* April 14, 1954.

3. Ollenhauer, *Die Freiheit,* November 13, 1953.

4. Beermann to Ollenhauer, December 3, 1953, "Ollenhauer Korrespondenz," file B; also, author's interview with Dr. Beermann in Bonn, August, 1970.

5. Schmidt to Ollenhauer, January 18, 1954, "Ollenhauer Korrespondenz," file Schm-Schz.

6. Ollenhauer to Schmidt, January 25, 1954, ibid.

7. Soell, *Erler,* 1:192-93.

8. Erler, *Verhandlungen des Deutschen Bundestages,* February 26, 1954, 18: 561-64 (hereafter cited as *Verhandlungen*).

9. Erler's comments are reported in Schmidt to Ollenhauer, March 6, 1954, "Ollenhauer Korrespondenz," file Schm-Schz.

10. Ollenhauer to Schmidt, April 8, 1954, ibid. There were seventeen on the committee, including SPD deputies Adolf Arndt, Helmut Bazille, Fritz Erler, Fritz Eschmann, Wilhelm Mellies, Carlo Schmid, Helmut Schmidt, and Herbert Wehner. *Jahrbuch der SPD, 1954-55,* p. 188.

11. For the Executive Committee's recommendation on European security, see *News from Germany,* May, 1954.

12. Schmidt at the May 8, 1954 security committee meeting, quoted in Löwke, *Für den Fall dass,* pp. 169-70.

13. Löwke, ibid., p. 170.

14. Erler's address to the Franken and North Hessen party conferences are reported in *Neuer Vorwärts,* June 4 and 17, 1954. Among his articles there was a four-part series published in the *Sozialdemokratischer Pressedienst,* June 4, 5, 10, and 11, 1954, and carried in the party's local newspapers; "Demokratie und bewaffnete Macht," *Gewerkschaftliche Monatshefte* 5 (June, 1954):355-61; "Nationalarmee—die falsche Alternative," *Neuer Vorwärts,* July 16, 1954.

15. Brandt, *Berliner Stimme,* June 19, 1954; Schmid, *Sozialist* (Hamburg), April 1, 1954; Carlo Schmid and Erwin Schoettle with Erler on the South German Radio Network, July 14, 1954, in "Erler Veröffentlichungen 1953-54," SPD archives.

16. The proposals (Anträge) can be found in *Neuer Vorwärts,* June 25, 1954.

17. Ollenhauer, *Protokoll der Verhandlungen des Parteitages der SPD vom 20 bis 24 Juli 1954 in Berlin,* pp. 53-62 (hereafter cited as *Berlin Protocols*).

18. Wehner, ibid., pp. 87-88; Schmidt, ibid., pp. 137-39; Brandt, ibid., pp. 89-91; Erler, ibid., pp. 79-80. Five members of the security committee spoke in favor of a positive statement. They were supported by delegates from the Berlin, Hamburg, and Bremen party organizations.

19. Fritz Wenzel (Braunschweig), ibid., pp. 75-76; Fritz Baade (Kiel), ibid., pp. 84-86; Ludwig Metzger (Darmstadt), ibid., p. 94.

20. Willi Birkelbach (Frankfurt), ibid., p. 77.

21. Heinz Kühn (Köln), ibid., pp. 80-83; Olaf Radke (Offenbach), ibid., p. 118.

22. Motion 113 was proposed by the party organizations from Hessen-Süd, Niederrhein, Braunschweig, Rheinland-Hessen-Nassau, and Hannover.

23. Ollenhauer, *Berlin Protocols,* pp. 143-47.

24. The members of the editorial committee represented a good cross-section of party opinion. They included Heinrich Albertz, Willi Birkelbach, Willy Brandt, Max Brauer, Fritz Erler, Heinz Kühn, Gerhart Luetkens, Ludwig Metzger, Helmut Schmidt, Georg Stierle, and Herbert Wehner.

25. According to the protocols, only about twenty delegates voted against the final resolution, *Berlin Protocols,* p. 203; however, Klaus Peter Schulz, "Resolutionen und Realitäten," *Deutsche Rundschau* 80 (September, 1954):918, claims that as many as sixty to eighty delegates remained stubbornly opposed to rearmament.

26. Max Lunze (Bassum), *Berlin Protocols,* pp. 140-42; also Birkelbach, ibid., p. 77, and Kühn, ibid., p. 83, who proposed the idea of a special party conference.

27. Eberhard Roterberg, *FAZ,* July 28, 1954.

28. Ollenhauer received 342 of 366 votes, 15 less than he won at the Dortmund conference. Mellies got only 279 votes, 39 less than he had received previously.

29. *Times* (London), July 26, 1954; *Stuttgarter Zeitung,* July 27, 1954; *Die Zeit,* July 29, 1954.

30. Ollenhauer, *Berlin Protocols,* p. 143; Erler on the Hessen Radio Network, July 25, 1954, "Erler Veröffentlichungen 1953-54."

31. Schiller, *Berlin Protocols,* p. 131; Löwke, *Für den Fall,* p. 182.

32. *Pressedienst,* July 22, 1954.

33. Bonn press conference, August 24, 1954, "Ollenhauer Reden Juli-Dezember, 1954."

34. *Sopade* 949 (September, 1954):1.

35. Statement by the Executive Committee, September 18, in *News from Germany,* October, 1954; Gleissberg, *Neuer Vorwärts,* September 3, 1954; Wehner, *SDZ,* September 4/5, 1954.

36. Bonn press conference, September 23, 1954, "Ollenhauer Reden Juli-Dezember, 1954."

37. Osgood, *NATO,* pp. 94-98; Wettig, *Entmilitarisierung und Wiederbewaffnung,* pp. 590-619.

38. Adenauer, *Verhandlungen,* October 5, 1954, 21:2227-34.

39. Kurt Georg Kiesinger (CDU), ibid., October 7, 1954, pp. 2274-79; Ollenhauer, ibid., pp. 2235-42.

40. For a description of the Bundestag debate, see *FAZ* and *SDZ,* October 8, 1954; *Die Welt,* October 9, 1954.

41. Ollenhauer to the parliamentary party, November 2, 1954, "Ollenhauer Reden, Juli-Dezember, 1954." See also his speech to the Party Committee, October 16, 1954, ibid; speech to the Executive Committee, *Neuer Vorwärts,* December 17, 1954.

42. Ollenhauer on Berlin radio, November 24, 1954, in *News from Germany,* December, 1954. Other SPD members severely criticized Western policy on German reunification; see Arndt in Bad Herzfeld, *FAZ,* November 25, 1954; Erler, *Pressedienst,* November 19, 1954; Wehner in Nuremberg, *SDZ,* November 8, 1954; resolution passed by the Executive Committee, December 13, 1954, in *Jahrbuch der SPD, 1954-55,* p. 330.

43. Robert Strobel, *Die Zeit,* October 7, 1954; *Die Welt,* December 10 and 15, 1954.

44. See the report on the combined meeting of the Parteivorstand, Parteiausschuss, and Kontrollkommission in Bonn, December 12, in *Neuer Vorwärts,* December 17, 1954.

45. *SDZ,* December 14, 1954.

46. *Pressedienst,* September 14, 1954; *Neuer Vorwärts,* December 3, 1954; *Sopade* 952 (December, 1954):10, carried an article titled "State Elections Confirm SPD Policy."

47. Richard C. Hottelet, "The Future of German Unity," *New Leader* 38 (May 2, 1955):6.

48. *New York Times,* November 25 and 28 and December 22, 1954, for reports on the demonstrations in Augsburg, Nuremberg, and Bremen.

49. For the resolutions of the federal youth congress of the DGB, the teenage socialist Falcons, and the Socialist German Student Union (SDS), see *Neuer Vorwärts,* October 1 and 15 and November 5, 1954.

50. Pirker, *SPD nach Hitler,* pp. 203-205; Gerald Braunthal, "West German Trade Unions and Disarmament," *Political Science Quarterly* 73 (March, 1958): 82-99.

51. *SDZ* and *FAZ,* October 8, 1954; Georg Schröder, *Die Welt,* December 10, 1954.

52. *FAZ,* January 8, 1955.

53. *Die Welt,* January 17, 1955; *SDZ,* January 18, 1955.

54. Ollenhauer on the Northwest German Radio Network, see *SDZ,* January 26, 1955. His letter to Adenauer is reprinted in *Jahrbuch der SPD, 1954-55,* pp. 330-32.

55. Ollenhauer on the Northwest German Radio Network, February 17, 1955, "Ollenhauer Reden, 1955." To prove the feasibility of a nationwide canvass, the Social Democrats gathered signatures in Aschaffenburg and Hof.

56. Adenauer quoted in *SDZ,* February 7, 1955; Strauss in *FAZ,* January 20, 1955. For the SPD response, see Ollenhauer in Dortmund, *Die Welt,* February 7, 1955; Arndt, *Pressedienst,* January 28, 1955.

57. Ollenhauer quoted in *Die Welt,* February 18; Brauer in *SDZ,* February 18, 1955.

58. Schmid speaking in Bielefeld, ibid.

59. Hans Ulrich Kempski, *SDZ,* February 28, 1955; Georg Schröder, *Die Welt,* February 28, 1955.

60. Ollenhauer to the Parteivorstand, Parteiausschuss, and Kontrollkommission, March 4, 1955, in "Ollenhauer Reden, 1955." For the resolution passed

by the committees, see *Jahrbuch der SPD, 1954-55,* p. 333.

61. Report of Ollenhauer's speech to the Fraktion in *Vorwärts,* April 29, 1955.

62. At the meeting of the parliamentary Fraktion during a break in the long Bundestag debate on the Paris Accords, Ollenhauer declared that the SPD would only consider ratification as one stage and not the completion of the rearmament debate. Erwin Schoettle immediately interrupted him to say that in continuing to oppose the accords "we are not thinking of departing from the grounds of parliamentary democracy." Ollenhauer was somewhat taken aback. He was not proposing a radicalization of the party's opposition campaign, but Schoettle wanted it made perfectly clear to those in the party who spoke of going back into the streets exactly where the SPD stood. Kempski, *SDZ,* February 28, 1955. Wehner also warned against going too far with a policy of extraparliamentary action; see Gaus, *Staatserhaltende Opposition,* p. 26.

63. Brandt warned against oversimplification in the party's campaign against the accords, *Parlamentarische Politische Presse,* February 18, 1955 (hereafter cited as *PPP*); similarly, Erler, quoted in Soell, *Erler,* 1:182.

64. Pirker, *SPD nach Hitler,* p. 205; H. J. Brauns et. al., *SPD in der Krise,* p. 219, complain about the timidity and shortsightedness of the SPD leaders. The authors claim that the German working class was ready to be led in an all-out campaign against rearmament.

65. On Carte Blanche and the German reaction, see Gordon A. Craig, "NATO and the New German Army," in William W. Kaufmann, ed., *Military Policy and National Security,* pp. 225-28; Speier, *German Rearmament,* pp. 188-93.

66. Edinger, *West German Armament,* p. 94. On the revision of NATO strategy, see Osgood, *NATO,* pp. 102-23.

67. Adenauer, *Verhandlungen,* February 25, 1955, 23:3736.

68. Richardson, *Germany and the Atlantic Alliance,* p. 12.

69. Henry A. Kissinger, *Nuclear Weapons and Foreign Policy,* p. 291.

70. Gleissberg, *Neuer Vorwärts,* August 14, 1953; Rudolf Gottschalk, ibid., April 23, 1954; Ollenhauer, ibid., June 17, 1954; Willi Eichler, "Bereitschaft zum Frieden," *Geist und Tat* 9 (February, 1954):33-36.

71. *Neuer Vorwärts,* May 1, 1954; *Berlin Protocols,* p. 53.

72. *Pressedienst,* June 10, 1954.

73. Felix, *Vorwärts,* January 7, 1955; *Pressedienst,* June 28, 1955.

74. Blank, *Verhandlungen,* July 16, 1955, 26:5588-89.

75. Strauss, ibid., pp. 5609-10; Erler, ibid., pp. 5611-12.

76. Ollenhauer, ibid., June 28, 1955, 26:5231; Peter Blachstein, ibid., July 16, 1955, 26:5597-5602.

77. On Bonin, see Adalbert Weinstein, *FAZ,* November 14, 1952; Dieter Schröder, *SDZ,* March 25, 1955; Ben Bern, *Die Zeit,* August 11, 1955.

78. On the Bonin Plan, see Speier, *German Rearmament,* pp. 76-81; Craig, "NATO and the New German Army," pp. 221-24.

79. Speier, *German Rearmament,* p. 79.

80. *Pressedienst,* April 1 and November 3, 1952, and April 1, 1955.

81. A German magazine reported that SPD criticism of Bonin had not been sanctioned by the Executive Committee but had been promoted by Beermann on his own initiative. *Der Spiegel* 9 (April 13, 1955):9. Wehner was apparently among those who wanted to look more closely at Bonin's ideas, and as late as 1959, Erler was recommending to Ollenhauer that the party discuss the question of cooperation with Bonin; see Erler to Ollenhauer, November 4, 1959, "Ollenhauer Korrespondenz," file E.

82. Ollenhauer, *Verhandlungen,* February 27, 1955, 23:3892.

83. Ollenhauer in Siegburg, *Die Welt,* March 28, 1955; Karl Wienand, *SDZ,* March 12/13, 1955; Erler, *Vorwärts,* March 4, 1955.

84. Erler, *Pressedienst,* April 13, 1955.

85. Criticism from the coalition parties in *SDZ,* April 16/17, 1955. Ollenhauer's response on the Bavarian Radio Network, May 4, 1955, "Ollenhauer Reden, 1955."

86. Erler, *Verhandlungen,* February 25, 1955, 23:3732; Fritz Erler, "Coexistence et Reunification de l'Allemagne," *Politique Etrangère* 20 (June/July, 1955):333-42.

87. Frieder Feldmann, *Vorwärts,* March 11, 1955.

88. Ollenhauer, ibid., May 27, 1955; similar statements by Mellies, ibid., June 24, 1955; Schmid, *Die Welt,* June 22, 1955.

89. *Jahrbuch der SPD, 1954-55,* pp. 340-47.

90. Adenauer, *Verhandlungen,* May 27, 1955, 24:4603-4607; Kiesinger, ibid., p. 4613-19.

91. Jaeger, ibid., February 26, 1955, 23:3738.

92. Adenauer, ibid., June 28, 1955, 26:5237.

93. Ollenhauer, *Times* (London), June 17, 1955; resolution by the SPD executive committees, June 30, 1955, in *News from Germany,* July, 1955.

94. Wehner, *Verhandlungen,* February 24, 1955, 23:3538.

95. Wilhelm Guelich, ibid., pp. 3786-88; Gerhart Kreyssig, ibid., pp. 3806-3809; Franz Barsig, *Vorwärts,* February 4, 1955; Heinrich Ritzel, ibid., June 17, 1955.

96. Mg., "Economic Implications of German Rearmament," *World Today* 11 (March, 1955):117-29; Edwin Hunter, "West Germany: Economic Aspects of Rearmament," *Swiss Review of World Affairs* 5 (July, 1955):3; H. J. Dernburg, "Rearmament and the German Economy," *Foreign Affairs* 33 (July, 1955):648-62.

97. Carolus (Jacob Altmeier), "Bonn's Disastrous Victory," *Nation* 180 (March 12, 1955):214.

98. Ollenhauer, *Verhandlungen,* October 7, 1954, 21:2240; and in Lübeck, *Vorwärts,* March 18, 1955.

99. Ollenhauer, *News from Germany,* October, 1954; Hans Manthey, *Vorwärts,* January 21, 1955.

100. Erler, *Verhandlungen,* February 24, 1955, 23:3723.

101. Fritz Baade, "Nur noch zwei Deutschlandkonzeptionen," *Aussenpolitik* 5 (December, 1954):763; Willi Eichler, "Von der Ko-existenz zur Kooperation," *Geist und Tat* 10 (February, 1955):40. Ollenhauer warned in an interview that an international system based on the balance of power was basically unstable. *News from Germany,* December, 1954.

102. Erich Mende (FDP), *Verhandlungen,* February 25, 1955, 23:3753.

Chapter 6

1. Hans Schmidt, *Vorwärts,* May 13, 1955. According to Grosser, *Bonner Demokratie,* p. 290, a poll taken in 1956 showed that 80 percent of the SPD supporters interviewed expressed the opinion that the new army would soon revert to the old ways.

2. *Die Welt,* May 27, 1955; *SDZ,* July 4, 1955; Ollenhauer, quoted in ibid., March 24, 1955.

3. Bernt Conrad, *Die Welt,* May 27, 1955. For critical comments from the party, see Peter Blachstein of the Bundestag Fraktion, *Hamburger Echo* (SPD), June 7, 1955; resolution of the Süd-Hessen party conference, *Vorwärts,* April 29, 1955; H. J. Heydorn of the Falcons executive committee, *Sozialdemokratischer Pressedienst,* May 11, 1955 (hereafter cited as *Pressedienst);* statement by the DGB delegation at a trade union conference in Brussels, *Economist,* April 2, 1955.

4. Erler on the Northwest German Radio Network, March 10, 1955; Erler, "Veröffentlichungen, 1955"; Erler, "Nüchterne Verteidigungsbereitschaft als erzieherische Aufgabe der Gesellschaft," *Zeitwende* 26 (March, 1955):151; Erler, *Pressedienst,* June 7 and 10, 1955.

5. Mellies, who was chairman of the party's security committee, told a local party conference in Westphalia that "the party would renounce all possibilities of influence if it stayed away from the deliberations" on the military legislation. *Vorwärts,* June 24, 1955; similarly, Schmid in Kaiserslautern, *SDZ,* March 28, 1955.

6. Gerhard Loewenberg, *Parliament in the German Political System,* pp. 290-91; Jürgen Domes, "Das Freiwilligengesetz im zweiten deutschen Bundestag" (Ph.D. diss., Heidelberg, 1960), pp. 47-49; *Der Spiegel* 9 (June 8, 1955):7-8.

7. Blank, *Verhandlungen des Deutschen Bundestages,* June 27, 1955, 26: 5213-20 (hereafter cited as *Verhandlungen);* Adenauer to Peter Altmaier, quoted in *Der Spiegel* 9 (June 22, 1955):8.

8. *SDZ,* May 11, 1955.

9. *FAZ,* May 31, 1955. Several weeks later the Social Democrats tried again. They called the government to put aside the Volunteers Bill and accept instead a full parliamentary debate on the military policy and defense needs of the Federal Republic. *Die Welt,* June 14, 1955; see also a resolution passed by the Executive Committee condemning the government's precipitate action. *Vorwärts,* June 10, 1955.

10. *Pressedienst,* May 31, 1955; FB, *Vorwärts,* June 3, 1955; Ollenhauer, quoted in *Die Welt,* June 8, 1955.

11. *Vorwärts,* June 10, 1955.

12. Erler, *Verhandlungen,* June 15, 1955, 25:4875, 4873; Erler, *Pressedienst,* June 7 and 10, 1955; *Vorwärts,* June 17, 1955; Executive Committee's resolution on the Volunteers Bill, June 4, 1955, in *News from Germany,* June, 1955.

13. Ollenhauer, *Verhandlungen,* June 28, 1955, 26:5231-35.

14. Jaeger, *Verhandlungen,* June 15, 1955, 25:4871; Domes, *Freiwilligengesetz,* pp. 49-55; *FAZ,* May 31 and June 16, 1955; *SDZ,* June 27, 1955.

15. *SDZ,* July 4, 1955; *FAZ, Die Welt,* and *Neue Züricher Zeitung,* June 29, 1955, all agreed that there was little chance of meaningful cooperation between the government and the opposition on military legislation.

16. *Die Welt* and *FAZ,* July 4 and 5, 1955. Adenauer agreed that: (1) the number of volunteers would be limited to six thousand; (2) none of these volunteers would be used to form tactical units; (3) their duties would be restricted to staff matters; (4) the government would create a personnel selection committee to screen officer candidates; (5) the permanent organization of the Defense Ministry would be established by later legislation rather than being determined by the government itself.

17. Among those most vigorously opposed to cooperation were Willi Birkelbach and Heinz Kühn, who had led the antirearmament forces at the Berlin party conference. Only about 20 of the 162 deputies supported them, however.

For a report on the caucus and the Fraktion's decision, see *Vorwärts*, July 15, 1955; *Die Welt* and *SDZ*, July 8, 1955.

18. Quoted in Loewenberg, *Parliament*, p. 340. For a discussion of the committee's work, see Domes, *Freiwilligengesetz*, pp. 69-86; *SDZ*, July 9/10, 1955; *Die Welt*, July 11, 1955; *FAZ*, July 12, 1955.

19. Mellies, *Verhandlungen*, July 15, 1955, 26:5532.

20. Loewenberg, *Parliament*, p. 340; Allemann, *Bonn ist nicht Weimar*, p. 366.

21. The *Times* (London), July 11, 1955, had already declared that the new measures were primarily the work of these two men. Similarly, Loewenberg, *Parliament*, pp. 337-39. Hans Merten, Helmut Schmidt, Herbert Wehner, Wilhelm Mellies, and Georg Kahn-Ackermann, however, were also active for the SPD.

22. Georg Schröder, *Die Welt*, February 28, 1955.

23. Soell, *Erler*, 1:200, reports that in the caucus of July 11, sixteen deputies voted against the decision to support the creation of a review board, and two abstained.

24. Erler, *Pressedienst*, July 15 and 16, 1955; JF, *Vorwärts*, July 15, 1955.

25. The Hamburg party organization passed a resolution calling on the Fraktion "to exhaust every possibility in parliament to protect the democratic order, even with military legislation." *Vorwärts*, July 8, 1955.

26. HGL, "The Four Powers and Germany: The Reunification Issue," *World Today* 11 (November, 1955):473-76; Frederick H. Hartmann, *Germany Between East and West*, pp. 67-86.

27. Executive Committee resolution, July 25, 1955, in *News from Germany*, August/September, 1955.

28. See the report on the Bundestag debate in K. H. Helfer, *SDZ*, October 13, 1955.

29. *News from Germany*, October, 1955.

30. Ollenhauer, *Verhandlungen*, December 2, 1955, 27:6155-62; Hans Manthey, *Vorwärts*, November 18, 1955.

31. Mellies, *Die Welt*, November 23, 1955; Willi Eichler, "Der Geist von Genf," *Geist und Tat* 10 (December, 1955):354.

32. CDU, *Deutschland Union Dienst*, November 9 and 17, 1955; Brentano *Verhandlungen*, December 1, 1955, 27:6101-11; Kiesinger, ibid., December 2, 1955, pp. 6165-71.

33. *Pressedienst*, November 15, 1955; Ollenhauer, *Verhandlungen*, December 2, 1955, 27:1655-62.

34. Jaeger in *Die Zeit*, December 8, 1955; also, commentaries in *SDZ*, November 23, and December 17/18, 1955; *FAZ*, December 19, 1955.

35. *SDZ*, September 14, 1955. On the SPD working groups, see Loewenberg, *Parliament*, pp. 177-79. For the membership of the working group for security questions, see *Jahrbuch der SPD, 1956-57*, p. 11.

36. In the Bundestag debate of February 26, 1954, the SPD raised eight specific demands for assuring civilian and democratic control of the armed forces. Later in the year the Executive Committee's advisory group on security matters presented seven more demands. *Jahrbuch der SPD, 1954-55*, p. 22.

37. Erler, *Vorwärts*, October 21, 1955; Erler, "Die ersten Wehrgesetze," *Geist und Tat* 10 (November, 1955):324-28; Erler, *Neue Rhein-Zeitung* (SPD), December 29, 1955; typescript of an article dated March 3, 1956, entitled "Demokratie und bewaffnete Macht in Westdeutschland," in Erler, "Veröffentli-

chungen 1955-Juni 1956."

38. *Pressedienst,* December 13, 1955; JF, *Vorwärts,* December 16, 1955. On how the committee functioned from July, 1955, to August, 1957, see John L. Sutton, "The Personnel Screening Committee and Parliamentary Control of the West German Armed Forces," *Journal of Central European Affairs* 19 (1959-60):389-401.

39. Erler, *Verhandlungen,* June 15, 1955, 25:4857-65; Erler, ibid., June 28, 1955, pp. 5286-87; Ollenhauer, ibid., pp. 5231-35.

40. Craig, "NATO and the New German Army," p. 210. For the debate in both the plenary and committee sessions on the powers of the Defense Committee, see: Detlef Dietz, "Einfluss und Haltung der SPD hinsichtlich der Entwicklung des Konzepts der Inneren Führung der Bundeswehr, 1949-57" (Diplom-Arbeit, Köln Universität, 1971).

41. Ernst Paul, in *Deutscher Bundestag, Protokoll der Ausschuss für Fragen der europäischen Sicherheit,* 26 and 32 sessions, March 5 and May 21, 1953 (hereafter cited as *Security Committee Protocols*).

42. Erler, *Verhandlungen,* February 26, 1954, 18:562-63; ibid., June 28, 1955, 25:5286-87.

43. For the views of the Christian Democrats, see *Die Welt,* September 14 and December 15, 1955; *FAZ,* February 9, 1956. On the debate in plenary and committee sessions, see Dietz, *Einfluss und Haltung der SPD,* pp. 184-92.

44. Erler, *Westfälische Rundschau* (SPD Dortmund), May 28, 1955; *Die Welt,* February 10, 1956; Arndt, *Verhandlungen,* March 6, 1956, 28:6823.

45. Schmidt on the South German Radio Network, September 29, 1955, in Helmut Schmidt, *Beiträge,* pp. 319-97.

46. Robert Strobel, *Die Zeit,* December 22, 1955; Dietz, *Einfluss und Haltung,* pp. 108-21. Under the Bonn constitution a vote of no confidence against the government would be valid only if Parliament could elect a new chancellor. Thus the sponsors of the motion could not irresponsibly provoke a major political crisis by leaving the country without a government.

47. *FAZ,* January 26, 1956; *Die Tat,* January 27, 1956.

48. *Die Welt,* February 1, 1956; *FAZ,* February 9, 1956.

49. For the Ollenhauer-Krone meetings, see *FAZ,* January 26, 1956. For the Security Committee debate, see ibid., January 13 and 19, February 9, 1956.

50. JF, *Vorwärts,* February 17, 1956.

51. *FAZ,* February 25, 1956; *SDZ,* February 25/26, 1956.

52. Mellies, *Verhandlungen,* March 6, 1956, 28:6823-26; Erler, ibid., pp. 6850-51.

53. On the caucus and the attitude of the twenty deputies who voted against the amendments, see Jesco von Puttkamer, *SDZ,* March 8, 1956. According to *Vorwärts,* March 9, 1956, the deputies collided in a "tough, but factual, verbal battle."

54. Wolfgang Wagner, *Hannoversche Allgemeine Zeitung,* March 29, 1956; George L. Rueckert, "Parliamentary Party Cohesion in the West German Bundestag" (Ph.D. diss., Wisconsin, 1962), pp. 345-49.

55. *Das Andere Zeitung,* March 1, 1956. Gleissberg published this paper in association with other dissident left-wingers who were opposed to the policies pursued by the SPD. See the resolution passed by the South Hessen party organization: *Die Welt,* March 12, 1956.

56. A resolution by the Parteivorstand, Parteiausschuss, and Kontrollkommission in *Jahrbuch der SPD, 1956-57,* p. 338. Walter Menzel then sent out a

circular to local party organizations explaining the Fraktion's behavior; Menzel, *Korrespondenz,* file R 14, SPD Archives.

57. Menzel, *Vorwärts,* May 25, 1956; Wehner, *Die Welt,* April 22, 1956; Ollenhauer, *Vorwärts,* May 18, 1956; Erler, ibid., June 15, 1956.

58. Blank's views can be found in memoranda released to the public by the Defense Ministry; *FAZ,* March 28, 1956; *Die Welt,* May 3, 1956.

59. The meeting of the Parteivorstand, Parteiausschuss, and Kontrollkommission at Bergneustadt, March 9-11, in *Vorwärts,* March 16, 1956.

60. Karl Drott, ed., *Sozialdemokratie und Wehrfrage,* pp. 187-90.

61. The commentary and the minutes of a combined meeting of the security committee and the parliamentary party's working group on security questions are dated April 11, 1956. SPD Bundestag Fraktion Archives, Bonn. See the comments by *Die Welt,* April 12, 1956; Alfred Rapp, *FAZ,* April 16, 1956.

62. *Die Zeit,* March 29, 1956.

63. Erler, *Verhandlungen,* May 4, 1956, 29:7493-7504.

64. Wehner, *Pressedienst,* March 7, 1956; Heinz Kühn, "Significant Chance," *News from Germany,* April, 1956.

65. Erler in Strasbourg, *Die Welt,* April 21, 1956. On the Hessen Radio Network, March 8, and May 3, 1956, in "Erler Veröffentlichungen 1955-Juni 1956."

66. Jaeger, *Verhandlungen,* May 4, 1956, 29:7535; Manteuffel, ibid., p. 7511.

67. *New York Times,* June 8, 1956; ze, *SDZ,* June 9/10, 1956.

68. Erler, *Verhandlungen,* June 22, 1956, 30:8203-10; sp., *Pressedienst,* July 2, 1956.

69. An elderly party worker told a reporter that the scene was as tense and agitated as the meeting before the Enabling Act, in March, 1933. Joachim Besser, *Die Welt,* July 5, 1956; Jesco von Puttkamer, *SDZ,* July 6, 1956.

70. Menzel, *Pressedienst,* June 15, 1956. During the second and third readings of the conscription bill, ten different SPD deputies spoke in defense of the rights of conscientious objectors.

71. Jaeger, *Verhandlungen,* July 6, 1956, 31:8848. For the debate in the plenary and committee sessions, see Dietz, *Einfluss und Haltung,* pp. 101-107.

72. Arndt, *Verhandlungen,* June 28, 1955, 26:5262; ibid., July 4, 1956, 31: 8704.

73. *Pressedienst,* July 2, 1956.

74. Adenauer, *Verhandlungen,* July 6, 1956, 31:8782-83; Erler, ibid., pp. 8774-82.

75. Kiesinger, ibid., pp. 8810-14. Hans Speier writes that by July, 1956, "the standard argument of the coalition parties that German rearmament would help to deter Soviet aggression had been replaced, in part, by the contention that the value of German soldiers consisted in helping to deter atomic war." This shift in emphasis occurred because in the popular mind fear of Soviet aggression had abated "and been replaced by the fear of nuclear weapons." Speier, *German Rearmament,* p. 210.

76. Wienand, *Verhandlungen,* July 7, 1956, 31:8869.

77. Erler, ibid., p. 8822.

78. Ollenhauer, ibid., pp. 8877-78.

79. See the critical resolutions from Unterbezirke Frankfurt and Munich, and Ortsvereine Velbert and Breitbrunn/Chiemsee, in *Vorwärts,* June 15, 1956. Fritz René Allemann wrote of a "de-socialization" of the SPD as it developed an economic policy closer to that of John Maynard Keynes than Karl Marx.

Allemann, "Die Krise in Bonn," *Der Monat* 8 (July, 1956):11-12.

80. Ollenhauer in the preface to *Jahrbuch der SPD, 1954-55.* See also the comments in R. H., "Eine Partei sucht eine Politik," *Die Gegenwart* 11 (June 30, 1956):403; Ilse Elsner, *Die Welt,* June 30, 1956.

81. The ninety-four conference resolutions, thirty-six of which dealt with foreign and military policy, are in *Vorwärts,* June 15, 1956. The most radical antimilitary demands came from such places as the Unterbezirk Frankfurt, Bezirk Mittelrhein, Ortsvereine Frelenberg, Breitbrunn/Chiemsee, and Dortmund-Aplerbeck, and Kreisverband Rosenheim-Land. The Kreisverband Koblenz-Stadt was the only district recommending a volunteer army.

82. From the minutes of the meeting held April 11, 1956. Fraktion Archives.

83. Beermann's memorandum is dated June 7, 1956. He was appointed military advisor to the SPD Bundestag Fraktion in January, 1955, on the recommendation of Helmut Schmidt and Fritz Erler. Fraktion Archives.

84. Ollenhauer, *Protokoll der Verhandlungen des Parteitages der SPD vom 10 bis 14 Juli in München,* pp. 47-72 (hereafter cited as *Munich Protocols*).

85. The resolutions are in *Munich Protocols,* pp. 344-51; and *Vorwärts,* July 20, 1956.

86. Alfred Rapp, *FAZ,* July 13, 1956. Writing before the Munich conference, Erler said that the party would have to formulate a policy which would be acceptable to other political parties; otherwise, "we will not be able to find allies to form a new government." Fritz Erler, "La politique extérieure de la Republique Fédérale," *Politique Etrangère* 21 (July/August, 1956):408.

87. Heinz Kühn (Mittelrhein), *Munich Protocols,* pp. 93-96; Franz Marx (Südbayern), ibid., pp. 96-98; Arno Beherisch (Franken), ibid., pp. 100-102.

88. Erler, ibid., pp. 112-15; Wehner, ibid., pp. 120-23; Brandt, ibid., pp. 108-10.

89. *Economist,* July 21, 1956. Erler proved to be a better party politician than Willy Brandt, who, although he was now President of the Berlin House of Deputies, failed again to be elected to the SPD's executive committee.

90. KM., "Ollenhauers Mannschaft," *Die Gegenwart* 11 (July 28, 1956):465. Ashkenasi states that the conditions for Erler's "absolution" by the party were (1) his brilliant attacks on NATO membership during the military debates; (2) his loyalty toward the Executive Committee; and (3) the loss of power by the traditionalists in the party after 1954. Ashkenasi, *Reformpartei,* p. 49.

91. Junius, *SDZ,* July 16, 1956. For the election results, see *Vorwärts,* July 20, 1956. In order of votes received, the top eight candidates were Knoeringen, Zinn, Steinhoff, Wehner, Schmid, Arndt, Menzel, and Erler.

92. *Time Magazine* 65 (February 28, 1955):19; *Der Spiegel* 8 (October 6, 1954):8-20; Walter Henkels, *FAZ,* November 6, 1954; Fritz Bruhl, *SDZ,* January 29/30, 1955.

93. Alfred Rapp, *FAZ,* July 10, 1956.

94. *Der Spiegel* 10 (July 18, 1956):15; *New Statesman* 52 (July 21, 1956):59; Klaus Peter Schulz, *Opposition als Politische Schicksal?,* p. 25.

95. There was no Rosa Luxemburg or Karl Leibknecht, no Pietro Nenni or Aneurin Bevan in the SPD. By the time of the Munich conference even Kühn and Birkelbach, who had led the antirearmers at Berlin two years before, had become supporters of the Ollenhauer line. *SDZ,* July 19, 1956; Robert Strobel, *Die Zeit,* July 19, 1956.

96. Klaus Schütz, "Die Meinungs- und Willensbildung in der Sozialdemokratie," *Die Neue Gesellschaft* 5 (September/October, 1958):366-68.

97. Gaus, *Staatserhaltende Opposition,* p. 36.

98. Pirker, *SPD nach Hitler,* pp. 216-18. Pirker also points out that Viktor Agartz, a radical leftist who was driven out of the DGB, and Wolfgang Abendroth, a Marburg professor, were attempting to maintain contact with leftists and pacifists within the SPD and the trade union movement—including Birkelbach, Blachstein, Baade, and Karl Bechert. See also Brauns, *SPD in der Krise,* p. 186.

99. Kurt Becker, *Die Welt,* July 16, 1956.

100. JF. *Vorwärts,* July 20, 1956.

101. Fritz Heine, *Parlamentarische Politische Presse,* May 24, 1956 (hereafter cited as *PPP*); Erler on the South German Radio Network, June 19, 1956, in "Erler Veröffentlichungen 1955-Juni 1956"; Willi Eichler, "Zeiten der Entspannung," *Geist und Tat* 11 (July, 1956):193-97. Ollenhauer, at an Executive Committee meeting in Bonn, called for "new proposals" from the government leading to "new and realistic negotiations on reunification." *SDZ,* October 19, 1956.

102. Peter Meyer, "Do the German Socialists Have a Policy?" *New Leader* 38 (January 17, 1955):7; Hans Morgenthau, "Notes on a German Journey," *New Republic* 135 (August 27, 1956):11. Hans Speier writes that the Social Democrats have justified their reunification policy in "pathetically unrealistic terms." Speier, *German Rearmament,* p. 173.

103. Wehner, *Vorwärts,* July 27, 1956; PM, ibid., October 26, 1956.

104. On Adenauer's response to the Radford Plan, named after the chairman of the Joint Chiefs of Staff, who was advocating a shift from conventional to nuclear weapons in American defense planning, see Richardson, *Germany and the Atlantic Alliance,* pp. 40-48; Hans Gert Pöttering, *Adenauers Sicherheitspolitik 1955-63,* pp. 62-82.

105. Erler, *Pressedienst,* July 27, 1956.

106. Erler on the West German Radio Network, May 9, 1956, and an address to the Rhein-Ruhr Klub, July 23, 1956, in "Erler Veröffentlichungen, Juli 1956-1957." By contrast, see Schmid, *FAZ,* April 6, 1956; FM, *Vorwärts,* July 13, 1956.

107. Erler, *Die Welt,* March 31, 1956; Erler, *Verhandlungen,* July 4, 1956, 31: 8587; Beermann, *Frankfurter Rundschau,* May 22, 1956.

108. On public opposition to conscription, see the reports by John Dornberg, "Defying the Draft," *Nation* 183 (December 8, 1956):494-97; *Manchester Guardian,* September 13 and 20, 1956.

109. *Economist,* March 17, 1956. On Adenauer's declining prestige, see *New York Times,* July 1, 1956; *SDZ,* July 9, 1956. On the public opinion polls, see *New York Times,* August 19, 1956; Alfred Rapp, *FAZ,* November 27, 1956.

110. *FAZ,* November 23, 1956.

111. Mellies, *Pressedienst,* August 23, 1956.

112. Hans Edgar Jahn, *Für und Gegen den Wehrbeitrag,* p. 130. The party leaders in Bonn did very little to discourage such remarks. In fact, throughout 1956 they themselves still insisted that social reconstruction should have priority over military rearmament. Ollenhauer in Hamburg, *Die Welt,* October 2, 1956. Mellies also called for new legislation on old-age pensions before a conscription law. *Vorwärts,* May 4, 1956.

113. *FAZ,* April 16, 1956.

114. Mellies, *Verhandlungen,* March 6, 1956, 28:6848. Erler at the Rhein-Ruhr Klub, July 23, 1956, in "Erler Veröffentlichungen Juli 1956-1957"; Brandt at a party conference in Berlin, *Berliner Stimme,* June 2, 1956.

115. Erler, "Die ersten Wehrgesetze," p. 328; Erler, *SDZ,* January 26, 1956; Erler, from the typescript of a manuscript, March 3, 1956, in "Erler Veröffentlichungen, 1955-Juni 1956."

116. Schmidt, *Verhandlungen,* May 4, 1956, 29:7559. In October, 1956, Schmidt became chairman of a Defense Committee subgroup on arms production and procurement, and one month later, he joined the Defense Committee itself. See also Mellies, *Berliner Stimme,* April 7, 1956. A speech by Fritz Erler in Berlin, February 5, 1957, reproduced as: Erler, "Heer und Staat in der Bundesrepublik," in Bundesministerium für Verteidigung, *Schicksalsfragen der Gegenwart,* 3:254-56.

117. Pirker, *SPD nach Hitler,* pp. 210-13.

Chapter 7

1. Adenauer, *Verhandlungen des Deutschen Bundestages,* November 8, 1956, 32:9259-64 (hereafter cited as *Verhandlungen*).

2. Wehner wrote a series of articles on the Hungarian Revolt and the Suez Crisis; see *Vorwärts,* November 2, 9, 16 and 23, 1956; Ollenhauer, *Sozialdemokratischer Pressedienst,* December 22, 1956 (hereafter cited as *Pressedienst*).

3. Erler in Strasbourg, January 9, 1957, in Fritz Erler, *Politik für Deutschland,* pp. 499-500; Schmid, *Vorwärts,* March 22, 1957; Willi Eichler, "Der Rückfall in die Barbarei," *Geist und Tat* 11 (December, 1956):355.

4. Mellies in Ingolstadt, *Die Welt,* November 26, 1956; Ollenhauer in Bonn, *Parlamentarische Politische Presse,* December 19, 1956 (hereafter cited as *PPP*).

5. *Pressedienst,* November 14, 1956; Parteivorstand resolution, November 7, 1956, in *Vorwärts,* November 9, 1956.

6. Erler, *Politik für Deutschland,* pp. 503-504; Wehner, *Pressedienst,* December 13, 1956.

7. PM, *Vorwärts,* December 14, 1956.

8. Mellies, *Verhandlungen,* November 8, 1956, 32:9267-69; Wehner, *Vorwärts,* November 16, 1956; PM, ibid., January 4, 1957; Erler on the Southwest German Radio Network, January 7, 1957, in "Erler Veröffentlichungen, Juli 1956-1957."

9. Ollenhauer, *Pressedienst,* December 22, 1956; Ollenhauer at the Asian Socialist conference, in *News from Germany,* October/November, 1956; Ollenhauer to the party leaders, January 24, 1957, "Ollenhauer Reden, 1957."

10. *Pressedienst,* November 19, 1956. The letter from Bulganin to Eisenhower, November 17, 1956, in *Documents, 1956,* pp. 605-12.

11. Wehner, *Vorwärts,* November 23, 1956. Wehner also discussed the Soviet note in a radio interview, November 19, 1956, with Karl Helfrich; see the Wehner file, *Presse- und Informationsamt der Bundesregierung, Pressearchiv* (hereafter cited as *Pressearchiv*).

12. Wehner quoted in *Frankfurter Rundschau,* December 4, 1956; Erler, *Neue Rhein-Zeitung* (SPD), January 26, 1957; Ollenhauer to the party leaders, January 24, 1957, "Ollenhauer Reden, 1957."

13. Brentano, *Verhandlungen,* January 31, 1957, 34:10649-50.

14. Erler, ibid., pp. 10717-25; Ollenhauer, ibid., pp. 10666-74.

15. Kiesinger, ibid., pp. 10652-63.

16. Strauss, ibid., pp. 10726-32.

17. Richardson, *Germany,* pp. 40-48; Pöttering, *Adenauers Sicherheitspoli-*

tik, pp. 82-90; Speier, *German Rearmament,* pp. 211-23.

18. A radio interview, September 12, 1956, Erler "Veröffentlichungen, Juli 1956-1957."

19. Mellies, *Pressedienst,* August 30, 1956; S, *Vorwärts,* September 14, 1956; statement by the Fraktion, quoted in *SDZ,* September 18, 1956.

20. Ollenhauer to the Parteivorstand, Parteiausschuss, and Kontrollkommission in Bonn, October 17, 1956, quoted in *SDZ,* October 19, 1956; resolution passed by the three committees, in *Jahrbuch der SPD, 1956/1957,* p. 340.

21. Schmidt, *Verhandlungen,* November 8, 1956, 32:9298-9303.

22. Erler, ibid., December 5, 1956, 33:9755. For a description of the scene in the Bundestag, see Kurt Becker, *Die Welt,* December 6, 1956; km, *Die Gegenwart* 11 (December 15, 1956):794-95.

23. Fritz Erler, "Die SPD ist anderer Meinung," *Das Neue Journal* 5 (December 19, 1956):1-2; *Nürnberger Zeitung,* December 31, 1956; interview with Walter Menningen, *Hannoversche Presse* (SPD), December 23, 1956; Erler, "Umrüstung," *Aussenpolitik* 8 (January, 1957):12-20.

24. On the "anti-Erler group," see *Der Spiegel* 11 (January 30, 1957):15; resolution passed unanimously by the Frankfurt Young Socialists in January, 1957, in "Ollenhauer Korrespondenz," file Bm-Bz.

25. See the reports of the press conference in *Die Welt, SDZ,* and *FAZ,* January 19, 1957.

26. Ollenhauer to the party leaders, January 24, 1957, "Ollenhauer Reden, 1957." Erler spoke of an army of 200,000 men; see "Die SPD ist anderer Meinung," p. 1. Beermann said the Bundeswehr should total about 150-200,000 men; see Fritz Beermann, "Sicherheit, Wiedervereinigung und Stärke der Bundeswehr," *Die Neue Gesellschaft* 4 (January/February, 1957):6. According to *FAZ,* January 24, 1957, other members of the security committee preferred an army of only 100,000 men.

27. Strauss, *Verhandlungen,* February 8, 1957, 35:10942-44.

28. Erler, ibid., December 5, 1956, 33:9756.

29. See the protocols of a security committee meeting on April 11, 1956, in Fraktion Archives, and Erler, *Verhandlungen,* April 12, 1956, 29:7175.

30. The Falcons met in Frankfurt several days after the Bad Godesberg meeting; *Vorwärts,* February 1, 1957. The Berlin Falcons discussed expulsion; *Die Welt,* April 12, 1957.

31. Mellies, *Vorwärts,* June 7, 1957. Heinz Pöhler, who led the Young Socialist delegation at Bad Godesberg, described the meeting in *Pressedienst,* January 30, 1957.

32. EE, *Vorwärts,* February 1, 1957.

33. PM, ibid., November 18, 1955; *Pressedienst,* August 30, 1955.

34. Schmidt, *Verhandlungen,* February 1, 1957, 35:10784-85. For the SPD's reaction to the so-called Zenker Affair, see Schmid, ibid., April 18, 1956, 29:7207-12.

35. General Adolf Heusinger gave a forty-one-page report to the committee on June 10, 1953, and Baudissin spoke to the committee on July 12, 1953, and June 14, 1954. *Security Committee Protocols.* Erler told Eric Waldman on July 20, 1960, that the problems of *Innere Führung* were thoroughly discussed and worked out in the committee meetings. Waldman, *The Goose Step is Verboten,* p. 64.

36. Wolf von Baudissin, "The New Germany Army," *Foreign Affairs* 34 (October, 1955):13; Dienststelle Blank, *Vom künftigen deutschen Soldaten.*

37. The views of the government parties and the opposition were expressed by Jaeger and Arndt in the Bundestag Judiciary Committee in February, 1956; Drott, *Sozialdemokratie und Wehrfrage,* pp. 63-65.

38. Arndt, *Verhandlungen,* February 7, 1957, 35:10912.

39. Erler, "Heer und Staat in der Bundesrepublik," p. 253; Schmidt, *Pressedienst,* August 29, 1955.

40. On the concept of Innere Führung, see Waldman, *The Goose Step,* pp. 101-86; George R. Moe, "A Survey of Politically Significant Innovations in the German Bundeswehr" (Ph.D. diss., American University, 1966), pp. 105-37.

41. Charles W. Thayer, "German Arms and the Men," *Reporter* 7 (April 21, 1955):27; Werner Picht, *Wiederbewaffnung.*

42. Erler in *FAZ,* June 25, 1956; EE, *Vorwärts,* June 7 and August 2, 1957.

43. *Economist,* February 2, 1957.

44. EE, *Vorwärts,* April 5, 1957; Erler, ibid., April 26, 1957.

45. Strauss, *Verhandlungen,* June 26, 1957, 37:12651.

46. Schmidt, *Pressedienst,* June 22 and 27, 1957; EE, *Vorwärts,* June 21, 1957; Eschmann, *Verhandlungen,* June 26, 1957, 37:12654-57.

47. Strauss, quoted in *FAZ,* June 24, 1957.

48. Ollenhauer, quoted in the *Times* (London), October 19, 1956; EE, *Vorwärts,* May 3, 1957. For a more moderate, but nonetheless critical, estimation of Strauss, see the contemporary reports of Fritz René Allemann, "Wehrminister Franz Josef Strauss: Der Mann und die Aufgabe," *Politische Meinung* 1 (December, 1956):51-56; Edmond Taylor, "The Powerhouse of German Defense," *Reporter* 9 (April 18, 1957):25-30.

49. See, for example, *Pressedienst,* October 7, 1953, and June 24, 1954; *Vorwärts,* April 1, 1955.

50. For the Göttingen Declaration and the response by government and public, see Hans Karl Rupp, *Ausserparlamentarische Opposition in der Ära Adenauer,* pp. 73-89. For the immediate response of Adenauer, see *Die Welt,* April 13, 1957.

51. *Pressedienst,* April 13, 1957; Ollenhauer in Wiesbaden, *Die Welt,* April 15, 1957.

52. EE, *Vorwärts,* April 26, 1957.

53. Erler, *Verhandlungen,* May 10, 1957, 36:12052-62. Also on this theme, Erler on German TV, Cologne Studio, March 11, 1957, and the West German Radio Network, February 10, 1957, in "Erler Veröffentlichungen, Juli 1956-1957"; Wehner on the Bavarian Radio Network, March 27, 1957, in Wehner File, *Pressearchiv;* Ollenhauer in Bonn press conferences, *Die Welt,* March 30, and *FAZ,* May 3, 1957.

54. Erler at Strasbourg, January 9, 1957, warned against the dangers of proliferation; Erler, *Politik für Deutschland,* p. 504.

55. Strauss, quoted in *Die Zeit,* April 18, 1957; Adenauer, *Verhandlungen,* May 10, 1957, 36:12130.

56. Erler, *Neue Ruhr-Zeitung,* March 28, 1957; *Vorwärts,* April 26, 1957.

57. Schmid, *Verhandlungen,* May 10, 1957, 36:12074-84.

58. Morton H. Halperin, *Limited War: An Essay on the Development of the Theory,* Harvard University, Center for International Affairs, Occasional Paper Number 3, May, 1962.

59. Ollenhauer on radio, April 10, 1957, in "Ollenhauer Reden, 1957"; GM, *Pressedienst,* May 25, 1957.

60. Strauss, *Verhandlungen,* May 10, 1957, 36:12066-74; Eugen Gerstenmaier

(CDU), ibid., pp. 12084-98.

61. Strauss, ibid., p. 12135; SPD response in *Pressedienst,* May 12, 1957; Ollenhauer in Bonn, *SDZ,* May 13, 1957.

62. See the reports of the interview in *Die Welt* and *Stuttgarter Zeitung,* May 18, 1957.

63. Erler, *Verhandlungen,* May 22, 1957, 37:12227.

64. GM, *Pressedienst,* April 1, 1957; FM, *Vorwärts,* May 24, 1957; Ollenhauer, "Wozu dient die NATO?" *Occident* 10 (June 19, 1957):11-12.

65. Ollenhauer, *Verhandlungen,* May 10, 1957, 36:12127-29; Ollenhauer in Bonn, *FAZ,* May 18, 1957, and *Die Welt,* May 27, 1957.

66. *Vorwärts,* May 31, 1957. Similar ideas were discussed by Erler, *Verhandlungen,* January 31, 1957, 34:10719.

67. *SDZ,* May 24, 1957.

68. Erler, ibid., May 25/26, 1957.

69. Ollenhauer, "Wozu dient die NATO?," p. 12. A similar but more cautious statement appeared in Fritz Erler, "Les Problèmes du Réarmament allemand du Point de Vue de l'Opposition," *Synthèses* 12 (June, 1957):33-46. Beermann, "Sicherheit, Wiedervereinigung und Stärke der Bundeswehr," p. 2.

70. Erler, "Sicherheit für Deutschland und Europa," *Dokumente* 1 (April, 1957):95. Carlo Schmid spoke of a "massive controlled disarmament" of the opposing forces; Schmid on the West German Radio Network, June 15, 1957, in Schmid file, *Pressearchiv.*

71. Erler spoke of Germany and her neighbours being sufficiently strong to balance the military strength of the USSR, which of course would be limited by an arms agreement. See *Westfälische Rundschau* (Dortmund, SPD), September 7, 1957.

72. Ollenhauer, quoted in *SDZ,* July 8 and August 17/18, 1957.

73. The confederation plan and the exchange of notes between West Germany and the Soviet Union are in *Documents, 1957,* pp. 81-112; see also Feld, *Reunification,* pp. 119-21.

74. Schmid on the West German Radio Network, June 15, 1957, in Schmid file, *Pressearchiv;* Ollenhauer in Vienna, July 3, 1957, "Ollenhauer Reden, 1957"; Hans Merten, *Die Welt,* August 9, 1957.

75. Ollenhauer, quoted in *FAZ,* July 30, 1957.

76. Adenauer in Hamburg, *FAZ,* June 3, 1957; in Nuremberg, *Die Welt,* July 10, 1957.

77. Fritz René Allemann, *Zwischen Stabilität und Krise,* pp. 109-10.

78. Ollenhauer to the Parteivorstand, Parteiausschuss, and Kontrollkommission in Bonn, January 24, 1957, in "Ollenhauer Reden, 1957."

79. *Die Zeit,* August 22, 1957; Terrence Prittie, *Manchester Guardian,* September 12, 1957.

80. PM, *Vorwärts,* September 20, 1957.

81. For a description of Ollenhauer on the hustings, see *Die Welt,* August 20, 1957; *Der Spiegel* 11 (August 21, 1957):13. Fritz René Allemann writes: "One has the feeling that between him and the masses who he addresses there is a glass partition which prevents contact." Allemann, "How the West Germans Voted," *New Leader* 40 (October 7, 1957):8.

82. On the SPD campaign, see Uwe Kitzinger, *German Electoral Politics,* pp. 126-50, 301; *Der Spiegel* 11 (September 25, 1957):14.

83. The manifesto is published in *Vorwärts,* June 21, 1957; see comments

of Fritz René Allemann, "Wahlkampf um Bonn," *Der Monat* 9 (July, 1957): 8-9.

84. David Childs, *From Schumacher to Brandt,* pp. 98-99; Kitzinger, *German Electoral Politics,* p. 133.

85. *Economist,* September 7, 1957; Allemann, "How the West Germans Voted," p. 7.

86. Fritz René Allemann, "Aussenpolitische Schattenboxen," *Der Monat* 9 (September, 1957):3; *Die Gegenwart* 12 (September 21, 1957):578.

87. Ollenhauer in Munich, *SDZ,* September 10, 1957; and in Essen, *Die Welt,* September 12, 1957. Hans Ulrich Kempski wrote that an institute making public opinion surveys for the SPD had already indicated that the public had altered its views of conscription. *SDZ,* June 4, 1957.

88. *Die Welt,* August 20, 1957.

89. On the impact of the Hungarian Uprising on West German thinking, see Kitzinger, *German Electoral Politics,* pp. 15-16; Claus Jacobi, "German Paradoxes," *Foreign Affairs* 35 (April, 1957):433.

90. Ollenhauer on the Hessen Radio Network, February 7, 1957, in "Ollenhauer Reden, 1957"; Ollenhauer, *SDZ,* August 17/18, 1957; Erler on the West German Radio Network, February 10 and June 15, 1957, in "Erler Veröffentlichungen, Juli 1956-1957."

91. Stefan Thomas, *Vorwärts,* August 30, 1957.

92. Werner Friedmann wrote that the West Germans preferred "a schnitzel in the hand to reunification in utopia." Werner Friedmann, *SDZ,* September 17, 1957; Hans Zehrer, *Die Welt,* September 17, 1957.

93. GM, *Vorwärts,* September 13, 1957.

94. Speaking in Vienna on July 3, 1957, Ollenhauer said: "I do not consider it to be my task to provide an answer" to the question of what would happen to NATO and the Warsaw Pact once the European security system came into existence. "Ollenhauer Reden, 1957."

95. *Die Welt,* August 20, 1957. Even the military experts said little on this during the campaign. See Erler on the West German Radio Network, June 15, 1957, in "Erler Veröffentlichungen, Juli, 1956-1957."

96. Ollenhauer in Hamburg, *Die Welt,* September 13, 1957.

97. PM, *Vorwärts,* November 30, 1956; Schmid, *FAZ,* September 21, 1957.

Chapter 8

1. *Economist,* September 7, 1957; or, by contrast, *Die Tat,* September 17, 1957; *Die Welt,* September 17, 1957.

2. *Der Spiegel* 11 (September 25, 1957):14. The proposals are listed in *Die Welt,* September 19, 1957. At the Executive Committee meeting held three days after the election, Schmid, Erler, Wehner, Kühn, Knoeringen, and Birkelbach all spoke in favor of party reform. *Die Welt,* September 26 and 28, 1957.

3. Heine reported in *SDZ,* September 20, 1957.

4. On the September 18 meeting, see *Der Spiegel* 11 (September 25, 1957): 16; Ollenhauer's address to the Parteivorstand, Parteiausschuss, and Kontrollkommission, September 25, 1957, in "Ollenhauer Reden, 1957."

5. Wolfgang Abendroth, *Vorwärts,* November 8, 1957; and "Die Chancen der deutschen Sozialdemokratie nach dem 15 September 1957," *Geist und Tat* 12

(November, 1957):366-74. For a discussion of the party left, see: Chalmers, *Social Democratic Party*, pp. 206-09.

6. For the views of the reformers, see Ulrich Lohmar, "Reform an Haupt und Gliedern?" *Deutsche Rundschau* 83 (December, 1957):1252-57; Klaus Peter Schulz, *Opposition Als Politisches Schicksal?*

7. On the elections, see *Der Spiegel* 11 (November 6, 1957):13-14; Richard Thilenius, *SDZ*, October 25 and 31, 1957; *Die Welt*, October 31, 1957. It is worth noting that Gustav Heinemann, who had recently joined the SPD, and Helmut Schmidt were elected to the twenty-one-man executive committee of the Fraktion. The deputies also elected Mommer, Menzel, and Arndt as parliamentary whips. These three men were prominent reformers and could be counted on to support the party's shift to the right.

8. *Die Welt*, November 2, 1957.

9. Dieter Schröder, *SDZ*, November 22, 1957.

10. For a discussion of the conflict between the party bureaucrats and politicians, see Hans Ulrich Kempski, *SDZ*, September 21/22, 1957; Paul Sethe, *Die Welt*, September 26, 1957; Fritz René Allemann, "The Great Debate Among German Social Democrats," *New Leader* 41 (February 17, 1958):15. The five in the Baracke on whom Ollenhauer relied were Fritz Heine, Willi Eichler, Max Kukul, Alfred Nau, and Herta Gotthelf.

11. Alfred Rapp, *FAZ*, November 27, 1957. Allemann, "The Great Debate," p. 16.

12. Mellies defended the bureaucrats in *Sozialdemokratischer Pressedienst*, November 3, 1957 (hereafter cited as *Pressedienst*). For the *Baracke's* view, see Willi Eichler, "Der 15 September 1957," *Geist und Tat* 12 (October, 1957): 321-23. For the reformers, see Erler quoted in *FAZ*, November 8, 1957.

13. Four months later, after a bitter intraparty battle, Brandt succeeded Neumann as chairman of the Berlin party organization. Ashkenasi, *Reformpartei*, pp. 143-52; *Die Zeit*, September 19, 1957 and January 16, 1958.

14. Gaus, *Staatserhaltende Opposition*, pp. 35-36; Hans Ulrich Kempski, *SDZ*, September 21/22, 1957.

15. Dieter Schröder, *SDZ*, November 22, 1957.

16. Adenauer, *Verhandlungen des Deutschen Bundestages*, October 29, 1957, 39:17-25 (hereafter cited as *Verhandlungen*).

17. Ollenhauer, ibid., November 5, 1957, pp. 45-55, 88.

18. For a discussion of the impact of Sputnik on Western military thinking, see *Survey 1957-58*, pp. 347-60, 501-504; Osgood, *NATO*, pp. 172-77 and 221.

19. Rapacki made his proposal in a speech to the United Nations; see *Survey 1957-58*, pp. 563-64. The Kennan lectures were subsequently published; see George Kennan, *Russia, the Atom, and the West*.

20. AE, *Pressedienst*, October 3, 1957; resolution passed by the Parteivorstand, November 20, 1957, *Jahrbuch der SPD, 1956-57*, p. 356.

21. *FAZ*, November 23, 1957. For a discussion of Adenauer's position on atomic weapons at this time, see Richardson, *Germany*, pp. 52-57.

22. Sigurd Paulsen, *Vorwärts*, November 15, 1957. EE, ibid., November 1, 1957. sp, *Pressedienst*, October 11, 1957.

23. *Survey 1957-58*, pp. 504, 546-47.

24. For the resolution, see *Jahrbuch der SPD, 1958-59*, p. 22; Erler, interviewed by J. R. Kaim, *Frankfurter Rundschau*, November 26, 1957.

25. On the NATO conference, see *Survey 1957-58*, pp. 504-506.

26. Ollenhauer on the Hessen Radio Network, December 19, 1957, "Ollenhauer

Reden, 1957"; Ollenhauer in Bonn, *SDZ,* January 16, 1958; and in Kiel, *FAZ,* January 20, 1958.

27. On the debate, see *Die Zeit,* January 30, 1958; *Die Tat,* January 24, 1958; Dieter Schröder, *SDZ,* January 24/25, 1958.

28. sp, *Pressedienst,* January 24, 1958.

29. Ollenhauer, *Verhandlungen,* January 23, 1958, 39:313-21; Schmid, ibid., pp. 356-63. His response to Kiesinger was, "Scratch a Communist and you will find a Russian."

30. Brentano, ibid., pp. 298-303; Kiesinger, ibid., pp. 321-31; Strauss, ibid., pp. 377-84.

31. Erler, ibid., pp. 369-75. The Social Democrats hoped that the Soviet Union would accept political change in the satellite counties as a natural consequence of military withdrawal or at least, as Erler described earlier, that political change would be carried out in an evolutionary rather than a revolutionary fashion so that the Russians would not have an easy excuse for intervention. See Erler on the Free Berlin Radio Network, December 7, 1957, "Erler Veröffentlichungen, 1957."

32. On the proposed summit conference, see *Survey 1957-58,* pp. 516-17.

33. Mommer, quoted in *SDZ,* March 6, 1958.

34. GM, *Pressedienst,* February 22, 1958; EE, *Vorwärts,* February 28, 1958.

35. A resolution passed by the Parteivorstand, Parteiausschuss, and Kontroll-kommission, March 5, 1958, in *Jahrbuch der SPD, 1958-59,* p. 387; Erler on the Hessen Radio Network, February 23, 1958, in "Erler Veröffentlichungen, 1958"; Ollenhauer on the South German Radio Network, March 12, 1958, in "Ollenhauer Reden, 1958."

36. Adenauer, *Verhandlungen,* March 20, 1958, 40:842-46.

37. *Times* (London), December 20, 1957.

38. Erler, *Vorwärts,* December 20, 1957; Mellies in Burgdorf, *Die Welt,* December 9, 1957.

39. The Executive Committee's announcement is in *SDZ,* January 31, 1958.

40. Karl Bauer, *Deutsche Verteidigungspolitik, 1945-63,* p. 153. For a discussion of SPD involvement in the campaign, see Rupp, *Ausserparlamentarische Opposition,* pp. 127-35.

41. CDU spokesman, quoted in *FAZ,* March 11, 1958.

42. Karl Bechert, *Deutsche Politik im Schatten der Atomdrohung.*

43. Günther Markscheffel, *Pressedienst,* March 26, 1958; Helmut Schmidt, *Hamburger Echo* (SPD), April 2, 1958.

44. Mommer, *Pressedienst,* March 27, 1958.

45. Gerstenmaier in Bonn, *SDZ,* April 16, 1958; Will Rasner, *Verhandlungen,* April 18, 1958, 40:1223.

46. Schmid, *Verhandlungen,* April 18, 1958, 40:1221-22.

47. Ollenhauer at a Bonn press conference, *FAZ,* March 28, 1958; and on the Hessen Radio Network, April 16, 1958, "Ollenhauer Reden, 1958."

48. Menzel, as parliamentary secretary of the SPD Bundestag Fraktion and chairman of the Kampf dem Atomtod committee, sent memoranda to SPD state party leaders on March 31 and April 30, 1958, telling them that since there was little chance of success in the Bundestag, they should promote opinion polls at the state and local level. "Menzel, Volksbefragung" (R 27), SPD Archives.

49. The government went to Karlsruhe on May 13, but its position had already been widely publicized. See the statements by the ministries of the interior and justice, *SDZ,* April 12/13, 1958.

50. On the rally, see Eberhard Bitzer, *FAZ*, March 25, 1958; Rupp, *Ausserparlamentarische Opposition*, pp. 153-56.

51. *SDZ*, March 29/30, 1958.

52. For the demonstrations from March to May, 1958, see Rupp, *Ausserparlamentarische Opposition*, pp. 162-212.

53. Brandt, quoted in *Der Tagesspiegel* (Berlin), April 19, 1958.

54. *Christ und Welt*, February 20, 1958; *Vorwärts*, January 3, 1958.

55. Ashkenasi, *Reformpartei*, pp. 153-58.

56. Erler, "Plebiszitäre Demokratie?" *Vorwärts*, April 18, 1958. Ollenhauer told a press conference in Bonn that a general strike was a legitimate weapon against the government. *FAZ*, March 28, 1958. Wehner responded that a general strike was "general nonsense." *Die Welt*, March 31, 1958.

57. *FAZ*, February 3, 1958.

58. Ibid., February 6, 1958. For the Beermann memorandum, dated January 19, 1958, and the advisory report, January 28, 1958, see SPD Fraktion Archives and my interview with Beermann, August, 1970.

59. *Der Spiegel* mentions a clash with the leaders over relations with Bonin, whom Beermann considered a dangerous reactionary; over acknowledgement of national defense at the Munich party conference; and over advocacy of a volunteer army in January, 1957. In each case Beermann was rebuked by the Parteivorstand. *Der Spiegel* 12 (February 26, 1958):22-27.

60. Schmid, Erler, and Merten met with Strauss on November 14. *Der Spiegel* 11 (November 27, 1957):13-14.

61. Erler on the South German Radio Network, November 17, 1957, Erler file, *Pressearchiv*. This was also discussed at a Parteivorstand meeting, but no decision was made. *FAZ*, November 21, 1957.

62. *Westdeutsche Allgemeine*, March 6, 1958; *Deutsche Zeitung und Wirtschaftszeitung*, March 8, 1958.

63. Fritz Erler, "Gedanken zur Politik und inneren Ordnung der Sozialdemokratie," *Die Neue Gesellschaft* 5 (January/February, 1958):3-4; Erler on the Southwest German Radio Network, November 15, 1957, Erler file, *Pressearchiv;* Erler on RIAS, February 25, 1958, "Erler Veröffentlichungen, 1958."

64. Political commentators and coalition deputies pointed out the contradictory views of Heinemann and Erler. See Alfred Rapp, *FAZ*, March 27, 1958; Wolfgang Wagner, *Hannoversche Allgemeine Zeitung*, February 18, 1958; Will Rasner (CDU), quoted in *FAZ*, February 8, 1958.

65. *Vorwärts*, February 21, 1958. SPD military experts were greatly concerned about the party's attitude toward the military, but they were unable to convince the leaders of the need to create better relations with the Bundeswehr. Ernst Riggert, a member of the Parteivorstand's security subcommittee, sent a series of letters to Ollenhauer on the subject and received an unenthusiastic response. Ollenhauer to Riggert, March 19, 1958, "Ollenhauer Korrespondenz," file R.

66. The resolution is in *Vorwärts*, May 9, 1958.

67. *Frankfurter Rundschau*, March 6, 1958.

68. *Christ und Welt*, March 13, 1958.

69. Speaking to a local party conference in Kelheim, Ollenhauer said that the Federal Republic would have to be ready to leave NATO if Poland and Czechoslovakia offered to leave the Warsaw Pact in order to realize the Rapacki Plan. *SDZ*, March 3, 1958. The following day, Erhard Eckert, who covered military affairs for *Vorwärts*, sent a telegram to Ollenhauer asking that he immediately publish a clarification of the statement he had made in Kelheim because the

CDU was using it against the SPD. Eckert to Ollenhauer, March 3, 1958, "Ollenhauer Korrespondenz," file E. The party's position had been that only a reunited Germany would leave NATO, not the Federal Republic. Carlo Schmid told the Bundestag earlier that, even while carrying out the Rapacki Plan, if reunification was not achieved, then West Germany could remain in NATO. *Verhandlungen,* January 23, 1958, 39:363.

70. Ollenhauer, *Protokoll der Verhandlungen des Parteitages der SPD vom 18 bis 23 Mai 1958 in Stuttgart,* pp. 36-51 (hereafter cited as *Stuttgart Protocols*).

71. Werner Stein (Berlin), ibid., pp. 61-64; Richard Boljahn (Bremen), ibid., pp. 73-75.

72. Ollenhauer, ibid., pp. 80-81.

73. Erler, ibid., pp. 92-106; Wehner, ibid., pp. 108-26.

74. Paul Nevermann (Hamburg), ibid., pp. 137-39; Max Seidel (Fürth), ibid., p. 152; Walter Möller (Frankfurt), ibid., pp. 141-43.

75. Hans Merten (Giessen), ibid., pp. 134-37; Ulrich Lohmar (Bielefeld), ibid., pp. 149-51.

76. Kurt Mattick, ibid., pp. 139-41.

77. Erler, ibid., pp. 166-69; Wehner, ibid., pp. 170-76.

78. Josef Grunner (Berlin), ibid., p. 444; Josef Neuberger (Düsseldorf), ibid., p. 396.

79. Eichler, ibid., pp. 170-77; Deist, ibid., pp. 178-92.

80. Willi Kinnigkeit, *SDZ,* May 23, 1958; Joachim Besser, *Die Welt,* May 23, 1958; Alfred Rapp, *FAZ,* May 23, 1958.

81. Quoted in Joachim Besser, *Die Welt,* May 24, 1958. For a commentary on Wehner's election, see Fritz René Allemann, *Die Zeit,* May 29, 1958; *Der Spiegel* 12 (May 28, 1958):20-22.

82. On the changes in the Executive Committee membership, see Schellenger, *SPD in the Bonn Republic,* pp. 157-59; *Der Spiegel* 12 (June 4, 1958):20. Among the new members were Helmut Schmidt, Gustav Heinemann, and Willy Brandt.

83. Alfred Rapp, *FAZ,* May 24, 1958; Kurt Becker, *Die Welt,* May 27, 1958; Fritz René Allemann, *Die Zeit,* May 29, 1958.

84. Jesco von Puttkamer, *Vorwärts,* March 28, 1958; Stefan Thomas, ibid., April 25, 1958; *Sozialdemokratischer Pressedienst,* May 8, 1958.

85. Fritz Erler, "The Reunification of Germany and Security for Europe," *World Politics* 10 (April, 1958):368.

86. Helmut Lindemann, *Vorwärts,* August 8, 1958; Puttkamer, ibid., July 25, 1958.

87. Ollenhauer, ibid., March 28, 1958.

88. Schröder, *Verhandlungen,* June 13, 1958, 41:1709-12.

89. Schmid, quoted in *SDZ,* July 5/6, 1958; Allemann, *Die Zeit,* July 4, 1958.

90. Fritz René Allemann, "Germany's Emerging Two Party System," *New Leader* 41 (August 4-11, 1958).18-19; Kurt Becker, *Die Welt,* July 8, 1958; Richard Thilenius, *SDZ,* July 8, 1958.

91. *FAZ,* July 8, 1958.

92. *Pressedienst,* July 10, 1958.

93. Gerald Braunthal, "Direct and Representative Democracy in West Germany: The Atomic Armament Issue," *Canadian Journal of Economics and Political Science,* 26 (August, 1959):319-21.

94. Criticism by Theodor Eschenburg, *Die Zeit,* April 3, 1958. Theo Sommer, ibid., April 17, 1958; Richard Thilenius, *SDZ,* April 26, 1958.

95. Günther Markscheffel, *Pressedienst,* March 26, 1958.

96. Erler, "Gedanken zur Politik," pp. 3-4.

97. *Pressedienst,* May 20, 1958; Wehner in Tutzing, *FAZ,* July 15, 1958.

Chapter 9

1. The letters can be found in *Vorwärts* under the section "Frei Tribune" from August 29 to October 24.

2. On the press conference, see *FAZ* and *Die Welt,* October 11, 1958.

3. Erler, SPD *Pressemitteilungen und Informationen,* October 10, 1958; Erler *Sozialdemokratischer Pressedienst,* October 17, 1958 (hereafter cited as *Pressedienst*); Schmidt, quoted in *Die Welt,* October 18, 1958.

4. The resolution is in *Vorwärts,* October 17, 1958. For reports of the Fraktion meeting, see *Die Welt,* October 15, 1958; *Der Spiegel,* October 22, 1958; Soell, *Erler,* 1:221-23.

5. Schmidt to Ollenhauer, July 2, 1958, in "Ollenhauer Korrespondenz," file Schm-Schz.

6. For the letters, see *Vorwärts,* October 31 to November 18, 1958.

7. Arno Beherisch, *Das Andere Zeitung,* October 16, 1958; the SDS, quoted in *Die Welt,* October 24, 1958; the Falcons, in *SDZ,* November 17, 1958.

8. On the meeting, see *Die Welt,* October 25, 1958; *SDZ,* October 27, 1958.

9. Kurt Becker, *Die Welt,* October 14, 1958; Adalbert Weinstein, *FAZ,* October 27, 1958; Marion Gräfin Dönhoff, *Die Zeit,* November 14, 1958.

10. Resolution passed by the Frankfurt Social Democrats in *Vorwärts,* January 9, 1959; and by the Frankfurt Falcons in ibid., April 3, 1959. The Cologne SPD called the Fraktion resolution a capitulation. *Industrie Kurier,* March 21, 1959.

11. See, for example, Erler at a Young Socialist meeting in Gelsenkirchen, *Die Welt,* February 6, 1959.

12. Recommendation of the security committee, July 3, 1959, in "Ollenhauer Korrespondenz," file E.

13. *Neue Rhein Zeitung,* October 21, 1958; Schmidt, *Verhandlungen des Deutschen Bundestages,* June 10, 1959, 43:3912-21 (hereafter cited as *Verhandlungen*); Merten on the South German Radio Network, October 20, 1959, in Merten file, *Pressearchiv.*

14. In a 1962 interview with William C. Nenno; Nenno, "The SPD and West German Rearmament, 1949-1959" (Ph.D. diss., Georgetown University, 1964). For a discussion of the duties and activities of the defense commissioner, see F. Ridley, "The Parliamentary Commissioner for Military Affairs in the Federal Republic of Germany," *Political Studies* 12 (February, 1964):1-20.

15. EE, *Vorwärts,* October 23, 1959; CG, ibid., July 16, 1958.

16. *Hannoversche Allgemeine Zeitung,* January 19, 1959.

17. For the Soviet note of November 27, see *Documents, 1958,* pp. 146-64. On the Berlin crisis, see Hans Speier, *Divided Berlin;* Jean E. Smith, *The Defense of Berlin.*

18. For the notes exchanged in September, see *Documents, 1958,* pp. 137-46.

19. Gradl, *Verhandlungen,* October 1, 1958, 42:2406-11.

20. Ollenhauer on the Bavarian Radio Network, September 10, 1958, in "Ollenhauer Reden, 1958"; Ollenhauer, *Pressedienst,* November 3, 1958. For a more optimistic view of the chances for reunification, see Ernst Wilhelm Meyer, "Gedanken zur Politik der Wiedervereinigung," *Aussenpolitik* 9 (October, 1958): 614-30.

21. PM, *Vorwärts,* November 7, 1958.

22. Declaration of the Parteivorstand on the Soviet notes, November 28, 1958, in *Jahrbuch der SPD, 1958-59,* pp. 393-94; GM, *Pressedienst,* November 29, 1958; Ollenhauer on the Bavarian Radio Network, December 10, 1958, in "Ollenhauer Reden, 1958."

23. Willy Brandt, "Crisis in Berlin," *New Leader* 42 (February 23, 1959): 3-4.

24. Quoted in Flora Lewis, "Leader of the Encircled and Defiant City," *New York Times Magazine,* December 7, 1958, p. 30. For Brandt's views, see his speech to the Berlin House of Deputies, *FAZ,* November 21, 1958; interview with Hans Ulrich Kempski, *SDZ,* December 5, 1958.

25. For the election and Brandt's strategy, see Ashkenasi, *Reformpartei,* pp. 159-61.

26. *Der Spiegel* 21 (December 17, 1958):21-22; declaration made by the Parteivorstand and the executive committee of the Bundestag Fraktion, December 13, 1958, in *Jahrbuch der SPD, 1958-59,* p. 394.

27. *Documents, 1958,* pp. 166-72.

28. *Documents, 1959,* pp. 1-9.

29. Wehner on the South German Radio Network, February 4, 1959, in Wehner file, *Pressearchiv;* see also the declaration of the Presidium, January 12, 1959, in *Jahrbuch der SPD, 1958-59,* p. 394.

30. Ollenhauer to the Parteirat, February 12, 1959, "Ollenhauer Reden, 1959."

31. Jesco von Puttkamer, *Vorwärts,* January 16, 1959; Wehner, ibid., February 6, 1959; Helmut Lindemann, ibid., March 6, 1959.

32. *Die Welt,* March 10, 1959. Ollenhauer on the South German Radio Network, March 11, 1959, "Ollenhauer Reden, 1959"; *Der Spiegel* 13 (March 18, 1959):13-15.

33. The plan is reprinted in *Jahrbuch der SPD, 1958-59,* pp. 397-401; *News from Germany,* April, 1959.

34. A statement by the government on the SPD plan, quoted in *Die Welt,* March 21, 1959.

35. Ernst Majonica in *Die Welt,* March 21, 1959; Kai Uwe von Hassel, ibid., March 23, 1959.

36. Wehner in *Vorwärts,* February 6, March 20, April 10 and 17, 1959. On Wehner's goals, see Fritz René Allemann, "Adenauer and the Others," *Encounter* 13 (August, 1959):66; Kurt Becker, *Die Welt,* June 4, 1959.

37. Adenauer in Brunswick, *Frankfurter Rundschau,* April 2, 1959; Rolf Handtke, "SPD auf Wehner Kurs," *Die Politische Meinung* 4 (April, 1959): 83-84.

38. Harold Hurwitz, "Confusion in Berlin," *New Leader* 42 (March 30, 1959): 6-7; WH, *Christ und Welt,* March 26, 1959; Robert Strobel, *Die Zeit,* April 3, 1959.

39. On the press conference, see *FAZ* and *Die Welt,* March 19, 1959. For Erler's impressions of the trip, see his article in *SDZ,* March 21/22, 1959.

40. Jesco von Puttkamer, *Vorwärts,* March 13 and 20, 1959. Erler on the Bavarian Radio Network, March 18, 1959, in "Erler Veröffentlichungen, 1959."

41. Wehner, quoted in *Die Welt,* March 20, 1959; Schmid, quoted in *New York Times,* March 19, 1959; Ollenhauer in *Frankfurter Rundschau,* March 16, 1959.

42. In an interview with Prague radio, Ollenhauer insisted on the need for a fixed timetable for the stages of reunification. *Frankfurter Rundschau,* February

24, 1959. Erler commented on the need to link military and political measures together in a speech to the Bundestag Foreign Affairs Committee, February 5, 1959, in "Erler Veröffentlichungen, 1959."

43. Wehner had recommended a political dialogue with the SED ever since 1954, but not until 1959, under the impact of the Berlin crisis, did the leadership accept the idea. *Der Spiegel* 31 (July 25, 1977):36-49. On his differences with Erler, see Soell, *Erler,* 1:375-77.

44. Conrad Ahlers, "Mit Wehner in den Abgrund?" *Der Spiegel* 13 (April 15, 1959):37. Erler said in Pforzheim that political changes would "automatically" follow a military detente. *Die Welt,* March 23, 1959.

45. Schmid, *Vorwärts,* March 27, 1959; Ollenhauer on the Bavarian Radio Network, April 15, 1959, "Ollenhauer Reden, 1959"; Erler, "Disengagement und Wiedervereinigung," *Europa Archiv* 14 (May 5, 1959):291-300.

46. Erler on the Southwest Radio Network, March 21, 1959, "Erler Veröffentlichungen, 1959"; Wehner, *Vorwärts,* April 17, 1959. Wehner and Carlo Schmid also counted on winning the support of moderate East German Communists. See the latter's comment in Dortmund that there were patriots as well as knaves in the SED. *Vorwärts,* May 15, 1959.

47. Freiherr zu Guttenberg, "Das kaudinische Joch," *Die Politische Meinung* 4 (May, 1959):61-66.

48. Ollenhauer in Hannover, *Die Welt,* March 23, 1959; Wehner, quoted in Ahlers, "Mit Wehner in den Abgrund?" *Der Spiegel* 13 (April 15, 1959):38.

49. SPD, *Deutschlandplan der SPD: Kommentare, Argumente, Begründungen,* p. 23.

50. On the Geneva foreign ministers conference, see Hartmann, *Germany Between East and West,* pp. 105-16; *Survey, 1959-60,* pp. 30-37.

51. See the reports from Geneva by Ulrich Blank in *Vorwärts,* May 22 and 29, June 5 and 12, 1959; Parteivorstand resolution, May 15, 1959, in *News from Germany,* June, 1959.

52. Brandt on RIAS, May 17, 1959 and the South German Radio Network, May 30, 1959, in Brandt file, *Pressearchiv.* A Brandt supporter, Joachim Lipschitz, warned the advocates of the plan not to be so naïve as to think that the monolithic character of the SED would crack in a confrontation with the forces of democracy. Ashkenasi, *Reformpartei,* p. 169.

53. For criticism of Brandt by the left wing, see *Frankfurter Rundschau,* May 11, 21, and 25, 1959.

54. Brandt to the Berlin party conference, May 23, 1959, in Brandt file, *Pressearchiv;* Ashkenasi, *Reformpartei,* pp. 165-70.

55. *Die Welt* and *FAZ,* April 11, 1959. Several days later at Göttingen, Carlo Schmid admitted that indeed there were differences of opinion within the SPD over the *Deutschlandplan,* quoted in *Die Welt,* April 14, 1959.

56. On the SDS, see Fritz René Allemann, *Die Zeit,* June 5, 1959; Klaus Günther, "Der andere Meinung in der SPD: 1949, 1955-56, 1958-61," *Archiv für Sozialgeschichte* 13 (1973):43-47.

57. *Die Welt,* May 29, 1959.

58. *Frankfurter Rundschau,* August 3, 1959; *Der Spiegel* 13 (August 2, 1959): 26-27.

59. *Die Welt,* May 29, 1959.

60. *Frankfurter Rundschau,* June 2 and 3, 1959; Dieter Schröder, *SDZ,* June 6/7, 1959. The intraparty dispute is discussed at length in *Der Spiegel* 13 (June 17, 1959):28-29.

61. Knoeringen in *News from Germany*, September, 1959; PM, *Vorwärts*, August 7, 1959; Helmut Lindemann, ibid., August 14, 1959.

62. Franz Barsig quoted in *FAZ*, August 22, 1959; a similar proposal by Wehner in an interview with *Izvestia*, August 22, 1959, in Wehner file, *Pressearchiv*.

63. *Vorwärts*, August 21, 1959; Knoeringen in Munich *SDZ*, January 7, 1959; Ollenhauer in Mainz, *Die Freiheit*, March 2, 1959.

64. Schmid in Bremen, *SDZ*, October 28, 1959.

65. Mommer, *Pressedienst*, September 7, 1959. Carlo Schmid made a similar trip the year before and drew similar conclusions. *Die Zeit*, March 20, 1958.

66. Meyer wrote a nine-page article with the approval of the Parteivorstand, in *Pressedienst*, September 1, 1959.

67. Ollenhauer on the Bavarian Radio Network, September 30, 1959, in "Ollenhauer Reden, 1959."

68. Puttkamer, *Vorwärts*, October 2 and 23, 1959.

69. Hanrieder, *West German Foreign Policy*, pp. 194-98. Richard Hiscocks, *The Adenauer Era*, pp. 273-83; Besson, *Aussenpolitik der Bundesrepublik*, pp. 196-213.

70. *Manchester Guardian*, October 29, 1959; Terrence Prittie, "Fear in West Germany of an Allied Sell-Out," *New Republic* 141 (November 16, 1959):8-9.

71. Schmidt, *Verhandlungen*, November 5, 1959, 44:4759-69. For a description of the debate, see H. W. Graf von Finckenstein, *Die Welt*, November 7, 1959; Dieter Schröder, *SDZ*, November 7/8, 1959.

72. Helmut Lindemann, *Vorwärts*, July 16, 1959. For other comments on de Gaulle and NATO, see Erler, *Pressedienst*, July 23, 1959; Merten, ibid., July 18, 1959.

73. On the evolution of the program debate since 1945, see Schellenger, *SPD in the Bonn Republic*, pp. 32-56; Chalmers, *Social Democratic Party*, pp. 53-67; Miller, *Vor und nach Godesberg*, pp. 34-38.

74. SPD, *Grundsatzprogramm der SPD*. See the commentary by Fritz René Allemann, "Farewell to Marx," *Encounter* 14 (March, 1960):67-69.

75. Möller, *Protokoll Der Verhandlungen des Ausserordentlicher Parteitages der SPD 13-15 November 1959 in Bad Godesberg*, pp. 151-52 (hereafter cited as *Godesberg Protocols*).

76. Stein, *Godesberg Protocols*, p. 84.

77. For the motions proposed by local party organizations, see *Vorwärts*, October 23, 1959. Twenty-two of the one hundred sixty motions dealt with the military policy section. Atomic weapons were by far the most pressing concern; conscription was a distant second. Only two districts drafted motions which rejected an SPD affirmation of national defense.

78. Erler, *Godesberg Protocols*, p. 159.

79. Wehner, ibid., pp. 143-44.

80. Willi Reiland (Franken), ibid., p. 145; Erler, ibid., pp. 156-58. See the more explicit statement by Joachim Lipschitz (Berlin), ibid., pp. 150-51.

81. Wehner, ibid., pp. 142-44; Erler, ibid., pp. 154-55.

82. H. W. Graf von Finckenstein, *Die Welt*, November 16, 1959. Even Erler admitted on radio the night the conference adjourned that it would not be easy to make the program a basis for action for all party members. Erler, *Politik für Deutschland*, p. 140.

83. For a statement by the reformers, see Ulrich Lohmar, "Zum Godesberger Programm der Sozialdemokratie," *Die Neue Gesellschaft* 6 (November/December, 1959):416; Willi Eichler, "Selbstverständnis der Sozialisten," *Geist und Tat*

14 (December, 1959):353-56.

84. Wolfgang Abendroth, *Vorwärts,* October 9, 1959; Herbert Graber, *Das Andere Zeitung,* October 29, 1959; Pirker, *SPD nach Hitler,* pp. 280-85.

85. Wehner in Gaus, *Staatserhaltende Opposition,* p. 40; Erler, *Politik für Deutschland,* pp. 138-41.

86. On Ollenhauer's resignation, see Dieter Schröder, *SDZ,* July 9, 1959; Eberhard Bitzer, *FAZ,* July 11, 1959; *Der Spiegel* 13 (July 15, 1959):13-15.

87. Helmut Lindemann, *Vorwärts,* December 11, 1959; Ulrich Blank, ibid., December 18 and 24, 1959.

88. Erler at the Tutzing Evangelical Academy, November 17, 1959, in Bundesministerium für Innerdeutsche Beziehungen, eds., *Dokumente zur Deutschlandpolitik,* Series 4, 3:640-48 (hereafter citcd as *Dokumente*); Erler, *Pressedienst,* December 28, 1959.

89. Ollenhauer, *Pressedienst,* December 29, 1959; Ollenhauer in Nuremberg, *SDZ,* January 11, 1960. On the Hessen Radio Network, January 6, 1960, Wehner said that whatever military value NATO had, politically it could not be used to promote reunification. Wehner file, *Pressearchiv.*

90. On the SPD response to the government's Spanish venture, see Schmidt, *Pressedienst,* February 26, 1960; Erler on the Bavarian Radio Network, February 24, 1960, in "Erler Veröffentlichungen, 1960."

91. On the restoration, see Erler, *Pressedienst,* December 19, 1959; Ollenhauer, ibid., December 29, 1959; HL, *Vorwärts,* March 4, 1960.

92. The guidelines are in *Jahrbuch der SPD, 1958-59,* pp. 407-409.

93. For the press conference at which Erler and Knoeringen announced publication of the pamphlet, see *FAZ* and *SDZ,* February 2, 1960. Knoeringen became the party's most active campaigner for a policy that emphasized non-military factors as a defense against the Communist challenge. See *Vorwärts,* February 12, March 4, and April 8, 1960.

94. Ollenhauer, *Mitteilung für die Presse,* February 7, 1960, in "Ollenhauer Reden, 1958-60."

95. *FAZ,* May 10, 1960; Günther, "Die andere Meinung in der SPD," pp. 43-49.

96. A further reminder of Soviet intransigence was Ambassador Smirnov's letter to Ollenhauer, January 13, 1960, in which he reiterated the proposal to make West Berlin a free city and the threat to sign a separate peace treaty with East Germany if a satisfactory agreement could not be reached with the Western powers. *Dokumente,* Series 4, 4:72-75.

97. Erler, *Verhandlungen,* February 10, 1960, 45:5406; Ulrich Blank, "Die kleinen Hoffnungen," *Vorwärts,* March 4, 1960.

98. Helmut Schmidt on the North German Radio Network, January 27, 1960, in Schmidt file, *Pressearchiv;* Ollenhauer in Berlin, *Vorwärts,* March 11, 1960.

99. Wehner, *Pressedienst,* March 17, 1960; Party spokesman Franz Barsig, quoted in *FAZ,* March 22, 1960.

100. On the valid parts of the plan, see Barsig, *SDZ,* March 22, 1960; Wehner, *Vorwärts,* March 25, 1960. For the new proposals, see Ollenhauer's letter to Adenauer, May 6, 1960, in *Jahrbuch der SPD, 1960-61,* pp. 447-50.

101. Ollenhauer in Bielefeld, *Vorwärts,* April 26, 1960. From February to April the East German regime carried out a policy of forced collectivization in the rural areas in order to complete as rapidly as possible a program which after a decade and a half had only been half-finished.

102. Erler, *News from Germany,* May, 1960.

103. Smith, *Defense of Berlin,* pp. 209-23; *Survey, 1959-60,* pp. 50-70.

104. Declaration of the Presidium, *Pressedienst,* May 18, 1960; Wehner, quoted in *Die Welt,* May 21, 1960; Ollenhauer to the Parteirat, May 25, 1960, "Ollenhauer Reden, 1958-60."

105. Ollenhauer, *Verhandlungen,* May 24, 1960, 46:6702; Wehner on the South German Radio Network, May 25, 1960, in Wehner file, *Pressearchiv;* Wehner, "Redliche Bestandsaufnahme," *Vorwärts,* May 27, 1960.

106. Strauss, *Politisch-Soziale Korrespondenz,* June 1, 1960, in *Dokumente,* Series 4, 4:1158-64.

107. Erler in *Pressemitteilungen und Informationen,* (SPD), March 19, 1960. Wehner stated frankly that NATO could never be used to promote reunification. *Pressedienst,* April 21, 1960.

108. Schmidt at the Hamburg-Nordwest party conference, in *Vorwärts,* May 27, 1960; Erler at the Franken party conference, ibid., June 17, 1960.

109. Ollenhauer at the Brunswick party conference, ibid., May 17, 1960; Knoeringen, *Pressedienst,* June 9, 1960.

110. Franz Barsig, *Pressedienst,* May 20, 1960; Ollenhauer, quoted by H. W. Graf von Finckenstein, *Die Welt,* June 4, 1960. Two weeks later the Parteivorstand confirmed the party's continued commitment to disengagement. Ibid., June 15, 1960.

111. In the June, 1960, Bundestag debate on the government's bill to improve the administration of the original conscription law, the Social Democrats stated that they would vote against the bill, not for military reasons but because of the powers it gave to the government. Not conscription but executive authority was their main concern. Erler, *Verhandlungen,* June 24, 1960, 46:6938-41; Hans Merten, *Vorwärts,* July 1, 1960.

112. Ollenhauer to Adenauer, *Pressedienst,* May 12, 1960; Wehner interviewed by Conrad Ahlers, *Frankfurter Rundschau,* June 18, 1960.

113. Ollenhauer, *Die Welt,* June 4, 1960.

114. Rolf Zundel, *Die Zeit,* June 3, 1960; Kurt Becker, *Die Welt,* May 24, 1960.

115. *Der Spiegel* 14 (June 29, 1960):13-14.

116. Wehner, *Verhandlungen,* June 30, 1960, 46:7052-61. His speech at a party meeting in Heilbronn, June 26, 1960, was republished as a pamphlet: *Das Gemeinsame und das Trennende.*

117. Guttenberg, *Verhandlungen,* June 30, 1960, 46:7076-85. He referred to equivocal statements by Puttkamer, *Vorwärts,* June 3, 1960; Knoeringen, *Pressedienst,* June 9, 1960; Erler, *Die Welt,* June 27, 1960.

118. See the comments by Eberhard Bitzer, *FAZ,* July 5, 1960; Alfred Rapp, ibid., July 15, 1960.

119. Soell, *Erler,* 1:401-402. At the Fraktion meeting on June 28, only three deputies voted against the foreign-policy statement Wehner was to deliver in parliament two days later.

120. *Die Welt* and *SDZ,* July 11, 1960. For a firsthand view of the Munich meeting, see Kenneth N. Skoug, "The Eastern Policy of the German Social Democratic Party" (Ph.D. diss., George Washington University, 1964), pp. 322-25.

121. Rolf Zundel, *Die Zeit,* July 22, 1960; al, *Die Tat,* July 17, 1960.

122. See, for example, Ollenhauer, *Die Freiheit,* September 26, 1960; Ernst Wilhelm Meyer, "Neue Wege Deutscher Aussenpolitik," *Die Neue Gesellschaft* 7 (July/August, 1960):247-54. For a contrasting view, see Wehner, *Die Freiheit,* September 26, 1960; Erler on the Hessen Radio Network, July 5, 1960, in "Erler Veröffentlichungen, 1960."

123. Wehner quoted in *Freie Presse,* Bielefeld (SPD), September 19, 1960; also articles by PM, *Vorwärts,* August 19, 1960; Stefan Thomas, ibid., November 11, 1960.

124. The foreign policy resolution is in *Jahrbuch der SPD, 1960-61,* p. 421.

125. Wehner, *Protokoll des Parteitages der SPD in Hannover vom 21 bis 25 November 1960,* pp. 182-89 (hereafter cited as *Hannover Protocols*); Erler, ibid., pp. 170-80.

126. Ollenhauer, ibid., p. 78.

127. Heinz Brakemeier (Hessen-Süd), ibid., pp. 142-44; Walter Möller (Hessen-Süd), ibid., pp. 165-66. The resolutions prepared by local party organizations for the Hannover conférence can be found in *Vorwärts,* October 28, 1960.

128. *Der Spiegel* 14 (November 30, 1960):25. Alfred Rapp commented that many delegates accepted the change which the SPD had undergone from Stuttgart to Hannover "with resignation." *FAZ,* November 26, 1960.

129. A CDU spokesman declared that his party would treat the atomic weapons question as "the criteria for judging the reliability of the Social Democrats" in foreign policy. *FAZ,* July 16, 1960.

130. The security policy resolution is in *Jahrbuch der SPD, 1960-61,* pp. 421-22.

131. Ollenhauer, *Hannover Protocols,* pp. 70-75. Observers at the conference offered a number of theories as to why Ollenhauer chose to speak out, but no one was really sure. Some suggested that the party chairman had allowed himself to be provoked by Adenauer, who, only a few days before the conference opened, had challenged the SPD to demonstrate its loyalty to NATO by arming the Bundeswehr with the weapons it needed to meet its treaty obligations. Others interpreted Ollenhauer's outburst as an attempt to protect himself and the party in case the new course failed to produce the votes they expected. Most observers agreed, however, that Ollenhauer was not motivated by selfish political purposes. The speech represented an honest expression of his feelings on the atomic weapons question. See H. W. Graf von Finckenstein, *Die Welt,* November 24, 1960; Jürgen Tern, *FAZ,* November 25, 1960; Hans Ulrich Kempski, *SDZ,* November 26/27, 1960.

132. The reformers had tried to take a flexible position toward the atomic weapons question after the June 30 debate, but the sudden outcry from the ranks of the party compelled them to move more cautiously. See Franz Barsig, a spokesman for the Parteivorstand, quoted in *SDZ,* July 5, 1960; Wehner, *Die Zeit,* July 8, 1960; Erler to Ollenhauer, July 13, 1960, in "Ollenhauer Korrespondenz," file E. On the idea of making NATO an atomic power, see Schmidt, *Vorwärts,* November 17, 1960.

133. Karl Vittinghoff (Hamburg), *Hannover Protocols,* pp. 148-51; Ludwig Metzger, (Darmstadt), ibid., pp. 158-61; Wilhelm Dröscher (Rheinland-Hessen), ibid., pp. 130-31.

134. Schmid, ibid., pp. 151-55; Wienand, ibid., pp. 135-37; Schmidt, ibid., pp. 138-42.

135. Erler, ibid., pp. 170-80.

136. Ollenhauer, ibid., pp. 146-48.

137. Brandt was chosen on July 13 by a seven-man commission which included Ollenhauer, Brauer, Erler, Deist, Schmid, Zinn, and Brandt himself. *SDZ,* July 14, 1960. On August 24, the party's three leading committees—Parteivorstand, Parteirat, and Kontrollkommission—approved the selection. *FAZ,* August 15, 1960.

138. Gaus, *Staatserhaltende Opposition,* p. 58. No one could doubt the sincerity of Brandt's declaration, at Hannover, that: "We are no wanderers between the

fronts. We know where we belong." A Brandt-led government would stand firmly in the Western camp. Brandt, *Hannover Protocols,* p. 659.

Conclusion

1. Grosser, *Bonner Demokratie,* p. 290.

2. *Deutsche Zeitung und Wirtschaftszeitung,* May 10, 1960; Letter from the Parteivorstand to the Kontakt Leute, May, 1960, file E, "Ollenhauer Korrespondenz." Eric Waldman, writing in 1964, stated that the leaders' more positive attitude toward the Bundeswehr and NATO had so far "failed to permeate downward through the entire party apparatus." Waldman, *Goose Step,* p. 95.

3. Narr, *CDU-SPD,* p. 118; Löwke, *Für den Fall dass,* p. 112; Speier, *German Rearmament,* p. 175.

4. Several authors have noted the SPD's anti-Adenauer complex. Narr writes of a negative "fetishization" over the policy of Konrad Adenauer. *CDU-SPD,* p. 126. Erdmenger comments on the SPD's "astonishing fixation" on Adenauer's policy. *Das folgenschwere Missverständnis,* p. 87.

5. Schulz, *Schicksal,* p. 122.

6. Most writers, while acknowledging the party's moral commitment to reunification, tend to emphasize tactical considerations. Typical is Richard Hottelet's comment: "Reunification enlists more than patriotic and humanitarian motives." Hottelet, "The Future of German Unity," *New Leader* 38 (May 2, 1955):5; also Ashkenasi, *Reformpartei,* p. 48; Patterson, *SPD and European Integration,* p. 6.

7. Erler, in an interview with Udo Löwke, July 6, 1966, in Löwke, *Für den Fall,* p. 240.

8. Ashkenasi, *Reformpartei,* p. 129. Fritz René Allemann pointed out much earlier that the SPD leaders had to call for one more conference in order to prevent a serious intraparty crisis. They had to show the pacifists and neutralists in the party that there was no chance for reunification because the Russians would not let it happen. Allemann, "Kein Urlaub von der Aussenpolitik," *Der Monat* 7 (November, 1954):109-11.

9. Willi Birkelbach in the Common Assembly, December 1, 1954, quoted in Patterson, *SPD and European Integration,* p. 118; see also Hrbek, *Die SPD,* pp. 372-76.

10. Ossip Flechtheim, "Die Anpassung der SPD," *Kölner Zeitschrift für Soziologie und Sozialpsychologie* 17 (1965):594; Ashkenasi, *Reformpartei,* p. 116.

11. Pirker, *SPD nach Hitler,* pp. 296-302; Brauns, *SPD in der Krise,* pp. 215-17.

12. Brandt, *Hannover Protocols,* p. 659. Besson rejects the notion that Wehner's June 30 speech could in any way be construed as an SPD capitulation to Adenauer. Although Wehner accepted the primacy of the Western connection, he believed that it was still possible—within the NATO framework—to pursue a more active German policy than the chancellor ever did. Besson, *Aussenpolitik der Bundesrepublik,* pp. 230-32.

13. Fritz René Allemann, "Bonn in der Defensive," *Der Monat* 12 (May, 1960): 16; Richard Thilenius, *SDZ,* May 24, 1960. Georg Schröder, *Die Welt,* July 12, 1960.

14. Peter Merkl, *The Origin of the West German Republic,* p. 108.

15. Löwke, *Für den Fall,* p. 240. The evidence does not support the SPD contention of a missed chance to negotiate with the Russians over reunification. Richardson, *Germany and the Atlantic Alliance,* pp. 24-27; Wettig, *Entmili-*

tarisierung, pp. 493-522.

16. On Kirchheimer's work, see the introduction. Also Loewenberg, *Parliament in the German Political System,* pp. 394-95; Gerald Braunthal, "The Policy Function of the German Social Democratic Party," *Comparative Politics* 9 (January, 1977):132-33.

17. Kirchheimer, "The Vanishing Opposition," p. 244; Gerhard Lehmbruch, "The Ambiguous Coalition in West Germany," *Government and Opposition* 3 (Spring, 1968):189; Ashkenasi, *Reformpartei,* p. 184.

18. Kirchheimer in his last article hardly touches on the vehemence of SPD opposition in the fifties. He moves rapidly from Schumacher's intransigent opposition to Brandt's appeal for a grand coalition. "The Vanishing Opposition," pp. 241-51.

19. Schumacher, *Verhandlungen des Deutschen Bundestages,* September 21, 1949, 1:32; see also Schmid, *Die Freiheit,* June 20, 1951; Mellies, *Neuer Vorwärts,* September 21, 1953.

20. Schumacher at the 1948 Düsseldorf party conference, quoted in Scholz, *Turmwächter,* 2:165; and in the Bundestag, September 21, 1949, *Verhandlungen,* 1:32; see also the discussion in Waldemar Besson, "Regierung und Opposition in der deutschen Politik," *Politische Vierteljahresschrift* 3 (September, 1962): 237.

21. Kralewski and Neunreither, *Oppositionelles Verhalten,* pp. 97-99.

22. Magathan, *Politics of German Rearmament,* p. 348; Gerald Freund, "Adenauer and the Future of Germany," *International Journal* 18 (Autumn, 1963):461.

23. *News from Germany,* October, 1959, 13:1. Similarly, Ollenhauer told the Bundestag in June, 1953, that in no Western parliament were the vital questions of the nation treated as they were in the Bundestag. Ollenhauer said he doubted that the chancellor had "a trace of good will for loyal cooperation with the opposition on foreign policy matters." *SDZ,* June 11, 1953; also Mellies on the Hessen Radio Network, quoted in ibid., January 14, 1955.

24. See the complaints by SPD deputies about the failure of the coalition parties to stand up to the government: Adolf Arndt, "Die Entmachtung des Bundestages," *Die Neue Gesellschaft* 6 (November/December, 1959):431-38; Walter Menzel, "Parliamentary Politics in the German Federal Republic, 1957-60," *Parliamentary Affairs* 13 (Autumn, 1960):509-19.

25. See the examples in other policy areas described by Michael Hereth, "Parlamentarische Opposition in Deutschland am Beispiel des Verhaltens der Sozialdemokratischen Bundestagsfraktion von 1949-66" (Ph.D. diss., Erlangen University, 1968), pp. 78-92.

26. Besson writes: "Die letzten 12 Jahren haben uns eine sehr kraftige wohldisziplinierte und nicht selten effektive Opposition im deutschen Bundestag beschert." "Regierung und Opposition," p. 234; similarly, Braunthal, "Policy Function of the German Social Democratic Party," p. 133.

27. Schmid, *Zukunft,* November, 1951, p. 304; newspaper article by Fritz Erler, September 15, 1949, in Erler, *Politik für Deutschland,* pp. 316-18.

28. Attempts to categorize types of opposition have in general proven unsatisfactory because political parties are not homogenous units and seldom follow a single course of action. See the categories proposed by Kirchheimer in "The Vanishing Opposition," p. 237; also Heino Kaack, "Opposition und Aussenpolitik," *Politische Vierteljahresschrift* 10 (1969):241-44.

29. Lewis Edinger, "The Comparative Analysis of Political Leadership," *Comparative Politics* 7 (January, 1975):253-71.

30. Robert Michels, *Political Parties* trans. Eden and Cedar Paul. For more recent studies of intraparty democracy, see Ulrich Lohmar, *Innerparteiliche Demokratie;* Ute Mueller, *Die demokratische Willensbildung in den politischen Parteien;* Bodo Zeuner, *Innerparteiliche Demokratie.*

31. Edinger, *Schumacher,* pp. 111-26.

32. Pirker, *SPD nach Hitler,* pp. 299, 326.

33. See Harry Nowka, *Das Machtverhältnis zwischen Partei und Fraktion in der SPD;* Hartmut Soell, "Fraktion und Parteiorganisation," *Politische Viertel-jahresschrift* 10 (December, 1969):604-26; Chalmers, *Social Democratic Party,* pp. 115-18.

34. Pirker, *SPD nach Hitler,* p. 167; Chalmers, *Social Democratic Party,* p. 138; Lohmar, *Innerparteiliche Demokratie,* p. 75.

35. On the role of the parliamentary party at the biennial conferences, see: Nowka, *Partei und Fraktion,* pp. 58-62.

36. Mueller, *demokratische Willensbildung,* pp. 83-86; Chalmers, *Social Democratic Party,* pp. 133-37; Jürgen Dittberner, "Die Bundesparteitage der Christlich Demokratische Union und der Sozialdemokratischen Partei Deutschlands von 1946 bis 1968" (Ph.D. diss., Free University of Berlin, 1969), pp. 31-49, 167-71.

37. Lohmar, *Innerparteiliche Demokratie,* p. 84; Dittberner, "Bundesparteitage," p. 229; Hans Schuster, "Die Heerschau der Parteien," *Politische Studien* 8 (August/September, 1957):57.

38. Zeuner, *Innerparteiliche Demokratie,* pp. 32-41, 68-82; Schütz, "Die Meinungs- und Willensbildung in der Sozialdemokratie," pp. 362-63.

39. Gunlicks, "Intraparty Democracy in West Germany," pp. 229-32.

40. Philip J. Cook, "Robert Michels' Political Parties in Perspective," *Journal of Politics* 33 (August, 1971):796; Gordon Hands, "Roberto Michels and the Study of Political Parties," *British Journal of Political Science* 1 (April, 1971): 155-72.

41. William E. Wright, ed., *Comparative Study of Party Organization,* pp. 46-49.

42. Lewis Edinger, "Political Science and Political Biography: Reflections on the Nature of Leadership," *Journal of Politics* 26 (August, 1975):652; Leon Dion, "The Concept of Political Leadership: An Analysis," *Canadian Journal of Political Science* 1 (March, 1968):4.

43. Nowka, *Partei und Fraktion,* pp. 83-84, argues that the deputies went beyond the limits set by party conference resolutions and, in their parliamentary work, did not always take into consideration the feelings of the party membership. See also Dittberner, *Bundesparteitage,* p. 263.

44. Kurt Becker, *Die Welt,* October 14, 1958.

Selected Bibliography

Primary Sources

The most important source of primary materials is the Friedrich Ebert Stiftung, the SPD archives, in Bad Godesberg. It contains a vast collection of SPD publications, as well as the private papers of many leading party politicians. For the rearmament debate in parliament, the office of the secretary to the Bundestag Defense Committee has the official reports on committee sessions, including the protocols for the earlier Committee for Questions of European Security. The government's press and information office has a press archive with files containing newspaper reports on the speeches and activities of parliamentary deputies. This was an important supplement to the collection at the party archives. Beyond these, the major West German newspapers were an essential source in tracing the course of the rearmament debate.

Government Documents

Federal Republic of Germany. Bundestag. *Ausschuss für Fragen der europäischen Sicherheit.* Bonn, July, 1952-August, 1953.
———. Bundestag. *Verhandlungen des Deutschen Bundestages,* Wahlperiode 1-3. Vols. 1-49. Bonn, 1949-61.
———. Parlamentarischer Rat. *Verhandlungen des Plenums.* Bonn, 1949.
———. Parlamentarischer Rat. *Verhandlungen des Hauptausschusses.* Bonn, 1949.

Collected Documents

Federal Republic. Bundesministerium für Innerdeutsche Beziehungen. *Dokumente zur Deutschlandpolitik.* Series 3, vols. 1-4, May 5, 1955-

November 9, 1958, Frankfurt, 1961-69; series 4, vols. 1-5, November 10, 1958-December 31, 1960. Frankfurt, 1971-73.

Royal Institute of International Affairs. *Documents on International Affairs, 1949-60.* 11 vols. London, 1953-64.

Ruhm von Oppen, Beate ed. *Documents on Germany Under Occupation, 1945-54.* London, 1955.

United States. Department of State. *Foreign Relations of the United States: The Conferences of Malta and Yalta, 1945.* Washington D.C., 1955.

————. Senate Committee on Foreign Relations. *Documents on Germany, 1944-61.* Washington, 1961.

Private Collections: SPD Archives

SPD. *Debatte um den Wehrbeitrag* (J37).

Erler, Fritz. *Veröffentlichungen.* 1953-61.

Menzel, Walter. *Korrespondenz, Volksbefragung, und Wehrfragen.* 1950-61 (R14 and R27).

Ollenhauer, Erich. *Korrespondenz, Aufsätze, und Reden.* 1945-61.

————. *Ollenhauer Aussenpolitik, 1951-55* (J34).

Schumacher, Kurt. *Korrespondenz, Interviews, und Reden.* 1945-52 (Q6-Q21).

Party Yearbooks and Conference Protocols

Jahrbuch der SPD. 1946, 1947, 1948-49, 1950-51, 1952-53, 1954-55, 1956-57, 1958-59, 1960-61.

Protokoll der Verhandlungen des Parteitages der SPD. Hannover, May 9-11, 1946; Nürnberg, June 29-July 2, 1947; Düsseldorf, September 11-14, 1948; Hamburg, September 21-25, 1950; Dortmund, September 24-28, 1952; Berlin, July 20-24, 1954; Munich, July 15-19, 1956; Stuttgart, May 18-23, 1958; Bad Godesberg, November 13-15, 1959; Hannover, November 21-25, 1960.

SPD Brochures and Publications

Bechert, Karl. *Deutsche Politik im Schatten der Atomdrohung.* Bonn, 1958.

Drott, Karl, ed. *Sozialdemokratie und Wehrfrage.* Hannover, 1956.

Erler, Fritz. *Soll Deutschland Rüsten?* Mannheim, 1952.

Ollenhauer, Erich. *Vor Entscheidungen für Jahrzehnte.* Mannheim, n.d. [1953].

————. *1953. Das Jahr der Entscheidung.* Bonn, n.d. [1953].

————. *Nach der Entscheidung.* Bonn, 1953.

Schulz, Klaus Peter. *Vor der schwersten Entscheidung: Deutschland und die Verteidigung Europas.* Dortmund, n.d. [1950].

Schumacher, Kurt. *Nach dem Zusammenbruch.* Hamburg, 1948.

————. *Deutschlands Beitrag für Frieden und Freiheit.* Dortmund, n.d. [1950].

————. *Die deutsche Sicherheit.* Hannover, n.d. [1950].

————. *Deutschlands Forderung.* Dortmund, n.d. [1951].

————. *Es Geht um die Freiheit.* Hannover, n.d. [1951].

————. *Macht Europa Stark.* Dortmund, n.d. [*1951*].

————. *Ein Winter der Entscheidungen.* Mainz, n.d. [1951].

————.*Die Staatsgewalt geht von den Besatzungsmächten aus.* Mainz, n.d. [1952].

SPD. *Aktionsprogramm. Bonn, 1952.*

————. *Deutschlandplan der SPD: Kommentare, Argumente, Begründungen.* Bonn, 1959.

————. *Dokumentation, Acht Jahre sozialdemokratische Kampf um Einheit, Frieden, und Freiheit.* Bonn, 1953.

————. *Grundsatzprogramm der SPD.* Cologne, 1959.

————. *Handbuch Sozialdemokratischer Politik.* Bonn, 1953.

————. *News from Germany.* English language newsletter. 1950-60.

————. *Sicherheit und Ruhrkontrolle.* Hannover, 1950.

————. *Sopade: Sozialdemokratische Parteikorrespondenz.* 1949-55.

————. *Sozialdemokratie und Bundeswehr.* Hannover, 1957.

————. *Sozialdemokratischer Pressedienst.* 1949-60.

Publications by Social Democrats

Abendroth, Wolfgang. "Die Chancen der deutschen Sozialdemokratie nach dem 15 September 1957." *Geist und Tat* 12 (November, 1957): 366-74.

Arndt, Adolf. "Die Entmachtung des Bundestages." *Die Neue Gesellshaft* 6 (November-December, 1959):431-38.

Baade, Fritz. "Wie kann Deutschland verteidigt werden?" *Aussenpolitik* 2 (July, 1951):254-62.

————. "Nur noch zwei Deutschlandkonzeptionen." *Aussenpolitik* 5 (December, 1954):753-64.

Beermann, Fritz. "Sicherheit, Wiedervereinigung, und Stärke der Bundeswehr." *Die Neue Gesellschaft* 4 (January February, 1957):3-8.

Brandt, Willy. "Crisis in Berlin." *New Leader* 41 (December 8, 1958): 3-4.

Eichler, Willi. "Ein Verteidigungsbeitrag fur die Freiheit." *Geist und Tat* 7 (March, 1952):65-73.

————. "Bereitschaft zum Frieden." *Geist und Tat* 9 (February, 1954): 33-36.

————. "Von der Ko-existenz zur Kooperation." *Geist und Tat* 10 (February, 1955):33-40.

———. "Zeiten der Entspannung." *Geist und Tat* 11 (July, 1956): 193-97.

———. "Der Rückfall in die Barbarei." *Geist und Tat* 11 (December, 1956):353-57.

Erler, Fritz. "Demokratie und bewaffnete Macht." *Gewerkschaftliche Monatshefte* 5 (June, 1954):355-61.

———. "Nüchterne Verteidigungsbereitschaft als erzieherische Aufgabe der Gesellschaft." *Zeitwende* 26 (March, 1955): 151-58.

———. "Coexistence et réunification de l'Allemagne." *Politique Etrangère* 20 (June-July, 1955):333-44.

———. "Die ersten Wehrgesetze." *Geist und Tat* 10 (November, 1955): 324-28.

———. "The Struggle for German Reunification." *Foreign Affairs* 34 (April, 1956):380-93.

———. "Les Problèmes du Réarmement allemand du Point de Vue de l'Opposition." *Synthèses* 12 (June, 1957):33-46.

———. "Gedanken zur Politik und inneren Ordnung der Sozialdemokratie." *Die Neue Gesellschaft* 5 (January-February, 1958):3-8.

———. "The Reunification of Germany and Security for Europe." *World Politics* 10 (April, 1958):366-77.

———. "Heer und Staat in der Bundesrepublik," in Bundesministerium für Verteidigung, eds. *Schicksalsfragen der Gegenwart.* Tübingen, 1958. 3:223-56.

———. *Politik für Deutschland.* Stuttgart, 1968.

Luetkens, Gerhart. "Die parlamentarische Opposition in der Aussenpolitik." *Aussenpolitik* 2 (September, 1951):398-407.

———. "Betrachtungen zu einem Deutschlandvertrag." *Aussenpolitik* 4 (March, 1953):141-51.

Menzel, Walter. "Parliamentary Politics in the German Federal Republic, 1957-60." *Parliamentary Affairs* 13 (Autumn, 1960):509-19.

Meyer, Ernst Wilhelm. "Gedanken zur Politik der Wiedervereinigung." *Aussenpolitik* 9 (October, 1958):614-30.

Ollenhauer, Erich. "Where We Stand." *New Leader* 37 (November 22, 1954):14-15.

———. "Wozu dient die NATO?" *Occident* 10 (June 19, 1957):11-12.

———. "German Socialism in Flux." *New Leader* 43 (March 14, 1960): 12-13.

Sanger, Fritz. *Erich Ollenhauer, Reden und Aufsätze.* Hannover, 1964.

Schmid, Carlo. "Germany and Europe: The SPD Program." *Foreign Affairs* 30 (July, 1952):531-44.

Schmidt, Helmut. *Verteidigung oder Vergeltung.* Stuttgart, 1961.

———. *Beiträge.* Stuttgart, 1967.

Schulz, Klaus Peter. *Sorge um die deutsche Linke.* Cologne, 1954.

———. *Opposition als politisches Schicksal?* Cologne, 1958.

Schütz, Klaus. "Die Sozialdemokratie im Nachkriegsdeutschland." In Max G. Lange et al. *Parteien in der Bundesrepublik.* Düsseldorf, 1955.

———. "Die Meinungs- und Willensbildung in der Sozialdemokratie."

Die Neue Gesellschaft 5 (September-October, 1958):361-70.

Wehner, Herbert. "Schwerpunkt sozialdemokratischer Politik im geteilten Deutschland." *Die Neue Gesellschaft* 5 (May-June, 1958): 209-12.

General Literature: A Selected List

Biographies and Autobiographies

Adenauer, Konrad. *Memoirs, 1945-53.* Chicago, 1965.

Brandt, Willy. *My Road to Berlin.* New York, 1960.

————, and Richard Löwenthal. *Ernst Reuter.* Munich, 1957.

Edinger, Lewis J. *Kurt Schumacher.* Stanford, Calif., 1965.

Heine, Friedrich. *Kurt Schumacher.* Göttingen, 1969.

Jahn, Gerhard ed. *Herbert Wehner: Beiträge zu einer Biographie.* Cologne, 1976.

Oschilewski, Walther G., et. al. *Erich Ollenhauer: Der Führer der Opposition.* Berlin, 1953.

Prittie, Terrence. *Adenauer.* Chicago, 1971.

Ritter, Waldemar. *Kurt Schumacher.* Hannover, 1964.

Scholz, Arno, and Walther Oschilewski, eds. *Turmwächter der Demokratie.* 3 vols. Berlin, 1953.

Schröder, Dieter. *Erich Ollenhauer.* Munich, 1957.

Soell, Hartmut. *Fritz Erler, Eine politische Biographie.* 2 vols. Stuttgart, 1976.

Wesemann, Fried. *Kurt Schumacher.* Frankfurt, 1952.

Weymar, Paul. *Adenauer.* Munich, 1955.

On the SPD

Ashkenasi, Abraham. *Reformpartei und Aussenpolitik: Die Aussenpolitik der SPD Berlin.* Cologne, 1968.

Brauns, H. J. et. al. *Die SPD in der Krise: Die deutsche Sozialdemokratie seit 1945.* Frankfurt, 1976.

Buczylowski, Ulrich. *Kurt Schumacher und die deutsche Frage.* Stuttgart, 1973.

Chalmers, Douglas A. *The Social Democratic Party of Germany.* New Haven, Conn., 1964.

Childs, David. *From Schumacher to Brandt.* London, 1966.

Dietz, Detlef. "Einfluss und Haltung der SPD hinsichtlich der Entwicklung des Konzepts der Inneren Führung der Bundeswehr, 1949-57." Diplom-Arbeit, Cologne University, 1971.

Gaus, Günther. *Staatserhaltende Opposition oder Hat die SPD kapituliert: Gespräche mit Herbert Wehner.* Reinbeck bei Hamburg, 1966.

Hrbek, Rudolf. "Die SPD, Deutschland, und Europe." Ph.D. dissertation, Tübingen University, 1968.

Kaden, Albrecht. *Einheit oder Freiheit: Die Wiedergründung der SPD, 1945-46.* Hannover, 1964.

Löwke, Udo F. *Für den Fall dass: SPD und Wehrfrage 1949-55.* Hannover, 1969.

Miller, Suzanne. *Die SPD vor und nach Godesberg.* Bonn, 1974.

Nowka, Harry. *Das Machtverhältnis zwischen Partei und Fraktion in der SPD.* Cologne, 1973.

Patterson, William E. *The SPD and European Integration.* Lexington, Mass., 1974.

Pirker, Theo. *Die SPD nach Hitler.* Munich, 1965.

Schellenger, Harold K. *The SPD in the Bonn Republic.* The Hague, 1968.

Theimer, Walter. *Von Bebel zu Ollenhauer.* Bern, 1957.

On Rearmament

Bauer, Karl. *Deutsche Verteidigungspolitik 1945-63: Dokumente und Kommentare.* Boppard, 1964.

Domes, Jürgen Otto. "Das Freiwilligengesetz im zweiten deutschen Bundestag. Ph.D. dissertation, Heidelberg University, 1960.

Dormann, Manfred. *Demokratische Militärpolitik: Die alliierte Militärstrategie als Thema deutsche Politik, 1949-68.* Freiburg, 1970.

Edinger, Lewis J. *West German Armament.* Maxwell Field, Ala., 1955.

Heydte, Freiherr von der. *Der Kampf um den Wehrbeitrag.* 3 vols. Munich, 1952, 1953, 1958.

Institut für Staatslehre und Politik. *Der deutsche Soldat in der Armee von Morgen.* Munich, 1954.

Jahn, Hans Edgar. *Für und Gegen den Wehrbeitrag.* Cologne, 1957.

Magathan, Wallace C. "The Politics of German Rearmament, 1949-53." Ph.D. dissertation, Princeton University, 1961.

McGeehan, Robert. *The German Rearmament Question.* Urbana, Ill., 1971.

Moch, Jules. *Histoire du Réarmament Allemand depuis 1950.* Paris, 1960.

Schubert, Klaus von. *Wiederbewaffnung und Westintegration: Die innere Auseinandersetzung um die militärische und aussenpolitische Orientierung des BRD, 1950-52.* Stuttgart, 1970.

Speier, Hans. *German Rearmament and Atomic War.* Evanston, Ill., 1957.

Tönnies, Norbert. *Der Weg zu den Waffen.* Rastatt, 1961.

Waldman, Eric. *The Goose Step is Verboten: The German Army Today.* New York, 1964.

Politics and Foreign Policy

Allemann, Fritz René. *Bonn ist nicht Weimar.* Cologne, 1956.

Baring, Arnulf. *Aussenpolitik in Adenauers Kanzlerdemokratie.* Munich, 1969.

Besson, Waldemar. *Die Aussenpolitik der Bundesrepublik.* Munich, 1970.

Dittberner, Jürgen. "Die Bundesparteitage der Christlich Demokratische Union und der Sozialdemokratischen Partei Deutschlands von 1946 bis 1968." Ph.D. dissertation, Free University, Berlin, 1969.

Erdmenger, Klaus. *Das folgenschwere Missverständnis.* Freiburg, 1967.

Feld, Werner. *Reunification and West German-Soviet Relations.* The Hague, 1963.

Grosser, Alfred. *Die Bonner Demokratie.* Düsseldorf, 1960.

Hanrieder, Wolfram F. *West German Foreign Policy, 1949-63.* Stanford, Calif., 1967.

Hartmann, Frederick H. *Germany Between East and West.* New York, 1965.

Hirsch-Weber, Wolfgang and Klaus Schütz. *Wähler und Gewählte.* Berlin, 1957.

Hereth, Michael. *Die parlamentarische Opposition in der Bundesrepublik Deutschland.* Munich, 1969.

Hiscocks, Richard. *The Adenauer Era.* New York, 1960.

Kitzinger, Uwe W. *German Electoral Politics.* London, 1960.

Kaufmann, William W., ed. *Military Policy and National Security.* Princeton, N.J., 1956.

Kralewski, Wolfgang and Karl Heinz Neunreither. *Oppositionelles Verhalten in ersten deutschen Bundestag, 1949-53.* Cologne, 1962.

Loewenberg, Gerhard. *Parliament in the German Political System.* Ithaca, N.Y., 1967.

Lohmar, Ulrich. *Innerparteiliche Demokratie: Eine Untersuchung der Verfassungswirklichkeit politischer Parteien in der Bundesrepublik Deutschland.* Stuttgart, 1963.

Michels, Robert. *Political Parties.* Translated by Eden Paul and Cedar Paul. New York, 1959.

Müller, Ute. *Die demokratische Willensbildung in den politischen Parteien.* Mainz, 1967.

Narr, Wolf-Dieter. *CDU-SPD: Programm und Praxis seit 1945.* Stuttgart, 1966.

Osgood, Robert E. *NATO: The Entangling Alliance.* Chicago, 1962.

Pöttering, Hans Gert. *Adenauers Sicherheitspolitik, 1955-63.* Düsseldorf, 1975.

Richardson, James L. *Germany and the Atlantic Alliance.* Cambridge, Mass., 1966.

Royal Institute of International Affairs. *Survey of International Affairs, 1949-60.* 8 vols. London, 1953-64.

Rupp, Hans Karl. *Ausserparlamentarische Opposition in der Ära Adenauer: Der Kampf gegen die Atombewaffnung in den fünfziger Jahren.* Cologne, 1970.

Schwarz, Hans Peter. *Vom Reich zur Bundesrepublik: Deutschland im Widerstreit der aussenpolitischen Konzeptionen in den Jahren der Besatzungsherrschaft, 1945-49.* Berlin, 1966.

Smith, Jean. *The Defense of Berlin.* Baltimore, Md., 1963.

Vali, Ferenc. *The Quest for a United Germany.* Baltimore, Md., 1967.

Wettig, Gerhard. *Entmilitarisierung und Wiederbewaffnung in Deutschland, 1943-45.* Munich, 1967.

Willis, F. Roy. *France, Germany and the New Europe, 1945-63.* Stanford, Calif., 1965.

Zeuner, Bodo. *Innerparteiliche Demokratie.* Berlin, 1969.

Articles

Allemann, Fritz René. "Kein Urlaub von der Aussenpolitik: Nach den Londoner und Pariser Abkommen." *Der Monat* 7 (November, 1954): 106-12.

———. "Aussenpolitisches Schattenboxen." *Der Monat* 9 (September, 1957):3-8.

———. "How the West Germans Voted." *New Leader* 40 (October 7, 1957):7-8.

———. "The Great Debate Among German Social Democrats." *New Leader* 41 (February 17, 1958):14-16.

———. "Adenauer and the Others." *Encounter* 13 (August, 1959):65-67.

———. "Farewell to Marx." *Encounter* 14 (March, 1960):67-70.

Baudissin, Count Wolf von. "The New German Army." *Foreign Affairs* 34 (October, 1955):1-13.

Besson, Waldemar. "Regierung und Opposition in der deutschen Politik." *Politische Vierteljahresschrift* 3 (September, 1962):224-41.

Braunthal, Gerald. "Direct and Representative Democracy in West Germany: The Atomic Armament Issue." *Canadian Journal of Economics and Political Science* 26 (August, 1959):313-23.

———. "The Policy Function of the German Social Democratic Party." *Comparative Politics* 9 (January, 1977):127-45.

Chalmers, Douglas, and Lewis Edinger. "Overture or Swansong: German Social Democracy Prepares for a New Decade." *Antioch Review* 20 (Summer, 1960):163-75.

Cook, Philip J. "Robert Michels' Political Parties in Perspective." *Journal of Politics* 33 (August, 1971):773-96.

Dernburg, H. J. "Rearmament and the German Economy." *Foreign Affairs* 33 (July, 1955):648-62.

Dirks, Walter. "Sozialdemokratische Alternativen." *Frankfurter Hefte* 8 (April, 1953):249-51.

Edinger, Lewis. "The Comparative Analysis of Political Leadership." *Comparative Politics* 7 (January, 1975):253-71.

Fishel, Jeff. "On the Transformation of Ideology in European Political Systems." *Comparative Political Studies* 4 (January, 1972):406-37.

Flechtheim, Ossip K. "Die Anpassung der SPD." *Kölner Zeitschrift für Soziologie und Sozialpsychologie* 17 (1965):584-604.

Freund, Gerald. "Adenauer and the Future of Germany." *International Journal* 18 (Autumn, 1963):458-67.

Gunlicks, Arthur B. "Intraparty Democracy in West Germany." *Comparative Politics* 2 (January, 1970):229-50.

Günther, Klaus. "Die andere Meinung in der SPD, 1949, 1955-56, 1958-61: Ein Beitrag zum Problem innerparteilicher Diskussionsfreiheit." *Archiv für Sozialgeschichte* 13 (1973):23-52.

Guttenberg, Freiherr zu. "Das Kaudinische Joch: Gefahren des sozial-demokratische Deutschlandplans." *Politische Meinung* 4 (May, 1959): 61-66.

Haerdter, Robert. "Eine Partei sucht eine Politik: Die SPD vor dem Munchener Parteitag." *Gegenwart* 11 (June 30, 1956):400-403.

Kaack, Heino. "Opposition und Aussenpolitik." *Politische Vierteljahres-schrift* 10 (1969):244-49.

Kirchheimer, Otto. "The Waning of Opposition in Parliamentary Regimes." *Social Research* 24 (Summer, 1957):127-56.

———. "Germany. The Vanishing Opposition." In R. A. Dahl, ed., *Political Opposition in Western Democracies.* New Haven, Conn., 1966, p. 237-59.

Kunz, Josef L. "The Contractual Agreements with the Federal Republic of Germany." *American Journal of International Law* 47 (January, 1953):106-14.

———. "Treaties Establishing the European Defense Community." *American Journal of International Law* 47 (April, 1953):275-81.

Lania, Leo. "Schumacher: Violent Martyr." *United Nations World* 6 (May, 1952):13-15.

Loewenstein, Karl. "The Bonn Constitution and the EDC Treaties." *Yale Law Journal* 64 (May, 1955):805-39.

Martin, Laurence W. "The American Decision to Rearm Germany." In H. Stein, ed. *American Civil-Military Decisions.* Birmingham, Ala., 1963.

Meyer, Peter. "Do the German Socialists Have a Policy?" *New Leader* 38 (January 17, 1955):7-8.

Petry, Richard. "Die SPD und der Sozialismus." *Frankfurter Hefte* 9 (September, 1954):663-76.

Ridley, F. "The Parliamentary Commissioner for Military Affairs in the Federal Republic of Germany." *Political Studies* 12 (February, 1964): 1-20.

Schuster, Hans. "Die aussenpolitische Konzeption der Sozialdemokratie." *Eckart* 26 (January-March, 1957):1-7.

————. "Die Herrschau der Parteien: Theorie und Praxis der Parteitage." *Politische Studien* 8 (August-September, 1957):57-72.

Sutton, John L. "The Personnel Screening Committee and Parliamentary Control of the West German Armed Forces." *Journal of Central European Affairs* 19 (January, 1960):389-401.

Vardys, V. Stanley. "Germany's Postwar Socialism: Nationalism and Kurt Schumacher." *Review of Politics* 27 (April, 1965):220-44.

Wahrhaftig, Samuel L. "Der Weg der Sozialdemokraten: Zum Dortmunder Parteitag." *Frankfurter Hefte* 7 (November, 1952):849-58.

White, Theodore H. "Kurt Schumacher: The Will to Power." *Reporter* 5 (December 11, 1951):12-16.

Index